Women in India and Central Asia

Women in India and Central Asia

Kamala Kumari

GYAN

Published, 2020

Published by

Gyan Publishing House
5, Ansari Road
Daryaganj, New Delhi-110002
Phone: 011-47034999, 9811692060
www.gyanbooks.com
E-mail: books@gyanbooks.com

Printed at: Gyan Press, Delhi.

Cataloging in Publication Data—DK
Courtesy: D.K. Agencies (P) Ltd. <docinfo@dkagencies.com>

Kamala Kumari, Author.
Women in India and Central Asia / Kamala Kumari.
pages cm
Includes bibliographical references.
ISBN 9788121220408 (HB)

1. Women in development—India. 2. Women in development—Asia, Central. I. Title.

LCC HQ1240.5.I4K36 2020 | DDC 305.420954 23

To
My Parents

and
All the Women
of
India and Central Asia

Contents

Foreword

With the disintegration of the USSR and beginning of wide-ranging economic reforms in India since 1990, many changes came about in Central Asia and India. Liberalisation, privatisation and the opening up of the economy in general brought many visible social and cultural changes. With new opportunities and business prospects some section of women found greater prosperity for themselves. Yet, many women are still struggling to survive in a competitive environment. In addition, tradition and patriarchy have put additional burdens on women despite the changes that have come about since 1990-91.

Central Asia women, who have higher level of education and skill, are still struggling to be relevant in the job market. Revival of religion and tradition, along with the burden of household chores have made life difficult for Central Asian women. The Soviet era social welfare and other benefits targeted at women have gone in all the Central Asian countries. India, which has a constitution that prevents discrimination on the basis of gender and has a robust democracy for nearly last seventy three years, has different problems associated with caste and community identities. This makes women's issues even more complex in the country.

The governments have tried some affirmative actions benefiting women like reservation for women in local bodies in India. In Central Asia, though the Soviet practice of one-third reservation in legislative bodies no longer exists, women still have relatively better representation in parliament compared to India. This could be due to the fact that political parties in some countries like Uzbekistan having reservation for women while deciding candidates for legislative elections. Yet, none of the five states in Central Asia today have even one-third representation, which used to be guaranteed during the Soviet period. In India, beyond the local bodies like Municipalities and *Panchayats*, there is no reservation for women in state and national legislatures. The bill for 33 percent reservation for women in Indian parliament is still pending.

The book by Dr. Kamala Kumari looks at the consequences of the political and economic transformations on the status of women in the socio-economic and political spheres in the countries under study. It takes into consideration the historical, geographical, ideological and cultural dimensions as well as national specificities. This study discusses the sociocultural prejudices and stereotyping that are still the main constraints to women's political and economic empowerment.

The book shows how the impact of globalisation and liberalisation is uneven across social and gender categories. Withdrawal of the state from welfare functions have negatively affected women more than men. Privatisation and structural adjustment resulted in cuts in social outlays like education, health, pensions, child allowances, unemployment benefits etc. Growing economic disparity and vulnerability in addition to cultural revivalism and resurgence of traditional institutions have created fertile grounds for further marginalisation of a large number of women. As the book underlines, the absence of women from the key posts is not because of lack of education alone as is generally perceived to be, but other socio-economic reasons like patriarchy and gender discrimination.

There are, however, positive trends so far as women are concerned. Both in India and Central Asia, women continue to have a better status than women in some countries in their immediate neighbourhood. In Central Asia, women have high levels of education and skill. Literacy rate of Central Asian Women (CAW) is remarkably high at around 98 percent; it competes with several developed countries. School and college enrolment for women remains quite high when compared internationally. In India, the literacy rate of women is gradually increasing and in the urban set-ups women have outperformed their male counterparts in several fields. The book discusses efforts to uplift the status of women in society, which include the role of the governments as well as non-governmental organisations (NGOs).

The research of Dr. Kamala Kumari, being based on materials collected through a field work of over two months in all the five Central Asian countries, is a serious effort to study the condition and status of women in Central Asia. The study of Indian experience helps the readers to understand how in certain aspects gender issues transcend political and economic systems.

The book helps us to understand the effects of liberalisation, market economy and privatisation on women in two different contexts with different historical legacy, political culture and levels of economic development.

There have been few research works in India on Central Asian women in the post-Soviet period and almost no published book on the subject of research that includes Central Asia and India. In that sense it is a rare and pioneering work.

Prof. Ajay Patnaik

Centre for Russian and Central Asian Studies,
School of International Studies,
Jawaharlal Nehru University,
New Delhi, India

Acknowledgement

For the successful completion of this work, I owe a considerable debt of gratitude to many people.

First and foremost, my sincere gratitude and heartfelt thanks to my supervisor and the guiding force, ***Prof. Ajay Kumar Patnaik*** *for his valuable guidance, support and encouragement. I am deeply indebted to him for the numerous suggestions made by him while the work was in progress.*

I would also like to thank, late Prof. Tulsi. Ram, Prof. Tahir Asgar, Prof. Gulshan Sachdeva, Prof. Archna Upadhyay, Prof. Rajan Kumar, and other faculties of my centre for their invaluable inputs and support.

My sincere gratitude to Prof. Nirmala Joshi, Mrs. Damayanti V. Tambay, Dr. Ramakant Dwivedi, (Ramakant Sir was instrumental in getting my Kyrgyz Visa) and Dr. Sowesh Patnaik for their best wishes, blessings, help, support and suggestions.

Special Thanks to Prof. Kiran Singh Verma, of CRS, School of Languages for all help and suggestions.

My thanks also to Thakur Sir, Handa Sir, Vijay Sir, Balram Sir, Ritu Ma'm, Gurpreet, Amit, Sonu, Roshni, Gauri di, Pritam Ma'm and Beli Ram Sir, Lalit, Pradeep for their help and cooperation.

My earnest thanks to staff of Jawaharlal Nehru University library, the staff at Teen Murti Library, Parliament Library, ICSSR Documentation, Central Secretariat Library, the Centre for Women's Developmental Studies (CWDS) Library for providing invaluable material for the research.

I also owe a sense of gratitude to ICSSR for granting me the field trip which helped me immensely in understanding Central Asia and Central Asian women better. In this regard, my heartfelt gratitude to late Prof. Ramesh Dadhich, Member Secy, ICSSR.

My special thanks to also to Dr. Harish Sharma, Mr. M.P. Madhukar, Rama Ma'm and Dr. S.M. Verma of ICSSR, for their suggestions, help, cooperation and support.

My work would not have been completed without the help, support and cooperation of several people in Central Asia, who helped me during my stay. I would especially like to thank everyone for their love, affection, all the help and support and for taking wonderful care of me during my field trip and never let me feel homesick. In this regard my special thanks in Kazakhstan to: Prof. Mara Gubailudina and Prof. Roza Sarabayeva, Department of International Relations, Al-Farabi Kazakh National University (KAZNU) Dr. Svetlana Shakirova, Director, Center of Gender Studies, Dr. Nazym Shedenova, Director, Center of Gender Studies, Department of Philosophy and Politology, KAZNU, Prof. Sattar Mazhitov, Dr. Yelena Rudenko, Prof. Laura Yerekesheva, Institute of Oreantal studies, Bagaeva Katerina- Director, Institute for Equal Rights and Equal Opportunities of Kazakhstan, Akbota Zholdasbekova, Eurasian National University, Astana.

In Kyrgyzstan: (in Bishkek) to Dr. Indira Musaeva, Prof. Ilhan Shahin, Prof. Hadicha Mamatbek, Ainura Asamidinova; (in Osh) Dr. Gulzada Bilbaeva.

In Tajikistan to Dr. Sofia R. Kasymova, Sociologist, Gender Education Center.

Prof. G.M. Maitdinova, Department of General History, Russian-Tajik (Slavic) University (RTSU) Dushanbe.

In Turkmenistan to, Gowher and Rahim, MFA, Turkmenistan, Director, Institute of History, Director and professors National Institute of Democracy and Human Rights, Professors at Turkmen National University, Academy of Sciences, Ashgabat.

The Indian Embassy, in all these countries. I would like to make special mention, about His Excellency Ambassador Ashok Sharma (Astana)

Mr. Rakesh Verma Consulate, Almaty

Mr. Ajay Kachroo Bishkek, Kyrgyzstan

Ambassador Sunil Jain, Ashgabat, Turkmenistan;

Mr. Saini, Second Secretary, Tashkent, Uzbekistan

My gratitude also to Ambassador Ashok Sajjanhar for his valuable inputs. My gratitude in Kazakhstan also to

Mr. Devender Singh, Almaty

Mr Mahendra Pandey, Shimkent,

Galiya, Khalida and Yusuf, Shimkent,

My lucky mascot Madiyar and Asien and her entire group (Hostel, 14), KAZNU

Monica, Marjan, KAZNU

Ulzhan Kabdelova, International Division, KAZNU

Akmaral Kainazarova, Almaty

Kyrgyzstan *Elina Schröder, works with UN agency, on Bishkek*
Ainura Aitibaeva, Zameera, Kamila,(Osh)

Tajikistan *Sophia, Dushanbe*
Host family, Dushanbe

Turkmenistan Serdar Shihiyev, Ishan Orazov (Turkmen Embassy in Delhi), Magtymguly Babayew, Nagmat Nazar, Ruslan Rajepov, Sheker, Gozel, Leyli, Sofia, Jennet, Ashgabat; Dildora, Landlady, Gulnuru guest house Tashkent, Uzbekistan.

My thanks also to the staff at Library Osh, Dushanbe, Almaty, Ashgabat, Bishkek

My heartfelt thanks to, all the Central Asian women and men, who spent their valuable time talking and sharing their experiences with me, specially all those whom I interviewed and had discussions with. Their comments and opinions have helped me immensely.

I also benefited considerably from the encouragement and suggestions of my friends–

I would particularly like to thank Niva (Susmita), Rajesh, Himani, OP Sir, Ruhil Sir, Bhaskar, Khushi (Khush-Hal), Neha (JNUMC), Sudhir, Jacob, Abhay, Mukesh, Dinesh, Arun, Radhika, Sangeeta, Vaishali, Deepika, Sushma, Suhasi, Rupesh, Geeta Bhabhi, for their friendly assistance and kind gesture. My thanks also to Happy, Neha, Archana, Akanksha, Lovey and all my CRS/SL/JNU friends.

I also want to thank all those people who helped me in their own little ways, though I have not been able to list their names here.

Last but certainly not the least I would like to thank my family and relatives for their constant encouragement, patience and support.

First of all I would like to express my gratitude to Dada and Maa, - the physical form of the 'supreme power' who are and have been the greatest source of my strength; for their blessings, love and affection. My gratitude and hearfelt thanks to my entire family-my brothers and sister-in-law (late Dr. Bhavna Singh, who I'm sure must be happy seeing this work;

Swati Rai, Diya (Titiksha) and Richa) and to Chhoti and Geeta, for their patience and constant support.

My thanks to Phuanani, Mamu, Mami, Mausa, Mausi for their blessings. My thanks, also to Ajay Bhaiya, Pinki, Pinku, Rekha, Pinnu, Chandrabhushan, Sippy, Tara, Shweta, Subbu, Khushboo, Khuspreet, Khushdil, Komal, Preeti and all my cousins for their best wishes.

I would also like to convey my special thanks, love and best wishes to Prerna- the Poetess. She has contributed a lot by keeping my spirit high with her smile and sometime sparing me and my time, so that I could focus on my work. My thanks also, to Pranav and Mohak- for refreshing my mind with their rare, but memorable little conversations. Garima- my Jaan and Mohak- my positive energy, have constantly supported me by keeping my spirit high and cooperating by giving me space to work without any disturbance, and my little Princess Akanksha, new member of our family, for bringing abundance of joy, positive energy and smile.

My thanks also, to Aditi, Kavya, Om, Kush, Vaibhavi, Saurabhi, Aaryan, Rudrapriya, Aditya, Rudrapratap, Harshiv; who gave me positive energy and motivated me with their smile. My thanks also to, Gadam, Ainur, Davut, Gulnur and Bezergen, my little Turkmen friends for their smile and affection.

New Delhi, India **Kamala Kumari**

Glossary

Hindi/Sanskrit/Urdu

Purdah : veil

Devadasi : a girl "dedicated" to worship and service of a deity or a temple for the rest of her life

Brahmavadinis: women who never married and cultured the Vedas throughout their lives

Sadyodvahas : women who studied the Vedas till they married

Upadhyaya : female teacher (as mentioned by Katyayana)

Upadhyayi : women teachers (as mentioned by Katyayana)

Upadhyayanis : wife of teachers (as mentioned by Katyayana)

Sati : when a woman burns to death on her husband's funeral pyre

Uttara Path: Nothern Route

Lathis : sticks made of bamboos

Dabba/Tiffin : box/lunchbox system

Swarajya : self-rule/self-governance

Grama : village

Taluka : block

Zilla : District

Sarpanch : head of a village

Lok Sabha (India) : Lower house of parliament

Rajya Sabha (India) : Upper house of parliament

Abala : feeble/weak woman

Sabala : strong/powerful

Gulabi : Pink

Karyalay : office

Russian/uzbek/turkmen/Kyrgyz/Persian/Tajik/Kazakh

Adat : local customary laws

Shariya : formal laws

Kalym : bride price

Jadids : reformists

Jadidism : reformist movement

Sura or Surah : chapter in Quran

kolkhozy : collective farms

kolkhoz : collective farming

zhensovety : women's councils

Zhenotdel : national and local women's sections of the Communist Party

delegatki : women delegates

Perestroika : economic restructuring

Glasnost : openness; transparency in work

peregruzhennost : overburdening

Zastoi : stagnation

zhenstvennost : womanliness

demokratizatsiya : democratisation

Goskomstat : The State Statistical Committee

matryoshka : gaily painted wooden dolls

trudnosti byta : the hardships of everyday life

Paranja : veil

Ichkari : section of the house where the females lived

hijab : veil traditionally worn by Muslim women

ala kachuu (Kyrgyz language): bride kidnapping

Mejlis (Turkmenistan): Parliament

Oliy Majlis (Uzbekistan): Parliament

Mazhilis: lower house of the bicameral Parliament of Kazakhstan

Jogorku Kenesh (Kyrgyzstan): the Parliament

velayet: Region

kustdepedi (Turkmen): dance

Mediniet (Turkmen): culture or ancient treasure

El-Ene: mother of the people

El Muras: People's Heritage

Bazaar: market

Zilyoni: Green

Zilyoni Bazaar: green vegetable market (in all countries; all day-to-day stuff available in this Bazaar)

Gaps/ chernaya kassa: something similar to kitty-party/ committee where elderly women come together and have heart to heart talk about important issues about themselves, family, money-matters etc./ Also every month or week they deposit some specified amount on cash and each month or week, one person will get the entire amount. And this is generally through a draw

Hujum: a programme/campaign to eliminate the hijab (veil) and liberate women

Salem: hello

Rakhmet: Thank you

Babushka: Grandmother

Atta: Grandfather

List of Tables

List of Maps

Graphs

Figure

Images

Map-1:

India: Political

India[1]: States and Union Territories, January 2019

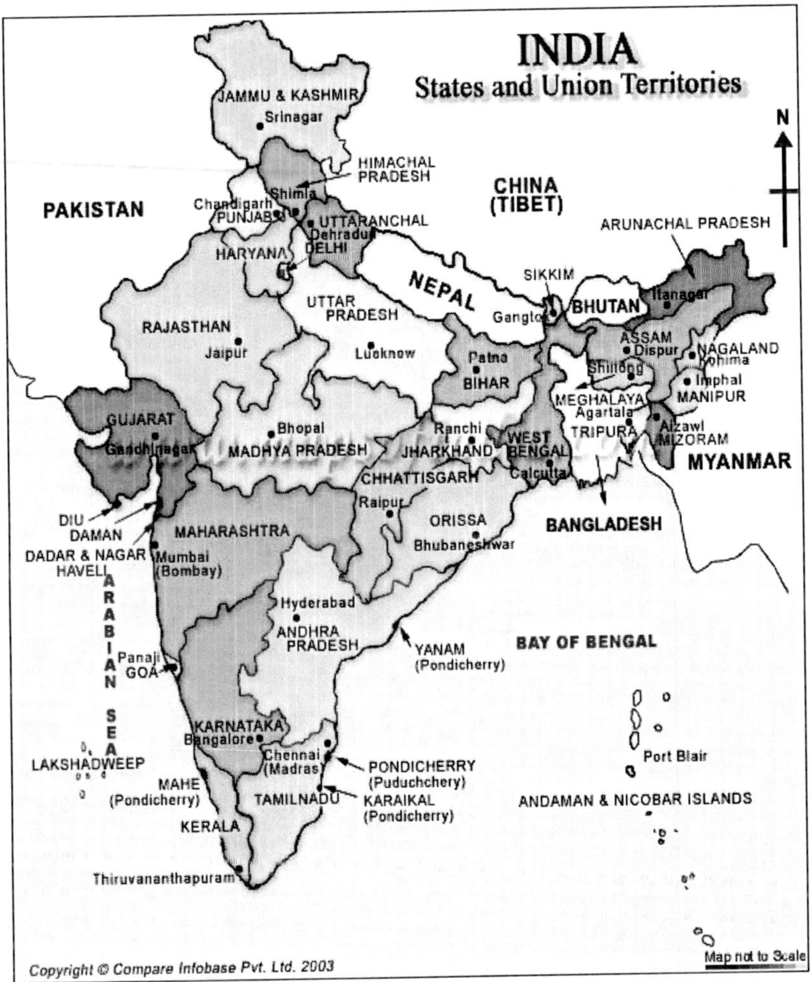

Source: http://www.mapsofindia.com/maps/india/india-political-map.htm. Accessed on 31 January 2019.

---

1. India is officially known as the Republic of India, is a peninsula and is in Southern part of Asia. India is the world's largest democracy and the second most populated country.

Map-2

Central Asia: Political

The geographical location and international boundaries of Central Asian Republics[1]

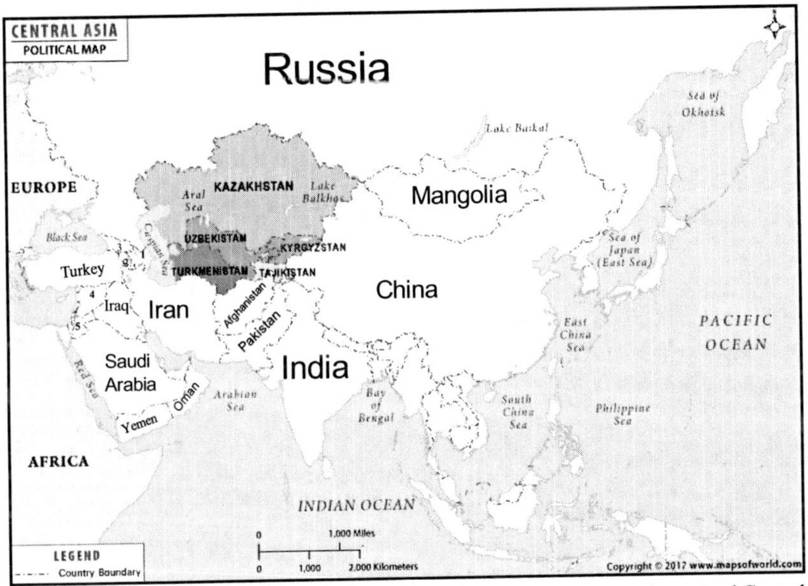

Source: Author has customised this Map, by filling the names of the countries around Central Asia, in the Map from Maps of world: http://www.mapsofworld.com/asia/regions/central-asia-map.html. Accessed on 27 November 2019.

Note: In the Map, the numbers marked corresponds to the following countries:

1. Azerbaijan, 2. Armenia, 3. Georgia, 4. Syria, 5. Jordan

---

1. Central Asia is located in the heart of Asia and comprises of five 'stans' (Kazakhstan, Kyrgyzstan, Tajikistan, Turkmenistan, Uzbekistan). They became independent in 1991.

Chapter 1

Introduction

> *"Empowerment of women and equality between women and men are prerequisites for achieving political, social, economic, cultural and environmental security among all peoples".*
>
> *– Beijing Platform of Action,*
> *United Nations Fourth World Conference,*
> *Women Beijing, 1995*

India and Central Asia have innumerable similarities as well as common values like, democracy and rule of law; and cultural and civilisational links. Besides, societies in India and Central Asia are primarily patriarchic like many other societies of the world having manifested male dominance in all walks of life. These countries have made great strides in terms of economic and social development. However, the economic progress made has not trickled down to the weaker sections of the society including majority of women. Apart from this, women face discrimination in terms of their role; economic, social and predominantly political and they need to work really hard with respect to women's participation in the political sphere. Political participation is an essential element of democracy and of paramount importance for the development of both, the individual and nation. Perhaps, that is why political participation of women is considered to be the hallmark of democracy and progressiveness of a nation. The present study is an attempt to study women in India and Central Asia with focus on changing role of women since 1991, a landmark year when India ushered in economic reforms which influenced the society as well as the approach of the political class towards women's issues and their role. Same year Soviet Union disintegrated and Central Asian Republics (CARs) gained independence. Central Asia, due to its dual experience of transition and development, is a fascinating region for research. Also this region is understudied, in part due to lack of availability of data on these countries; and lack of literature; and of the literature available, it is mostly from the western perspective.

The choice of India and Central Asia for this study has been made keeping a number of factors in mind. First, in all these countries women have had equal rights for a considerable part of their recent history. In other words, there is substantial history to women's rights including political. However, in both cases, as has been the trend world over, the rights on paper, in practice did not automatically translate into power in the hands of women. Third, countries under study have witnessed an increase in the intensity of democratisation; CARs, since independence and India following the rise of public interest litigations and the Panchayati Raj legislation. Also, there have been significant changes following liberalisation of the economy in the 1990s. Another reason that influenced the choice of these countries is the relatively important positions of these countries in their respective regions; India as the biggest democracy in the world and CARs as a part of former global superpower and strategic location with abundance of natural resources.

Status of Women

Gender equality and women's empowerment is the third of eight UN Millennium Development Goals (MDGs). However, according to the UN data and reports, due to the persistent disadvantages, women accounted for two-thirds of the world's 774 million adult illiterates till early into this century. Gender disparities in adult literacy rates remain wide in most regions of the world. According to the UN, globally, 123 million youth (aged 15 to 24) lack basic reading and writing skills. 61 percent of them are young women, though, the gender gaps in youth literacy rates is narrowing globally; there were 95 literate young women for every 100 young men in 2010, compared with 90 women in 1990,[3] which has further improved over the years.

There is a reason to look towards future decades with optimism as improvement in access to education eventually raises literacy levels. As improvements in youth literacy rates have been accompanied by declining gender disparities.[4] Women in India and Central Asia continue to have a better status than women in their immediate neighbourhood, as the condition of women in many West Asian societies and some of the South Asian countries are even worse.

In India, there have been major transformations in terms of policy and programmes regarding women in the post-1990s particularly for women's empowerment; education and economic independence. According to 2001 census, the overall literacy rate is 64.8 %, the male female ratio of literacy rate is 75.3:53.7 percent, however, the literacy rate of women is gradually increasing[5] and in the urban setups, women have outperformed their male counterparts in several fields. Women in India have also made a mark in terms of economic independence. They are contributing not only to the source of income of the family but contributing in a big way in the development of the country. However, majority of population resides in the rural areas, where women are not encouraged to study, work independently and away from home. Though in recent years, there have been some signs of dilution in this thinking, it would still take a long time for this attitude to go away altogether.

In Central Asia, the disintegration of the Soviet Union caused political and economic crises, and these countries underwent transition in social, political, cultural and economic spheres. The transition to democracy, privatisation and a free market economy, opened many opportunities for the Central Asians, including integration into the global economy. And as rapid social change in transitional societies leads to social upheavals, in the case of Central Asian societies, wide ranging changes in social stratification occurred resulting in women being among the worst affected. As privatisation and structural adjustment resulted in cuts in social outlays like education, health, pensions, child allowances and unemployment benefits, the impact of these changes was first felt by women, both at work and at home.

However, with regard to literacy rate of Central Asian Women (CAW), it is remarkably high; as high as at 98 percent, which is comparable with several developed countries. School and college enrolment for women remains the highest when compared internationally. Despite rising unemployment, CAW are majorly engaged in some sort of economic activity contributing to the overall economy of their family and country. Besides, all the Central Asian countries covered under this study have constitutional provisions of equality of sexes (see Appendix 1.A, B, C, D, E).

With regard to women in politics and other decision-making positions in the countries under study, the picture is not very encouraging. Women's participation and representation has shown some positive results in last ten years though. Women's political participation, has been slowly improving, for example, the rate of participation in Parliaments has grown and as of February 2019, the world average was 24.3% and Asian average at 19.8%. With regard to women heads of state or government, as of June 2019, 11 women were head of state and 12 as head of government. Earlier, there were 20 women heads of state or government, and women held about 16% of ministerial portfolios across the world. As of February 2019,

20.7% women were ministers, in another word one in five ministers is a woman.[6]

There is under-representation of women in political sphere, though, it is not because of the lack of education alone as sighted most of the times, but also other socioeconomic factors such as traditional patriarchal psyche and gender inequality in terms of opportunities, for example, despite several decades of active democracy in India, women's political participation remains disappointing owing to socioeconomic and cultural reasons. However, Panchayati Raj Institution has politically empowered Indian women by ensuring fixed number of constituencies and seats for them resulting in more and more women becoming aware about the ongoing political developments and showing their willingness to come forward. And with time, it has started to show an upward trend, at least, at the very basic level of governance. Such provisions are yet to be replicated at state and national level. In India, despite the best of intentions, the Women's Reservation Bill introduced in 1998 has ended up on the side of controversy and has been practically buried.

In Central Asia, women's participation in the political process is generally influenced by the regime in power. Post-independence Central Asia witnessed new trends of cultural nationalism and re-Islamisation of the society. This was adverse to women's overall development and has emerged as a major hindrance to the political participation of women, though, women in Central Asia has better representation rate than India.

Review of Literature

Going through variety of literature it is quite clear that the involvement of women and their role in position of power or society is generally examined through the prism of international economic forces, nationalism, religious fundamentalism and the feminist movements etc. Women in India and Central Asia, has and had most of these elements.

Lincoln Chen et al, bring forth the issue and the result of economic, social and political reforms and how the related crisis gets tackled.[7] Education, employment, and political participation are considered essential to the achievement of gender equality and women's empowerment and certainly has the potential to bring about positive changes in women's lives, says Naila Kabeer.[8]

From the economic aspect, state has failed to remove inequality and provide socio-economic justice to women after economic liberalisation.

In a structural manner, the miserable conditions of women in terms of work place insecurity and violence, low wages in manual jobs and in some instances preference of men over women speaks volumes regarding the prevailing psyche and mindset.[9] Janaki Nair introduces the theoretical foundations of the legal juridical framework that was evolved under colonial rule and the paradox of the lack of a suffrage movement in India of the nineteenth and twentieth century. Nair makes the point, that the unevenness that marks access to the legal system in India as far as women are concerned is a result of their generally low economic status and low education. These do not allow them to translate legal provisions into practice, or challenge and change some of these provisions.[10]

Rajeswari Rajan analyses the intricately woven "relationship between the post-colonial, democratic Indian nation state and Indian women's actual needs and lives and how the state is central to understanding women's identities and how, reciprocally, women and 'women's issues' affect the state's role and function. In India, law and citizenship define for women not only the scope of political rights but also cultural identity and everyday life". Rajan exposes the contradictory position of the Indian state vis-à-vis its female citizens and brings out the inadequacy of its commitment to women's rights.[11]

Segregation of women combine to reinforce, not only the view that society is dichotomised into public and private spaces but also the stereotyped gender roles that assign women to the seclusion of the domestic sphere. Jinee Lokeneela questions the political agenda of empowerment of women, which have come into vogue as methods of redressing gender discrimination. She argues that empowerment of women emerges as an extremely limited concept and that empowerment should imply a power to participate in all decision-making and in all spheres of society without the separation of the public and private. She emphasises her point of view by noting the fact that political parties with no political commitment towards struggle for women's rights not only fail to transcend the state's agenda, but further collaborate with the state in order to keep the patriarchal process intact.[12]

Najma Chowdury, et al, however, underscore that, women all over the world have never had equality with men in terms of political status, access or influence. The politics of everyday life is studied in terms of patriarchy, female representation in political parties, reproductive health, and domestic violence. They argue that wherever women exercise political power, the situation is always exceptional.[13] Political power is linked to social and economic power. As Pargunan analyses the political status of Indian women and the power with a broader interpretation. The State, Pargunan feels, has resorted symbolic policy-making and in the process has co-opted women's movement without bringing any real changes in the lives of women and depoliticised women's movement.[14]

Linda Richter, while analysing the effects of patriarchy on the chances of women becoming political leaders, believes that the ideology of patriarchy has had a decisive impact on the fate of women in most cultures around the globe as male dominance has been legitimated in law and custom. Patriarchy also determines the role of women in the political sphere, which is considered natural for men but women are made to struggle.[15] Rehana explores the impact of globalisation on Indian women and the struggle for gender equality and gives insight into gender identity, gender relations and conceptions of violence against women by women. She presents the relation between women and the media and draws a clear picture of politics and women's political participation.[16]

Letha Kumari argues that the focal point of resistance must be against male abuse of power and subjection of women to the personal satisfaction of men. She opines that women all over the world continue to be marginalised in the game of political administrative power. Equal opportunities for both men and women remain to be created. Economic exploitation and social oppression towards women is not only rampart but shocking as well.[17]

Kiran Saxena highlights the limited choices Indian women are left with owing to the domination of patriarchy. She also focuses on the existing contradictions among constitutional provisions ensuring equality and widespread gender discrimination. Only few extraordinarily courageous and fortunate women could carve some niche for themselves. Such women rose to the upper echelons of power rarely and that is why very seldom women are visible in social and political life.[18] According to Thompson, the rareness of female leaders has been explained by traditional stereotypes about women's nonpolitical role in the family.[19]

Mohini Giri, contests that, while "women constitute half the country's population the dismal figure of female representation in Lok Sabha speaks volumes of gender bias". She further stresses that the rough and challenging world of politics does not attract more enthusiastic participants; but for an effective functioning of democracy, a larger participation of women is essential. Citing the example of Mahatma Gandhi's call which inspired even women to leave their homes and join the freedom struggle argues that thereafter, perhaps, politics has not enchanted women to the extent to which other areas have done.[20]

Raichel Mathai points out to the practice and failure of women's political participation measures. The number of women filling their nomination paper in any election, national or state level, is only a fraction of the corresponding number of men; the membership of women in the political parties are extremely low; the representation of the women in the higher cadres of the political parties is lower. In some cases, women are not much aware of the mainstream activities of their respective parties at all.[21] And women political participation at panchayat level has been symbolic in many cases.

Likewise, in Central Asia the views and opinions are no different. Rafis Abazov says, "Central Asian society has many hidden, invisible social and cultural customs, religious traditions, family experiences and the history of local developments". Women had legal rights both under *Adat* and *Shariah* laws, but these rights were not literally being practiced or followed. For example, women had the right to divorce, but they had to prove their case against their husband (of being impotent or abusive etc.) before the local court.[22] During Soviet time, at least there were accesses to facilities like childcare, healthcare etc, even though these were tied to labour force participation and in fact it did not automatically serve the purpose of easing the burden of women.[23]

Women in Soviet Central Asia though, were in much better condition than women in the most developed countries of the world during soviet period. Ajay Patnaik's study highlights women's emancipation in the Soviet period with special stress on women labour force and through his remarkably chronicled and scholarly work (probably one of the first on such a broad based theme) has highlighted the achievements of Central Asian women.[24] Transition to privatisation post-disintegration, Mehrangiz Najafizadeh feels, resulted in the elimination of several incentives including healthcare which were previously taken care of by the state. And among the worst affected areas were education and public services.[25]

Besides, the factors influencing women's role in public and decision-making, Marifat Abodullaeva identifies, as role of few Islamic groups in promoting partial or full veiling and voluntary seclusion as another significant reason. She says, in some countries of the region there is a tendency to form such a stereotype among the young and relatively educated men, which promotes the views like prohibiting wives to work. There are increasing number of cases where husbands require their wives to wear *paranja* or *hijab* (big kerchief), and seldom be out of home.[26]

Caroline Sweetman, notes the positive implications of self-employment which is widespread in Central Asia. She says, even, "paid-work carried at home have the potential to shift the balance of power within the family."[27] Anuradha Chenoy contests that, "despite the rising statistics of women in political roles, the secondary status of women in places of power is evident in Central Asia".[28]

Nazneen Kanji argues that, "CAW's workload has increased manifolds and conflict in household relations is constantly growing". Kanji further compares and contrasts the condition of CAW during pre-disintegration and post-disintegration period. In the aftermath of the disintegration, "women had been compelled to retreat into subsistence production, housework, and when possible, petty trading in order to cope with the very difficult situation". CAW no longer have time to participate actively in public decision making arenas, even at the local level.[29] Susana Fried analyses, "how women's organisations, over the past three decades, have created a paradigm shift in understanding and acting to end violence against women".[30]

These works of literature provide the basis for this research. All these, and various other literature reviews shows that, there is no dearth of literature on women related issues in India and Central Asian Republics. However, a study of the changing role of women's in society with reference to political role has not been attempted. Therefore, a study focusing on this aspect of women's role is essential. This study underscores the factors behind women's inadequate representation and role in societies in India and CARs.

This topic is also relevant because there are clearly identifiable reasons why women were not able to take full advantage of their rights in these countries. Patriarchy and the obvious gendered notions of what a woman's place should be, sometimes have specific agencies in these countries that contrive to keep women tied down to what are considered traditional roles. In India, the continuing patriarchal, caste and religious structures hinder women's emancipation. Despite continued lip-service to the ideal of political and social equality for women in these countries, things have not moved forward as much as the women themselves would have liked; the campaigns for change that women have had, with regard to women's empowerment; or their continued lack of representation in the political arena; the kind of initiatives they have taken and their consequences. It is in this context that this study becomes more important. The scope of the work covers, in general, the situation of women in India and Central Asia and particularly focuses on the changing role of women in society and their participation in the political and public sphere.

Objectives and Research Questions

The chapters are based on the analysis of some of the issues mentioned above. To have an insight of the issues, the objectives and research questions were conceived at the outset of this research. The present study analyses the implications of sociopolitical changes on women in the countries under study and seeks to understand the changing roles of women in these societies post-1991. The study also looks into the nature and extent of the decline or improvement in the status of women in the countries under study. The present study also tries to examine the institutions which are effective in women's campaign for change and strengthening political participation and issues which prevent them from playing a more prominent role.

Some of the other important research issues analysed in this study includes; how have social and economic conditions affected the role of women in societies in these countries including political? What are the distinctive features of the participation of women in the political processes in India and Central Asia since 1991? How have the governments and societies in each of these countries responded to the question of women in politics and what do the findings presage for women's political participation elsewhere? What are the commonalties and differences in political role of women in these countries?

Methodology and Sources

Descriptive and analytical approach has been followed in this study. The study has taken into consideration the historical, geographical, ideological and cultural dimensions, as well as national specificities relevant to the objectives of the study. The area of enquiry is India and Central Asia. In Central Asia, the focus is on the five Central Asian Republics- Kazakhstan, Kyrgyzstan, Tajikistan, Turkmenistan and Uzbekistan. The study has been carried out through extensive perusal of literature such as books, articles, and unpublished works, documents, speeches, government releases, proceedings of conferences and policy papers from both governmental and non-governmental sources available in Hindi, English as well as in Russian, Kazakh and Turkmen languages.

Literature in the native languages of the CARs, are not available and translated in English widely. Therefore, the literatures which the author could get translated in English from the available literatures in Turkmen and Kazakh languages have been used. The sources majorly used for analysis are people, documents, observations and websites visits (Of all websites, mostly accessed several times between, March 2012-July 2014; some in April-May, 2017; and October-November, 2019; March-May, 2020). The Analysis is based on the Author's perspectives and understanding of the region through lectures, discussions and interactions with her supervisor and other experts on this subject. Keeping in mind the local perspective and besides, truth being relative, the Author has tried to use as much as possible the available literatures which reflect the local perspective to the maximum. For this, the Author took extensive Field work to these countries. The Author was in Central Asia from 17th October to 14 December 2012 for field research and again visited in August 2014. Visits were made to various places; Kazakhstan- Almaty, Chimkent, Turkistan, Taras, Sairam, Astana; Kyrgyzstan- Bishkek, Ata-Beyit, Burana fort near Tokmok, Osh, Uzgen; Tajikistan- Dushanbe, Kurgan; Turkmenistan- Ashgabat; Uzbekistan- Tashkent and Samarkand.

As part of Field work interviews were conducted with various stakeholders such as officials in Ministries, Diplomats and Academicians; Bureaucrats, Organisational heads and journalists. In due course, there were discussions and interactions as the Author also visited universities, institutes, head offices of organisations, libraries, pilgrimage sites, museums, archeological sites, Zilyoni bazaars, Tolkuchka bazaar etc. In India, visits took place to as many cities possible during research period. However, due to financial constrains the research in India was carried out mostly during stay for conferences and workshops. In fact, conference participations were used also for the purpose of this research-work. Though, it was kept in mind to use the same methodology and similar questionnaire and list of questions as in case of Central Asia, (See Appendix V). Apart from this, communications with prominent individuals in academia, involved in women's movements, and working in related areas, through email and correspondence has also been part of the process and their opinions have been duly incorporated.

Economic liberalisation in India and the disintegration of USSR impacted the entire population in India and Central Asia, but the most drastic effects came with changing economy, politics; and in case of Central Asia also the resurgence of Islam and traditional beliefs; that can be seen in the changing status of women in these countries. In the following chapters, the changing role of women, are analysed. The next; **Chapter Two**, describes the implications of sociopolitical and economic changes on women post-1991 under the broad categories of education and employment. This is followed by **Chapter Three,** which deals with women's political participation and their representations in decision-making institutions, along with the factors determining their participation and challenges they face. **Chapter Four** discusses women's campaign for change, the role of different actors be it the government, NGOs or Women Organisations in shaping the role, life and lifestyle of women. The challenges to women's campaign have also been touched upon in this chapter. This chapter also has a section which elaborates the **field trip experience and observations of the Author along with the highlights of the research**. The **Concluding Chapter** sums up the findings of the research.

Notes

1. India is officially known as the Republic of India, is a peninsula and is in Southern part of Asia. India is the world's largest democracy and the second most populated country.
2. Central Asia is located in the heart of Asia and comprises of five 'stans' (Kazakhstan, Kyrgyzstan, Tajikistan, Turkmenistan, Uzbekistan). They became independent in 1991.
3. See http://www.gsleducation.com/news-28-UN-Millennium-Development-Goals-and-Education—.html. Accessed on 14 March 2014; Also see http://www.un.org/millenniumgoals/education.shtml. Accessed on 14 March 2014.
4. The World's Women 2010, United Nations, New York, 2010.
   http://unstats.un.org/unsd/demographic/products/Worldswomen/WW_fullreport_color.pdf. Accessed on 24 June 2014.
5. As many as 560,687,797 persons in the country are literate. Of these 336,533,716 are males and 224, 154,081 are females. The gap is more in the rural areas. In the urban areas, higher literacy rate has been recorded both for males and females and the difference among the sexes is lower (13 percentage points). See http://censusindia.gov.in/Census_And_You/literacy_and_level_of_education.aspx, Accessed on May 2014.
6. As according to 2019 IPU/UN Women Map. https://www.ipu.org/news/press-releases/2019-03/one in five-ministers-woman-according-new-ipuun-women-map. Accessed on 15 November 2019.
7. Lincoln, C Chen, et al., "Health Crisis in Central Asian Republics," *Economic and Political Weekly*, Vol. 27, No. 23, June 6, 1992, pp. 1197-1202.
8. Naila Kabeer, Gender Equality and Women's Empowerment: A Critical Analysis of the Third Millennium Development Goal, *Gender and Development*, Vol. 13, No. 1, March 2005, pp. 13-24.
9. Anupam Ghosal, "Gender and Poverty: A Case Study of India", *Jadavpur Journal of International Relations*, 11(12), 2008, 302-316.
10. Janaki Nair, "Women and Law in Colonial India: A Social History," in Kiran Saxena (ed), *Women and Politics*, New Delhi: Gyan Publishing House, 2000.

11. Rajeswari Sunder Rajan, *The Scandal of the State: Women, Law, and Citizenship in Postcolonial India*, Durham: Duke University Press, 2003.
12. Jinee Lokeneela, "Women Empowerment: Redefining Agenda" in Kiran Saxena, (ed.), *Women and Politics*, New Delhi: Gyan Publishing House, 2000.
13. Najma Chowdury, et al, "Redefining Politics: Patterns of Women's Political Engagement from a Global Perspective," in Barbara J Nelson and Najma Chowdhury, *Women and Politics Worldwide*, New Haven: Yale University Press, 1997.
14. M. Pargunan, "Political Empowerment of Women: An Illusion", *Kurukshetra*, 55(5), 2007, pp. 12-18.
15. Linda K Richter, "Exploring Theories of Female Leadership in South and Southeast Asia," *Pacific Affairs*, No. 4, Winter 1990-1991.
16. Rehana Ghadially, (ed), *Urban Women in Contemporary India: A Reader*, London: Sage Publications, 2007.
17. R. Letha Kumari, *Women in Politics: Participation and Governance*, Delhi: Researcher's Press, 2006.
18. Kiran Saxena (ed), *Women and Politics*, New Delhi: Gyan Publishing House, 2000.
19. Mark R Thompson, "Female Leadership of Democratic Transitions in Asia", *Pacific Affairs*, Vol. 75, No. 4, Winter, 2002-2003, pp. 535-555.
20. Mohini Giri, "Women and Politics," in Yashoda Bhat, (ed.), *Beyond the Threshold: Indian Women on the Move*, New Delhi: B R Publishing Corporation, 1995.
21. Raichel Mathai, "Political status of Indian Women: Progress since Independence", *Mainstream*, Xliv (1), 2006, pp. 83-86.
22. Rafis Abazov, *Culture and Customs of Central Asia*, London: Greenwood, 2007.
23. Tatyana Teplova, "Welfare State Transformation, Childcare and Women's Work in Russia", *The Researcher* 2007, Oxford: Oxford University Press, 2007.
24. Ajay Patnaik, *Perestroika and Women Labour Force in Soviet Central Asia,* New Delhi: New Literature, 1989.
25. Mehrangiz Najafizadeh, "Women's Empowering Carework in Post-Soviet Azerbaijan," *Gender and Society*, Vol. 17, No. 2, April, 2003, pp. 293-304.
26. Marifat Abdullaeva, Background paper prepared for the "Education for All", Global Monitoring Report 2006, Literacy for Life, Review of Central Asian countries, UNESCO, 2006. http://unesdoc.unesco.org/images/0014/001459/145934e.pdf. Accessed on 11 March 2013.
27. Caroline Sweetman, "Gendpublicer and the Millennium Development Goals", Oxfam, 2005, p. 17.
28. Anuradha M Chenoy, "Islam, Women and Identity in Contemporary Central Asia," *Economic and Political Weekly*, Vol. 31, No. 9, March 2, 1996, pp. 516-518.
29. Nazneen Kanji, "Trading and Trade-Offs: Women's Livelihoods in Gorno-Badakhshan, Tajikistan", *Development in Practice*, Vol. 12, No. 2 (May, 2002), pp. 138-152.
30. Susana T Fried, "Violence Against Women," *Health and Human Rights*, Vol. 6, No. 2, 2003, pp. 88-111.

Chapter 2

Socio-economic Transformation and Women

The worth of a civilisation can be construed from the position it assigns to women, as women's wellbeing is important for the wellbeing of society and for the nation to prosper!
"In order to change the condition of life, we must learn to see them through the eyes of women" – LEON TROTSKY

Implications of any transformation; sociopolitical or socioeconomic, are not only felt by women first, but impacts directly their role and status in society. This is due to the fact, that, women world over, play and are expected to play pivotal role in shaping the society and the nation. In fact women have time and again, had more responsibility bestowed upon them, more so in this globalised world.

Historical background

India

India could best be described in its first Prime Minister Jawaharlal Nehru's words, "India is a geographical and economic entity, a cultural unity amidst diversity, a bundle of contradictions held together by strong but invisible threads".[1] India has been home to "the ancient Indus Valley Civilisation and a region of historic trade routes and vast empires and cultural wealth for much of its long history". India as an amalgamation of several cultures, spans across the Indian subcontinent and includes traditions that are several millennia old. India's great and rich cultural heritage has four of world's religions- Hinduism, Buddhism, Jainism, and Sikhism which originated here, and Zoroastrianism, Christianity, and Islam arrived from elsewhere. All these helped India shape its highly diverse culture with many languages, cultures and religions; making India one of the most religiously diverse nations in the world. India being a multicultural and multi-religious society, people here celebrate holidays and festivals of all religions with zeal and enthusiasm.[2] In fact, India's unique feature is its unity in diversity. Even Mark Twain was mesmerised by cultural heritage of India, and said, "India is the cradle of human race, the birthplace of human speech, the mother of history, the grandmother of legend, and the great grandmother of tradition. Our most valuable and most astrictive materials in the history of man are treasured up in India only!"[3]

Women in India have had their share of ups and downs in their status at different times, as is evident, through the wide angled view of the evolution of women and their unique cultural identity in Indian history. As land of diversity and opportunity, India, has always been an attractive destination for invaders like the Kushans, Mughals and others. "Each of these invaders brought their own distinct culture and perceptions of womanhood to this country".[4] Of the several factors that justify the greatness of India's ancient culture, one of the greatest is the honoured place ascribed to women. Manu, said long ago, '*Yatra naryastu poojyante ramante tatra devataha*' (Where women are worshipped there reside the Gods).[5] The "Rig Vedic Women, enjoyed high status in society".[6] However, from enjoying free and respected positions in the Rig Vedic society, women started being discriminated against in later periods.

Women in Ancient India

The role of women as in Ancient Indian Literature is immense. In terms of education, there are some bright exceptions. Ancient India had many learned women. There were two types of scholarly women; the Brahmavadinis, and the Sadyodvahas.[7] Panini in his *Ashtadhyayi* (the ancient text: 6.2.86) takes notice of female students and mentioned of them studying Vedas. Katyayana in his *Vartika* (4.1.48) refers to women teachers who were called *Upadhyaya* or *Upadhyayi*, as distinguished from *Upadhyayanis* (wives of teachers). It also shows that there were quite a large number of women teachers.[8] Ashoka 'the great', got his daughter Sanghamitra, inducted into preaching Buddhism. Even from the Jain texts, we learn about the Kousambi princess, Jayanti, who remained a spinster to have studied religion and philosophy. Various literature mentions that, often, Buddhist nuns even composed hymns. Also some women wrote Sanskrit plays and verses, excelled in music, painting and other fine arts.[9]

During ancient times women were treated at par with men even in political and philosophical spheres. Women often enjoyed prominent roles in public sphere too. Megasthenes mentioned of Pandya women running the administration. The *Satavahana* queen, "Nayanika ruled the kingdom on behalf of her minor son. So did Pravabati, daughter of Chandragupta II, on behalf of the minor prince Vakataka. A little after the Gupta period, queens used to rule in Kashmir, Orissa and Andhra. Princess Vijaybhattarika acted as the provincial ruler under the Chalukya King and Vikramaditya I. Women were provincial and village administrators in the Kannada region".[10] Though it is believed that, only women from the aristocratic classes enjoyed education and other privileges and the common woman were still far from many of such activities. And "down the centuries, women were pushed to the background"[11] and the overall the position of women in society deteriorated.

Unlike, in the ancient period, the position and status of women in the Mughal period was not high. *Purdah* and child marriage had become common. Though, the overall position of women in Mughal period was low, there were many women of outstanding ability, whose fame is still well-known, as they played an important part in the affairs of that time, notably Rani Durgawati of Gondwana, Rani Karmawati, Mira Bai, Tarabai, Razia Sultan (Sultanate and the Mughal period), Mariam-uz-Zamani Begum, also known as Heer Kunwari, Hira Kunwari or Harka Bai (also mentioned as Jodha Bai in some literaure), Nur Jahan, Mumtaz Begum (Arjumand Banu Begum), Chand Bibi, Jahanara, Raushanara, Zeb-un-nisa.[12]

Second half of nineteenth century and the early years of the twentieth century witnessed rapid progress in breaking down prejudices against women's education and their role in society for example, Rama Bai (Pandita Rama Bai), who dedicated her life and strove hard for the upliftment of women and their education. Annie Besant also played very pivotal role in promoting women's education. Socio-religious reform movements like the Arya Samaj, the Brahmo Samaj and the Theosophical Society added impetus to this awakening. After provincial autonomy came into effect as the result of the Government of India Act of 1935, many women became ministers in Congress Governments. Many women started studying economics, sociology, science, mathematics, etc. which they could not do earlier. Social hindrances like *Purdah* began to disappear gradually.[13]

Ever since Rani Lakshmi Bai took to the throne and fought the British, women have been seen in public sphere. Thousands of women both educated and uneducated took part in the freedom movement under Gandhiji's leadership, fearlessly facing police's *lathis* and guns and were very active in different aspects. In fact, India's freedom struggle movement had more women in positions of importance than in Russian or Chinese revolutions.

"Sarojni Naidu was elected as first woman president of Congress as early as 1925, even long before United Kingdom elected Margaret Thatcher as first and only woman leader of Conservative Party".[14]

Post-Independence

Post-independence in 1947, several measures were taken by the Government of India to assign equal status to women in the economic, political and social sphere. More avenues were opened to women to show their talents and have a sense of participation in national activities. Today, women in India participate in politics, lead political parties and make crucial decisions affecting millions. Legacy and vision of modernity of India's first woman prime minister Indira Gandhi continue even today. By 1990s literacy rate of women grew and women were more visible both in politics and economy. The governments through different policies and programmes made sure that women also got their due. Women movements also helped in this to some extent.

India has come a long way from the days immediately after independence in 1947, when its economy and population both were in highly unimpressive conditions. It had many challenges to overcome; however, India has managed to meet those successfully and reach to a level where it could influence the global economic and political arena. Today India has become one of the fastest growing economies of the world, following the market based economic reforms in 1991. Although India continues to face the challenges, but these are of different kind like corruption and terrorism. Though, further developments of society including that of women, gets hampered.[15]

Central Asia

Through the ages, history of different people and races has been shaped by their topography and environment; the climate, terrain and water resources have influenced people and racial characteristics, which became the roots of distinct cultures. One has to search their respective roots to understand different cultures; and in case of Central Asia these are embedded in religion.[16] These Central Asian Republics, besides geography, share a similar history, culture, legacy and a common vision for the future. Central Asia's location between Europe and Asia has also contributed to the diversity of this region. The Uttara Path (northern Route) and during the Roman Empire, the famous 'Silk Road' which was a series of trade routes for valuables, developed in the southern region of Central Asia connecting India, China and Europe.[17] Commodities, including silk, were traded over these routes. However, some of the treasures exchanged along the Silk Road were more enduring and significant than commodities. And these treasures were the art, literature, religion, language and values of many cultures. Exchanges of both culture and commodities have enriched lives for centuries, and continue to do so today.[18] This resulted in an increased interest in the people, culture and the region's resources as it grew commercially and culturally. A variety of groups competed to influence the region but it was the Arabs and Turks who brought the religion of Islam to the people of Central Asia.[19]

Women in Pre-Soviet Central Asia

Central Asians had actively participated in Islamic civilisation, producing many of its great dynasties and cultural achievements, as the vast majority of Central Asians were Muslims.[20] Therefore, it is no chance that Central Asian people prior to 1917 had Islamic culture and practices. By the year 750, Arabs had completed the conquest of Central Asia, imposing Islam and new culture.[21] Islam became a dominant religion from the 8th century onwards. When Islam was introduced in the social landscape of Central Asia, it was redefined to suit the ethnic and tribal peculiarities that had shaped the life of people for centuries. These people observed the Islamic practices in accordance with Quranic percepts. The combination of formal laws of *Sharia* and the local customary laws of *adat* were intimately related to the social structures and dominant forms of social life in these societies.[22]

Large extended family was a norm. There was considerable age difference between husband and wife. Women though, made important contribution to the family income, but their most important duty was child-bearing. Proverbs suggests that, daughters were considered as burdens, but large number of sons were considered prosperous for the household. Female mortality was also high. Child marriage, *Ichkari*, *Paranja*, polygamy, violence were common. Marriage was a property transaction between the relatives of the bride and groom including *kalym*. Husband had unlimited authority over his wife.[23]

Society in the pre-Soviet era was in general very patriarchal with women generally confined to the home and excluded from most activities including formal education. Men were the breadwinners while women carried out all the domestic chores.[24] There was no attempt in the Tsarist period to raise the educational and cultural level of the indigenous population. In fact the local population was left to be taken care of by the religious institutions, which did not have modern curriculum, and also did not encourage girls to study. Literacy rate was extremely low in Central Asia and as far as women were concerned it was dismal. Sanctified by religion, host of traditions and customs kept women away from having a life outside the household.[25]

Barring few exceptions like Merv in Turkmenistan, where, even as early as the end of eighth century, there was a possibility to study of science. Centres were opened up, for example, a library by Govher Hatyn, sister of Sultan Sandjar. In this library, however, there were also books on beauty and morals, female character (aesthetics) and women being glorified, and there was possibility of women to be engaged in creative work. Creativity of Mehesti, the female poet of the middle ages, is a distinct example; she was a poet and also master of song performances and music. She was also a very good chess player and was awarded by Sultan for her talents.[26] Even in Uzbekistan, some literature suggests, that there were efforts on the part of the *jadids/jadidism* (reformists/reformist movement) intellectuals regarding educating women and in some areas women were considered as important agents of change.[27]

Few of these countries had nomadic culture and women played a very important role in the nomadic group. The economic structure of the nomadic organisation could not be sustained without them. Women carried out all the chores and labour. The so called 'barbarians', as designated by the Chinese, were far advanced in terms of women's rights. In later periods of nomadic history women had right to own property and animals, which was unique in traditional times. They had a right to divorce. While the men could focus on warfare and fighting against enemies, the women would take care of economic basis of the entire economy of the nomadic group.[28] And moreover, nomadic women had far more freedom and responsibility than is allowed to the women of the settlements.[29] In few of these countries like, for example, Kazakhstan and Turkmenistan which had nomadic culture, women did not cover their faces.[30] However, over all, a host of traditions and customs sanctified by religion kept women away from having a life outside the household. Even after the Russian Revolution, during the initial few years people of the region maintained their identity and pursued religious beliefs.[31]

Soviet Central Asia

With the Russian conquest of Central Asia especially after the establishment of communist rule in 1917, the situations changed considerably for the Muslims especially so for women, keeping in mind, the perturbing picture of the social position of women in this region. As mentioned before, women in Central Asia during the Tsarist period were left untouched and uncared for and lived life without human dignity. They were dependent on men for everything, as they did not have any access to education or culture.[32] Regarding the social condition of Central Asian Muslim women Lenin had said that they "were the most oppressed of the oppressed and the most enslaved of the enslaved".[33]

To uplift the condition of women in this region was a challenge for the Soviet government. The attempt to liberate Central Asian women from both men and their religion was however much in line with the overarching political ideology that was created by the Soviet system. The early Soviet period was characterised by the attempt to liberate women from their prescribed gender roles in the Islamic society. Russian observations of female seclusion and the strong patriarchal system, led the Soviet policy makers to adopt the project to liberate Central Asian Muslim women.[34]

With the advent of Soviet control of Central Asia in the early twentieth century, government programmes were designed and instituted to increase the power of the lower and middle class segments of society. By the 1920s, only few Tajiks had received a formal education and according to the first Soviet census, the literacy rate was 4 percent for Tajik men and 0.1 percent for Tajik women.[35] The programmes designed, were for the upliftment of the people in the society in general and women in particular.

These programmes included land redistribution, educational reform and public work programmes, such as the construction of libraries and cultural centers and thereby decrease the power and influence of religious leaders and the local oligarchs. Through the Soviet education programmes primary education was made compulsory for the entire population. Network of schools and teacher training colleges was expanded. In 1919 Islamic institutions like Muslim schools were gradually closed and replaced with Soviet-run schools that were mandatory for youth of both sexes to attend. The Soviet policies of the 1920-1930s were aimed to bring about the radical transformation of Central Asian society. Positive measures such as the introduction of mass literacy, compulsory education, provision of social welfare services and the emancipation of women[36] were taken up.

The most striking thing was that in most urban areas traditional customs and gender stereotyping, as well as practices like *kalym*, and women's confinement to reproduction and housekeeping had been abandoned and women participated in public sphere. The veil, worn by many devout women in the region, was a public display of spirituality and, therefore, condemned by the Soviet leadership. On March 8, the International Day of Women, in 1927 women throughout the Soviet Union were, encouraged to publicly shed and burn their veils. On that day, over 10,000 women burned their veils in Uzbekistan alone.[37] Isolated, marginalised, and reduced to silence in the pre-Soviet era, women in Central Asia in the soviet period had clearly gained some degree of gender equality in the field of legislation. They had free access to education and employment both of which were compulsory. The system provided them with sufficient social benefits, access to free basic health and social care.[38]

The Soviet policies resulted in many opportunities for women to participate in the socio-economic sphere which previously had not been available. As a result, over 90 percent of working age women were either employed or studying and this rate of women employment was probably the highest in the world.[39] Lenin, spoke at great length regarding the Soviet government's efforts and achievements, in particular, regarding women. He said that,

> "The Soviet government, as the government of the toilers, brought about during the first months of its existence a complete revolution in the laws affecting women....And we can now proudly say without the slightest exaggeration that except for Soviet Russia there is not a single country in the world in which there is complete equality between men and women and in which women are not placed in a degrading position, which is particularly felt in everyday family life....The position of women in Soviet Russia is now an ideal position from the point of view of the most advanced states." He pointed out, however, that "even with the fullest equality women are still in actual inferiority because all housework is thrust upon them. Most housework is the most unproductive, most barbarous and most arduous work that women perform. This labour is extremely petty and contains nothing that facilitates the development of women. As long as women are engaged in housework their position is still a restricted one. In order to achieve the complete emancipation of women and to make them really equal with men, we must have social economy and the participation of women in general productive labour. Then women will occupy the same position as men....Lenin in his speech at a conference of women workers in Moscow in 1919 reversed traditional values. And the task of the woman's movement was thus described by him: "The main task of the proletarian woman's movement is the struggle for woman's economic and social equality, and not merely a formal one. To draw woman into socially productive work, to pull her out of domestic slavery, to liberate her from submission-degrading and stultifying- to the eternal and exclusive surroundings of kitchen and nursery- that is the main goal.[40]

Equal political rights and women emancipation programmes for women in Muslim Central Asia were the biggest achievements of the Soviet era.[41] Several scholarly works deal with the issue of women and treatment meted to women during the Soviet era. Primarily, Bolshevik discourse assumed that socialism had solved 'the woman question' and that continuing attention to feminist issues revealed a bourgeois attitude. Indeed, as Amy Bug puts it, data on the number of female scientists in socialist Eastern Europe (based on her own field, physics) suggests that planned economies did relatively well at getting women into the professional 'pipeline' and keeping them there.[42]

During Soviet times, these countries had good literacy and employment rate and social security measure as part of socialist policies of USSR. The data from the 1959 and 1970 censuses of the USSR showed three aspects of the improved position of Soviet women of Central Asia in terms of educational attainment, non-agricultural labour force participation, and the burden of child dependency.[43] By the end of the Soviet period, almost all women were literate and majority of working age women were working outside home. Even in the most traditional society like Tajikistan women were literate and the majority had access to higher education and employment.[44] Women's status in these countries improved considerably during Soviet period; and was better off than women of many other Muslim countries.

Post-Soviet Central Asia

Past experiences and reminiscences of the pre-Soviet era influenced the development of these post-Soviet, independent Central Asian Republics significantly. As mentioned earlier, Islam had remained central to the identity and culture for societies in this region over a thousand years before they became part of USSR. Even Soviet authorities could not completely eliminate Islam from the minds and souls of Central Asian people. While the Soviet period affected society in Central Asia in many ways, at the same time, it is also true that the resurgence of traditionalism and Islam following the collapse of the Soviet Union has had a profound impact on the role of women in Central Asian society. The traditional role, status and dress code of women were quickly embraced by large sections of the female population, with the result that even young girls, who had scarcely memorised a single *sura* of the Koran, started to accuse their friends of impiety.[45] Uzbekistan has since sought to move away from the West and their Soviet past by adopting traditionalism, which has led gender to become a fundamental issue concerning identity.[46] And Islam continues to be the predominant religion in the region and dominate the sociocultural fabric and polity even today.

The collapse of the Soviet Union caused a complex series of events. The economic problems in post-Soviet Central Asia had direct impacts on the daily lives of all citizens, in particular of women. The Soviet period's policies, including gender quotas, which had assisted women in the public sphere, were quickly disbanded. The cost of education has become a large obstacle for female attendance. The Soviet Era provisions such as paid maternity leave for up to one year, or up to three years unpaid with hundred percent guarantee of job retention (the time also counted as working time for the calculation of her pension) have deteriorated over a period of time. The institutions like obstetric clinics, gynecology, sanatoriums, and delivery centers which were free of charge for women or low cost childcare system (free for disabled or sick children) during soviet time, could not be sustained in the post-Soviet transition phase and eventually had to be closed. Other welfare activities like free public education; government allowances for families with children; and state support for families with many children, including additional allowances; inexpensive children's clothing; housing privileges and so on which were being provided by the state have been hit hard.[47] Few of these facilities have been stopped altogether.

In the post-Soviet period these countries have their own policies in place for education, employment etc. Though, there is not much change in terms of literacy rate, but there are lots of changes in term of employment and availability of social services. Some of these countries are doing well in terms of economy, with Kazakhstan, Uzbekistan, and Turkmenistan doing well, but Kyrgyzstan and Tajikistan in comparison not faring that good. The transition from planned to market economy, from social engineering under the Soviets to an open and democratic civil society, have led to a religious and traditional revival that has had negative impact on women's status.[48] The main challenges of these new independent countries, has been to sustain their economic growth; to create more jobs and improve the welfare of its citizens, for example, the policy of infrastructure development focuses mainly on transport and communication, energy, water resources, water supply, and other municipal infrastructure and services, and access to financial services so as to cater to the population's basic requirements.

According to the selected social indicators amongst these countries as shown in the Table 2.1, Uzbekistan had the lowest per capita GDP in the group, however in terms of the social indicators such as infant mortality rate, literacy rate it is better than the countries with higher GDP per capita in 1990. Similarly, Kyrgyzstan also records high primary school enrolment, life expectancy, adult literacy and low infant mortality rate compared to its relative lower per capita income in the group. This indicates a higher level of human development in Uzbekistan and Kyrgyzstan.

The various dimensions of Gender Development Index (GDI) report 2018, indicates that, there has been progress in decreasing the gender disparity in India and the life expectancy rate of female is better than male; male 68.2 and female 70.7.[49]

Table 2.1
Selected social indicators in 1990

Country	*Primary School enrollment (gross)***	*Life expectancy at birth (years)****	*Infant mortality rate per 1000 live births ****	*Adult literacy rate (% of people aged 15 and above)**	*PPP GDP per capita USD*****
India	93	59	88	48.2	1,210
Kazakhstan	89	68	63.0	97.53	**4650**
Kyrgyzstan	**92**	68	58.0	96.71	**2038**
Tajikistan	77	63	**91.0**	97.67	2002
Turkmenistan	82	63	80.0	98.96	4405
Uzbekistan	78	64	**57.0**	96.22	**1499**
Least developed Countries	63.7	45.6	121.0	52.4	1053

Source: Table prepared by the Author with the help of data from: Dari Khongorzul, "Mongolia and Central Asia in Transition", http://www.apu.ac.jp/rcaps/uploads/fckeditor/publications/journal/RJAPS_V26_Dari.pdf and
http://www.uis.unesco.org/Education/Documents/UIS-literacy-statistics-1990-2015-en.pdf
*http://unesdoc.unesco.org/images/0021/002174/217409e.pdf/
** http://data.worldbank.org/indicator/SE.PRM.ENRR?page=4
*** http://wdi.worldbank.org/table/2.21
**** https://data.undp.org/dataset/GDP-per-capita-2005-PPP-/navj-mda7

Graph 2.1
BTI country report 2014[50]: Rank and score of each country under study

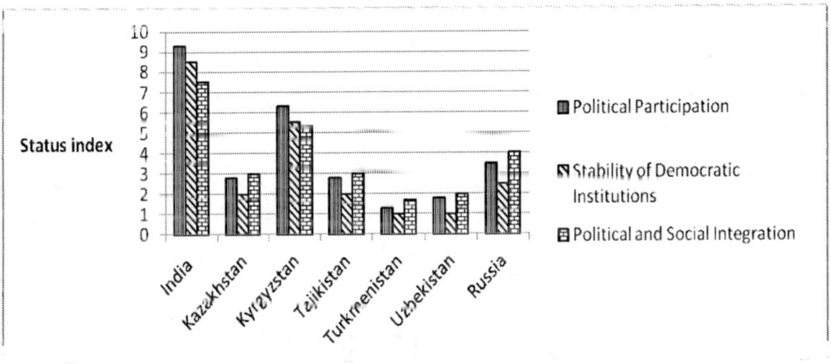

Source: Prepared by the Author with the help of data in Appendix. II.A
*scale: 1-10; Rank: out of 129 countries

Graph 2.2

BTI country report 2014: Rank and score of each country under study

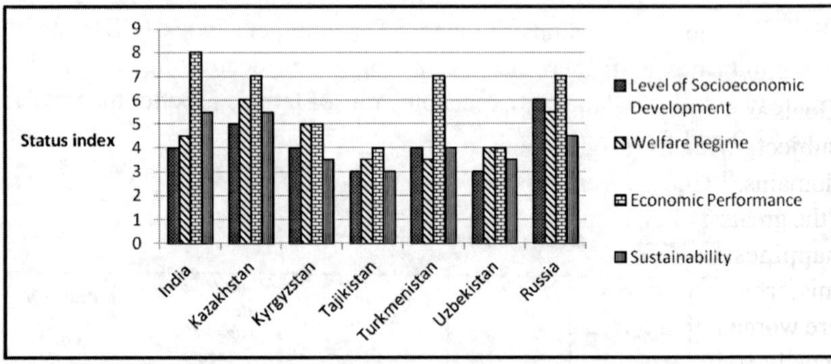

Source: Prepared by the Author with the help of data in Appendix. II. A
*scale: 1-10; Rank: out of 129 countries.

The graph above (2.1 and 2.2) indicates the rank and score of each country under study in terms of status Index, political and economic transformation and management Index in the year 2014. These figures suggest that India has done better vis-à-vis political transformation and amongst Central Asian Republics only Kyrgyzstan has fared well. Economically India, Turkmenistan and Kazakhstan are better placed than others. And Kyrgyzstan and Uzbekistan's socioeconomic development have deteriorated over the period 1990-2014 as compared to the other countries in the region.

Graph 2.3

Rate of Growth of GDP percapita (PPP $) 2005-2011.

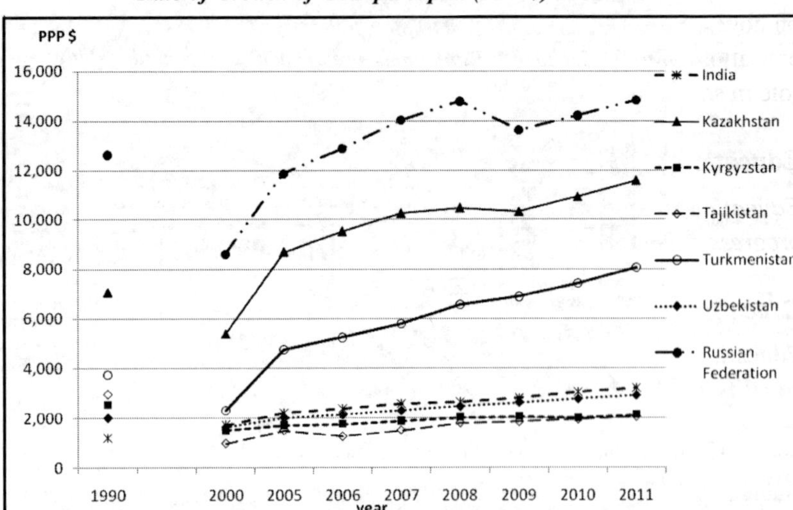

Source: Prepared by the Author with the help of data from table. See, Appendix: II.B

Equally important is the GDP growth of these countries as is shown in the graph below (2.3). Only Kazakhstan and Turkmenistan has performed well.

Poverty eradication is one of the eight UN Millennium Development Goals as poverty is a multidimensional problem and a kind of very complex subject, with its origins both in the national as well as international domains.[51] George Bernard Shaw argued more than 100 years ago that, "the greatest of evils and the worst of crimes is poverty". Lives are battered, happiness stifled, creativity destroyed, freedoms eradicated by the misfortunes of poverty.[52] More than one billion, the great majority of whom are women, in the world today, live in unacceptable conditions of poverty, mostly in the developing countries including few countries under study. Poverty has various causes, including structural ones.[53] And women both in India and Central Asia share this burden. About 70% of populations in the Kyrgyz Republic live in rural area and 64% of villagers are women. The most specific feature of the rural population today is its growing poverty. Among poor in the country, 70% are women. Tendency of feminisation of poverty is increasing.[54] As per a 2011, World Bank report, 76.6% people in Kyrgyzstan and 76.9% of citizens in Tajikistan were living under three dollars a day.[55] Things have improved over the years, though the improvement is not that significant.

Keeping these social, economic and political indices, indicators and contexts in the background, present situation of women vis-à-vis impact of socio-economic transformation in these countries will be discussed, focusing on how women are faring with respect to education and employment. As education and employment facilitates women's empowerment and their role in society.

Education and Employment

Education and employment are indicators which not only explain the progress of society but also the overall progress of the nation.

Education

Education is a basic right and an essential tool for achieving the goals of equality and development and further lays a foundation for sustained economic growth. Equality of access and attainment of educational qualifications is necessary if more women are to become the agents of change in the development of society and nation. And it is a well known fact that, non-discriminatory education facilitates both girls and boys, thereby contributes to equal relationships between women and men and ultimately benefits society.[56] It is important to note that literacy of women is an important key to improving health, nutrition and education in the family and to empowering women to participate in developmental process of society and nation.[57]

India

In India, there have been significant changes taking place especially in the context to education. Several new policies and measures have been taken in this regard. Higher education system in India is supposed to be the third largest in the world, after China and the United States, and is often cited as one of the main contributors to the economic rise of India. Much of the progress, especially India's improved education system; higher education and scientific research have been credited to various public institutions.[58] Education in India is mainly provided by the public sector, with control and funding coming from three levels: federal, state, and local. Education in India falls under the control of both the Union Government and the states, with some responsibilities lying with the Union and the states having autonomy for others. Most universities in India are Union or State Government controlled.[59] Three Indian universities were listed in the Times Higher Education list (2005, 2006) of the world's top 200 universities; Indian Institutes of Technology, Indian Institutes of Management, and Jawaharlal Nehru University etc. The University of Mumbai was ranked 41 among the Top 50 Engineering Schools of the world by America's news broadcasting firm Business Insider in 2012 and was the only university in the list from the five emerging BRICS (Brazil, Russia, India, China and South Africa) nations.[60] In recent years however, many private universities and Institutions of India have come up and are doing quite well namely, the Indian Institutes of Technology (IITs), Indian Institutes of Management (IIMs), National Institute of Technology (NITs), International Institute of Information Technology (IIIT-H), University of Mumbai and Jawaharlal Nehru University, have been globally recognised for their standard of education.

The graph 2.4 shows, the growth of total students in higher education in India over the years and the share of girl/women's enrollment. There had been a phenomenal growth in the number of women students enrolled in higher education, since independence. Women enrolment which was less than 10 percent of the total enrolment on the eve of Independence had risen to 43.28 percent in the academic year 2012-2013. The pace of growth has been particularly faster in the last two decades.

Graph 2.4
Higher education enrolments in India (1947-2013)

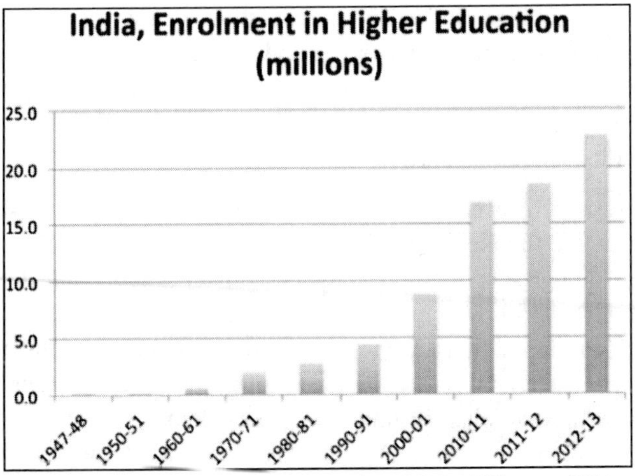

Source: India's University Grants Committee 2013, UGC report 2014.

Graph 2.5
Higher Education in India over the years

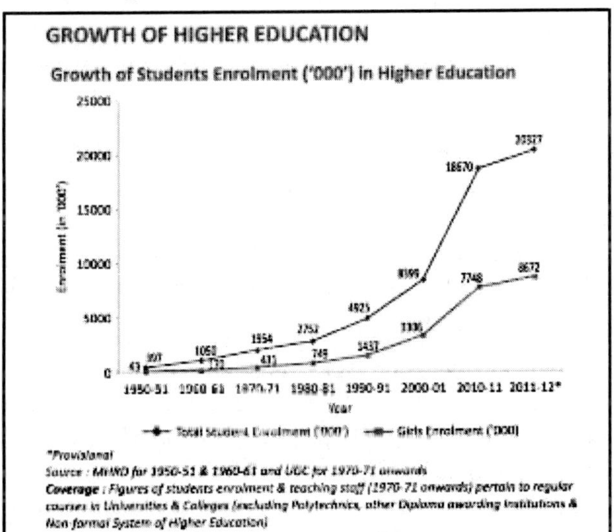

Source: www.ugc.ac.in/pdfnews/6805988_HEglance2013.pdf

India possesses a very large and diverse higher education system with programmes in almost all areas of traditional and modern learning. Despite this growth, the issue of deteriorating quality and social inequity still persists. An insight into prospective higher education demand stresses an explicit focus on the supply parameters that influence the higher education from the perspectives of various stakeholders. These include not only sources and quantity but also quality and access. With the increase in the number of students who complete higher secondary schooling, the transition rate from secondary to higher education in absolute terms is also increasing. Therefore, the demand from disadvantaged groups will rise dramatically through their increased participation along with women.[61]

There is gender equality in school attendance in urban areas, but, in rural areas, the female disadvantage in education is marked and increases with age. Though school dropout beyond primary school is a major problem for both girls and boys,[62] and in both cases the reasons are different for dropout. In terms of literacy and educational attainment among adults, the percentage of adults who are literate is much lower in rural than in urban areas; nonetheless, even in urban areas one-fourth of women and more than one-tenth of men are not literate. Gender disparity in literacy is much greater in rural than in urban areas and declines sharply with household wealth. Forty-one percent of women and 18% of men in the age group of 15-49 had never been to school by the year 2005-06.[63] Educational attainment remained very low: even among the 20-29 age groups, only 27% of women and 39% of men had 10 or more years of education in 2005-06.[64] Though, the percentage of ever-married women with 10 or more years of education has risen very slowly from 11% to 17%.[65]

However, according to a 2019 survey report, India's gender parity index (GPI) shows that, there has been improvement in girl's education at all levels of education, except higher education. And the focus now is to eliminate gender disparity by 2030, in education and ensure equal access to all levels of education and vocational training to the vulnerable.[66]

In India, there are policies like Economically Weaker Sections (EWS) under the Right to Education (RTE) Act. Apart from this, several other schemes are there specially, for girls, to encourage parents to send their daughter to school like, *Ladli*, *Kishori*, *Sarv Shiksha Abhiyan (SSA)* schemes etc.[67] Facilities for girls have increased over the years, so as to facilitate girls to attend school, for example, schools having Girl's toilets (all Schools) was 72.16 percent in 2011-12.[68] There is also drastic change in attitude of parents and the Government in India; in terms of policy on the government's part and responsibility on the part of parents. The government is doing its part by bringing in policies which benefits all school going age group children. And parents of today are more aware of the benefits that education brings with it, thereby more and more parents are sending their children to school. It is important to note that parents today are more than happy to send even their daughter to school and also pamper her when she performs well.[69]

During an individual interaction with a government school teacher, she said that, "the policies implementation will reap result only when the parents also take the responsibility of sending their daughters to school. The enrolments of girls have increased in last couple of years and once in school, they perform better than the boys; however, the onus lies still with the parents".[70] Some said that actually not only have the enrollment of girls increased but also that girls seem to be more serious about their studies and performance. Also there is visible change in attitudes of parents about sending their daughters to school and at the same time also very appreciative of the fact that their daughters are better in studies than their sons".[71]

During last seven decades, India has improved in terms of school education as well higher education. Higher education in India has undergone remarkable transformation from elite to a mass system. Total enrollment increased from a meager 0.1 to 1923 million between 1947 and 2013.[72] Higher education became more for the masses and democratised after 2000 with more than 50% of enrolments coming from lower socio-economic strata and women comprising more than 40% of total enrolment. The female enrollment share in the total higher education has also increased; in 1950 it was 11%, in 1990 to 29%; in 2000 it was 39 % and reached to 42% by 2011.[73]

Central Asia

At the end of the 1980's Central Asian countries had a sustainable and effective system of education which was a result of the long existence of the Soviet Union. The system had a common structure for all Soviet republics and it was managed centrally. It is necessary to note that the USSR's education system was able to reach a high level of coverage to almost all the adult population of the republics. The level of literacy of the adult population was about 96-100%.[74] Post 1991, after their independence there was severe deterioration of state sponsored secular educational systems across the region. This posed a threat to social cohesion. Although the region does share a deep history of cultural syncretism, religious pluralism, and ethnic coexistence, all of these traditions are under strain because of educational deterioration, economic crisis, poverty etc. It often seems that little of that history of tolerance and pluralism is reflected in their nationalistic exclusionary language policies and emerging inequities based on ethnicity, gender, clan, and religion.[75]

There are continuities as well as changes in Central Asian education development since the collapse of the Soviet Union in 1991. Two decades of post-socialist transformations, reveal that education systems in Central Asia has responded to the rapidly changing political, economic, and social environment in profoundly new and unique ways. The political nature of the transformation processes and the uniqueness of historical, political, social, and cultural contexts of each of these Central Asian Republics portray post-Soviet education transformations to be complex and multidimensional. The governments in these countries believe that, higher education is one of the best ways to make these countries a part of the world economy.[76] While some countries moved towards Western models, others went backwards, and still others followed entirely new courses. Though, some elements of the old system remain.

According to 1989 USSR census data, the number of people having incomplete secondary, secondary, secondary special and higher education in Central Asian countries were as in the Table 2.3.

Table 2.2
Number of people having education above incomplete secondary education (% of the total population above 15 yrs)

Country	*Total (% of the population above 15)*	*Including*				
		Higher	*Incomplete higher*	*Secondary special*	*Secondary*	*Incomplete secondary*
Kazakhstan	83.8	9.9	1.8	18.5	33.8	19.8
Tajikistan	83.7	7.5	1.4	11.0	42.7	21.1
Turkmenistan	86.4	8.3	1.4	13.5	41.9	21.3
Uzbekistan	86.7	9.2	1.9	15.0	40.8	19.8
Kyrgyzstan	84.2	9.4	1.6	15.7	39.1	18.4

Source: Table prepared by Author with help of data from DVV Review of Central Asian Countries, Marifat Abdullaeva, 2006.

http://www.dvv-international.de/index.php?id=809&L=1; http://unesdoc.unesco.org/. Accessed on 23 March 2014.

Note: The proportion of people having incomplete secondary education includes **the number of persons having primary education according to the existing Soviet educational system** and correspondingly these indices are taken into account while calculating the final index.

At the end of 2000 the scenario of literacy level in Central Asian countries was as shown in the Table 2.3. As visible every country had close to 100 percent literacy rate.

The governments of the Central Asian countries have been making an attempt to improve the situation in the sphere of education via the development of effective and financially viable education reforms.

Table 2.3
Comparative table of coefficient of the level of literacy of the population of Central Asian countries in 1990, 2000

Country	*1990*		*2000*	
	Men	*Women*	*Men*	*Women*
Kazakhstan	100	98	100	99
Kyrgyzstan		95	--	--
Tajikistan	99	97	100	99
Turkmenistan	--	--	--	--
Uzbekistan	100	98	100	99

Source: Table prepared by Author with help of data from DVV Review of Central Asian Countries, Marifat Abdullaeva, 2006, http://www.dvv-international.de/index.php?id=809&L=1 ; http://unesdoc.unesco.org. Accessed on 23 March, 2014.

Unequal access to education exists in all these countries. Gender representation in education is not balanced in any of these countries; some have lower level of boys' education because of the early involvement of boys in maintaining families. Some countries show the level of girl's education as low, which is because of the low education prestige among the girls, early marriage and the religious code. A part of the population prefers to provide girls with religious education via private lessons conducted by religious people instead of formal school education. Another reason of gender disbalance is the ingrained concept about the gender roles in the society, which also influence the school education due to the stable stereotype of the teachers towards this issue.[77]

For many years, higher education in these countries mirrored the former Soviet Union model of education, to which it belonged for more than seventy years. This model was characterised by a high degree of specialisation and the rigidity of the curriculum. Once they became an independent nation, some of the country's educational institutions began to look towards the West and tried to import some aspects of their model of education. These include the use of new technologies like the Internet, which are slowly being introduced in higher education institutions. With the help of USAID, a Promotion of Information Communication Technology in Turkmenistan (PICTT) programme has been implemented. This programme aids the learning of students, including in higher education in Turkmenistan, and strives to include Information and Communications Technology (ICT) as an important aspect of education in the country. Turkmenistan President, Gurbanguly Berdimukhamedov is keen to make his country more computer literate with greater Internet access available for its citizens.[78] Whether general or vocational, higher secondary education is provided free of charge, as it is included in the budget allocated for education by the government and university education is partly funded by the government, although private universities charge higher tuition fees. Till the end of 2002, Turkmenistan had a literacy rate of 98 percent, but in the recent years there have been a decline in standards due to financial cutbacks and lack of investment.[79] Uzbekistan reportedly spends about 12% of its GDP on education, which is the highest percentage in the region. This level of spending surpasses even the average OECD spending, which is 6%, and nears the level spent on education during the Soviet era. The increase in expenditure on education is part of the government's efforts to show commitment to achieving the, 'Education for All' (EFA) and Millenium Development Goals.[80]

Amongst these countries, few have some specific problems. For example, in Tajikistan, part of the problem is that 93 percent of the country is mountainous and this makes it difficult to develop the country's infrastructure. However, thanks to the proactive steps taken by the government in this regard. Tajikistan has created Tajik Academician Research and Educational Networks Association (TARENA), which is an online corporative educational and scientific network to promote the use of computer technology in education. This network connects all the higher education institutions in the capital. However, there are further opportunities for improvement.[81]

Traditionally, "literacy has been quite high in Kazakhstan. Right now there is free education up to 11 standard and provision for Grant for higher education. More measures are being taken with respect to education".[82] The country's adult literacy rate according to the UNDP Human Development Indicators was: of those of age 15 and over that could read and write in 1999-2006 was, 97.9%; 99.0% for men and 96.7% for women and resulting in women to men parity rate of 98%.[83] For 2007 the youth (15-24 years) literacy rate of Kazakhstan with 99.8% was close to the maximum; young females scored 99.9%, against 99.8% for the young males. Already in 1999, these scores were 99.9% and 99.8% respectively.[84]

The data from a March 2012 Women in Muslim Countries (WIMC) report by Stephen Hornbeck, indicates that, "in Kazakhstan, 67% of women who have enrolled in or have completed a university education currently live in urban areas compared to 33% who live in rural areas. Similarly, in Kyrgyzstan, 59% of university students or graduates are living in urban areas compared to 44% living in rural areas. In Tajikistan, which has a similar urban and rural population as Kyrgyzstan, the opposite situation exists where 65% of college students or graduates live in rural areas and

35% live in urban areas. The difference in Tajikistan may be due to the lack of employment opportunities currently available in urban Tajikistan as well as displacement of the urban population as a result of the Tajik civil war which left over 1 million people displaced".[85]

Post 1991, these countries realised that, to improve their socioeconomic condition, radical reforms in their education system was a must as the education system was required to serve national interests and at the same time be globally competitive. Despite the education reforms, there are issues which Central Asian countries need to tackle. These issues include financial crunch, need to re-train staff and teachers to improve their teaching abilities and, thereby, enhance the quality of teaching etc. Few of these countries have integration with international education community, setting up universities in conjunction with Russia and setting up distance learning centre's for some of the higher education institutions in association with the other CIS countries.[86]

There are other attempts to improve the situation. Many non-governmental national and international organisations are having an influence on the improvement of access for separate levels of population. For Example, 'Open Society Institute' (OSI) activity in the Central Asian countries has a series of educational programmes which include provision of schools, universities and libraries with the modern textbooks; support in preparation and publication of up-to-date books for the particular region, replenishment of library funds and training of library specialists and many other issues.[87] 'Agency for Technical Cooperation and Development' (ACTED) in Tajikistan, Kyrgyzstan and Uzbekistan implements the programme of school feeding in the border districts of Fergana valley, which fosters the significant growth of school attendance.[88] This is quite similar to the mid-day meals scheme in India, which off course, is provided by the government, whereas, in Fergana region it is by other agencies.

UNICEF and Save the Children Fund (UK) support the projects for disabled children in Kyrgyzstan, Uzbekistan and Tajikistan. Some other nongovernmental development organisations over the years, with the support of international donors, have conducted many educational activities and helped these countries.[89]

Many reforms suggest the solution of the important task, which is the provision of quality education. Solving of this task depends on the condition of the education system itself, availability of the high level professionals, funding, improvement of the system etc. As was mentioned earlier, the majority of national reform in the area of education is oriented towards the improvement of the formal education in all these countries of the region. The Ministry of Education and Science of Kazakhstan began to take part in the realisation of programmes of international organisations like The United Nations Educational, Scientific and Cultural Organisation (UNESCO), Peace Corps, University Studies Informational System (USIS), German Academic Exchange Service (DAAD) etc.[90] However, one of the main problem is the lack of development of education in masters programme, in fact at the master level the strength is only 2.3 percent of total number of students in Kazakh universities.[91]

All in all, it is worth mentioning that, almost all the countries under study are making efforts for the improvement of the education system and finding solutions to the specific problems related to education. And there are reforms conducted by the state which are mainly oriented towards the improvement of the formal education system. The main problems however, with implementing reforms, are lack of funds, deficit of qualified specialists, low quality of management of the education system and low participation of citizens in the education reform. For examples, there are various obstacles for female attendance; social stereotypes and the cost of education being two of most important factor in this aspect.[92]

It is thereby significant to look at the level of education and literacy rate at different time span of countries under study as shown in the Table 2.4.

According to the 2019 report, the youth literacy rate for the world for 2010-19 periods for male was 93% and female was 90%. And the adult literacy rate of male female ratio was also close with 90 to 83%. All Central Asian Republics has 100% literacy rate for both male and female, with exception of Kyrgyzstan where in adult literacy rate male-female ratio is 100:99%. India with all its improvements had male-female ratio of youth literacy at 93:90 and adult literacy rate at 82:66.[93]

It is clear from the facts and figures above that there indeed have been lot of improvement in terms of closing the gender gap however, it cannot be ignored that still discrimination in girls' access to education persists. Even UN documents and reports acknowledge this discrimination. However, the low education level among women and girls to some degree vary from country to country and may depend on public opinion, traditions and life style, specially, in rural areas, where family connects the welfare of the house with male. So given a choice the preference is given to boys. "Girls in any case will get married and will live in another family and sons have to support parents in future". Besides, especially in rural areas it seems the

Table 2.4

Level of Education and literacy rate of countries under study

Countries	Primary completion rate						Youth literacy rate				Adult literacy rate			
	Total		Male		Female		Male		Female		Male		Female	
	% of relevant age group		% of relevant age group		% of relevant age group		% of ages 15-24		% of ages 15-24		% ages 15 and older		% ages 15 and older	
	1999	2011	1999	2011	1999	2011	1985-94	2005-11	1985-94	2005-11	1985-94	2005-11	1985-94	2005-11
India	70	96	78	96	61	97	74	88	49	74	62	75	34	51
Kazakhstan	95	108	94	109	95	108	100	100	100	100	99	100	96	100
Kyrgyz Republic	94	96	94	96	93	95	..	100	-	100	..	100	..	99
Tajikistan	91	103	..	104	..	101	100	100	100	100	99	100	97	100
Turkmenistan	..	..	..	..	..	..	..	100	..	100	..	100	..	99
Uzbekistan	96	92	101	93	100	91	..	100	..	100	..	100	..	99

Source: Table prepared by the Author with help of data from http://wdi.worldbank.org/table/2.10. Accessed on 27 June 2014.

demand for educated women has been declining.[94] Apart from these, there are some other reasons as well; from customary attitudes, early marriages and pregnancies to inadequate and gender biased teaching, sexual harassment or lack of adequate accessible schooling facilities. Several other factors like few girls undertaking domestic work at a very early age also prevent girls from attending school. In some other instances like in India, girls and young women are expected to manage both educational and domestic responsibilities, either resulting in absence from school or if attending school then often having poor performance, thereby resulting in early dropout.

In some cases, young women mostly in central Asian countries, would want to earn and settle down early in life; have a family; have to do two jobs at two different place to have sufficient income so cannot devote time for study; in fact few people start to look for a job immediately after completing the first year of graduation to add some extra money to their pocket, this was very much prevalent in Almaty, Kazakhstan.[95]

All these have long lasting consequences for all aspects of women's lives and, as a result, to society. In this regard, particularly in India, an effort is needed from the parent's side to shoulder the responsibility and to make the use of governmental policies, provisions, and schemes like *Ladli*, EWS and SSA. And in Central Asia, though, the plans for future development of the higher education system is under way and various measure are being taken to improve modern education system, however, what is important is that, there is first of all, a need to have widespread adoption of the English language as a medium for instruction[96] or at least as an additional language apart from its own national language and may be Russian if it is in the syllabus. In fact, Russian school is preferred by parents for their children, primarily, so that children will learn English.[97]

Women's participation in the labour market to a large extent; apart from education, is another important factor to understand women's status in society.

Women and Employment

> *"There is no chance of the welfare of the world unless the condition of women is improved. It is not possible for a bird to fly on one wing"*
>
> – Swami Vivekananda

Women's employment is also a social indicator which, not only reveals about women's status in society but also provides essential understanding of the societal make up, particularly in low income and transition countries.

The last decade of the twentieth century brought about enormous changes in the lives of the people world over, especially so in India and Central Asia due to economic liberalisation in India and due to disintegration of USSR and independence of countries in Central Asia.

India

Since the liberalisation period, Indian women are increasingly occupying relatively larger space in almost all the spheres of economic activities. For the year 2012, percentage of female employment in India was in agriculture 59.8, Industry: 20.7; services: 19.5.[98] According to a 2014 report, women's share in the teaching was 43.8 percent, which is the ninth fastest growing occupation for women. Though, in recent times from the policy point of view, more women are encouraged to enter into otherwise male dominated occupations including managerial roles.[99] However, women constitute less than 50 percent in each of India's fastest growing occupations even though female employment in India grew by 8.7 million between 1994 and 2010.[100] It will, may be, take more time before it starts to show results in this regard.

World Development Indicators (2008) highlighted that there are many differences in how countries define and measure employment status, particularly members of the armed forces, self-employed workers, and unpaid family workers. Where members of the armed forces are included, they are allocated to the service sector, causing that sector to be somewhat overstated relative to the service sector in economies where they are excluded.[101] In India, men still make up the majority of people employed in all three sectors, but the gender gap is biggest in industry. Many service jobs, such as nursing and social and clerical work are considered 'feminine' because of a perceived similarity to women's traditional roles. Women often do not receive the training needed to take advantage of changing employment opportunities. And the greater availability of part time work in service industries lures more women.[102] It is noteworthy that in post-liberalisation India, initially there was an unparalleled situation, where ample of opportunities for women had been created in terms of employment etc. However, overtime, it changed to more about being competent.

Central Asia

In the initial years after independence each of these countries apart of having similar traits had their own unique problems related to women's work or employment. Yet, within a short time span the familiar elements of the economic and social make up of the Soviet period were overhauled with the introduction of market principles into the economy and the revision of the extensive social protection system etc. Though, this created exciting opportunities for the people, there were uncertainties and challenges as well, as several people were not prepared for these challenges in their lives, especially livelihood related. Worst affected were the rural women as very little alternative for income generating opportunities were available to them with limited help from the state in terms of employment provision and social support. They needed to cope with the triple burden of looking after the family, agricultural plots and carrying out household responsibilities and generating an income outside the house.[103]

During the Soviet times, the economy, which heavily depended on female workers, provided an array of subsidised social services for women and children; liberal abortion laws and family planning programmes to raise a 'healthy generation'. It is worth pointing out that during the 1930s, there was a sharp increase in female employment and urban unemployment was reduced to negligible levels. And majority of the rural population, previously been engaged in peasant farming, joined *kolkhozy* (collective farms). And this was significantly higher than in most European states; unemployment rates were on average much lower than in other developed and developing economies. These characteristics of the Soviet labour market were preserved until the collapse of the system at the beginning of the 1990s.[104]

As early as 1930s, Soviet Union witnessed the first generation of female doctors, lawyers, and scientists covering important economic spaces. Women emancipation regardless of its flaws was the biggest contribution of the Soviet Era despite the Islamic dominance of the society in Central Asia. However, the nexus between Islam and national identity remained unbroken throughout seventy years of Soviet rule.[105] In the 1936 constitution, female employment was underlined as a right. A woman in the USSR had equal rights with a man in all areas of economic, civil, cultural and socio-political life. They had legal guaranty of equal pay for equal work and several other benefits.[106]

However, in the post-Soviet period, the economic problems decreased the state's ability to provide child and maternity allowances; and all the social security and welfare schemes were either withdrawn or became non-operational.[107] The reemergence of Islamic traditions and family and community values since independence, and with absence of subsidised social services, women were further burdened with extra responsibility. Besides, several industrial units employing about 90% of women were shut down while economy underwent restructuring for example, in Kazakhstan.[108]

The status of women in post-Soviet Central Asia depends much on the economic situation and the policies being followed by the individual country. Women in these countries are more actively pursuing opportunities to contribute to the economy of the family, however, in few countries pressures on women to return to more traditional roles have resulted in considerably fewer opportunities for female involvement in spheres beyond the home. There are different levels of female involvement in these countries, despite their shared history as former Soviet Republics and the similar economic problems experienced with the transformation of their societies in post-Soviet period, which explains the divergent paths of these countries. Major factor in the development of gender relations is due to the pre-Soviet traditions that have resurfaced in the post-Soviet era with the development of each state's national identity. Each Central Asian Republic has its own set of policies and regulations impacting socioeconomic status of women.

There are many barriers to women's economic participation. The most pertinent reason is the patriarchal and traditional society in few of these countries and off course the lack of access to markets, training and technology are among the main obstacles that stand in the way of women managing businesses etc. Some women in Central Asia do not have inheritance or property rights or the ability to conduct independent transactions.[109]

Economic Status of Women in 2009 as reported in GID-DB is shown in table below.

Table 2.5
Economic Status of Women According to Institutions and Development Database 2009 (GID-DB)

Country	*Ratio of estimated Female to male earned Income*	*Estimated earned income (PPP US$), female*	*Estimated earned income (PPP US$), Male*
India	0.32	1,185	3,698
Kyrgyzstan	0.58	1,333	2,306
Tajikistan	0.58	1,182	2,041
Uzbekistan	0.60	1,646	2,727
Turkmenistan	0.64	3,461	5,420
Kazakhstan	0.68	8,039	11,782

Source: Table prepared by the Author with help of data from Gender, Institutions and Development Database 2009 (GID-DB*),
http://stats.oecd.org/Index.aspx?DatasetCode=GID2, accessed on Nov 15 2013.
* For detailed methodology of GID-DB, please visit.
http://www.genderindex.org/sites/default/files/Backgroundpaper.pdf. Accessed on 27 March 2014.

Lower participation of women in the economy can be judged by the decreasing rate of female labour force in almost all the Central Asian Republics with Kazakhstan as an exception.[110] In Kazakhstan, availability of large number of jobs, which do not require significant physical labour, makes possible for many people specially, with higher education to receive full or partial employment resulted in decrease of serious unemployment problems and even the situation of disabled people is to a certain degree positive.[111] In Kazakhstan, "there are measure and policy so that women's economic situations do not decline; to see that youth after university get involved in government work, 2011-20; unemployment less than 5.2 %. It was said that, the condition of women has become better in last five years (2007-12) and it is more visible. People seem to be happy. More measures are being taken for social protection, education etc.[112] Also, "there are developments in agriculture. To encourage entrepreneurship there are provision of credit, 'to develop entrepreneurship'. Infrastructure in villages, are being increased so as to help women".[113] Also, "the policy of '*Salamte* Kazakhstan' is being implemented so as to have overall *salamat* Kazakhstan".[114]

In Uzbekistan, according to Zulfiya Tursunova, women at times exercise multi-dimensional empowerment by joining social and economic saving networks such as *gaps* and *chernaya kassa*. These social networks enable women to express their voices and build relationships with women whose economic situations are similar or different to their own. Women re-organise their physical spaces for such social networks and economic empowerment.[115] This was also witnessed by the author in Osh in Kyrgyzstan (See Image 14.B, in Chapter Four).[116]

Globally, women's participation in the labour market remained steady in the two decades from 1990 to 2010, hovering around 52 percent. In contrast, global labour force participation rates for men declined steadily over the same period, from 81 to 77 percent.[117] However, in Kazakhstan, women still had much to worry about as in the year 2008, 30% of the female labour force was in commercial services, of which over half in wholesale and retail. In international perspective, notably the high female share in finance is surprising. But in contrast perspective, with 45% the female share in public administration is rather low.[118]

According to a UNIFEM Gender Equality Employment 2007 report, only 59% of 2.2 million able-bodied Tajik women were employed, compared to 75% of men. There is lack of employment opportunities in urban areas in Tajikistan, Women in Muslim Countries (WIMC) data reveals that women with higher education living in rural areas actually have a higher rate of employment.[119]

Women's rights to productive resources have been linked to increases in household food security, economic development and children's education. And access to land and natural resources confers economic benefits through agricultural production; access to collateral, rental and sales income. When women have rights to land and natural resources, they have a semblance of economic security, the benefits of which are realised by the entire household. Yet, customary practices restrict women's rights to these critical resources. Like, while women's rights to land are supported by formal law, customary rules prevail in regards to the use, allocation and inheritance of land, making it difficult for women to exercise ownership and control rights.[120] It is more or less the same situation in India as well.

In remote areas and traditional families even in few cities specially, in Tajikistan and Uzbekistan, men disapprove women occupying economic sphere as they believe that women should concentrate on the traditional roles and confine themselves, to the domestic issues. In some regions there is a tendency to form a stereotype among the young and relatively educated men; prohibiting wives to work, and there are few cases, where husbands require their wives to wear a *hijab* or cover their faces when in public.[121] Otherwise also women are mostly employed in the education sector.

In spite of so many similar obstacles or restriction it is very interesting to note that, there are different levels of female involvement in the economy in these countries. But the most important thing about these countries is that; in Central Asia women have the culture of doing business; small or big is irrelevant, whereas in India it is a recent development however, it is picking up at quite a fast pace. Central Asian women are involved in some economic activities; some women who are not into salaried employment have some sort of business. At times, women sit on the roadside with fruits or vegetables plucked right from their garden and earn some money. Most of the local shops and markets near metro etc are actually run by women, and even if it is owned by men, the women are running it. The famous *Zilyoni Bazaar* is full of women, either as owners or as workers and at times as customer too. See image: 5;14a; 18a; 27b.[122] In India, it's a recent trend, though it has progressing remarkably and is giving good results specially, in metro cities and southern states in India. There are many examples of women doing good business both small and big, which ranges from *Dabba* or *Tiffin* system to leather and jewellery business.[123]

Key Economic indicators for the countries under study as of 2014, is as in the Table 2.6. Kazakhstan is the most economically developed country in the group, which has a high per capita income and almost no poverty whereas Kyrgyzstan has the lowest per capita income in the group and a low poverty ratio. Turkmenistan though doesn't have a low per capita income, has a high poverty ratio which indicates high level of economic inequality in the economy.

Table 2.6
Key Economic Indicators 2014

	India	*Kazakhstan*	*Kyrgyzstan*	*Tajikistan*	*Turkmenistan*	*Uzbekistan*
Population, total (millions)	1,252.14 2013	16.84 2013	5.66 2013	8.21 2013	5.24 2013	29.75 2013
GNI per capita, Atlas method (current US$)	$1,550 2012	$9,780 2012	$990 2012	$880 2012	$5,410 2012	$1,720 2012
Poverty headcount ratio of $1.25 a day (PPP) % of population	32.7% 2010	0.1% 2009	5.0% 2011	6.6% 2009	24.8% 1998	N/A

Source: Table prepared by author with help of data from World Bank, 2013. http://datatopics.worldbank.org/gender/country/india. Accessed on 6 June 2014.

The details regarding women in development according to the World Development Indicators (WDI), is as in the Table 2.7. It highlights the situation of women in India and Central Asian Republics vis-à-vis their life expectancy, access to pre-natal care, percentage of women workers in the non-agricultural sector, female legislators and high officials etc. And it is noteworthy that female life expectancy is more than male. Kazakhstan is better placed than the others in terms of other indicators as well, and Kyrgyzstan close by in second place.

Table 2.7
Women in Development: World Development Indicators (WDI)

	Female population % of total 2011	*Life expectancy at birth (years) 2011*		*Pregnant women receiving prenatal care % 2006-11*	*Teenage mothers % of women ages 15-19 2006-11*	*Women in wage employment in nonagricultural sector % of nonagricultural wage employment 2009*	*Unpaid family workers % of male and % female employment 2011*		*Female legislators, senior officials, and managers % of total 2006-11*	*Women in parliaments % of total seats*	
		M	*F*				*M*	*F*		*1990*	*2012*
India	48.3	64	68	75	16	..	11.0	33.9	14	..	11
Kazakhstan	51.8	64	74	100	7	50	0.8	0.8	38	..	24
Kyrgyzstan	50.7	66	74	97	..	43	..	..	35	..	23
Tajikistan	49.7	64	71	80	..	29	0.5	0.3	..	..	19
Turkmenistan	50.8	61	69	99	..	..	..	..	..	..	17
Uzbekistan	50.3	65	71	99	..	39	..	..	..	..	22

Source: Table prepared by author with help of data from World Bank, 2013. http://datatopics.worldbank.org/gender/country/india. Accessed on 6 June 2014.

Table 2.8b*

The labour force structure of women as according to WDI

Country	*Labour force participation (%) Ages (15 and older)*					
	Male			*Female*		
	2000	*2012*	*2018*	*2000*	*2012*	*2018*
India	**83**	**81**	**78.6**	**34**	**29**	**23.6**
Kazakhstan	76	78	77.1	**65**	**68**	**65.1**
Kyrgyzstan	74	79	75.8	56	56	48.0
Tajikistan	75	77	59.7	58	59	27.8
Turkmenistan	74	77	78.2	48	47	52.8
Uzbekisatn	**72**	**75**	**78.0**	**47**	**48**	**53.4**
Russia	68	71	70.5	54	57	54.9
Norway	72	70	66.7	**60**	**62**	**60.2**

Source: Table prepared by the author with help of data from World Bank and WDI reports. (2009), http://databank.worldbank.org/data/views/reports/tableview. aspx; (2000, 2012, 2018) http://wdi.worldbank.org/table/2.2.

* For details see table: 2.8b in appendix: II.D.

The Table 2.8b shows the labour force structure of women as according to WDI of various years. It shows a comparison of labour force participation rate between men and women in India and Central Asian countries. It is to be noted that Kazakhstan has the highest participation rate even better than Norway and its other neighbours including Russia. In Uzbekistan, the participation rate is the lowest, and in India participation rate of women is the least.

The total labour force growth rate in 2014 is illustrated in Graph 2.6. Tajikistan and Uzbekistan show a higher rate of growth in total labour force as compared to other countries of the region.

Graph 2.6

World Development Indicators 2014: Labour force growth rate

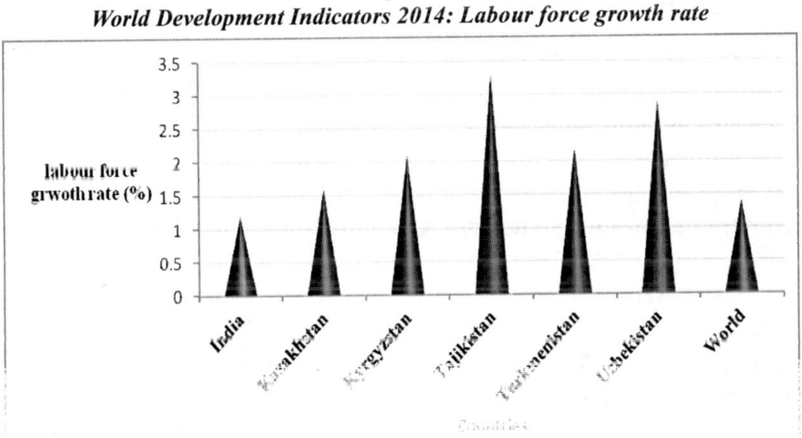

Source: Prepared by the Author with the help of data in Table in Appendix. II.C.

And as of 2019, the labour force growth rate of these countries 2009-18 for World is 1.1. India is 1.2; Kazakhstan 0.9; Kyrgyzstan 1.0; Tajikistan 2.3; Turkmenistan is 1.8; Uzbekistan is 2.4.[124]

In the labour sector, be it agriculture, industry or services, women are less in strength. The agriculture sector is underperforming in many developing countries, in part because men and women do not have equal access to the resources and opportunities, to be productive. Across countries and contexts: women have consistently less access than men to agricultural assets, inputs and services and to rural employment opportunities.[125] This exists despite the fact that, women are the backbone of the rural economy in many societies more so in the developing countries. Yet they receive only a fraction of the land, credit, inputs (such as improved seeds and fertilisers), agricultural training and information compared to men. Empowering and investing in rural women has been shown to significantly increase productivity, reduce hunger and malnutrition and improve rural livelihoods, not only for women, but for everyone.[126]

Likewise, there are considerable differences in women's and men's access and opportunities to exert power over economic structures in their societies. In most parts of the world, women are virtually absent from or are poorly represented in economic decision-making, including the formulation of financial, monetary, commercial and other economic policies, as well as tax systems and rules governing pay.[127] One report noted that although Asia's economic growth of 6.2 percent in 2000-2007 exceeded the global average of 4.2 percent, the average growth in women's employment was just 1.7 percent, below the world average of 2 percent.[128]

The role of women in families, local communities and societies began to shift in the early 1990s. Liberalisation of economy in India had tremendous impact on people in society including women. Women suddenly had lot of option both in education and labour market. In Central Asia likewise independence brought in many changes along with it. In few countries family and community values reemerged, along with traditional marriage practices. Women's role in these societies changed and started to be seen purely in reproductive terms, education was only meant for equipping girls to be better wives and mothers, or increasing their chances of getting a suitable husband. These could be genuine aspirations, given the realities of these societies. However, they do little to equip girls and women to question the world around them, and the subordinate status assigned to them.[129]

Besides, one must keep in mind that, when women are educated and can earn and control income, a number of good results follow: infant mortality declines, child health and nutrition improve, agricultural productivity rises, population growth slows, economy expands, poverty reduces and as a result the country prospers.

However, the persistent gender gaps in access to education, healthcare and income; and above all these, a lack of basic rights and pervasive violence against women keep women from being fully productive members of society. This challenge seems dauntingly large for women to lessen that gap; be it in education, employment or politics. The entrenched gender discrimination remains a defining characteristic of life for the majority of the world's people, helping sustain the gap between the most destitute and everyone else who shares this planet.[130]

Furthermore, the exclusion of women from certain occupations prevents the efficient allocation of labour with negative consequences for productivity and income distribution. In India, women aged 15 and above comprise only 27 percent of all employed persons. As according to 2009 ILO report, young girls account for 42 percent of all, in employment. These findings raise grave concerns about the impact of the economic crisis on the working poor, and especially on women.[131]

Women also often face legal and institutional barriers to economic activity outside home, including laws or customs and practices that deny them the right to own land, inherit property, to have access to policy and decision making power etc.[132] Within the family, women usually have the primary responsibility of both childcare and housework tasks which they usually have in addition to their productive labour.

According to a report of The Association for Women's Rights in Development (AWID), women of Central Asia suffered unequal access to economic and financial resources and decision-making with more than 85% of the wealth in Central Asian countries owned by men. Amongst the most vulnerable groups are working class women and rural women from poor families; women working in education and healthcare systems; women owning small and medium textile enterprises; women working for export-oriented industries; women in the informal economy and nonworking women in households dependent on remittances.[133] In fact, Tajikistan, Turkmenistan, Kyrgyzstan, and Kazakhstan, all have passed gender equality legislation and all Central Asian Republics have ratified International Labour Organisation (ILO), Conventions No. 100 (on equal pay) and No. 111 on discrimination in labour and employment. However, several reforms and proper implementation of these conventions are required.[134]

In Central Asia, in addition to the already existing evils of society like gender disparities, inequalities, violence against women have increased, there are some very unique and different kind of issues that are prevalent, which challenges the role of women in general and is also detrimental for society; for example, bride kidnapping (*ala kachuu* in Kyrgyz), in Kyrgyzstan, some part of Kazakhstan and Uzbekistan.[135] And this has been a real challenge not only for women and governments in the concerned countries but Non-Governmental Organisations and International Organisations too. The struggle is still on with no respite visible in near sight.

Education, employment, and political participation are considered essential for the achievement of gender equality and women's empowerment and bring about positive changes in women's lives. And moreover, economic participation and political participation, is not divorced from each other. In fact, they are parallel arenas for women's empowerment and women's ability to become agents of change in their own communities for the better. The economic and social changes impact women's political leadership and participation. So, women's political participation and representation will be dealt with, in the next chapter.

Notes

1. Jawaharlal Nehru, 'The Discovery of India', Centenary Edition, Delhi: Oxford University Press, 1989, p. 562.
2. According to a 2002 census of India, the religion of 80% of the people is Hinduism. Islam is practiced by around 13% of all Indians. The country had over 23 million Christians, over 19 million Sikhs, about 8 million Buddhists and about 4 million Jains.
3. James P. Stobaugh, World History: Observations and Assessments from Creation to Today, New Leaf Publishing Group, 01-Mar-2012, p. 129.
4. Rushoti Roy, "The Changing Roles of Women- An Overview into the Perception of Women Over Time in India", The Institute of Chartered Accountants of India, Jan 2010, p. 1103.
5. Manu Smriti chapter 3, exclusively deals about women and their status in society; 3.56:Where women are honoured, there the gods are pleased; but where they are not honoured, no sacred rite yields rewards; 3.57: Where the female relations live in grief, the family soon wholly perishes; but that family where they are not unhappy ever prospers; 3.58: The houses on which female relations, not being duly honoured, pronounce a curse, perish completely, as if destroyed by magic; 3.55: Women must be honoured and adorned by their fathers, brothers,

husbands, and brothers-in-law, who desire (their own) welfare. Also see, https://docs.google.com/file/d/0Bz1OumJznV7ucmwyelNvQy1CcUU/edit; for more detail see http://www.vedicsanskriti.com/2016/04/manusmriti-in-hindi-pdf.html. Accessed on May 6, 2014.

6. Ramesh Chandra Majumdar, Ancient India, Motilal Banarsidass, 1977, ISBN 978-81-208-0436-4. Also see Olivelle, Patrick (Trans), Upanishads, Oxford University Press, 1998, ISBN 978-0-19-283576-5.
7. The Brahmavadinis, or the women who never married and cultured the Vedas throughout their lives; and the Sadyodvahas who studied the Vedas till they married. R. C. Majumdar and, A. D. Pusalker eds., "The history and culture of the Indian people". Volume I, The Vedic age. Bombay: BharatiyaVidya Bhavan 1951, p. 394.
8. Kanjiv Lochan, Medicines of Early India: With Appendix on a Rare Ancient Text, Varanasi, Chaukhambha Publications, 2003, p-100. Also see. R C Majumdar, The Age of Imperial Unity, Bombay: Bharatiya Vidya Bhavan, 1953, p. 563.
9. R. C. Majumdar and A. D. Pusalker eds., "The history and culture of the Indian people", Volume I, The Vedic age. Bombay: BharatiyaVidya Bhavan 1951, p. 394, Jyotsna K Kamat, "Perspectives in Education", Sadashiva Wodeyar's 50th Birthday Felicitation Volume, Dharwad 1980. Also see, Upinder Singh, A History of Ancient and Early Mediaeval India: From the Stone Age to the 12th Century, Pearson Education India, 2008, ISBN: 978-81-317-1120-0.
10. T.M.P. Mahadevan, The Religio-Philosophic Culture of India, The Cultural Heritage of India, Vol. I, The Rama Krishna Mission, Calcutta, 1975. Also see, V.K. Gokak, India and World Culture, Sahitya Akademi, New Delhi, 1994. Many Queens like Nayanika of the Satavahana Dynasty (2nd century B.C.), Prabhavati Gupta of the Vakataka family (4th century A.D.), Vijaya Bhattrika of the Chalukya house (7th century A.D.) and Sugandha and Bidda of KashmirdOth century A.D.), successfully administered extensive kingdoms during the period of the minority of their sons. Queen Nayanika was the head of the administration of the extensive Satavahana Empire of Deccan when her son was a minor in the second century B.C. In the 4th century A.D. Prabhavati Gupta administered the Vakataka kingdom in Madhya Pradesh for over 10 years after her husband's death, for the sake of her minor son. In Medieval Kashmir Queen Sugandha was actively governing the country. Also see http://shodhganga.inflibnet.ac.in/bitstream/10603/102290/8/08_chapter%201.pdf
11. http://rajyasabha.nic.in/rsnew/publication electronic/reserv_women_pers 2008.pdf
12. Raja, C. Kunjan, Vedic Culture, The Cultural Heritage of India, Vol. I, The Ramakrishna Mission, Calcutta, 1975. Also see, T.M.P. Mahadevan, The Religio-Philosophic Culture of India, The Cultural Heritage of India, Vol. I, The Rama Krishna Mission, Calcutta, 1975.
13. Vikash Mehra, "Women in India: Status, Position and Condition of Women in India", February 17, 2014.
14. The Changing Roles of Women: An overview into the Perception of Women over Time in India, January, 2010, p.1104, https://womenportal.icai.org/wp_articles/ChaD5C8pdf216aa.pdf. Accessed on 27 March, 2014.

15. Fatimah Kelleher, "Women and the Teaching Profession: Exploring the Feminisation Debate", Commonwealth Secretariat and UNESCO 2011, p. 26, http://www.ungei.org/files/212200e.pdf. Accessed on 5 May, 2012.
16. Soonu Kochar, "Geo-Political Diversity" in Kurt April & Marylou Shockley, eds, "Diversity New Realities in a Changing World", Palgrave, N Y, 2007, p. 154.
17. The 'Ancient Silk Route' (300 BC-AD 100), which was an extensive interconnected network of trade routes across the Asian continent connecting East, South, and Western Asia with the Mediterranean world, as well as North and Northeast Africa and Europe. The Ancient Silk Route formed the first bridge between the East and West and was an important vehicle for trade between ancient empires of India, China, Persia and Rome. The route was a channel for contact between people and cultures, inspiring the exchange of dialogue, art, religion, ideas and technology. Some of the world's most acclaimed explorers such as Alexander the Great, Marco Polo and Ibn Battuta have treaded on these routes.
18. Gustavo Henrique Feddersen, Giovanna Esther Zucatto, "Infrastructure in Central Asia: Energy and Transportation Controversies", UFRGSMUN/UFRGS Model United Nation Journal, Vol. 1, 2013, pp. 159-181, p. 159. Also see, Linda Buskirk, "The Silk Road", Quest Paper, Presented on 31October, 2008, p. 2. http://www.fwquestclub.com/welcome_files/papers/the_silk_road.pdf. Accessed on 5 May, 2012
19. Glenn E. Curtis, ed., Kazakstan, Kyrgyzstan, Tajikistan, Turkmenistan, and Uzbekistan country studies, Federal Research Division, Library of Congress, 1997, p. xxxii. https://ia601903.us.archive.org/18/items/kazakstankyrgyzs00curt_0/kazakstankyrgyzs00curt_0.pdf.

    Accessed on 6 May 2014. Also see G. Kidayator, "Uzbekistan: Between the Past and Future", *Contemporary Central Asia*, 1 (1), 12-25, 1997, p-15. See also, D. Sinor, "The Cambridge History of Early Inner Asia", London: Cambridge University Press, 1990, p. 344.
20. Daniel Pipes, "The Third World Peoples of Soviet Central Asia", in W. Scott Thompson Ed., The Third World: Premises of U.S. Foreign Policy, San Francisco: Institute for Contemporary Studies, 1983, pp. 183-203.
21. Glenn E. Curtis, area handbook series Kazakstan, Kyrgystan, Tajikistan, Turkmenistan, and Uzbekistan, country studies, 1997, p. xix. http://www.marines.mil/Portals/59/Publications/Kazakstan,%20Kyrgystan,%20Tajikistan,%20Turkmenistan,%20and%20Uzbekistan%20Study_1.pdf. Accessed on 6 May 2014.
22. Reza Banakar, The Politics of Legal Cultures, 53, Scandinavian Studies in Law, 2008. p. 40. http://www.retfaerd.org/gamle_pdf/2008/4/Retfaerd_123_2008_4_s37_60.pdf. Accessed on 6 May, 2014.
23. Kamala Kumari, "Identifying women's issues in Central Asia: Problems and Prospects" *Contemporary Central Asia*, Vol.xiv, No. I, March 2010, pp. 45-62, pp. 45-46.
24. Muborak Sharipova, One more war against Women: Historical and socio-cultural aspects of violence against women in Tajikistan, in Hämmerle, Christa, Nikola Langreiter, Margareth Lanzinger, and Edith Saurer, eds., Gender Politics in Central Asia: Historical Perspectives and Current Living Conditions of Women. Germany: Behlau, 2008, pp. 67-94.

25. Ajay Patnaik, Perestroika and Women Labour Force in Soviet Central Asia, New Delhi: New Literature, 1989, pp. 8-9.
26. "Razvitiye matiryalnoi i dukhovnoi kulturi crednebekobovo Merva" v matiryali mejhdunarodnoi nayuchnoi konferentsii na Srednebekobiye goroda turkmenistana v sisteme evraziiskoi tsivilizatsii, 28-30 Marta, 2012, pp. 547-48.
27. Suad Joseph, Afsana Nagmabad, eds, "Encyclopedia of Women and Islamic Cultures: Family, Law and Politics", p. 50. Also see, Colette Harris, "identity politics: Central Asia" in Suad Joseph, Afsāna Nag mābādī, ed., Encyclopedia of Women and Islamic Cultures: Family, Law and Politics, 2004, pp. 283-284. Also see Timur Kocaoglu, The Past as Prologue? Challenging the Myth of the Subordinated, Docile Woman in Muslim Central Eurasia, p. 177. http://www.iccrimea.org/scholarly/kocaoglu-gender.pdf. Accessed on 6 May, 2013.
28. Morris Rossabi, "Central Asia: A Historical Overview",

    http://asiasociety.org/central-asia-historical-overview?page=0,0. Accessed on 6 May, 2014
29. Gulnara Mendikulova, "Kazakh Women: the Impact of Three Different Socio political Systems within Two Centuries", in Christa Hämmerle, ed. "Gender Politics in Central Asia: Historical Perspectives and Current Living Conditions of Women", Germany: Böhlau Verlag Köln Weimar, 2008, p. 21-34.
30. During one of the discussions of Author with Director, Dr. Nazym Shedenova and other professors and research scholars, Center of Gender Studies, Department of Philosophy and Politology, KAZGU, Almaty (22 October, 2012), See Image: 11c & d; and at the Institute of Culture Studies, Ashgabat (28 November 2012).
31. Kamala Kumari, "Identifying women's issues in Central Asia: Problems and Prospects", *Contemporary Central Asia*, Vol. xiv, No. I, March 2010, pp.45-62.
32. Ajay Patnaik, Perestroika and Women Labour Force in Soviet Central Asia, (New Delhi: New Literature, 1989), p. 10.
33. Lenin, "Soviet Power and the Status of Women 1919", in Lenin, V. I., On the Emancipation of Women. Moscow: Progress Publishers, 1974. http://icl-fi.org/english/ssa/5/women.html. Accessed on 14 March 2012.
34. Northrop, Douglas, "Veiled Empire: Gender and Power in Stalinist Central Asia", 1st ed. Ithaca: Cornell University Press, 2004, p. 11.
35. Glenn E. Curtis ed., Kazakstan, Kyrgyzstan, Tajikistan, Turkmenistan, and Uzbekistan, Country Studies, Area Handbook Series, Federal Research Division Library of Congress, 1997, p. 243.
36. Shirin Akiner, Islam, the State and Ethnicity in Central Asia in Historical Perspective, Religion, State & Society, Vol. 24, Nos. 2/3, 1996, p. 108. http://www.biblicalstudies.org.uk/pdf/rss/24_2-3_091.pdf. Also see T. Saidbayev, Islam i obshchestvo (Nauka, Moscow, 1984), p. 79.
37. Armine Ishkanian, "Gendered Transitions: The Impact of the Post-Soviet Transition on Women in Central Asia and the Caucasus", Perspectives on Global Development and Technology, Vol. 2, no. 3-4, 2003, pp.475-496, p. 480, http://booksandjournals.brillonline.com/content/journals/15691497/2/3. Accessed on March 14, 2013.

38. Muborak Sharipova, "One More War Against Women: Historical And Socio-Cultural Aspects Of Violence Against Women In Tajikistan", in Hämmerle, Christa, Nikola Langreiter, Margareth Lanzinger, and Edith Saurer, eds., Gender Politics in Central Asia: Historical Perspectives and Current Living Conditions of Women, Germany: Behlau, 2008, p. 67-94, p. 69.
39. Kathleen R. Kuehnast, Carol Nechemias, Eds., Post-Soviet Women Encountering Transition: Nation Building, Economic Survival, And Civic Activism, Woodrow Wilson Center Press, 2004, p. 4.
40. Complete edition of Lenin's works in Russian (2nd ed., Moscow 1928) Vol. 25, p. 64 Also see Lenin, Selected Works (New York 1935-38) Vol. 9, pp. 494-9. Also see "The Woman Question: Selections from the Writings of Karl Marx, Frederick Engels, V. I. Lenin, Joseph Stalin", Printed in 1951 in the United States of America.
41. Timur Kocaoglu, "The Past as Prologue? Challenging the Myth of the Subordinated, Docile Woman in Muslim Central Eurasia", in Linda Racioppi and Katherine O'Sullivan See eds.,Gender politics in post-communist Eurasia, East Lansing : Michigan State University Press, 2009, pp. 169-208, p-199.
42. Amy Bug "Has Feminism Changed Physics?", *Signs*, 28.3 (2003), pp. 881–99. http://books.openedition.org/obp/1239. Accessed on 14 March, 2013.
43. D M Heer, Youssef N., "Female Status Among Soviet Central Asian Nationalities: The Melding Of Islam And Marxism And Its Implications For Population Increase", Population Studies, Mar, 31(1), 1977, pp. 155-73.
44. During one of the discussion, with Professor G Maitdinova; Director, Centre for Geopolitical Studies, RTSU. She is also the Executive Director, 'Central Asian Expert Club, Eurasian Development' in Dushanbe, 12-17 August 2014(this field work was for another project on Central Asia). Also seehttps://islamic-family-law/socialcultural-information-by-region/central-asia-and-caucasus/`. Accessed on 27 November, 2014.
45. Marfua Tokhtakhodzhaeva, "The Re-Islamisation of Society and the Position of Women in Post-Soviet Uzbekistan", 2008, E-ISBN: 9789004213241, http://booksandjournals.brillonline.com/books/9789004213241, Accessed on 14 May 2014.
46. Güneş-Ayata, Ayşe, and Ayça Ergun, "Gender Politics in Transitional Societies: A Comparative Perspective on Azerbaijan, Kazakhstan, Kyrgyzstan, and Uzbekistan", Gender Politics, 2009, p. 211. Also see, D M Heer, Youssef N., "Female Status among Soviet Central Asian Nationalities: The Melding of Islam and Marxism and Its Implications for Population Increase", Population Studies, Mar, 31(1), 1977, pp. 155-73.
47. Galiya Khassanova, "On the Way to Democracy: Women's Activism in Kazakhstan".

    http://www.gwu.edu/~ieresgwu/assets/docs/demokratizatsiya%20archive/08-3_Khassanova.PDF. Accessed on 23 March 2014.
48. Muborak Sharipova, "One More War Against Women: Historical And Socio-Cultural Aspects Of Violence Against Women In Tajikistan", in Hämmerle, Christa, Nikola Langreiter, Margareth Lanzinger, and Edith Saurer, Eds., "Gender Politics In Central Asia: Historical Perspectives And Current Living Conditions Of Women", Germany: Behlau, 2008, p. 67-94.

49. https://timesofindia.indiatimes.com/india/india-tad-better-than-south-asia-in-gender-equality/articleshow/72448804.cms. Accessed on 15 March 2019.
50. The Bertelsmann Stiftung's Transformation Index (BTI) analyzes and evaluates the quality of democracy, a market economy and political management in 129 developing and transition countries. It measures successes and setbacks on the path toward a democracy based on the rule of law and a socially responsible market economy. In-depth country reports provide the basis for assessing the state of transformation and persistent challenges, and to evaluate the ability of policymakers to carry out consistent and targeted reforms. The BTI is the first cross-national comparative index that uses self-collected data to comprehensively measure the quality of governance during processes of transition. The Status Index ranks the countries according to their quality of democracy and market economy as of January 31, 2013. www.bti-project.org Also see, http://www.bertelsmann-stiftung.de/. For details of methodology see appendix. II.A.i.
51. For details see, Report of the Fourth World Conference on Women, Beijing, 4-15 September 1995), http://www.un.org/documents/ga/conf177/aconf177-20en.htm. accessed on 5 May 2012.
52. George Bernard Shaw, (1907), in the preface to his play "Major Barbara", https://archive.org/details/BernardShawsMajorBarbaraTheCompletePreface. Accessed on 23 May 2014. Also see Duncan Green, "From Poverty to Power: How active citizens and effective states can change the world", 2nd ed. Rugby, UK: Practical Action Publishing and Oxford: Oxfam International, 2012, p. ix.
53. http://www.un.org/womenwatch/directory/women_and_poverty_3001.htm. Accessed on 23 May 2014.
54. http://www.ucis.pitt.edu/nceeer/2009_824-02h_Clement.pdf. Accessed on 23 May 2014.
55. World Bank Report, 2011.
56. See, CEDAW document, http://www2.ohchr.org/english/bodies/cedaw/docs/CEDAW-C-50-4.pdf, accessed on 23 May 2012.
57. Investing in formal and non-formal education and training for girls and women, with its exceptionally high social and economic return, has proved to be one of the best means of achieving sustainable development and economic growth that is both sustained and sustainable. See, "Beijing Platform for Action". Chapter IV. B. Education and training of women. p. 69. http://www.un.org/esa/gopher-data/conf/fwcw/off/a 20.en, accessed on 6 May, 2012.
58. see http://www.nuepa.org/Download/Publications/UnPriced/NUEPA_SAsia%20models_Final_Full.pdf

    https://www.scribd.com/document/233313295/India-Education-Report-January-2012.
59. For details see http://shodhganga.inflibnet.ac.in/bitstream/10603/40092/9/09_chapter1.pdf. Accessed on 23 May 2014.
60. See p. 11, http://shodhganga.inflibnet.ac.in/bitstream/10603/37480/7/07_chapter%201.pdf. Accessed on 23 May 2014.
61. Kishore M Joshi, "Higher Education, Social Demand and Social Equity in India", in Simon Schwartzman, Rómulo Pinheiro, Pundy Pillay, eds., "Higher Education

in the BRICS Countries: Investigating the Pact between Higher Education and Society", Higher Education Dynamics, Volume 44, 2015, p. 125-142.

62. Sandeep Kumar Sharma, *International Journal for Research in Education*, Vol. 2, Issue: 9, October- Nov. 2013. http://raijmr.com/wp-content/uploads/2014/01/4. Accessed on 14 March 2013.
63. "Gender Equality and Women's Empowerment in India", Ministry of Health and Family Welfare, Government of India, National Family Health Survey (NFHS-3), India, 2005-06. http://www.rchiips.org/nfhs/a_subject_report_gender_for_website.pdf, accessed on 14 May 2014.
64. Amtul Waris, B. C. Viraktamath, "Gender Gaps and Women's Empowerment in India: Issues And Strategies", *International Journal of Scientific and Research Publications*, Volume 3, Issue 9, September 2013. http://www.ijsrp.org/research-paper-0913/ijsrp-p21116.pdf, accessed on 14 May 2014.
65. "Gender Equality and Women's Empowerment in India", Ministry of Health and Family Welfare, Government of India, National Family Health Survey (NFHS-3), India, 2005-06. http://www.rchiips.org/nfhs/a_subject_report_gender_for_ website.pdf. Accessed on 23 May 2014.
66. https://www.shethepeople.tv/news/economic-survey-2019-women-empowerment. Accessed on 27 November 2019
67. ***Ladli* scheme:** Department of Women and Child Development, Govt. of NCT of Delhi has launched a new scheme for protection of the girl child called 'Delhi Ladli Scheme'. The scheme aims at enhancing the social status of girl child in the society as well in the family, ensuring proper education to make the girls self-reliant, ensuring her economic security and protecting them from discrimination and deprivation. This scheme is enforced in Delhi w.e.f. 01.01.2008. The girls born on or after this date will get benefit immediately after their birth. The other girls born before this date will get benefits under this scheme w.e.f. the academic year 2008-09 on their admission to the Ist ,VIth, IXth, XIIth class and after getting passed the Xth class. in the Govt. recognised Schools. ***Kishori*** scheme's main objective is to improve the nutritional and health status of girls in the age group of 11-18 years; to provide the required literacy and innumeracy skills through the non-formal stream of education, to stimulate a desire for more social exposure and knowledge and to help them improve their decision making capabilities. For details see Department of Women & Children Developmen, Govt. of NCT of Delhi. **Sarva Shiksha Abhiyan** (SSA) is Government of India's flagship programme for achievement of Universalisation of Elementary Education (UEE) in a time bound manner, as mandated by 86th amendment to the Constitution of India making free and compulsory Education to the Children of 6-14 years age group, a Fundamental Right. SSA is being implemented in partnership with State Governments to cover the entire country and address the needs of 192 million children in 1.1 million habitations. See Ministry of Human Resource Development, Dept of School education & Literacy, GOI. http://wcddel.in/ksy.html. Accessed on 14 March 2013.
68. Arvind Kumar, "Privatisation of School Education: A Social Welfare Program or Industry for Profit", *European Academic Research* - Vol. II, Issue 1 April 2014, p. 1552. for details regarding facilities in schools see, DISE Report

2011-12, Flash Statistics National University of, Educational Planning and Administration Delhi, 2013.

69. At least all parents the author interacted during the research had similar opinion. Few even went on to say that girls perform better that their sons and makes them proud.
70. During, a discussion with Dr. Sangeeta Gahlot (lecturer, Govt. Sr. School, Delhi), on Change of attitude toward a girl child, her education etc.
71. Dr. Susmita Sahu, Consultant, TERI; Geeta, Social worker, *Naaz* Foundation; Deepika, Consultant, Electronic Media house, during interactions and discussion on Changes in attitudes towards girl child in Indian society.
72. http://mhrd.gov.in/statistics_data. Accessed on 14 March 2014.
73. UGC report, 2013-14. p. 58. Also see, Kishore M. Joshi, Higher Education, Social Demand, and Social Equity in India, in Schwartzman, Simon, Pinheiro, Rómulo, Pillay, Pundy eds, Higher Education in the BRICS Countries, Higher Education Dynamics Volume 44, 2015, pp. 125-147.
74. Marifat Abdullaeva, Review of Central Asian countries, Background paper prepared for the Education for All Global Monitoring Report 2006, Literacy for Life, 2006. http://uncsdoc.unesco.org/images/0014/001459/145934e.pdf. Accessed on 14 March 2013.
75. Iveta Silova, Mark S. Johnson, And Stephen P. Heyneman, Education and the Crisis of Social Cohesion in Azerbaijan and Central Asia, May 2007 p. 176, http://www.vanderbilt.edu/peabody/heyneman/PUBLICATIONS/Ed.%20and%20the%20Crisis%20of%20Social%20Cohesion%20in%20Azerbaijan%20and%20Central%20Asia.pdf. Accessed on 27 March 2014.
76. Negmatullo Mirsaidov, 20.07.2012., http://centralasiaonline.com/en_GB/articles/caii/features/main/2012/07/20/feature-01, accessed on 23 January 2014.
77. Marifat Abdullaeva, Education For All And Literacy: Review of Central Asian Countries, Adult Education and Development, Number 66, DVV Publications, http://www.dvv-international.de/index.php?article_id=207&clang=1. Accessed on 14 March 2013; http://unesdoc.unesco.org/images/0014/001459/145934e.pdf. Accessed on 14 March 2013.
78. The Condition of Higher Education in Turkmenistan, http://www.silkproject.org/highereducationinturkmenistan.htm. Accessed on 14 March 2013.
79. There are around 150 universities and higher education institutions spread throughout Kazakhstan. Almaty has the highest concentration of facilities and also the most varied choice of subjects. A 2007 World Bank report pointed out that Kazakhstan's high degree of specialisation as one of the country's main strengths for future areas for improvement in Kazakhstan's higher education system. However, further investment is essential to improve the quality of education within the country. Uzbekistan boasts of 34 high educational institutes and all of them responsible to the Ministry. However there are challenges in higher education in Uzbekistan like re-training the teaching staff at higher education institutes, so that they are well-versed with the latest pedagogical methods etc. Also see http://www.silkproject.org/highereducation.htm. Accessed on 27 March, 2014.

80. Education in Uzbekistan Country Profile, UNICEF, p. 4, http://www.unicef.org/ceecis/Uzbekistan.pdf. Accessed on 14 March 2013. The Education for All (EFA) movement is a global commitment to provide quality basic education for all children, youth and adults. At the World Education Forum (Dakar, Senegal, 26-28 April 2000), 164 governments pledged to achieve EFA and identified six goals to be met by 2015. Governments, development agencies, civil society and the private sector are working together to reach the EFA goals. http://www.unesco.org/new/en/education/themes/leading-the-international-agenda/education-for-all/the-efa-movement/dakar-2000/. Accessed on 27 March 2014.
81. Discussion with Dr. Sofia Kasymova, Sociologist, Gender Education Center, Dushanbe, Tajikistan, November 11, 2012. Also see http://www.silkproject.org/highereducation.htm. Accessed on 27 March, 2014.
82. Interview with Ms. Zhuldyz Smagulova, Expert Social Policy Department in the Ministry of Economic Development and Trade, 20 November 2012.
83. UNDP Report, 2008.
84. Maarten van Klaveren, Kea Tijdens,Melanie Hughie-Williams, Nuria Ramos, "An Overview of Women's Work and Employment in Kazakhstan. Decisions for Life", MDG3 Project, Country Report No. 10, University of Amsterdam / Amsterdam Institute for Advanced Labour Studies (AIAS), Netherlands, March 2010, p. 41 www.uva.nl/aias . Accessed on 23 May 2014.
85. Data from Women in Muslim Countries (WIMC) http://www.unescap.org/Rural/doc/women/index.htm, and http://www.d3systems.com/wp-content/uploads/2010/09/WIMC-Educational-Attainment-in-Central-Asia-Final1.pdf. Accessed on 14 March 2014.
86. http://www.marines.mil/Portals/59/Publications/Kazakstan, Kyrgystan, Tajikistan, Turkmenistan, and Uzbekistan Study_4.pdf. Also see http://www.silkproject.org/highereducation.htm. Accessed on 27 March 2014.
87. Open Society Institute (OSI) was created in 1993 to support Soros foundations in Central and Eastern Europe and the former Soviet Union. In August 2010, the Open Society Initiative changed its name to Open Society Foundations (OSF) to better reflect its role as a funder for civil society groups around the world. http://www.dvv-international.de/index.php?article_id=207&clang=1; http://unesdoc.unesco.org/images/0014/001459/145934e.pdf. Accessed on 27 March 2014.
88. ACTED (Agency for Technical Cooperation and Development) is a non-governmental organisation with headquarters in Paris, founded in 1993. Independent, private and not-for-profit, ACTED respects a strict political and religious impartiality and operates according to principles of non-discrimination and transparency. Marifat Abdullaeva, "Review of Central Asian Countries",

    http://www.dvv-international.de/index.php?article_id=207&clang=1; http://unesdoc.unesco.org/images/0014/001459/145934e.pdf. Accessed on 27 March 2014.
89. International donors like USAID, Counterpart Consortium, OSI - Soros Fund, International Labor Organisation, Eurasia Fund, UNESCO, UNICEF, UNDP, Asian Development Bank, WHO, UNFPA, IOM, INTRAC, World Bank, Mercy Corps, TASIS, OSCE, IIZ/DW, Friedrich Ebert Fund, ACCELS, Embassy of USA, Switzerland, Norway. See. http://pdf.usaid.gov/pdf_docs/pdabu135.pdf.;

http://www.marines.mil/Portals/59/Publications/Kazakstan, Kyrgystan, Tajikistan, Turkmenistan, and Uzbekistan Study_4.pdf. Accessed on 27 March 2014.

90. Zhakenov G., The national report on the development of the system of higher education of the republic of Kazakhstn, 2008. http://www.unesco.kz/education/he/kazakh/kazakh_ru.htm. Accessed on 23 May 2013.

91. Gosudarstvennia programma razvitija obrazov, http://www.edu.gov.kz/.../gosudarstvennia_programma_razvitija_obrazov. Accessed on 14 March 2013.

92. During Author's Field work discussions; these were few of the reason cited for proper implementation of policies. The Author met several undergraduate Students, Research Scholars, who were of the similar opinion, in Almaty, Bishkek and Dushanbe, Astana, Ashgabat and Tashkent; during her field work visit. The author was in Kazakhstan, Kyrgyzstan and Tajikistan, Turkmenistan and Uzbekistan from 17 October to12 December, 2012, where she visited various Institutes/ Universities/ Libraries/ Organisations.

93. http://wdi.worldbank.org/table/2.10. Accessed on 31 January 2020.

94. See http://www.dvv-international.de/index.php?id=809&L=1, accessed on 14 March 2013.

95. The Author met several undergraduate students who were studying and working in Almaty, Bishkek and Dushanbe, during her field work visit to Kazakhstan, Kyrgyzstan and Tajikistan from 17 October to 12 December, 2012, where she visited various Institutes/ Universities/ Libraries/ Organisations.

96. G. Philip, Altbach, Patti Mcgill Peterson Eds, "Higher Education In The 21st Century: Global Challenge And National Response", April 1999. www.iie.org/.../Research-Report-029. Accessed on 23 March 2014.

97. Author's experience during discussions and interaction sessions, during field trip.

98. http://www.oitbrasil.org.br/sites/default/files/topic/gender/doc/getwomen2012_963.pdf, accessed on 14 March 2013; http://databank.worldbank.org/data/views/reports/tableview.aspx?isshared=true, accessed on 14 March 2013.

99. S. Kapsos and A. Silberman, "Female Labour Force Participation in India", ILO, Geneva, 2013.

100. Steven Kapsos, Evangelia Bourmpoula, Andrea Silberman, "Why is female labour force participation declining so sharply in India? ILO Research Paper No. 10, 2014, p. 31 http://www.ilo.org/wcmsp5/groups/public/—dgreports/—inst/documents/publication/wcms_250977.pdf. Accessed on 23 June 2014.

101. See https://www.scribd.com/doc/17512075/World-Development-Indicators-2008. Accessed on 14 May 2014.

102. This is also detrimental to men, when job losses are concentrated in industries dominated by men and job growth is centred in service occupations, where women have better chances, as has been the recent experience in many countries. http://databank.worldbank.org/data/views/reports/tableview.aspx?isshared=true. Accessed on 14 May 2014.

103. For details see http://www.unescap.org/rural/doc/women/index.htm, accessed on 14 May 2014.

104. Alastair McAuley, "Development Strategy, Welfare Regime and Poverty Reduction in the Former Soviet Union", United Nations Research Institute for Social Development (UNRISD), 2008, p. 11, http://www.unrisd.org/80256B3C005BB128/%28httpAuxPages%29/61A3639B57518A12C125773D004A78AA/$file/USSRweb-3.pdf. Accessed on 14 May 2014.
105. Yvonne Corcoran-Nantes, "Lost Voices: Central Asian Women: Confronting Transition", London and New York: Zed Books, 2005. 208 pages, p. 63.
106. Ajay Patnaik, Perestroika and Women Labour Force in Soviet Central Asia, (New Delhi: New Literature, 1989), pp. xv-xvi. Also see, Deniz Kandiyoti, "The politics of Gender and the Soviet paradox: Neither Colonized, nor Modern?", Volume 26, 2007 - Issue 4, pp. 601-623 http://www.tandfonline.com/doi/abs/10.1080/02634930802018521. Accessed on 14 May 2014.
107. Shirin Akiner, "Between Tradition and Modernity: the Dilemma Facing Contemporary Central Asian Women", in Mary Buckley ed., "Post-Soviet Women: from the Baltic to Central Asia", New York: Cambridge University Press, 1997, p. 288.
108. Address by Statement By H.E. Mrs. Aitkul B. Samakova, Minister of the Republic of Kazakhstan, Chairperson of the National Commission on Family and Women's Affairs Under the President of the Republic of Kazakhstan, To the 23rd Special Session of the United Nations General Assembly, "Women 2000: Gender Equality, Development, and Peace for the Twenty-First Century.", New York, June 8, 2000, Permanent Mission of the Republic Of Kazakhstan to the United Nations, http://www.un.org. Accessed on 23 March 2014.
109. "Women And Economy in Central Asia", http://editorials.voa.gov. Accessed on 23 March, 2014.
110. Magdalena Rokicka, "Gender Gap in the CIS…", *Center for Social and Economic Research (CASE) Network Studies & Analyses*, No. 376, Warsaw, 2008, p. 48.
111. Yelena I. Rudenko, "Public Issues and Social Initiatives for the differently abled people of Kazakhstan", in Mondira Dutta ed., Gender and Human Development in Central and South Asia, Delhi: Pentagon Press, pp. 87-98.
112. Interview with Ms. Zhuldyz Smagulova, Expert Social Policy Department in the Ministry of Economic Development and Trade, 20 November 2012.
113. Interview with Mrs. Smagulova Alma Kurmetovna, in the 'Ministry of women and Labour and social Development/ Ministry of Labour and Social Protection', on 20 November, 2012.
114. Interview with Mrs. Bermaganbetova Gazima Nurashevna, in the 'Ministry of Health/ Healthcare on 19 November 2012.
115. *Gaps (something similar to kitty-party or committee)* and *chernaya kassa* are women's spaces of empowerment and social networks like these represent a collective movement and action against economic dependency of women on men and the state micro-loan bank system. For details see, Zulfiya Tursunova, Women's Lives and Livelihoods in Post-Soviet Uzbekistan: Ceremonies of Empowerment and Peacebuilding, Lexington Books, 2014, p. 115.
116. Author had first-hand experience, as she participated in one such *Gaps* in Osh, Kyrgyzstan, during Field Trip.

117. In 2010, Women's labour force participation rates remain below 30 percent in Northern Africa and Western Asia; below 40 percent in Southern Asia; and below 50 percent in the Caribbean and Central America. The gap between participation rates of women and men has narrowed slightly in the last 20 years but remains considerable. The smallest gender gaps are in the early adult years and the widest in the prime working age. See "The World's Women", United Nations, New York, 2010. http://unstats.un.org/unsd/demographic/products/Worldswomen/WW_full report_color.pdf. Accessed on 14 March 2014.
118. Maarten van Klaveren, Kea Tijdens,Melanie Hughie-Williams, Nuria Ramos, "An Overview of Women's Work and Employment in Kazakhstan. Decisions for Life", MDG3 Project, Country Report No. 10, University of Amsterdam / Amsterdam Institute for Advanced Labour Studies (AIAS), Netherlands, March 2010, p. 40. www.uva.nl/aias . Accessed on 23 May 2014.
119. Overall, 62% percent of Tajik women with a college degree living in rural areas are employed full-time compared to 45% of their urban counterparts. Furthermore, these educated Tajik women living in rural areas are more likely to work in areas of public health (28% rural women, 17% urban women) and education or culture (38% rural women, 20% urban women) while their educated urban counterparts have higher rates of working in trade (14% urban women, 3% rural women) and commercial services (14% urban women, 7% rural women). See Stephen Hornbeck, "Educational Attainment and its Impact on Women's Status in Central Asia", March, 2012. http://www.d3systems.com/wp-content/uploads/2010/09/WIMC-Educational-Attainment-in-Central-Asia-Final1.pdf. Accessed on 23 May 2014.
120. During her Field work visit, the author attended a Public Lecture, October 30, 2012, on the topic, "Women's Rights to Land and Natural Resources in Kyrgyzstan: Findings from Batken, Chui, Naryn and Jalalabad Oblasts" by Ailey Hughes, Fulbright Research Scholar, University of Central Asia, Bishkek, Kyrgyzstan. For details see http://www.ucentralasia.org/news.asp?Nid=415. Accessed on 6 December 2012.
121. During field work discussions with professors, in Osh, Dushanbe, Tashkent (November 2012).
122. This is a common sight in all the countries of Central Asia. Author's personal observation during Field Work Trip (October- December, 2012).
123. Author's personal observations, during visits to different cities in India. Also, there are Literatures available regarding, women in business etc.
124. http://wdi.worldbank.org/table/2.2 . Accessed on 27 November 2019.
125. See www.fao.org/sofa/gender/en/ ; Accessed on 23 March 2014. Also see http://www.un.org/womenwatch/directory/women_and_poverty_3001.htm, Accessed on 23 March 2014.
126. www.fao.org/gender/infographic/en, Accessed on 23 March 2014. Also see http://www.un.org/womenwatch/directory/women_and_poverty_3001.htm, Accessed on 23 March 2014.
127. See http://www.un.org/documents/ga/conf177/aconf177-20en.htm, Accessed on 14 March 2014.

128. "Women and Labour Markets in Asia: Rebalancing for Gender Equality", http://www.indianexpress.com/news/asia-needs-to-improve-employment-options-for-women-adb/783426/, Accessed on 23 March 2014.
129. Naila Kabeer, "Gender equality and women's empowerment:a critical analysis of the third Millennium Development Goal",Gender and Development, Vol. 13, No. 1, March 2005, 17.
130. Isobel Coleman, May/june issue, 2010.

     http://www.foreignaffairs.com/articles/66206/isobel-coleman/the-global-glass-ceiling. Accessed on 27 March 2014.
131. Global Employment Trends for Women, March, 2009, p. 19, International Labour Organisation 2009. Also see http://www.oitbrasil.org.br/sites/default/files/topic/gender/doc/getwomen2012_963.pdf. Accessed on 27 March 2014.
132. See http://www.unfpa.org/modules/6billion/populationissues/empower.htm. Accessed on 27 March 2014.
133. Nurgul Djanaeva, The Systemic crisis′ impact on women: sub regional perspectives, AWID:Women's Rights, Brief 5, p. 5. http://www.awid.org, accessed on 14 March 2014.
134. Megan Bick, EU- Central Asia Civil Society Seminar on Women's Rights, Brussels 21-24 June 2010, Final Report, September 2010, p. 14, http://eeas.europa.eu/human_rights/civil_society/docs/2010_ca_final_report_en.pdf, accessed on 14 March 2014.
135. Author, during her field research with whom so ever, interacted did mention (mostly women) that bride kidnapping in Kyrgyzstan is an evil of society and an issue of concern. Bride kidnapping involves the taking of an unwilling young woman by a young man for the purpose of non-consensual marriage; is still prevalent. Kidnappings can occur in rural and urban areas. It has been estimated that up to a third of all ethnic Kyrgyz women in Kyrgyzstan may have been wedded in non-consensual bride kidnappings. The Gender Equality Law of Kyrgyzstan applies to family members and to relatives who reside with a family member (Article 5) from whom they experience physical, psychological or other forms of harm.

Chapter 3

Women's Participation in Political Sphere

"A woman is the companion of man gifted with equal mental capacities. She has the right, to participate in the minute details of the activities of man. She has the same right of freedom and liberty as he" - MAHATMA GANDHI

While education and economic independence are the two most important parameters of appraising women's status in any given society, higher degree of political participation and representation enables women to influence policy-making and governance. Worldwide more electoral democracies exist today than at any time in history, where almost half of all governments are considered to be democratic. As a result, one of the most important political developments of the past century has been the increasing representation of women in politics. At the turn of the 20th century, there was not even one woman who held political positions at national level. In the second decade of 21st Century, women are represented in all democratic parliaments.[1] However, there are differences and inequalities in most countries between women and men in terms of responsibilities assigned, activities undertaken, access to and control over resources, as well as decision-making opportunities.[2]

In Asia, socio-cultural factors as 'Asian values'; traditional, patriarchal or social structure, are often cited as factors for women's under-representation. Consequently, dominant explanations for Asian women's rise to political leadership tend to focus on non-institutional family or dynastic ties.[3]

Despite, the shift in the global power dynamics to Asia in the 21st Century, many countries still remain in the back seat of development due to lack of governance reforms. It is imperative for the developing countries to implement good governance policies to ensure sustainable and inclusive growth and development. Otherwise corruption and poor public service delivery, which are considered to be the biggest issues hindering the developmental process, would delay the overall progress.[4]

The table below is self explanatory showing the different Bertelsmann Stiftung's Transformation Index (BTI) Key Indicators. It is clear that Kazakhstan fares better than the other Central Asian Republics. Also the Central Asian Republics are better placed than India, however, as shown in chapter 2, (Graph 2.1 and 2.2) India is much ahead of these Republics in several other indicators.

Table 3.1
BTI Key Indicators

	India	*Kazakhstan*	*Kyrgyzstan*	*Tajikistan*	*Turkmenistan*	*Uzbekistan*	*Russia*
UN Education Index	0.459	**0.839**	0.721	0.710	0.743	0.716	0.862
Gender inequality2	0.610	**0.312**	0.357	0.338	-	-	0.312
Gini Index	33.9	**29.0**	33.4	30.8	-	36.7	40.1
Poverty3 %	68.8	**1.1**	21.6	27.7	-	-	0.1

Source: Table prepared by the Author with help of data from BTI reports and The World Bank, World Development Indicators 2013 | UNDP, Human Development Report 2013.

Footnotes: (1) Average annual growth rate. (2) Gender Inequality Index (GII). (3) Percentage of population living on less than $2 a day.

Table 3.2
Social Institutions and Gender Index of 2012 and 2009*

		India	*Kazakhstan*	*Kyrgyzstan*	*Tajikistan*	*Turkmenistan*	*Uzbekistan*
SIGI RANK	2012 2009	57 96	14 3	33 30	40 35	-- --	56 --
SIGI VALUE	2012 2009	0.304458 0.318112	0.121157 0.0034778	0.175566 0.0292419	0.22345 0.0326237	-- --	0.304442

Sources: prepared by the Author with help of data from: http://genderindex.org/country/india/kazakhstan/kyrgyzsatn/tajikistan/turkmenisatn/uzbekistan, accessed on 14 March 2014.
*In 2012 out of 86 countries; In 2009 out of 102 countries.

As per SIGI ratings (Table 3.2), four out of five CARs have better rankings than India. Kazakhstan followed by Kyrgyzstan is doing really well in relative terms. Uzbekistan is very close to India. Tajikistan is somewhere in the middle and for Turkmenistan, there is no data available. India has significantly improved its SIGI ranking in 2012 as compared to 2009. These figures are also reflective of the efforts of the Governments to ensure good governance and gender equality (for more about the methodology of reports see Appendix: II.A.i).

The social attributes, opportunities, gender roles and relationships are all socially constructed and are learned through socialisation processes.

They are at times contextual, time-specific and changeable.[5] As mentioned before, democratic practice enhances and encourages political participation. Political participation of women in the selected countries is discussed taking into consideration their respective social and political set up, and nature of democracy.

Democracy

> *"I understand democracy as something that gives the weak the same chance as the strong".*

And

> *"Democracy is an impossible thing until the power is shared by all...Even a pariah, a labourer, who makes it possible for you to earn your living, will have his share in self-government Swarajya or democracy".*
>
> **- Mahatma Gandhi** *(Young India, December 1, 1927)*

Democracy is defined as a government 'of the people, by the people and for the people', and in fact, considered the finest form of government in which, every individual knowingly participates. And the benchmark of democratic system is said to be in the fact that, the voice of the common man does not go unheard and is accordingly conveyed through proper channel to those in power. In view of the fact that, it is not possible for all people to be part of the government, thereby, they exercise their franchise and elect their representatives at regular intervals. These elected representatives then form the government.

India

India is the largest democratic country in the world and soon after its independence in 1947, got its written constitution declaring India as a democratic federal republic. The first democratic election on the basis of universal adult franchise was held in 1952 and the latest in 2019 (national). India's acievements in the last seven plus decades is commendable. India's institutions are quite robust and the economy has seen rapid growth over recent decades, and so has the policies aimed at the welfare of its rather huge population. The electorate remains enthusiastic in its political participation, especially at the time of elections. In fact, India with its experiments of democracy has also taught the world a few lessons, like the successful workings of coalition governments and the importance of an autonomous responsive electoral commission.[6] India is taking a lead in spreading democratic values and helping other nations to follow the path of democracy.

"Made in Central Asia" Concept of Democracy

Democracy is an evolving process and these Central Asian Republics are at various level of that evolving process. Also, the idea of democracy has been articulated in different ways in most Central Asian Republics. Central Asian concept of democracy varies from the existing Western liberal concept. As per Islam Karimov, then President of Uzbekistan, "there is no unified democratic model, which equally fits for all states and takes into account all peculiarities and conditions. Any democracy must be based on historical, national and religious features of each country". Despite variations, the power in these countries rests with the executive.[7] Political culture in the Central Asian Republics depicts imprints of "Made in Central Asia" concept of democracy and this bears resemblance to Russia's 'sovereign democracy' which was articulated very well by Vladislav Sukrov while addressing the media in 2006.[8] All these imply that democracy is an ongoing process and at various stages it takes various forms. Thereby, Central Asian Republics also have legitimate forms of democracy and these countries have reasons and arguments for their kind of politics, policy and procedures.

The promotion of democracy, good governance, human rights and the rule of law are all fundamental for the long term political stability and also very vital at the same time for conflict prevention and security. All these factors continue to be seen and linked to long term patterns in sustainable economic development.[9] And Central Asia is the region in example. Central Asian Governments have made significant efforts to implement citizen centric and citizen friendly policies. Being relatively new polities, each government is committed to nation building, democratisation and has succeeded to a great extent.

However, unlike India which is a pluralistic and multi-lingual society and allows the freedom of press, Central Asian Republics have fewer political assets in terms of allowing assembly and associations, addressing gatherings, meetings, canvassing etc. This may be due to their historical experiences. In the pre-Soviet period, in fact, economic and social life was organised around clans, tribes and communities of neighbours. In traditionally nomadic communities, kin-based bonds regulated relations with the outside world and provided a guarantee of physical security. Religious leaders thus, played a prominent role in forming public opinion.[10] Prior to 1917, ethnic identities in Central Asia were relatively unimportant, instead, tribal designations were far more significant to individual identity than broader categories such as 'Turk' or 'Tajik'. These tribes, or clans, were essential for the functioning of society and engaged in social, economic, and political activity. For instance, leaders of clan in villages were responsible for implementing customary law before the emergence of the modern state. Despite, Soviet attempts to root out clans, it persisted throughout the Soviet period and even today Central Asian countries are all dominated by 'the hegemony of clan politics' and have dominated the region for centuries.[11]

However, in recent years, post-Soviet changes have had major impact on their institutions, identity and culture. It would be appropriate to say that Central Asian Republics are fast changing their systems and institutions to ensure better governance. Good governance ensures equality of gender, equal opportunity to all without any discrimination, constitutional remedies for grievances, inclusiveness, accountability, freedom to expression, and equitable distribution of resources and so on.

Governance

The concept of governance is not new. It is as old as human civilisation. When talking about governance in Central Asia; yes it has been an issue though, mainly from western lens. There is however, a need for understanding the historical, cultural and social contexts of a given society or community when talking about it. As it is, very few countries and societies have come close to achieving good governance in its totality. Thereby, bad governance has increasingly been regarded as one of the root cause of all evils within such societies.[12]

The United Nations Economic and Social Commission for Asia and the Pacific (UNESCAP) has defined characteristics of good governance as Figure 3.1 sums it up. Good governance can also be judged from the

Figure 3.1
Characteristics of good governance

Source: http://www.unescap.org/pdd/prs/ProjectActivities/Ongoing/gg/governance.asp. Accessed on 27 June 2014.

interactions between formal and informal actors and formal and informal institutions of the state.[13]

Participation by both men and women is a key cornerstone of good governance. Human rights protection particularly of minorities is another hallmark of good governance. Democracy at all levels including the very basic institutions of any polity are must to ensure adequate women participation and representation in all spheres of life.[14] Electoral democracy is the most preferred mode of polity in the whole world and as a result, more women are occupying the political space across the globe.[15]

On the basis of the above mentioned parameters of good governance, one can say that, India has travelled so far with its good democratic governance, where as governance in Central Asia is evolving, and each country is making policies and procedures to achieve higher degree of good governance.

Women in Political Participation

Political participation is one of the factors or characteristics of good governance and women's participation in politics is one of the core areas of women empowerment. Women's low rate of participation at the highest levels of politics is an enduring problem. Women's active participation in the mainstream political processes is believed to have a bearing on the good governance, nation-building and development of a country. Women's political participation is also indicative of the inclusiveness and broad based decision making.[16]

Political participation is not only about participating in the electoral process and contesting elections, but much more than that; it includes many activities like, forming the political and non political associations having bearing on political process. This also includes, contesting and getting elected at various level of government. And it is also not confined to a single party's activities, rather many parties participate. Then, there is network of professionals, pressure groups, media, business houses etc. In a nutshell, political participation is the over encompassing process of influencing or facilitating government's decisions.

Conventional participation is relatively a routine behaviour that uses the channels of representative government. Unconventional participation is relatively an uncommon behaviour that challenges or defies government channels or the dominant culture. In the conventional political participation, socioeconomic position plays a dominant role. The higher the income and social status of an individual or certain section of the society the higher is likelihood of their taking part in the political process.[17]

Education, religion, race, caste and gender are intertwined with political participation. These factors influence the political process and women's participation in all societies, including India and Central Asia.

In the contemporary context, low representation of women in parliament affects its representativeness and undermines the quality, inclusiveness, and effectiveness of the democratic debate on policy issues. And, the promotion and protection of the rights of women, is a key element in welfare policy of any country. The principle of gender equality is enshrined in the Constitution of all the countries under study (For CARs See Appendix. 1.A-E). Women's participation in political sphere is a basic human right and gender equality in elected office is the basis of democracy. There are enough studies to substantiate that women's increasing participation in the decision-making bodies have reduced the levels of corruption in several countries. Countries with greater representation of women in the decision-making bodies are economically more prosperous than the countries where, women's voices remain unheard. Despite this, the gender gap in the political sphere is the toughest to close.[18]

Women have always proved to be good, if not better, in whatever opportunity has come their way even though it always came after much of struggle. There have been several women in history, who were great leaders; showed tremendous courage and their rule have been prosperous and successful. Olga's reign, for example, was an amicable, profitable era and had peaceful alliances with the powerful Khazar State of neighbouring Constantinople, during which Kiev became one of the most prosperous states in Europe.[19] Similarly, even in Asia there have been several extra ordinary women. For example, in India rulers like Rani Lakshmi Bai (1835-1858 A.D.), Chand Bibi (1550-1599 A.D.), Razia Sultan (1205-1240 A.D.) and many others mentioned in Chapter 2, who were great and outstanding women (Also, see Appendix: III.E).

India

The basic tenets of the Indian Constitution are liberty, fraternity, equality and justice and Equality also includes gender equality. Indian women are given equal rights to participate in the political process constitutionally as India has a unique standing on ensuring Universal adult franchise to all its citizens without any discrimination. This feat was achieved during the very first general elections held in post-Independence India. Indian women in fact, had raised the issues of universal adult franchise, as early as 1917. In 1920 Sarojini Naidu and Margaret Cousin led a group of women which demanded equal rights of representation for the fair sex in the Indian Legislatures. Although, the British Government turned down the demand for women's franchise, the Indian National Congress in 1931 adopted a resolution in favour of women's franchise and representation.[20] And the Act of 1935 provided all women above 21 years the right to vote (later on the age for voting was changed to 18 years). Constitutional equality has been supplemented by legal equality through enactment of series of laws.

There are many provisions in the Indian Constitution which lay stress on equality between men and women. Many laws have also been enacted by the Central Government and State Governments to protect the rights of women, and to provide equal opportunity for them. India in 1993 also ratified the UN International 'Convention for the Elimination of All Forms of Discriminations Against Women' (CEDAW). Yet, politics for women remains to be that extra mile, which they have so far not been able to walk, resulting in very few women joining politics.

There have been endeavours from leaders from time to time to encouraged women to take part actively along with men. Gandhiji wished that, women should play a meaningful role in politics, making it more accountable, transparent and corruption free. He prophetically said, "there can be no salvation for India, as long as women do not take part in public life".[21] In the 20th century, under the leadership of Mahatma Gandhi during the freedom movement, many women joined the movement and women's involvement in politics was accepted as the natural course. As a result, several women not only played very pivotal role in India's freedom movement but also in the post-Independence period, they were very actively involved in politics as well in the progress of India. Women have held important political and administrative positions.[22]

Despite the fact that, Indian women have held important positions both at the national and international levels, women's political participation is not in proportion to their population, except in the local bodies, as India reserves seats for women in local government. However, at the national level, the Women's Reservation Bill is still pending in parliament. The way the quotas are applied makes a difference to whether the presence of women is a token or a legitimate form of representation.[23] In India, close to forty percent of the elected representatives in the village and municipal councils are women. Thanks to the introduction of reservation and 'quota system' that was adopted in 1993, today more than a million women across

India have been elected at the local level to serve in Panchayats (village councils) and in municipal councils. Their success has been described as a silent revolution in democracy of India.[24] The Panchayat Raj Institutions (PRI), is a three tier system. It consists of:

1. *Grama Panchayat*: for a village or a group of villages having population of not less than 5000 and not more then 7000 or the geographical distance of an area within a radius of five kilometers from the center.
2. *Taluka Panchayat:* for every block.
3. *Zilla panchayat*: for every district.

With women at the panchayat level in such large numbers, can be considered a new beginning in the direction of legislative empowerment of women. These women led councils deliver the public services more effectively. From health, sanitation to education, they utilise the public resources available to benefit the community and are responsible for considerable gains at the local level.[25] However, their effective participation, even in these bodies, leaves much to be desired. Although, gender based quota is important to raise the level of female representation in the politics, it has also raised several questions on the legality and constitutionality of this provision. Few people contest that, quotas are as good as nomination. Often, it has been seen that gender based electoral quota is more of a symbolic nature and actual power is wielded in the hands of the males of the families especially in the rural India.[26] There are opinions like- mostly they are related to the power game i.e., de facto council head. "Even though the wife is the *sarpanch*, it is believed that, it's the husband who dictates everything". This could be true, keeping in mind that, women are ignorant about political practices or the know-how of politics.[27] However, the important thing is that atleast they are there, and moreover, in the last decade or so women have shown their grit, growth and understanding of their office and efficiency in their work. Even though, for some they might be just symbolic in nature, but many draw inspiration from them.

However, the challenges to increased participation of women in politics in India, particularly at the local levels are manifold: poverty, patriarchal mindset, social set up and uncertainty of support and success. Though, the scope for women's public activism varies across class, caste and region in India, the collective effect of all these have been that, women still tend to lack the required opportunities, skills and self-confidence, needed to function effectively in the public sphere.[28]

The predominant socio-religious and cultural practices further add to women's dilemma of active participation. Apart from these, there are some overarching challenges to women's participation in politics. The main and the most pervasive challenge lies in the form of deep rooted negative stereotyping of women's role and position in society. Gender disparities are more due to the lack of proper understanding of capabilities of women than any real frailty of will and wisdom among them.

Central Asia

Like India, Constitution in all Central Asian Republics guarantees to all women, the fundamental right to equality under which, they have equal right to political participation as well. During the last two plus decades, the transition to market economy and political democracy was the primary challenge of Central Asian Republics. This transition affected and influenced all sections of society; young and old, rich and poor, male and female. The transformation that took place can be viewed from a number of perspectives and socio-political is the most important one. Even though, the transition impacted everyone, the situation of women is of genuine concern keeping in mind the regional specifics of women's engagement in politics or policy making. Women's participation in the political process and their representation reflects the societal sentiment; outdated customs, traditions and social structures which are patriarchal and hierarchal.[29] And these at times, restrict women's active participation in politics. Poverty and discrimination against women remain major concerns for the Central Asian Republics to establish stronger roots of democracy as Central Asia Republics have witnessed varying degrees of economic and political changes which have played out differently to men and women across the region.

With a historical culture founded on Islam, religion had shaped the daily lives of Muslim women in the region for several centuries prior to Soviet rule and continues to do so today. As mentioned in the earlier chapter, the traditional *adat* laws and religious *shariat* laws governed the lives of the people of Central Asia due to the influence of Islam in the region. Women had no intellectual culture, as they were never sent to schools. Like chattels, women were bought by *kalym*. Early marriages were the common practice and marriages between minors and between a minor girl and an old man were wide-spread. Women were in *Paranja*, which basically symbolised the enslavement of woman, her ignorance and their subjection to men.[30]

This was more common in sedentary societies, for example, the Uzbek and Tajik women as per the traditional and societal norms were supposed to cover themselves in *paranja* as they stepped out of the women's portion of the house. On the contrary, nomadic Kazakh and Kyrgyz women were relatively freer especially of veils. As per the societal norms and professional compulsions, Kazakh and Kyrgyz women had to ride horses and do outdoor activities including herding along with their men. And women in Kazakhstan and in Turkmenistan never covered their faces.[31] Even, in Kyrgyzstan nearly everyone is Muslim though, Islam is practiced more as a way of life rather than as a religion. They celebrate Islamic holidays but do not strictly follow Islamic practices daily.[32] Similarly in Turkmenistan covering the face was never a part of their tradition. In fact, young or newly wedded women would cover their mouth as a mark of respect for the elders.[33]

However, women's contribution to society so far cannot be ignored. From Shamanism to Sufism women have played a decisive role in the interplay between religious belief and the cultural heritage of music and dance. Ritual and music has been at the heart of Central Asian and Islamic culture, not only at weddings and funerals but in all aspects of everyday life.[34] Nowhere, the role of women was more important than in the Ferghana Valley, which is considered to be the cradle of female Islamic culture and a centre for women's poetry and music.[35]

It is contemplated that, female seclusion, or the removal of women from public life, began as early as the late sixteenth century. Women were not even included in some historical narratives. The few individuals who promoted women's activities in the public sphere were viewed as acting in opposition to Muslim law and were accused of being 'infidels'.[36]

However, as mentioned earlier women did play an important role in 20th century Central Asia under the Soviet rule both in economic and public sphere. In fact in the 'First All Russian Congress of Muslims', that took place in Moscow on May 1, 1917, there were some 1,000 delegates out of whom, 200 were women,[37] who endorsed the emancipation of Muslim women.[38] Thanks to these women, the Congress voted for an eight hour working day, the abolition of private landed property, confiscation without indemnity of large properties, equality of political rights for women, and an end to polygamy and *purdah*. This meant that Soviet Union's Muslims were the first in the world to free women from the restrictions typical of Islamic societies of that period.[39] Lenin stressed that, "women must be drawn into local Soviets in both the towns and the villages, and they must be given practical tasks and knowledge. Particular attention must also be given to the development of those institutions which lighten the burden of motherhood".[40] Very much in line with Lenin's view, women were educated also in law and were trained to take political posts. Women were also elected to local and central governing bodies because of its new policies; however, like in Russia, rural areas of Central Asia were slow or unwilling to accept equal roles for men and women.[41]

In 1925, Soviets worked to create more opportunities for women to participate at all levels of public and political life. The Communist Party took steps to enable Muslim women to be active in public and political life. For this it was essential to increase female representation in public office. Throughout Soviet history, women's participation was increasing, though, only at lower level unlike their male counterparts who rose to high position of power. Though, Yadgar Nasretddinova did manage to reach high position of Chair of Supreme Soviet in Uzbek SSR and Chair of Upper Chamber of Supreme Soviet of USSR during 1940s to 1970s.[42] However, women in general were stereotyped as incapable of making decisions. Actually women's identity within the society was traditionally centered on their roles as mother and wife, their obligation to feed the family and take care of children, both materially and emotionally.[43]

It is true, that with Sovietisation, women of Soviet Central Asia had a much different role in the Society including political sphere. Apart from being educated and part of the soviet labour force, they were part of political sphere also. However, guaranteed representation did not allow women representatives to nurture their leadership qualities, effectiveness to carry out coordinated election campaigns and constructive debates on the issues relevant to women and so on. And in post-Soviet Central Asia including Kazakhstan underwent rapid transformation and modernisation.[44] As a result, women began losing ground as traditional gender stereotypes returned in few of these newly independent Central Asian Republics.[45] Besides, the quota system practiced by the Soviet regime was abolished in 1989 and as a result many women lost their positions in the government. Thereby, impacting the role and the effectiveness of women in political sphere.

As mentioned earlier, political participation is constitutionally guaranteed, without any discrimination on any grounds. The national governments made international commitments after the Central Asian Republics gained independence, in terms of protecting and promoting gender equality. In compliance with them they established institutional mechanisms and are working towards further improvement of national legal frameworks in these countries. For example, equal rights and opportunities laws have been drafted in Kyrgyzstan and were approved by the parliament in early 2003. However, the traditional patriarchal attitudes that replaced communist ideology prevail and women remain associated primarily, with 'social' or 'women and family' issues; public office usually is stranded in secondary positions.[46]

Kazakh President Nursultan Nazarbayev, very rightly confessed that, "Men are preventing the progress of women into managerial positions in key bodies and posts, because it immediately becomes clear that women work better than men". And in 2011, he called on his government to provide increased opportunities for women to serve in politics and government. At the first Women's Congress, he said, "I instruct the government, together with the Presidential administration and the national commission for women's affairs, the leadership of the Nur Otan Party, to form a concrete plan for the promotion of women in taking decisions".[47]

Turkmenistan after independence, implemented active gender policy since its very first year, aimed at women possessing equal rights in all spheres of social and political life. Turkmenistan in 1999 became a member to the UN assembly, which had adopted the Convention on the Political Rights of Women on 31 March 1953.[48] Various forms of social guarantees allow women to combine successfully family and work responsibilities.[49] However, in Turkmenistan great attention is attached to family development, maternity and children protection. Though, the violation of gender equality is considered as an offence.[50] In fact every year on women's day the president congratulates women, applauding the achievements of doctors, diplomats, deputies and teachers. The President begins by addressing women as, "Dear mothers, Dear ladies", appreciating their contribution in different sphere of production, science, education, health and bringing up young generation.[51]

Share of women in the population is 50%, but women account only for 17% deputies in *mejlis* (Parliament). Higher level of education and activity explains large scale involvement of women in all spheres of economy especially in education, culture art, public health services and social welfare.[52] Speaking at a conference organised on the issue of Turkmen folklore in the Epoch of Might and Happiness, the director of theatres and the head of *velayet (region)* spoke about the importance of women in keeping alive the tradition of women's poetry and the *'kustdepedi'* (dance).[53] In fact, the role of women in preserving of the cultural heritage of Turkmenistan has always been appreciated every now and then by the president.[54] These kinds of statements are found in journals like *Medinlet* which means culture or implies ancient treasure. There is always lot of talk and appreciation for girls and women who have expertise on carpet weaving etc.[55]

In spite of having drafted laws on 'equal rights and opportunities', in these countries, women are still stuck in secondary positions because of traditional patriarchal views of both men and women. And the advent to democracy in these Central Asian republics does not seem very promising specially so when talking about women in political process. During the author's interaction with women and men alike, many opined 'there is no need for women to be part of politics, when they are already doing so much. Also, politics is not safe for women'.[56]

Despite the existing provisions, women do not enjoy the rights and liberties at par with their men counterparts.[57] And regardless of having higher educational qualifications and significant contribution to their respective economies, women's political participation remains low.[58] It has been found in a worldwide survey of female politicians that the societal values and beliefs about the gender roles determine levels of women's political representation. This applies across societies,[59] including countries under study. Besides, religion and regionalism also plays a vital role in determining women's political representation.[60]

Women's participation in politics and governance structures in Kazakhstan has been rather low keeping its developmental rate in mind. Like for example, the average life expectancy in Kazakhstan according to World Bank report (2012) was 66.2 years, including 60.6 for men and 72.0 for women.[61] And according to Word Bank 2014 report it was 65 years for men and 74 years for women. Women live longer than men (Appendix: II.D, Table: 2.8a). Of course, there are several reasons as to why women do not opt to be full time politician. These include patriarchal nature of society and unwillingness of women themselves to be part of politics; owing to family and other responsibilities and traditional mindset.[62] The number of women in power is decreasing depending on the high order of the position.[63]

At times, ideological factors are more important than political ones in determining women's political representation. In few societies, including few of the under study societies, low level of women's participation is because of their lower levels of exposure to the political process, political orientation and upbringing.[64] The traditional belief system in these societies, that, women are meant only to become homemakers and take care of children prevents them to enter into active politics. During discussions, for example, while interacting with the author, young women in Dushanbe opined that family responsibility is important, "If we women do not take care of house, children, who will? -We (women) cannot expect our men to do these 'woman's job'. First we have to bear children and then bring them up, and simultaneously take care of husband, his family, his relatives and household work".[65] And this is not limited only to societies in developing countries but in several societies across the world.[66]

Similar kinds of beliefs also influence party elites who decide whether to field and support a female candidate or not.[67] Most of the times political parties, cite lack of skills, capacities, and merit of their political candidates, as reasons for not nominating women as candidates for election. However, this only highlights the fact that, these are mere process for screening or eliminating women. Women in political parties face other challenges as well. For example, they are often not promoted to higher party positions, they do not have access to funding, or have the social support to promote themselves for office, and also they don't attract the attention of the media.[68]

And as already discussed in chapter 2, after independence due to economic transition there was resurgence of traditional practices. Also, the declining access of jobs to women have coincided with a rising burden for women at home, which is a result of shrinking childcare provisions and other social safety nets. Majority of women have suffered economic setbacks, in the form of unemployment, as well as growing economic insecurity and exploitation.[69] All these, coupled with lack of support, funds and finances, prevent women from playing active role in politics.

Some of the national MDG reports in the region also call for attention to the glass ceiling in business and the need to stimulate women's interest in seeking public office. Women's increased economic dependence along with a lack of access to economic resources has discouraged them from actively engaging in politics.[70]

At times, these along with violence and other kind of crisis, also impact women in the areas of employment, social safety networks, health, education and migration. All this affects the enabling environment, which is fundamental for women's participation in public life.[71]

In Central Asia, ironically, lack of interest has also played quite an important role so far, even though, there seemed to be surge of activism for few years following the independence. This however, could not be sustained for long as today also people seem to be very docile and indifferent to participation in any political activity.[72]

Throughout the region, policies aimed at promoting equal participation of women and men in decision-making processes and positions have to take into account, how to challenge, existing stereotypes and perceptions that have affected women's participation in political life. These stereotypes influence the unequal sharing work time between women and men; income and family responsibilities. Also, these create barriers to women's career advancement and appointment to decision making positions.

Women, despite the constitutional provisions, unlikely get representation at higher levels of legislative apparatus. However, it is important to keep in mind that, for the success of democracies it is imperative to have a higher political participation and representation of women, as the numbers are important for any section of the society including women to make a difference in the legislative process.

Political Representation

As a result of globalisation, rapid urbanisation and modernisation in several societies across the globe, there is visible change in the societal values and beliefs. This has to some extent, impacted political representation as well and several women candidates have been elected as political representatives across the globe. The results are more visible in the last couple of decades due to the introduction of electoral gender quotas. "Although the first quotas for women were adopted in the 1930s, these policies became increasingly popular in the 1990s and 2000s in all major regions of world".[73] Women's participation is essential not only from the political and electoral perspective but also from economic perspective. International organisations including World Bank have been suggesting that, larger number of women's participation is pertinent to change established beliefs and integrating societies, with the modern market economies.[74] Several studies have shown that electoral quotas have been instrumental in reducing gender disparities and boosting gender balance in politics.[75]

According to Inter-Parliamentary Union (IPU) statistics, the international situation as far as political representation of women in the world is concerned is not very encouraging. However, there has been a slow increase in last decade or so. In January 2019, there were total of 24.3% in lower or single house; 24.1% in upper house and 24.3% of both houses combined and the Asian average at 19.8%.[76] And in January 2014 report, World average of women in parliament was 17.7% and Asian average 16.7 %.[77]

India

In India, over the years, it has been observed that the overall performance of women elected representatives at the local level has been better than that of their male counterparts which is encouraging for them to assume higher responsibilities in later years. Despite these efforts and significant changes over the years, social constraints appear to be serious obstacles in giving the dues to the women folk.[78]

In India the local level representative bodies have given the much needed political platform and space to women, thereby enabling them to take part in planning and development at the grassroots level, laying a strong foundation for women's participation in decision-making processes in India. The country has around 37 percent representation of women in its local bodies, which is higher than the mandated 33 percent.[79] To give more representation to women in local bodies, some of the States in India have enacted legislations providing for half of the seats for women in local bodies.

As far as women's participation in local governance is concerned, their representation in the local elected bodies in India reveals the story of a mature and flourishing democracy that has evolved over the years. Though, the origin of the local self-government in India goes back to the ancient times, the 73rd and 74th Amendments to the Indian Constitution in 1993 gave a new dimension to local self-governing institutions in the country by providing for representation of women in at least one-third of their total membership.[80] Even though elections are held every five years at the state and national level (See, Appendix: III.B and III.C), women's representation in parliament is not heartening. As far as the percentage of women in parliament is concerned, according to January 2019 report India stood at 149 rank with 12.6 (66) out of 524 in Lok Sabha and 11.5 (28) out of 244 in Rajya Sabha. However, in ministerial positions, India ranked 78 with 23.1% total of 6 out of 26.[81] Earlier, post-2014 Lok Sabha election, India ranked 107 with 9.1 % (49) women representative in Lok Sabha out of 541 and 9.9 % (24) women representatives in Rajya Sabha out of 243. And according to January 2014 report, India's average representation was less than 10 %. In ministerial positions, it stood at number 68 as far as its ranking in giving number of ministerial berths to women is concerned. In India, out of total 39 ministerial positions, only 4 (10.3%) were held by women representatives. Only place where India performed fairly well was the position of the head of the state. India figured among the top 7 (4.7%) countries out of 150 to have a woman as the head of the state.[82]

Political empowerment of women has now been attached utmost priority and their participation in other spheres such as governmental bodies, public administration, Judiciary and corporate and technical bodies has been recognised as equally important. As the pioneer of championing the cause of the women, Indian Parliament enacted the National Commission for Women Act, 1990, paving way for the establishment of the National Commission for Women in 1992 to safeguard the interests of women in Indian society. The Joint Parliamentary Committee on Empowerment of Women is yet another parliamentary initiative aimed at monitoring, examining and reporting on the varied aspects of gender related issues.

Central Asia

Despite economic and social challenges, progress in bringing women into political positions is being made. The proportion of women members of parliament in most countries of the region is slowly rising, though, it is still below the critical mass of 30 percent considered necessary for women to meaningfully influence political debates.[83] There is variation in terms of participation in the region. Throughout the region, women hold too few senior level political positions (See Table 3.6). During the Soviet period, due to the continuous intervention of the Soviets, efforts were made to separate religion from the politics and state affairs. Women were beneficiaries of such interventions and propaganda which were further endorsed by the state laws to improve and strengthen economic and social position of women. Since the political representation of women was ensured through the quota system in Soviet Central Asia, as shown in Table 3.3, women's representative participation within Central and local Government was high by international standards. Quota ensured balanced representations between genders in the machinery of government, the Party and State enterprises. A specific number of seats were reserved for women candidates so that, their voice did not remain unheard. However, in reality men dominated the key decision making positions.[84]

In the post-Soviet period, the political representation of women varies from country to country. In January 2019, in terms of women's political representation in the Parliament, Kazakhstan ranked 61 had 27.1% (29) out of 107 in Lower house and 10.6% (5) out 47 in Upper house. Kyrgyzstan was at 108 with 19.2% (23) out of 120 in Lower house. Turkmenistan ranked 69 with 25.0% (31) out of 124 in Lower house. Data for Upper house for Kyrgyzstan and Turkmenistan was not available. With 110 rank Tajikistan had 19.0% (12) out of 63 women in Lower house and 21.9% (7) out of 32 in Upper house and Uzbekistan stood at rank 129 with 16.0%

(24) out of 150 in Lower house and 17.0% (17) out of 100 in Upper house. In ministerial positions; Kyrgyzstan stood at rank 123 with 14.3% (3) out of 21. Uzbekistan stood at rank 155, with 7.7% (2) out of 26. Turkmenistan stood at rank 157 with 7.1% (2) out of 28. Tajikistan stood at 167 with 5.9% (1) out of 17 and at rank 168 stood Kazakhstan with 5.6% (1) out of 18.[85] Earlier till June 2014 the percentage ranging between less than 15.9 % to almost 26.4% of women's political representation in the Parliament in Central Asia. Turkmenistan ranked 46 with 26.4%, Kazakhstan at 53 with 25.2 %, Kyrgyzstan at 62 with 23.3%. Uzbekistan not far behind was ranked 67 with 22.0% and Tajikistan ranked 89 with 15.9 % women parliamentarians. Data included only the Lower house, as data was not available for the Upper house.[86]

The earlier representation till 2005 was: 26% of the members in the Turkmenistan parliament were women. In Uzbekistan 9.9% members were women and 14.9% of the members in Tajikistan parliament were women in 2000.[87] In 2009, in Kazakhstan, there were two women in the 47-seat senate (4.3%), and 19 women in the 107-member *Mazhilis* (17.8%). From 2000 to 2007, women occupied eight seats in the then 77-member parliament, or 10.4%.[88] In 2009, Kazakhstan had one woman in the cabinet and one chaired a national agency.[89] In Tajikistan, after the election of 2000, the percentage of elected women in parliament was about 14.9, and in administrative and managerial posts 15.5 percent. In Uzbekistan, women had a representation in the parliament of only 9.9 percent. The percentage of women in supreme organs of government stood at the beginning of 2002 at only 13.7.[90]

In Kyrgyzstan till 2009, three women held cabinet level positions, the post of Vice Prime Minister; Minister of Labour and Social Development, and the Chair of the State Agency on Migration and Employment. Women also held the following posts in Kyrgyzstan: the Chair of the Supreme Court, the Constitutional Court and the National Academy of Science. [91] In Kyrgyzstan's 2005 election, no women were elected to parliament. But, due to the quota system and the new Elections Code adopted in 2007 in Kyrgyzstan, women now make up 25.6 percent of representatives in parliament in Kyrgyzstan. See (Table 3.7). This is the highest percentage amongst any Central Asian state and second place in the CIS region. This is a result of the long term involvement of civil society organisations.[92]

In Kyrgyzstan there is the 'Presidential Decree on Measures to Improve Gender Policies' targeting the 'Introduction of a 30% quota' for women in political positions (2006). There is law on Basic State Guarantees for Ensuring Gender Equity (2003). There is also law on Social and Legal Protection against Family Violence (2003). Institutional Framework for gender equality like National Council on Women; Family and Gender Affairs under the President and its working body; Legislative and National Institutional Frameworks for Gender Equality and Women's Political Participation.[93] The results of the elections held till 2014, in the region confirm that proportional representation together with some form of quota system and accompanying measures to reduce obstacles to women entering politics are a key to women's election to parliament as in the case of Kyrgyzstan.[94]

Table 3.3 shows the representation of women in national legislature's by region during the period 1975-97. It is evident that Central Asian region had a much higher representation at 23.3 percent which was much higher than other regions. Even developed countries had a representation of 5.1 percent and the egalitarian Nordic countries had 16 percent women in legislatures. However, women's representation has declined in the post-Soviet space, one of the reason being, disappearance of the guaranteed representation to women in polity.

Table 3.3
Women in National Legislatures, By Region (%), 1975-97

	1975	*1987*	*1997**
Arab States	3.5	2.8	3.3
Asia	8.4	9.7	13.4
Asia excluding China, Mongolia, North Korea, Vietnam**	(3.8)	(6.2)	(6.31)
Central and Eastern Europe and **Former Soviet Union**	**23.3**	**23.1**	**11.5**
Developed countries (excluding East Asia]	5.1	9.6	14.7
Latin America and the Caribbean	6.0	6.9	10.5
Nordic Countries	16.1	28.8	36.4

Source: Kumari Kamala, Women in New Russia, 2012, p. 182; Also see The World's Women, 1970-1990: Trends and Statistics, New York: United Nations, 1991 and Democracy Still in the Making: A World Comparative Study, Geneva: Inter-Parliamentary Union, 1997.

* 1997 statistics for lower houses and single house systems, (Mongolia excluded.)

** women's representation under party control

*** Single house

As visible in the table 3.4 there is increase in world average from 2014: Lower house 22.2% in 2014 to 25.1% in 2020; Upper house 19.5% to 24.7% and both house, combined from 21.8% to 25.0%. In 2010, the world average was 19.0% in Lower house; 17.8% Upper house and 18.8% both houses combined.

Table 3.4
Women in National Legislatures, By Region* (%) 2014 and 2020**

	Single House or Lower House		*Upper House or Senate*		*Both Houses combined*	
	2014	***2020***	***2014***	***2020***	***2014***	***2020***
Nordic countries	42.1	43.9	--	--	--	43.9
Americas	25.8	31.7	26.4	32.3	25.9	31.8
Europe (Nordic countries included)	25.3	30.1	22.8	29.1	24.8	29.9
Europe (Nordic countries not included)	23.7	24.1	22.8	17.8	23.5	23.3
Sub-Saharan Africa	22.6	24.7	19.8	24.0	22.2	24.6
Asia	19.0	20.7	13.9	17.2	18.5	20.3
Arab States	17.8	14.5	7.7	12.3	15.9	14.3
Pacific	13.4	16.7	38.6	43.8	16.2	19.6
World Average*	**22.2%**	**25.1**	**19.5**	**24.7**	**21.8**	**25.0**

Source: Table prepared with the help of data from http://www.ipu.org/wmn-e/world.htm, accessed on 14 March 2014 and 15 March 2020.
* The regional groupings used are those of IPU.
** From November 2019 onwards.

Table 3.5
Women in parliament 2010* and 2014 and 2019**

Country	***Rank***		***Lower or single house % Women***			***Upper house or Senate % Women Women/Seats***		
	2014	***2019***	***2010***	***2014***	***2019***	***2010***	***2014***	***2019***
Rwanda	1	1	56.3	63.8	61.25	34.6	38.5	38.46
Turkmenistan	46	73	16.8	26.4	25.0	..	..	..
Kazakhstan	53	65	17.8	25.2	27.1	4.3	6.4	10.64
Kyrgyzstan	62	116	**25.6**	23.3	19	..	..	..
Uzbekistan	67	44	22.0	22. 0	32	15.0	15.0	24.74
Tajikistan	89	82***	17.5	15.9	19.0	23.5	11.8	21.9
India	111	142	11.4	11. 4	14.36	11.9	11.4	10.42

Source: Table prepared by Author with help from data from http://www.ipu.org/pdf/publications/wmnmap14_en.pd, accessed on 14 March 2014; https://www.unwomen.org/en/what-we-do/leadership-and-political-participation/facts-and-figures.; https://data.ipu.org/women-ranking?month=5&year=2020. Accessed on May 2020
*See Appendix: III.D
**till 15 May 2020
***Election held in March 2020

The Table 3.5 above, shows number of women in Parliaments of the countries covered under the purview this study. In January 2019, no country had 50% or above representation. The highest was obviously in Rwanda at 38.5%. In January 2014, two countries were above 50% representation of women and in 2010 only one country above 50%. The CARs has more than 15 percent of women representatives in the Lower house. In India the figure has barely managed to cross the double digit.

Indian Parliament has however, witnessed gradual increase as well as decrease of women representatives since the first national election post-independence in 1952. In 1977, it was lowest ever with only 3.4 percent and in 1991 it touched its peak with 15.5 percent representation. Later in the year 1998 it was again quite low with only 6.1 percent, however 1998 onwards, women's participation in Indian parliament has gradually increased to nearly 12 percent.[95] In the National election in 2014, 11% women were elected for *Lok Sabha*. In total 8% of women contested in 2014 general election.[96] And in 2019 General election total of 724 women contested and 78 women were elected.[97]

Representation of the women in Indian parliament at the best has been just around 15 percent in 1991 and 11.4 percent in 2014. This is in contrast with the higher proportion of women representation in the local bodies as discussed earlier in this chapter.

With respect to women in ministerial position, according to IPU 2014 report Rwanda, ranked 13th position with 39.3% women in ministerial positions having 11 out of 28 ministers. Turkmenistan ranked 80th position with 6.3 % ministerial berths for women in which there were 2 out of 32 ministers. This trend explains that just numbers do not translate into ministerial berths and hence power.[98]

Table 3.6
Women heads in the world

	2010	*2012*	*2014*	*2019**** *
Women heads of state*	6.0%	5.3%	5.9%	6.6%
Women heads of government	5.7%	7.3%	**7.8%**	**5.2%**
Women speakers of parliament**			14.8%)	19.7%
Women deputy speakers of parliament***			26.5%	28.2%
Women with portfolios	**1056**[b]	**1065**[b]	**1096**[a]	**1412**[b]

Source: Table prepared by Author with data from http://www.ipu.org/pdf/publications/wmnmap14_en.pdf. Accessed on 14 March 2014.

and https://www.unwomen.org/en/what-we-do/leadership-and-political-participation/facts-and-figures. Accessed on 27 March 2019.

* Only elected heads of state have been taken into account

** Of the total 189 parliaments, 76 are bicameral. One bicameral parliament has no speakers and is not included in the Percentage

*** 88 parliaments out of 188 have women deputy speakers.

**** As of 01 January 2019.

a: in 189 countries; b: in 188 countries

As shown in Table 3.6, other than 'women heads of government' there have been an increase over the years, in percentage of women as heads of state, women speakers, deputy speakers and portfolios held by women ministers.

Table 3.7 gives rank of country and percentage of women in Ministerial positions in 2014 and 2019 for the selected countries. India has the best rank at 134th position and Turkmenistan least at 179th rank. Other than in India and Kazakhstan there is decline in percentage ministerial position of women in other countries.

Table 3.7
Women in ministerial positions 2014 and 2019*

	Rank		*% of Women*	
	2014	*2019*	*2014*	*2019*
India	73	**134**	**9.3**	**12.5**
Kyrgyzstan	60	152	14.3	9.5
Tajikistan	69	173	11.1	5.9
Uzbekistan	70	158	10.3	8.0
Turkmenistan	75	**179**	**8.8**	3.7
Kazhakhstan	40	174	**2.0**	**5.0**

Source: Table prepared by Author with help of data from http://www.ipu.org/pdf/publications/wmnmap14_en.pdf, accessed on 14 March 2014 and https://www.unwomen.org/en/what-we-do/leadership-and-political-participation/facts-and-figures. Accessed on 27 March 2019; https://www.unwomen.org/-/media/headquarters/attachments/sections/library/publications/2020/women-in-politics-map-2020-en.pdf?la=en&vs=827. Accessed on 15 May 2020.

* as of 27 November 2019.

As evident from the fact and figures reflected above, there has been increase in representation of women in parliaments. This trend has been visible since the first decade into the 21st century. According to the January 2012 MDG Report, women accounted for nearly 20 percent of parliamentarians worldwide; a 75 percent increase since 1995 when women held only just over 11 percent of seats worldwide, and a 44 percent increase over 2000.[99] The increase has also been seen over the years, in the portfolios held by women. According to January 2014 report, a total of 1096 portfolios in 189 countries were held by women ministers. In 2012, 1065 women held ministerial portfolios across 188 countries, whereas in 2010 women ministers held 1056 portfolios across 188 countries.[100]

The last two decades have seen an increase in women's political participation worldwide, but conditions are still far from equal, and progress toward goals set in the '1995 Beijing Platform for Action' and the '2000 MDGs' remains slow. Women account for half of the population yet hold only one fifth of the positions in national governments. They are significantly outnumbered in parliaments, local councils, and more often than not missing from the negotiating tables where conflicts are to be resolved. Often women are not included in decision making even in issues that affect women, their families, and societies.[101] And this trend is so true in the case of India and Central Asia.

Even when elected, women ministers are often given portfolios such as socio cultural functions including social affairs, health, women and children, sport, youth, education, science, culture, labour; leaving all the key portfolios including finance, trade, industry, agriculture, infrastructure, transport, communications, environment, foreign and internal affairs, defence and justice for men.[102] In India, though, there have been women having some key portfolios; Vijaya Lakshmi Pandit- First woman diplomat to Moscow, USSR; US and UK. She was also the Presidents of the General Assembly, from 15 September 1953-21 September 1954 for which she was lator honoured of being the first woman and the first Asian to be elected president of the U.N. General Assembly[103]; Indira Gandhi- Prime Minister from 1966 to 1977 and 1980-1984, Minister of Finance in 1970, Minister of Home Affairs in 1970, Minister of External Affairs from 1967-69; and Sushma Swaraj, Minister for Foreign Affairs, 2014. Nirmala Sitharaman is serving as the current Minister of Finance and Corporate Affairs and earlier she served as the Defence Minister.

However, overall there is need for more representations so as to give women their due share. Though, there are several reasons behind women being at helm of affairs, like for example; political parties often do not promote women to leadership positions. And this holds true even for India except in cases where the woman herself has constituted the party: Mamata Banerjee, Trinamool Congress, (TMC) and J. Jayalalita, All India *Anna Dravida Munnetra Kazhagam*,(AIADMK). Mayawati of Bahujan Samaj Party and Sonia Gandhi of Congress party is an Exception. Political parties are generally critical for ensuring women's political participation. In many cases, parties recruit women, mainly engaging them in organisational work, especially in election campaigns. Women are often portrayed as having little political knowledge, political experience or skills. This creates an unfavourable environment for women's political participation and gender equality. As a consequence, there are many women party members, but few are able to move into positions of power.

Another major challenge is lack of women friendly policies and laws that ensure that more women are elected to parliament and take more decision making positions in public administration, the judiciary, and state sectors by using mechanisms and strategies such as temporary special measures including quotas.[104] Violence, or the threat of violence, has also been identified as a significant impediment to women's political participation including representation. Violence occurring at the local level, remains underreported and undocumented.[105] Sometime even the lack of proper implementation of laws to prevent gender based violence is the reason, as implementation of laws to prevent gender based violence, is a prerequisite for providing a positive environment for gender equality and for overcoming barriers to women's political participation, and for mobilising women to become more involved in political life.[106] This is despite the fact that, CEDAW Article 744 obliges states parties to 'take all appropriate measures to eliminate discrimination against women in political and public life and to ensure that they enjoy equality with men in political and public life'.[107]

The basic problem is that these barriers at the national level, goes far beyond the legislative frameworks. Although the justice systems, national, regional and international, guarantee the protection of women's human rights, they often fail when it comes to addressing most common, gender specific violations of women's rights. A characteristic feature of these violations is that they are deeply rooted in tradition and or religion of the societies and hence, are not recognised as human right issues. It is often that these patent violations are considered by the public, including women themselves, as a normal consequence of the natural gender roles where a woman is subordinate to a man and his family, and is subjected to social control.[108]

The traditional and or religious value systems also influence the attitude of the law enforcement institutions towards the acts of discrimination against women that, happen in the family. They are reluctant to 'interfere' in the so called family issues even though it is where most of the acts, including all forms of violence against women, take place. For a woman, questioning widely accepted codes of conducts at times result in social ostracism, exclusion from the family, and in consequence the loss of livelihood as she is often economically dependent on a man,[109] this is visible in several cases in India.

The numbers and enthusiasm is, however, different in different country owing to the mindset of majority of people in these societies. For example in India, women are too tied up with household chores and sometime lack of social and financial support prevents women from coming in mainstream political affairs. This does not imply that young educated and financially independent women are eager to participate in political affairs rather they give more importance to career and personal growth. However, there has been change of minds and mindset in last few years. Amongst the CARs, in Uzbekistan, people in general, acknowledge the role of women in their life and society and even in the developmental process of the nation, but only in context to maintaining the community's sense of Uzbek Muslim's identity; in maintaining traditions and safeguarding Islam; role of women as intergenerational transmitters of cultural traditions, customs, and songs is valued more.[110] In fact, in 1997 President Karimov had admitted, "We do not fully meet many democratic stands" blaming the traditionalism of the people and had stated that "he will change this way of thinking gradually and in stages".[111] In Kyrgyzstan on the other hand the view is totally different, "only women can understand women's problem and can take right decision to solve them".[112] People young and old alike working/non-working, in most of these countries would simply, say, "women already have much to do, why would they want to take unnecessary botheration of politics. Anyway, politics is not good option for women because politics always has problems and women will always be out of house because of that. What will happen to children and family?"[113]

In spite of a long tradition of active participation in the workforce by a vast majority of women, both women and men in CARs see motherhood and marriage as the most important goals in a woman's life. A common standpoint is that "politics is a man's business", and that women are too emotional to deal with affairs of the state.[114] This mentality is due to the stereotyped and traditional structure of society. And as Khalid notes, that, "one aspect of the Islamic revival in post-Soviet Central Asia is a new emphasis on traditional roles for women... that feeds the rhetoric of redefining women's place in society".[115]

So, simply lack of education and economic independence alone is not the real reason rather, apart from this stereotype, there are other things to blame as well; the mindset and psyche of the society at large. As, in spite of women being, as educated as their male counterparts, sometimes even more qualified, do not make to the seat of power. For example, in Scandinavian countries, with their long tradition of egalitarianism, score lower than other countries on negative gender attitudes.[116] Thus, apart from education, economic independence, the change of mind set and psyche is also equally if not more important, to ensure political participation of women and good representation, which so far has not happened in the countries under study and in many societies across the globe, that is why, it is still believed that women are too sentimental to carry out the functions of the state which often require tough decisions.

Quotas as practiced in India at local level and in Central Asia as was practiced earlier during Soviet times and in the present time as is practiced in Kyrgyzstan are important means to enhance women's representation.[117] Quota, if implemented and thereupon monitored properly can play a significant role in enhancing women's political participation. Also each political party across the states should have women cells which could work towards greater unity among women members within the parties.[118]

Another factor that should be given utmost importance is, to sensitise people across the spectrum about the importance of gender equality particularly in the elected offices. The social, economic and political bodies and media could play a significant role in this regard. Each government should take adequate measures to ensure that women get their due share, equal opportunities and support to become part of political decision making machinery. Civil society and political activists should also be encouraged to bring not only the women related issues but women representatives to the forefront.

On the issue of international commitments for quotas, even some women's organisations in post-Soviet Central Asian Republics in initial stage were reluctant to talk and promote women's role in public sphere. Even, now not everyone is comfortable in talking or dealing with this aspect of women's role. As a result, the issue of participation of women in public sphere remains marginalised and the link to democratic and people-centered development remain outside general public discourse. Unless proper attention is given to these issues at the highest level and comprehensive national programmes are designed and implemented, there is a potential danger[119] of women not being there at all.

Political power is a tool to get women's issues resolved and their demands fulfilled. Civil society organisations can play a pivotal role in this regard. Therefore, with the help of machineries like civil society and encouraging them, including public boards and local councils and the activities of organisations such as political parties; trade unions; professional or industry associations; civil society organisations; community based organisations and other organisations concerned with public and political life, will certainly make a difference.[120]

On this promising note, this study would explore women's campaign for change and the impact of these on women in the next chapter.

Notes

1. Andrew Roberts, Jason Seawright, Jennifer Cyr "Do Electoral Laws Affect Women's Representation?", Comparative Political Studies, 46: 1555, November, Sage Publications 2013. p. 1.
2. United Nations Office of the Special Adviser on Gender Issues and Advancement of Women. http://www.un.org/womenwatch/osagi/pdf/factsheet1.pdf, accessed on 14 March 2014.
3. Netina Tan, Ethnic Quota and Unintended Effects on Women's Political Representation in Singapore, p. 3-4, 1 This paper was first presented at "Electoral Quotas and Political Representation: Comparative Perspectives", ECPR Joint Session Workshop, Mainz, Germany,11-16 Mar 2013, https://www.cpsa-acsp.ca/papers-2013/Tan1.pdf, accessed on 14 March 2014.
4. Lean Alfred Santos, "How Central Asia can improve governance for development", 9 October 2013, https://www.devex.com/en/news/how-central-asia-can-improve-governance-for/82046, accessed on 14 March 2014.
5. United Nations Office of the Special Adviser on Gender Issues and Advancement of Women. http://www.un.org/womenwatch/osagi/pdf/factsheet1.pdf, accessed on 14 March 2014.
6. Mukulika Banerjee, Democracy, http://www.lse.ac.uk/IDEAS/publications/reports/pdf/SR010/banerjee.pdf, accessed on 14 March 2014.
7. Cited in Ajay Patnaik, "Democracy Debate in Central Asia: Missing the Social Dimension", *Contemporary Central Asia,* Vol. XVII, No. 3, 2013, pp. 2-3.
8. Vladislav Surkov, "Vladislav Surkov Divides Democracy", June 29, 2006, http://www.kommersant.com/p686274/r_1/Vladislav_Surkov_Divides_Democracy/, accessed on 14 March 2014
9. Todd Landman, Marco Larizza, EU Policy Discourse: Democracy, Governance, and Human Rights, International IDEA, Stockholm, Sweden, 2010) p. 8.
10. http://www.intrac.org/data/files/resources/412/Praxis-Paper-15-Organisational-Capacity-Building-in-Central-Asia.pdf, accessed on 14 March 2014.
11. Kathleen Collins, Clan Politics and Regime Transition in Central Asia, Cambridge University Press, 2006, p. 74; See also 2009 edition. Also see Adeeb Khalid, The Politics of Muslim Cultural Reform: Jadidism in Central Asia, Berkeley: University of California Press, 1998, p. 190; see also Danielle Kane, Ksenia O. Gorbenko. "States and Women's Rights in Central Asia." Paper presented at the American Sociological Association. Las Vegas, NV, 22 August 2011.
12. Naila Kabeer, Gender equality and women's empowerment: a critical analysis of the third Millennium Development Goal, *Gender and Development,* Vol. 13, No. 1, March 2005.
13. What is Good Governance?, United Nations Economic and Social Commission for Asia and the Pacific, July 10, 2009, http://www.unescap.org/pdd/prs/ProjectActivities/Ongoing/gg/governance.asp, accessed on 14 March 2014.
14. Presentation on 'Women's Participation in Politics in the Asia Region – A Case Study of Local Governance' for the use of Indian Parliamentary Delegation at the 10th Commonwealth Women Affairs Ministers Meeting to be held in Dhaka, 17-19 June 2013.

    Also see: http://www.idea.int/, accessed on 14 March 2014.

15. Andrew Roberts, Jason Seawright, Jennifer Cyr "Do Electoral Laws Affect Women's Representation?", Comparative Political Studies, 46: 1555, November, Sage Publications 2013. p. 1. http://www.sagepublications.com, accessed on 14 March 2014. Also see Pippa Norris, Driving Democracy Do Power-Sharing Institutions Work? Cambridge: Cambridge University Press, 2008, p. xi.
16. Presentation on 'Women's Participation in Politics in the Asia Region - A Case Study of Local Governance' for the use of Indian Parliamentary Delegation at the 10th Commonwealth Women Affairs Ministers Meeting held in Dhaka, 17-19 June 2013.
17. Conventional politics is primarily dominated by the older generation whereas younger generation remains averse to participating in the political process. Unconventional participation has been successful in influencing government decisions- civil rights movement, the Vietnam War, People participating in unconventional ways (such as direct political action) tend to share three characteristics: (1) Distrust of the political system (2) A strong sense of political efficacy (3) A highly developed sense of group consciousness. See Jan W. Van Deth, José Ramón Montero, Anders Westholm, (eds), Citizenship and Involvement in European Democracies: A Comparative Analysis, Routledge Research in Comparative Politics, 2007, p- 343-387. Also see Joakim Ekman, Erik Amnå, "Political Participation And Civic Engagement: Towards A New Typology", *Human Affairs* 22, 283–300, 2012, pp. 286-92, http://www.degruyter.com/downloadpdf/j/humaff.2012.22.issue-3/s13374-012-0024-1/s13374-012-0024-1.xml, accessed on 14 March 2014.
18. World Economic Forum's (WEF) Gender Gap Report 2013.
19. The Varangians who established Russia's first political legacy allowed women to inherit the throne from a male relative. Olga, the widow of the Kievian prince Igor, became the first woman ruler of Russia in 945 and ruled Kievan Rus for the 27 years. Kamala Kumari, Women in New Russia, 2012, p. 19.
20. AICC Resolution, of Fundamental Duties and economic programme, Bombay, 1931. See "Reservation Of Seats For Women In Legislative Bodies:Perspectives, Occasional Paper Series, 1/2008, Rajya Sabha Secretariat, New Delhi, July 2008, p-2, http://rajyasabha.nic.in/rsnew/publication_electronic/reserv_women_pers 2008.pdf, accessed on 23 March 2014. Also see Prabhat Datta, Payel Sen, "Women in Urban Local Governance:

    Empowerment Through Participation, Journal of Governance and Public Policy, Vol. 4, Nos. 3 & 4, October 9, 2009, pp. 48-61.
21. Speech at Women's Conference, Sojitra, Gujrat, in *collected works of Mahatma Gandhi*, Vol. 30, 27 December 1924, 21 March (1925), p. 108.
22. For instance, Smt. Indira Gandhi guided the country as Prime Minister for more than one and half decades. Women have also served as President, Governors, Chief Ministers, Ministers in Union and State Governments, Presiding Officers of Legislative Bodies, Judges of the High Courts and Secretaries to the Government of India. Also see http://rajyasabha.nic.in/rsnew/publication_electronic/reserv_women_pers2008.pdf, accessed on 14 March 2017.
23. Naila Kabeer, "Gender Equality and Women's Empowerment: A Critical Analysis of the Third Millennium Development Goal", Gender and Development, Vol. 13, No. 1, March, Millennium Development Goals 2005, pp. 13-24, p. 21.

24. It was during Rajiv Gandhi's tenure as PM that the idea of decentralising power and empowering women at the grassroots was discussed and debated. And during PV Narasimha Rao's tenure as PM, the one-third reservation for women in panchayats came through the 73rd and 74th constitutional amendment. Panchayats were expected to serve as nurseries for women leaders, preparing them for tasks they may have to shoulder in case the addiction for politics endures. The 73rd and 74th Constitutional Amendment Acts in December 1992 became effective on 24th April 1993.
25. Ambassador Melanne Verveer, The Political and Economic Power of Women, 2011 http://www.cipe.org/sites/default/files/publication-docs/071511.pdf, accessed on 14 March 2014.
26. During discussion and interaction with people from academia, professional, research scholars, students etc. as part of Field work. Author while interacting and discussing with people (both sexes) in all countries under study had more or less same opinion with some variations. All interactions and discussions in India were during January 2012 to May 2014 and 2018-2019.
27. While interacting with gender experts at a conference in JNU December 2013 and other academicians at Political Science congress December 2013 and various other conferences and workshops during period of research.
28. Presentation on 'Women's Participation in Politics in the Asia Region- A Case Study of Local Governance' for the use of Indian Parliamentary Delegation at the 10th Commonwealth Women Affairs Ministers Meeting to be held in Dhaka, 17-19 June 2013.
29. Ismagilova Nuria Rifkatovna, "Women in Politics and Gender-Based Corruption in Central Asia: Realities and Responses", http://www.10iacc.org/download/t1-05.pdf, accessed on 14 March 2014.
30. Ajay Patnaik, Perestroika and Women Labour Force in Soviet Central Asia, (New Delhi: New Literature, 1989), p. 10.
31. During one of the discussions with Director, Dr. Nazym Shedenova and other professors and research scholars, Center of Gender Studies, Department of Philosophy and Politology, KAZGU, Almaty, 22 October, 2012, (See Image: 11c & d) and Professors and Research Scholars at the Institute of Culture Studies, Ashgabat, 28 November 2012. Also see Megan Bick, EU – Central Asia Civil Society Seminar on Women's Rights, Brussels 21-24 June 2010, FINAL REPORT, September 2010, http://eeas.europa.eu/human_rights/civil_society/docs/2010_ca_final_report_en.pdf, accessed on 14 March 2014.
32. Zainura Rysalieva, "Kyrgyzstan: Culture and Identity in the process of Globalisation", in Mondira Dutta ed., gender and human development in Central and South Asia, Delhi: Pentagon Press, 131-139.
33. During discussions, with Professors and Research scholars, in Turkmenistan, November, 2012. For more see, Matiryali, Academiya nauk Turkmenistana, institute istori, Ashgabat, Turkmenistan, 2012.
34. Razia Sultanova has done in-depth analysis of these facets of cultural life within Central Asian society. She offers important insights into the lives of the societies in the region. Razia Sultanova, From Shamanism to Sufism: Women, Islam and Culture in Central Asia, International Library of Central Asia Studies, N Y, 2011.

35. Tazim R Kassam, "Those who Sing pray Twice", *American Academy of Religion,* Vol. 16, No. 2, 2001, https://www.aarweb.org/sites/default/files/pdfs/Spotlight/Teaching/Issues/2001-02SPRING.pdf, accessed on 14 March 2014.
36. Tokhtakhodjaeva, Marfua, Balchin, Cassandra and Shirkat Gah, "Between the Slogans of Communism and the Laws of Islam", Shirkat Gah Women's Resource Centre, Lahore, Pakistan, 1995. p. 21, 43.
37. Dave Crouch, "The Bolsheviks and Islam", Issue: 110, April 2006, http://isj.org.uk/the-bolsheviks-and-islam/, accessed on 14 March 2013.
38. Erich W.Bethmann, "The Fate of Muslims under Soviet Rule", http://www.bjpa.org/Publications/downloadFile.cfm?FileID=16761, accessed on 14 March 2014.
39. A Bennigsen and C Lemercier-Quelquejay, Islam in the Soviet Union (London, 1967), p. 78; R Pipes, The Formation of the Soviet Union (New York, 1954), p. 77.
40. Vladimir Ilyich Lenin. Reminiscences. 1900-1922, Moscow, 1963, pp. 221-223.
41. Alexandra Kollontai, V.I. Lenin and the First Congress of Women Workers, https://www.marxists.org/archive/kollonta/1918/congress.htm, accessed on 14 March 2014. Also see, Vladimir Ilyich Lenin: Reminiscences,1900-1922, Moscow, 1963, pp. 221-223.
42. Dono Abdurazakova, "Political-Social Movements: Unions and Workers' Movements", in Suad Joseph ed.Encyclopedia of Women & Islamic Cultures: Family, Law and Politics, Vol. II, brill Leiden - Boston, 2005, p. 680.
43. Ismagilova Nuria Rifkatovna, "Women in Politics and Gender-Based Corruption in Central Asia: realities and responses", http://www.10iacc.org/download/t1-05.pdf, accessed on 14 March 2014.
44. Galiya Khassanova, Women in Democratic Institutions, in Kazakhstan, http://pdc.ceu.hu/archive/00001809/01/Khassanova.pdf, accessed on 14 March 2014.
45. Megan Bick, "EU- Central Asia Civil Society Seminar on Women's Rights", Brussels 21-24 June 2010, Final Report, September 2010, p. 5, http://eeas.europa.eu/human_rights/civil_society/docs/2010_ca_final_report_en.pdf, accessed on 14 March 2014.
46. Suad Joseph ed.Encyclopedia of Women & Islamic Cultures: Family, Law and Politics, Vol. II, brill leiden – boston, 2005, p. 680.
47. Kazakh President, "Calls For More Women In Politics", at the first women's congress, 05/03/2011, http://en.ria.ru/world/20110305/162871147.html, accessed on 14 March 2014.
48. The convention on women's political rights was approved by the United Nations General Assembly during the 409th plenary meeting, on 20 December 1952, and adopted on 31 March 1953. The article 20 of this convention says, men and women have equal civil rights. http://www.un.org/womenwatch/daw/cedaw/history.htm, accessed on 14 March 2014.
49. Demokratiya i Pravo, Turkmensnkii natsionalnii institut demokratii u prav cheloveka pri prezidente turkmenistana, 2, 2012.st.-156.
50. Zhenshina, Simiya, obshestvo, Ashgabat, Turkmenistan, 2011, st. 137, 139-154.

51. Zhenshina, Simiya, obshestvo, Ashgabat,Turkmenistan, 2011 p. 68-70.
52. Zhenshina, Simiya, obshestvo, Ashgabat, Turkmenistan, 2011, str.- 160.
53. Medeniyet, 4,(yul-avfgust) 2012, Ministriterestva kulturi turkmenistana, Ashkhabad, Turkmenistan, p. 55.
54. *Medeniyet*, 2,(mart-apriel) 2012, Ministriterestva kulturi turkmenistana, Ashkhabad, Turkmenistan.
55. *Zenan* 7, 2012, Hatiya Begim, pp. 23, 29.
56. During, discussions with professors and interactions with people in Almaty (October 2012), Osh, Dushanbe, Tashkent, Chimkent and Ashgabat (November 1- 12, December, 2012), as part of field work to Central Asia (Kazakhstan- Almaty, Chimkent,Turkistan, Taras, Astana; Kyrgyzstan- Bishkek, Osh; Tajikistan- Dushanbe; Turkmenistan- Ashgabat; Uzbekistan- Tashkent and Samarkand) from 17th October to 14 December 2012.
57. An Overview of Women's Work and Employment in Kazakhstan. Decisions for Life MDG3 Project, Country Report No. 10, University of Amsterdam / Amsterdam Institute for Advanced Labour Studies (AIAS)www.uva.nl/aias Maarten van Klaveren, Kea Tijdens,Melanie Hughie-Williams, Nuria Ramos, Netherlands, March 2010.
58. Currently 182 countries allow women to run for office. Yet women constitute less than 20% of elected representatives in the great majority of these countries. Pamela Paxton, Sheri Kunovich, "Women's Political Representation: The Importance of Ideology", *Social Forces*, Volume 82, Number 1, September 2003, pp. 87-113.
59. http://www.ipu.org/english/surveys.htm, accessed on 14 March 2014.
60. Pamela Paxton, Sheri Kunovich, "Women's Political Representation: The Importance of Ideology", Social Forces, Volume 82, Number 1, September 2003, pp. 87-113, p. 88.
61. Zhenshini I mushini kazakhstana, gendernaya statistika- almati: Agenstvo RK Po statistike, 2012.
62. Discussion with Prof. Roza Sarbayeva, KAZGU, Almaty, Kazakhstan, during FT, Oct-Dec, 2012.
63. Roza Sarbayeva, "Post- Soviet and modern gender politics in Kazakhstan", in Mondira Dutta ed., "Gender and human development in Central and South Asia, Delhi: Pentagon Press, 227-234.
64. Inter-Parliamentary Union (IPU), "Politics: Women's Insight". Geneva, Switzerland: Inter-Parliamentary Union, 2000a, p. 23.
65. During interactions and discussion with people (particularly women) in all these countries people had more or less same opinion with some variations. The author was in Central Asia(Kazakhstan- Almaty, Chimkent,Turkistan, Taras, Astana; Kyrgyzstan- Bishkek, Osh; Tajikistan- Dushanbe; Turkmenistan- Ashgabat; Uzbekistan- Tashkent and Samarkand) from 17th October to 14 December 2012 for field research.
66. Inter-Parliamentary Union (IPU), "Politics: Women's Insight". Geneva, Switzerland: Inter-Parliamentary Union, 2000a, p. 25.

67. Pamela Paxton, Sheri Kunovich, "Women's Political Representation: The Importance of Ideology", *Social Forces*, Volume 82, Number 1, September 2003, pp. 87-113.
68. Kamala Kumari, Women in New Russia, 2012, p. 181, 212.
69. UNECE, Countries in Figures, http://www.unece.org/stats/profiles2009/Welcome.html,June2009, accessed on 14 March 2014;

    http://www.unece.org/stats/gender/genpols/keyinds/genpols-2work.htm, June 2009, accessed on 14 March 2014.
70. http://europeandcis.undp.org/gender/gendermainstreaming/show/66F1EDBD-F203-1EE9-B3F12FEA5C87F079, accessed on 14 March 2014.
71. Louise Sperl, The Crisis and its Consequences for Women, in: Development and Transition Newsletter, 2/2009, http://www.developmentandtransition.net/index.cfm?module=ActiveWeb&page=WebPage&DocumentID=728, accessed on 14 March 2014.
72. During author's interactions and discussion with people (both sexes) and from all walks of life, in all these countries, had more or less the same opinion regarding women's involvement in political sphere, with little variations, during her Field work to Central Asia (Kazakhstan- Almaty, Chimkent,Turkistan, Taras, Astana; Kyrgyzstan- Bishkek, Osh; Tajikistan- Dushanbe; Turkmenistan- Ashgabat; Uzbekistan- Tashkent and Samarkand) from 17th October to 14 December 2012, where she visited various Institutes/Universities/Libraries/Organisations.
73. Mona Lena Krook, "Electoral Gender Quotas: A Conceptual Analysis", *Comparative Political Studies,* Vol. 47(9), 2014, 1268–1293.
74. Dorothy E. McBride (Review), Ann E. Towns, "Women and States: Norms and Hierarchies in International Society", New York: Cambridge University Press, 2010, *Politics & Gender*, 7 (2011), Florida Atlantic University, 605–613.
75. Julie Ballington and Azza Karam, eds., "Increasing Women's Political Representation: New Trends in Gender Quotas", International IDEA, 2005. Also see Julie Ballington and Azza Karam eds., "Women in Parliament: Beyond Numbers", (revised edition), International IDEA, 2005; and Drude Dahlerup, ed., "Women, Quotas and Politics", Routledge, 2006.
76. Appointments are up to 1 January 2019. Inter-Parliamentary Union (IPU) Report, www.ipu.org. Accessed on 15 March 2019.
77. Inter-Parliamentary Union (IPU) Report 2014. See, www.ipu.org, Accessed on June 2014.
78. At present, there are three Constitutional Amendment Bills under consideration in the Indian Parliament. While one seeks to provide for at least one-third seats for women in the national and state legislatures, the other two Bills seek to mandatorily provide for half of the seats for women in all the local level representative bodies. India has the local self governance bodies in both the rural and the urban areas. In rural areas, they are called Panchayati Raj Institutions (PRI) and in the urban areas they exist in the form of Municipalities. At present, these local self governing institutions- both rural and urban - derive their powers and functions directly from the Constitution. See, Presentation on 'Women's Participation in Politics in the Asia Region- A Case Study of Local

Governance' for the use of Indian Parliamentary Delegation at the 10th Commonwealth Women Affairs Ministers Meeting to be held in Dhaka, 17-19 June 2013.

79. Through this affirmative action, a silent revolution has taken place wherein more than a million women have entered politics across the country. For more see., Presentation on 'Women's Participation in Politics in the Asia Region- A Case Study of Local Governance' for the use of Parliamentary Delegation at the 10th Commonwealth Women Affairs Ministers Meeting to be held in Dhaka, 17-19 June 2013, p. 3.
80. Julie Ballington and Azza Karam eds., "Women in Parliament: Beyond Numbers", (revised edition), International IDEA, 2005, p. 175.
81. Appointments are up to 1 January 2019. Inter-Parliamentary Union (IPU), www.ipu.org. Accessed on 15 March 2019.
82. Inter-Parliamentary Union (IPU) Report 2014. See, www.ipu.org, Accessed on June 2014.
83. "Enhancing Women's Political Participation: A Policy Note for Europe and the Commonwealth of Independent States", UNDP Regional Bureau for Europe and the Commonwealth of Independent States, 2010, p. 8.
84. Kamala Kumari, "Identifying women's issues in Central Asia: Problems and Prospects" *Contemporary Central Asia*, Vol.xiv, No. I, March, 2010, pp.45-62, p. 46. See also, Genia K.Browning, "Women & Politics in the U.S.S.R: Consciousness Raising and Soviet Women's Groups", Sussex: Wheatsheaf Books, 1987, p. 34. Also see, Gail W Lapidus, "Women in Soviet Society", Berkeley: University of California Press, 1978, p. 205.
85. Reflecting appointments up to 1 January 2019. Inter-Parliamentary Union (IPU). IPU. Data obtained from national governments, permanent missions to the United Nations and publicly available information. See, www.ipu.org, Accessed on 31 January 2019.
86. Reflecting appointments up to 1 January 2014. Inter-Parliamentary Union (IPU). IPU. Data obtained from national governments, permanent missions to the United Nations and publicly available information. Inter-Parliamentary Union (IPU). See, www.ipu.org, Accessed on June 2014.
87. Suad Joseph ed. Encyclopedia of Women & Islamic Cultures: Family, Law and Politics, Vol. II, brill Leiden -Boston, 2005, p. 680.
88. http: www.parlam.kz/ru/legislative-act/1666, accessed on 14 March 2014.
89. Inter-Parliamentary Union (IPU) Women in Parliaments, March, 2010. www.ipu.org/wmn-e/classif.htm; Also see United Nations (UN) Millenium Development Goals (MDG), March, 2010, http://mdgs.un.org/unsd/mdg/Default.aspx, accessed on 14 March 2014.
90. Suad Joseph ed. Encyclopedia of Women & Islamic Cultures: Family, Law and Politics, Vol. II, brill Leiden -Boston, 2005, p. 680.
91. This trend is also seen in the European Union where almost half of all women ministers hold responsibility for socio-cultural functions and only less than 15 percent were responsible for economy or other functions. Men still dominate defence, police and security. At parliamentary level, planning for police reform

is often confined to the political party leaders, over which women have little power or influence. Women are better represented in regional assemblies or parliaments or councils, though it is difficult to make broad comparison as there are different levels of regional and local structures in different countries. For details see, "Enhancing Women's Political Participation: A Policy Note for Europe and the Commonwealth of Independent States", UNDP Regional Bureau for Europe and the Commonwealth of Independent States, 2010, p. 9-11. Also see "Women and Men in Decision-Making", Analysis of the Situation and Trends, European Commission 2007. http://ec.europa.eu/employment_social/publications/ 2008/ke8108186_en.pdf, accessed on 14 March 2014.

92. Anara Moldosheva, "Kyrgyzstan National Report on Women & Governance", Bishkek, November 2008.

93. Kyrgyzstan can also provide a number of examples of women's parties including the Women's Democratic Party (1994, renamed in 2005 the Democratic Party of Women and Youth, New Power) and the Party of Women *El-Ene* (2000), which literally means mother of the people. In addition, women leaders founded: *El Muras* (People's Heritage 2002), Agreement (2002) and the Communist Party of Kyrgyzstan (2000). In the parliamentary elections of 2000, the Women's Democratic Party won two seats in the Legislative Assembly. One of the two MPs- Ms. Toktokan Borombaeva - became a strong advocate of two important laws on gender equality- the 'Law on State Guarantees on Equal Rights and Opportunities of Men and Women', and the 'Law on Social and Legal Protection against Family Violence', which were approved by parliament in 2003. In Kyrgyzstan, women account for 10 percent of high ranking party leaders. And now there is a move among political parties to create women's sections, as a response to the introduction of gender quotas in the election system based on party lists. See., www.quotaproject.org; http://www.stopvaw.org, 2009, accessed on 14 March 2014.

94. During, discussion with gender experts in Bishkek (October, 2012), as part of field work interview/interaction/discussion; on "Women in Central Asian Society". The author was in Central Asia from 17th October to 14 December 2012 for field research, where she visited various Institutes/Universities/Libraries/Organisations.

95. Kamala Kumari, "Political Participation of Women in India", in Alok Kumar Gupta and Asha Bhandari, Eds, "Women and Political Participation in Indian Democratic System", Author's Press, 2010, p. 6.

96. http://eci.nic.in/, accessed on 14 March 2014.

97. https://eci.gov.in/files/file/10947-24-participation-of-women-candidates-in-poll/ Accessed on 27 November 2019.

98. Inter-Parliamentary Union (IPU), 2014 Women in Parliaments, March, 2010. www.ipu.org/wmn e/classif.htm, accessed on 14 March 2014.

99. Millennium Development Goals Report 2012, p. 24. Also see Democracy and Gender Equality: The Role of the UN, Discussion Paper September 2013, https://eudevdays.eu/sites/default/files/Democracy-and-Gender-Equality-The-Role-of-the-UN-PDF.pdf, accessed on 14 March 2014.

100. Kamala Kumari, "Globalisation and Women in India", Tuesday, 27 July 2010. www. paxindica.in/. Also see, www.worldbank.org/opendata/women-ministerial-positions-worldwide-looking-data-close, accessed on 14 March 2014. Also see Women in Politics: 2010, IPU, 2010, http://www.ipu.org/pdf/publications/wmnmap10_en.pdf, accessed on 14 March 2014.
101. Ambassador Melanne Verveer, "The Political and Economic Power of Women", Ambassador-at-Large for Global Women's Issues, Center for International Private Enterprise, Washington, D.C., 06-20-2011, http://www.humanrights.gov/dyn/ambassador-verveer-on-the-political-and-economic-power-of-women.html, accessed on 14 March 2014.
102. This trend is also seen in the European Union where almost half of all women ministers hold responsibility for socio-cultural functions and only less than 15 percent were responsible for economy or other functions. Men still dominate defence, police and security. At parliamentary level, planning for police reform is often confined to the political party leaders, over which women have little power or influence. Women are better represented in regional assemblies or parliaments or councils, though it is difficult to make broad comparison as there are different levels of regional and local structures in different countries. For details see, "Enhancing Women's Political Participation: A Policy Note for Europe and the Commonwealth of Independent States", UNDP Regional Bureau for Europe and the Commonwealth of Independent States, 2010, pp. 9-11. Also see European Commission, Women and Men in Decision-Making, Analysis of the Situation and Trends, 2007. http://ec.europa.eu/employment_social/publications/2008/ke8108186_en.pdf, accessed on 14 March 2014.
103. http://worldleadersindex.org/InternationalOrganisations/UN.html
104. During, discussions with professors and interaction with people in Almaty (October 2012), Osh, Dushanbe, Tashkent, Chimkent and Ashgabat (November 2012), as part of field work to Central Asia (Kazakhstan- Almaty, Chimkent, Turkistan, Taras, Astana; Kyrgyzstan- Bishkek, Osh; Tajikistan- Dushanbe; Turkmenistan- Ashgabat; Uzbekistan- Tashkent and Samarkand) from 17th October to 14 December 2012, where the author visited various Institutes/Universities/Libraries/Organisations.
105. Consolidated response from the E-Discussion on Violence Against women in politics, *iKNOW Politics*, http://www.iknowpolitics.org/files/Consolidatedreply_violenceagainstwomen inpolitics_.pdf, accessed on 14 March 2014.
106. See for example Sonja Lokar, in http://www.iknowpolitics.org/files/Consolidated reply_violence against women in politics_.pdf., accessed on 14 March 2014.
107. Article 1 provides definitions of domestic violence, physical domestic violence, psychological family abuse and sexual domestic violence. Articles 23 and 24 address temporary restraining orders, and Articles 25 to 27 address protective court orders. Monitoring of the law is the responsibility of the police and court system. See http://www.wilpf.int.ch/publications/CEDAW_Report_Jan_2004.html., accessed on 14 March 2014 http://daccessdds.un.org/doc/UNDOC/GEN/N07/264/90/PDF/N0726490.pdf?, accessed on 14 March 2014.
108. Women's Access to Justice in Central and Eastern Europe and Central Asia, KARAT, Coalition with Partners, 2012. http://www.karat.org/wp-content/

uploads/2012/01/Women_Access_To_Justice_ENG_final_version.pdf., accessed on 14 March 2014.

109. Women's Access to Justice in Central and Eastern Europe and Central Asia, KARAT, Coalition withPartners, 2012. http://www.karat.org/wp-content/uploads/2012/01/Women_Access_To_Justice_ENG_final_version.pdf, accessed on 14 March 2014. Also see, Yvonne Corcoran-Nantes, "Lost Voices: Central Asian Women: Confronting Transition", London and New York: Zed Books, 2005. 208 pages, p. 63.
110. Nick Megoran, "Theorizing Gender, Ethnicity and the Nation-State in Central Asia", *Central Asian Survey*, 18, No.1, 99-110, p. 103.
111. http://www.nationsencyclopedia.com/World-Leaders-2003/Uzbekistan-domestic-policy.html, accessed on 14 March 2014.
112. Nazgul Abalova and Almeiiz Abalov, "Women as apolitical Resource: Kyrgyzstan and India", in Mondira Dutta ed., Gender and human development in Central and South Asia, Delhi: Pentagon Press, pp. 235- 252.
113. During author's discussions with women in *bazaar*/markets, metro, parks, in Tashkent, Samarkand, Uzbekistan; Osh, Kyrgyzstan; Dushanbe, Tajikistan, Chimkent, Ashgabat, Turkmenistan (3 November-3 December, 2012).
114. As part of field work interview/interaction/discussion with people from all walks of life, young and old alike, working/non-working, in most of these countries had the same opinion on the issue of "Women's involvement in political sphere in Central Asian Society". Also see http://www.unhcr.org/publ/PUBL/3eaff4422.html, accessed on 14 March 2014.
115. As cited in Michele E. Commercio, "The politics and economics of "retraditionalisation" in Kyrgyzstan and Tajikistan", *Post-Soviet Affairs*, 2014, p. 2. For details see, Adeeb Khalid, "A Secular Islam: Nation, State, and Religion in Uzbekistan", *International Journal of Middle East Studies*, 35 (4): 2003, pp. 573-598.
116. M. Jill Bystydzienski, "Women in Electoral Politics: Lessons from Norway", Praeger. 1995.
117. Gender quotas can be classified into two types. One is constitutional / legislative and second is voluntary quotas. While constitutionally a specific number of seats can be reserved for women representatives, the political parties have their own constitution to govern party's internal affairs distribution of tickets on the basis of various criteria. It is important that political parties voluntarily allocate a certain portion of posts and seats for women. For instance, in India, the Bharatiya Janata Party has reserved 50 percent of organisational posts for women(year).
118. Malgorzata Fuszara, Kobiety w polityce [Women in Politics], Warszawa 2007. Also see Anara Moldosheva. Kyrgyzstan National Report on Women & Governance. Bishkek, November 2008; See also Enhancing Women's Political Participation: A Policy Note for Europe and the Commonwealth of Independent States, UNDP Regional Bureau for Europe and the Commonwealth of Independent States, 2010, p. 34-38 . Also see Consolidated Response on Women's Party Sections, *iKNOW Politics*, http://www.iknowpolitics.org/files/consolidatedresponsewomen'spartysection iknowpolitics.pdf. Accessed on 14 March 2014.

119. Suad Joseph ed.Encyclopedia of Women & Islamic Cultures: Family, Law and Politics, Vol. II, brill leiden -boston, 2005, p. 680.

120. Article 7 (political and public life) states that 'Parties shall take all appropriate measures to eliminate discrimination against women in political and public life of the country and, in particular, shall ensure that women, on equal terms with men, have the right: (a) To vote in all elections and public referenda and to be eligible for election to all publicly elected bodies; (b) To participate in the formulation of government policies and the implementation thereof and to hold public office and perform all public functions at all levels of government; (c) To participate in non-governmental organisations and associations concerned with the public and political life of the country. UN Committee for the Elimination of Discrimination of Women, CEDAW General Recommendation No. 23 (UN Committee for the Elimination of Discrimination of Women, CEDAW General Recommendation No. 23 16th session, 1997). http://www.un.org/womenwatch/daw/cedaw/recommendations/recomm.htm#recom23. Accessed on 14 March 2014.

Chapter 4

Women's Campaign for Change

Campaign for Change; to Empower Women Economically, Socially and Politically; Transform Communities, Societies and to Build a Great Nation!

"When woman, whom we call, abula becomes, sabala, all those who are helpless will become powerful" - **Mahatma Gandhi**

Women's campaign for change through movements and various other activities are among the most global form of modern social actions. Women's issues have been the concern not only of women, but of concern to all revolutionary leaders, male and female. Mahatma Gandhi advocated for women's empowerment. He transformed the outlook of politics and society in India.[1] Even Russian revolutionaries like V.I. Lenin and Leon Trotsky wrote on women's issues.[2]

In the 1990s, women from the global south led the women's movement which began to interrogate western assumption of shared oppression of patriarchy and sexism. Despite the fact that sexism impacts women globally, the experience and impact of sexism and patriarchy is experienced very differently across the world, nations and within communities. Thereby, the goals and structures of women's movements reflect the commonalities as well as the differences among different women movements. Women in these different societies experience not just sexism but oppressive practices based on race, nationality, religion, class, (dis)ability, caste, sexual orientation, parental status, marital status, political beliefs and practices, appearance, geographic location etc.[3] Even though, due to the technological developments especially in the information technology domain and rise of the national and international institutions and legal frameworks, the socioeconomic and political status of women have changed across the societies. However, lot remains to be done.

When talking about the equality between women and men, equality here does not necessarily means that, women and men are or will become the same but that women's and mens rights, responsibilities and opportunities should not be gender based. Ensuring gender equality and elimination of discrimination against women has been on top of the agenda of governments as well as multilateral conventions working under the aegis of United Nations. Gender equality implies, that the interests, needs and priorities of both women and men are taken into consideration, recognising the diversity of different groups of women and men. Gender equality is not only a womans issue but concerns and fully engages both women as well as men. Equality between women and men should be seen both as a human rights issue and as a precondition for, and an indicator of sustainable, people centered development.[4]

Gender equality has quantitative as well as qualitative aspects. The quantitative aspect implies that for women and men, an equal distribution in all areas, such as education, work, recreation, and position of power. The qualitative aspect implies that the knowledge, experiences and values of both women and men are given equal weight and further used to enrich and direct all social areas and endeavours.[5] However, despite the legal provisions and increasing awareness about gender equality, women in several societies are yet to get their due share. And it is very rightly said that, "if half of the worlds population remains vulnerable to economic, political, legal, and social marginalisation; as the majority of the worlds unhealthy, unschooled, unfed, and unpaid are women and girls; the hope of advancing democracy and prosperity will remain in serious jeopardy".[6]

On paper, no constitution or family code of any country discriminates against women, but no country in the world can vouch that there is no discrimination against women, however less degree it may be; it exists even in developed countries. And the transition at the turn of the century, brought with it many opportunities as well as challenges which impacted societies particularly women all over the world and India and Central Asia were no exception. Women in all these countries were affected to a great extent, even though few of these challenges were region specific and affected women differently in their respective country.

According to the June 2013 report, edition (16), most of the Central Asian countries were either in the sustainability evolving or sustainability impeded and none of them in sustainability enhanced category even though their individual score or rank remained the same or even if it improved.[7]

Table 4.1
BTI Country Status* 2014 and 2019**

		India		*Kazakhstan*		*Kyrgyzstan*		*Tajikistan*		*Turkmenistan*		*Uzbekistan*		*Russia*		*China*	
		2014	***2019***	***2014***	***2019***	***2014***	***2019***	***2014***	***2019***	***2014***	***2019***	***2014***	***2019***	***2014***	***2019***	***2014***	***2019***
Status Index	Score	7.19	6.7	5.05	4.9	5.61	5.9	3.59	3.3	3.45	2.7	3.09	4.1	5.24	5.3	5.01	5.0
	Rank	26	34	83	87	66	59	113	120	115	129	118	107	77	73	84	81
Political Transformation	**Score**	**8.10**	**7.25**	3.85	3.78	**5.80**	**6.10**	3.60	2.92	2.78	2.75	2.85	3.63	**4.40**	**4.50**	**3.33**	**3.33**
	Rank	20	29	102	100	64	57	108	124	123	128	122	105	86	85	113	114
Economic Transformation	Score	**6.29**	**6.14**	**6.25**	**6.04**	5.43	5.64	3.57	3.71	4.11	2.63	3.32	4.54	**6.07**	**6.11**	**6.68**	**6.75**
	Rank	45	48	47	54	70	66	113	113	104	128	116	98	48	50	35	30
Management Index***	Score	**6.32**	**5.9**	4.67	4.6	4.69	4.6	3.58	3.4	2.19	2.3	1.79	3.6	3.90	3.5	4.94	4.7
	Rank	20	32	75	80	74	80	110	116	122	123	125	108	104	114	66	77

Source: Prepared by the Author with help of BTI Country Reports 2014 and 2019 (https://atlas.bti-project.org/1*2020*) Accessed on 15 May 2020. For details see Appendix II.A and II.A.i

*scale: 1-10; Rank: out of 129 countries

**out of 137 countries

*** For 2019 Governance index

The status of respective countries under study in terms of status Index, political and economic transformation and management Index/ government index, and their rank and score under these indicators are as in the Table 4.1. These figures suggest that India vis-à-vis political transformation is much ahead of Central Asian Republics which have not fared that well and even Russia and China are behind India. Amongst CARs only Kyrgyzstan has managed to score more than 5. Even in terms of Management index and Governance index India is much ahead of others including Russia and China. Economically India and Kazakhstan are better placed than other CARs and close to Russia and China. And the Gender Gap Index, as per the Table 4.2, it is very much clear as to how each of these countries stands as of 2019 and has managed so far. India has improved its score in Educational, Health and Survival and Political Empowerment. The striking feature in this table is that all countries under study have has scored less in terms of Economic participation and opportunities since 2013. No data available for Turkmenistan and Uzbekistan.

Table 4.2
Gender Gap Index 2013* and 2020**

Countries		*Overall*		*Economic Participation and Opportunity*		*Educational Attainment*		*Health And Survival*		*Political Empowerment*	
		Rank	*Score*	*Rank*	*Score*	*Rank*	*Score*	*Rank*	*Score*	*Rank*	*Score*
India	2013	101	0.655	124	0.446	120	0.857	135	0.931	9	0.385
	2020	112	0668	149	0.354	112	0.962	150	0.944	18	0.411
Kazakhstan	2013	32	0.722	20	0.771	69	0.991	1	0.980	65	0.146
	2020	72	0.710	37	0.742	63	0.995	74	0.975	106	0.130
Kyrgyzstan	2013	32	0.722	20	0.771	69	0.991	1	0.980	65	0.146
	2020	72	0.710	37	0.742	63	0.995	74	0.975	106	0.130
Kyrgyzstan	2013	63	0.695	60	0.679	77	0.989	75	0.973	71	0.138
	2020	93	0.689	88	0.654	82	0.990	1	0.980	105	0.130
Tajikistan	2013	90	0.668	38	0.728	110	0.899	123	0.956	100	0.089
	2020	137	0.626	134	0.496	123	0.942	72	0.976	128	0.088

Source: Table prepared by Author with help of data from World Economic Forums (WEF) Gender Gap Report, 2013 and 2020 reports.

*(out of 136 countries)

**(out of 149countries)

***Data not available for Turkmenistan and Uzbekistan.

According to the 2020 Gender Gap Report, at the global level, the gender gaps vary significantly across four dimensions: health and survival; educational attainment; economic participation and opportunity; and political empowerment. So far, in Educational Attainment and Health and Survival, 96.1% and 95.7% of the gap (respectively) have already been closed. Even on Economic Participation and Opportunity, there seems to improvement, where 58.8% of the gap has been closed. However, in terms of Political Empowerment the gap between women and men remain significantly larger, where only 24.7% of the gap has been closed. Even though, there is improvement, only 25% of the gap has been closed and no country has been successful in fully closing this gap yet. Not even in Iceland, where the presence of women across parliament, ministries and heads of states is the most widespread compared to all other countries assessed by the index; with approximately 70% of its Political Empowerment gap closed and score of 10 percentage points, which is higher than the second-ranked Norway and being almost four times higher than the global average. This clearly explains that keeping in mind the gender gap size, the Political Empowerment is one area where women are severely under-represented.[8]

Table 4.3
CSO Sustainability Index Country Scores 1997–2012

	Kazakh-stan	***Kyrgyz-stan***	***Tajiki-stan***	***Turkmeni-stan***	***Uzbeki-stan***	***Average***	***Eurasia & Central Asia Average***
1997	4.6	4.6	N/R	N/R	N/R	4.6	4.1
1998	4.4	3.9	6.6	N/R	4.7	4.9	4.7
1999	4.8	4.1	6.1	6.6	5.3	5.4	5.0
2000	4.7	4.3	5.4	6.0	5.1	5.1	4.9
2001	4.3	4.3	5.1	5.8	4.6	4.8	4.6
2002	4.1	4.0	4.6	5.6	4.7	4.6	4.5
2003	3.9	4.1	4.6	5.7	4.7	4.6	4.5
2004	4.1	4.2	4.7	5.5	5.3	4.8	4.6
2005	4.1	4.1	4.6	5.7	5.6	4.8	4.6
2006	4.1	4.1	4.7	5.7	5.7	4.9	4.6
2007	4.0	4.1	4.8	5.6	5.7	4.8	4.6
2008	4.0	4.1	4.9	5.7	5.7	4.9	4.6
2009	4.0	4.1	4.8	5.7	5.7	4.9	4.6
2010	4.0	4.1	4.8	5.6	5.7	4.8	4.6
2011	4.1	4.1	4.7	5.6	5.7	4.8	4.6
2012	4.1	4.0	4.8	6.4	5.7	5.0	4.6

Source: Table prepared by the Author with help of data from 2012 CSO Sustainability Index for Central and Eastern Europe and Eurasia, 16th Edition - June, 2013, http://www.usaid.gov/sites/default/files/documents/1863/2012CSOSI_0.pdf, accessed on 5 July 2014 N/R=Country was not studied in that year.

And the Table 4.3 shows the Civil Society Organisation (CSO) Sustainability Index, Country Scores, 1997-2012, for Central Asian Republics and Table 4.4 shows the NGO Sustainability Index Scores for the year 2010 and 2012 for Central Asian Republics. The CSO sustainability index and the NGO Sustainability Index Scores is only available for a country in transition, so there is no such ranking or score available for India. And it is a well-known fact that, in India the NGOs are very effective in raising awareness and highlighting issues through systemic process.

Table 4.4
NGO Sustainability Index Scores 2010 And 2012

		Kazakh-stan	*Kyrgyz-stan*	*Tajiki-stan*	*Turkmeni-stan*	*Uzbeki-stan*	*Average*	*Eurasia Average*
Legal Environment	2010	3.8	3.9	4.9	**6.3**	6.0	5.0	4.7
	2012	4.1	3.8	5.0	**6.2**	6.0		
Organisational Capacity	2010	4.1	4.3	4.6	5.3	5.4	4.7	4.4
	2012	4.2	4.3	4.5	6.4	5.5		
Financial Viability	2010	4.6	5.1	5.6	6.0	6.1	5.5	5.3
	2012	4.5	5.3	5.6	6.0	6.1		
Advocacy	2010	3.8	3.5	5.1	6.1	5.9	4.9	4.5
	2012	4.0	3.1	4.8	6.0	5.9		
Service Provision	2010	4.0	4.0	4.5	5.2	5.4	4.6	4.4
	2012	4.0	4.0	4.4	6.4	5.4		
Infrastructure	2010	3.7	3.7	4.6	5.2	5.6	4.6	4.3
	2012	3.7	3.7	4.6	6.8	5.6		
Public Image	2010	4.1	4.2	4.5	5.5	5.6	4.8	4.6
	2012	4.2	4.0	4.5	6.7	5.6		
Overall Score Country rank	2010	4.0	4.1	4.8	5.7	5.7	4.9	4.6
	2012	4.1	4.0	4.8	6.4	5.7		

Source: Table prepared by author with help of data from 2009 NGO Sustainability Index for Central and Eastern Europe and Eurasia, 13th Edition, June 2010 and 2012.
http://www.icnl.org/research/resources/regional/NGOSICEE2009.pdf, accessed on 23 March 2014.

For the development and , by CSOs and for them to be able to carry out their critical work, they require at a minimum, the freedom to exercise three interdependent rights: the rights to peacefully assemble, freely associate, and openly express themselves. Impediments to exercise any of these rights undermine civil society's ability to contribute in any significant manner. Reviews reveal that, in an increasing number of countries, local and international CSOs engaged in critical development work are constrained from fully exercising their internationally protected rights, and thus, from serving the communities that need and depend on them.[9] And as visible in the tables above, the CARs have barely managed to keep up with respect to CSO and NGO sustainability index.

With this picture we will now look at women's campaign for change in terms of democratisation, economic, politics as well as social developments in the countries under study.

Women, particularly in the developing countries are continuously striving to get their rights and recognition in the society. And women movements in these societies are using information and communication technologies to propagate their cause. Though, such tools to sensitise society in general and women in particular exists sparsely. However, the Civil Society Organisations (CSOs) including non-government organisations (NGOs), advocacy organisations, a range of professional and community associations, faith-based organisations, and academia, in developing countries have had a long history of involvement and an important role in public sphere.

As democracy remains a universal human aspiration and has been a powerful force of political mobilisation for change, citizen led movements as witnessed, are demanding democratic reform.[10] Therefore, strong civil society is must to ensure good governance and accountability in the governmental apparatus. Strong civil societies play a significant role in ensuring that the governmental and societal institutions are doing enough to adequately safeguard women's' rights and liberties. These institutions cannot be strengthened without active participation of women. Empowered women can bring about sustainable change and contribute meaningfully towards societal growth and nation building. On the contrary, women issues would remain unaddressed even by the policy-makers if women are marginalised in the socioeconomic and political sphere.[11] Post 1975, according to some research, there has been a significant undulating effect on women's legislative representation due to democratisation within developing nations. There is initial decline in legislators, which is tied to pre-democratic regime types, and the upward trajectory is slow and mostly connected to a nations electoral experience.[12] As mentioned in Chapter three there has been an increase in women political representation more so the last few decades.

In many countries of Central Asia including Kazakhstan, the political system transformation and social-economic changes sufficiently influenced the change in political culture, and was a catalyst to different social layers of activism. And since the 1990s, the governments in the countries under study including India, have put in place various policies and affirmative actions to enhance gender equality.

In the modern context, burgeoning of women organisations, their activities and initiatives forced researchers to study new social phenomena such as women's movement and women's activism. However, even today, rare attention is paid to this social problem, especially in connection with historic and culture traditions, national peculiarities, mentality etc.,[13] hence, despite scientific development and recognition of women's movement during 1960-80s, the form, types and peculiarities have remained different in different countries.

Women's Movement for Change

India

Most of the movements on women's issues in India have been successful both before and since independence. The campaign for women's issue and rights, have been happening since a long time. In the 19th century reformers like Raja Ram Mohan Roy, Swami Dayananda Saraswathi, Ranade, Ishwar Chandra Vidyasagar and many others championed the cause of women emancipation. Even in the 20th century Gandhiji was the biggest propagator for women emancipation. The post-1991 period though, has witnessed structured growth of women NGOs, and the women movements have imprint of the western influence.

Mahatma Gandhi was one of the first few leaders to have advocated women's role and their importance in public sphere. Others like Bal Gangadhar Tilak was of the view that political action on the part of women could be independent of their social status and that political action was possibly more important than social reform in empowering women. In fact, as mentioned in Chapter 3, Indian women had raised the issues of universal adult franchise early as 1917 and in 1920 which demanded equal rights of representation for the fair sex in the Indian Legislatures. Though, this demand was turned down by the British Government, the Indian National Congress in 1931 adopted a resolution in favour of women's franchise and representation.[14] In post-Independence era also women's campaign for change continued. There have been several campaigns like, *Mahila Samakhya*, a literacy programme for women, was a successful campaign of women's against alcoholism[15]; *Chipko Andolan*, against deforestation and cutting of trees; The *Narmada bachao andolan* against a number of large dams being built across the Narmada river, etc.[16]

Several women's movements have been successful in making an impact; and some despite having good intentions, could not leave behind a significant mark in terms of societal or institutional changes. However, there have been several successful movements all over India here only few important women movements amongst many such movements would be discussed.

The Gulabi Gang Movement

The *Gulabi* Gang was formed in 2006 by Sampat Pal Devi in the Banda District of Uttar Pradesh in Northern India. Being, one of the most neglected and poorest districts in the country, with, a traditional male dominated society. Sampat Devi formed the *Gulabi* Gang to fight injustice and violence. *Gulabi* means Pink and the *Gulabi* Gang members wear bright pink saris

(Indian traditional attire for women) and wield bamboo sticks. See Image: 4.1. The leader of this Group describes the gang as group of women committed to a cause and that is justice.[17]

The '*Gulabi* Gang' has tens of thousands of women members. Surprisingly, the '*Gulabi* Gang' has also won admirers among men. The Pink sisterhood has stood up against all kind of injustice. Initially this movement was only intended to collectively punish oppressive husbands, fathers and brothers, and combat domestic violence and desertion. The offenders were first made to listen to reason and if this did not work, the hardened offenders were publicly shamed. Women even took up the *lathis* if men resorted to the use of force. Over the years the group has also helped streamline public distribution system and disbursal of governmental aid to poor and aged through simple methodology-immediate action and confrontation, wherever necessary. They have also fought against the issues of human rights violation.[18]

Image 4.1

Sampat Lal (in centre with lathi) and her Gulabi Gang

In 2003, three years before the trust was formally set up, Sampats just ways and enterprising streak helped Prema Rambahori, a dalit woman, set up a leaf-plate making business in Bangalipura community of Badausa village, a tribal area barely 15 kms away from '*Gulabi* Gangs' '*Karyalay'* (office in Atarra). These leaf-plates are environment friendly and are sourced to adjacent towns and communities for weddings and various other functions. The work has expanded, and currently Prema employs 500 women of the community, each earning upto Rs. 150 per day.[19] Today they provide facilities for a complete wedding within local community with cost-effective solutions to cater to the modest means of the community.[20]

Issue of Women's Reservation Bill in the Parliament

The most prominent manifestation of women movement in India at the national level has been seen on the issue of Women's Reservation Bill in the Parliament. The Bill was introduced in the Lok Sabha on September 12, 1996. Although, it has been introduced in Parliament several times since then, the Bill could not be passed because of lack of political consensus.[21] Eventually, it was passed in the Upper House in March 9, 2010 after long struggle; though it is still pending in the Lok Sabha. To get the bill through the Lok Sabha, women representatives from all the political parties, came together to support the Bill. Over 500 women and men, representing 350 women's groups and civil society organisations, marched to the Indian Parliament before the Monsoon Session on July 29, 2010.[22]

Brinda Karat, Member of Parliament (MP) and General Secretary, All India Democratic Women's Association (AIDWA), said that, "nobody underestimates the challenge in achieving such an outcome. While the Bill has been passed in the *Rajya Sabha*, (Upper House), its fate in the adjoining chamber, the all important *Lok Sabha*, (House of the People) is rather less certain" as unfortunately, due to the vested interest of the few patriarchs, the Bill could not be passed in the lower house of the parliament. However, women groups and women parliamentarians have not given up yet. They voiced the opinion that, "This struggle for the Bill is not just for women alone, it is for society as a whole". Jyotsna Chatterji of the Joint Women's Programme (JWP), who has also long been associated with the Young Women's Christian Association (YWCA) movement in India, recalled to the media, "We have been struggling from 1995 for this bill and we are determined to see it translated into law".[23] See the Image 4.2.

However, there isn't much change in the status of the bill till date, as it is still pending in the parliament.

Indian women have also played a significant role in the complete eradication of polio from India, as in the year 2011, WHO had officially removed India from the list of the countries where polio was actively transmitted.[24]

Image 4.2
Women's March to Parliament in support of 33% Women's Bill

Source: Pamela Philipose, India–Battle for the Women's Bill: Bring in the Umbrellas, Alliance for 33%, http://apwld.org/wp-content/uploads/2013/09/APWLD-Forum-News-Vol. 32 No. 2-Web.pdf, accessed on 23 March 2014.

In India, there is a government body, the National Commission on Women (NCW) in place which exclusively deals with all women's issues. Also, each state has a State Women Commission (SWC). These commissions have power to take *Suo Motto* action and ask explanation from anyone, if any discrimination takes place against women. Due to the consistent pressure, from civil society groups and women movement, a stringent law to curb the incidents of rape have been passed by the Indian parliament. In the section below few of the Organisations and NGOs Working for Women's Issues will be discussed.

Organisations and NGOs Working for Women's Issues

There are many women organisations and NGOs working for women's issues in India and Central Asia. However, here only few of them will be mentioned for the purpose of elaborating their significance in respect to the theme of this chapter.

Centre for Women's Development Studies (CWDS), is a research centre comprised of a group of professionals working for the realisation of women's equality and development in all spheres of life. The centre maintains a specialised library with a collection on women and development in India, which is open for reference, to students, research scholars, gender consultants, policy-makers, journalists etc.[25]

Centre for Social Research (CSR), founded in 1983, is a non-profit, non-governmental organisation based in New Delhi. Its mission is to empower women and girls; guarantee their fundamental rights, and increase understanding of social issues from a gender perspective. They operate on local, national and regional levels in an effort to enhance the capacities of individuals, communities and institutions for creating a humane, equitable and gender-just society.[26]

The Young Women's Christian Association (YWCA) of Delhi was established in 1912. This is an umbrella organisation affiliated to the World YWCA with 65 local associations in India. The organisation works for women's empowerment through a variety of programmes, the most important of which are leadership training for women, advocacy work on all women's issues, and community development work. The YWCA also runs 40 women's residences across the country providing housing for working women as well as emergency shelter for women. The YWCA of India is also a part of a network of 7 women's organisations based in Delhi and works together with them on common issues.[27]

All India Coordinating Forum of the Adivasi/Indigenous Peoples (AICAIP), was established as a forum for Adivasi/indigenous peoples movements all over India. There are five working groups of AICAIP, one of these working group has established to focus on Adivasi Women's Issues. Its objective is to strengthen the process of building solidarity and alliances amongst struggle oriented indigenous peoples organisations. AICAIP aims to identify shared issues and problems, to generate debate on these issues and to provide support to help deal with them.[28]

Maitreyi is another organisation whose major objective is to develop a feminist perspective in understanding women's issues and the women's movement, and to sensitise everyone about women's issues. *Maitreyi* sponsors and indirectly supports activities like: women's studies workshops, research, documentation, support centers for women in distress, mobilisation of women in villages to join Ladies Club, and publication of books and annual reports.[29]

Akshara is a Resource Centre for women. *Akshara* began informally in 1987 as result of the women's movement and its campaigns in Bombay. It started by producing low cost publications for women's organisations and activists. In 1995, *Akshara* establish a library and reference centre for women through funds. It now apart from library facilities, offers gender training and workshops, and publishes educational and movement oriented materials in English and Marathi.[30]

Forum against Oppression of Women (FAOW), was formed in 1979 as a platform to respond to an extremely unjust judgment on a rape case. FAOW is part of what in India is recognised as the Autonomous Women's groups which has played a crucial role in the women's movement from 1979 onwards. Today it is mainly a campaign group consisting of members from varied background- students, housewives, professional women, lecturers etc. There are no paid staffs. The members meet regularly once in a week and every one puts their voluntary time in the work that needs to be done.[31]

Majlis is a legal and cultural resource centre working in the area of women and minority rights. The legal centre of Majlis is a group of lawyers providing legal assistance to women. Majlis is also involved in reasearch and documentation on issues concerning women. India Women Scientists Association (IWSA) promotes women's participation in Science.[32]

Sanhita Gender Resource Centre is an initiative of women activists in West Bengal and was born out of a need for information activism and networking among grassroots organisations working towards the empowerment of women. *Sanhita* aims to increase women's access to information. *Sanhita* conducts gender trainings, publishes, provides a referral service, and produces advocacy materials. *Sanhita* also collects, processes, and disseminates information through action research programmes and by means of a library and documentation centre.[33]

Organisations like **Kali for Women**; **Diverse Women for Diversity; Centre for Women's Development Studies; Centre for Documentation and Research on Women** (Aalochana) also contributes to issues of Women by doing research, workshops, programmes, publications etc.[34]

Central Asia

The current situation of post-Soviet Central Asia is largely the consequence of three elements-the restoration of Islamic values; the revival of pre-Soviet institutions; and the reinstatement of the patriarchal sentiment. And each of these elements is significantly tied to an attempt to create a new historical narrative and national identity for states that have existed for close to three decades and the leadership in the respective nations has played an important role in shaping the direction of their nation state.[35]

The common past of USSR, the post-Independence transitions, Russian language, culture, education, geographic proximity, human connections, etc. all unite these countries; however there are certain differences in the approach to these ideas of the individual country in their own unique ways. They have their own set of political regime, level of economies, difference of culture, national language, mixed populations, historical prejudices and ethnic stereotypes. For example, the Turkmen people have chosen their specific way of development in the building of democratic, legal, secular society of justice, based on the ancient national traditions of the Turkmen people; their national peculiarities and mentality, taking into account the generally accepted principles of democracy in a society.[36]

All these countries are secular, where, religion is separated from the state. For instance, Kazakhstan is a multinational state where different ethnic groups freely practice various religions. These are the main values of this country and are the basis of stability of the Kazakh society. In modern Kazakhstan, Islam is one of the factors of cultural self-identification and of the search for spiritual identity.[37] These factors are more or less common to all the countries. It has been observed that there is a "growing complexity of the inner Islamic situation as well as the growth of religious feelings amongst the population. Being one of the forms of ethnic identity, Islam plays a major role in ethnic consolidation".[38]

The end of the 20th century saw the spreading of feminist ideas in newly independent Central Asian countries, where systemic transformation caused the processes of new public consciousness. This in turn made space for women's activities in various unique ways. Women in many Asian countries including Central Asia have in fact, been the backbone of their countries economic development. Women's contribution to the economy has strengthened the economies and process of nation building.

Central Asia due to disintegration of USSR in 1991, underwent transition or transformation which was influenced by sociopolitical and religious changes including democratisation and Islamisation. Given its geo-strategic importance, the region attracted attention of all major global powers. Therefore, the changes could not take place in isolation. As a result several groups including women groups mushroomed in Central Asia and today in each society they are running campaigns for change; women empowerment and community transformation. These groups are very much part of nation building process even though, several disagreements may exist within each society.

It has to be kept in mind that the case of Central Asia is different in the sense that in the Soviet era, the history of women's emancipation in Central Asia was said to have begun in 1928 with *hujum,* a programme to eliminate the *hijab* (veil) and to liberate women. Though, in reality, the change was under way well before that, says Marfua Tokhtakhodjaeva. In the 1920s one could see the mental shift among the middle class. There were opportunities for studies and a modern way of life. She cites "a portrait from 1915 which showed 'Aisha', a high school student in Ferghana, wearing her hair, a white dress and hat in a completely European style; a group of women are all carrying suitcases as they travel to Tashkent for the 1928 Congress of Women in Central Asia; and a photo from 1929 showing microbiologist Maria Vavilova sitting on a donkey cart during a research trip in *Surkhondarya* province".[39]

During the Soviet era, socialism engulfed the Central Asian region, which brought in egalitarian concepts as equality and female emancipation. The Soviet styled modernisation of entire Central Asia injected through the socialistic principles of secular institutions of education; and governance altered the very outlook of the people but basic socio-cultural fabric of the region did not undergo much change. The campaign for the emancipation of Central Asian Women was inspired by activities and writings of activist like Nadezhda Krupskaya, Klara Zetkin, Inessa Armand and Aleksandra Kollontai. Despite, the best efforts of the government during the Soviet era, religious identities and practices prevailed, though covertly, and patriarchy remained dominant in the personal lives.[40] Post-independence transition to market economy was accompanied by new problems for women's lives, but also gave new opportunities for women to unite, organise and campaign for gender equality and women's NGOs development.

Even though, women's activism is not new to Central Asia, however, it has acquired new dimensions and like India most of the activism in Central Asia is mostly guided by western influence. Since the early years post-independence, laws on groups or organisations have been quite similar throughout Central Asia.[41]

The struggle of women's movements for gender equality and women's rights had its challenges and victories in Central Asia. Women's NGOs have been integrating women's human rights approach and women's rights initiatives at various levels in the last two and a half decades in Kyrgyzstan, Kazakhstan, Tajikistan, and Uzbekistan. The Beijing Platform for Action (BPFA) and CEDAW, formatted women's movement development and gave it a legal angle in the new post-Soviet space, especially when leaders of most of these countries encouraged return of traditionalism. Networking led to strengthening of consolidation among women's groups and movement building. Role of women's NGOs is critical in increasing women's empowerment: economic and political, however, in Central Asia there is continuing problem with national and local implementation of BPFA, CEDAW, MDGs from State and donors sides. Women's NGOs have done tremendous job for increasing women's role and visibility of women's voice in society. In Kyrgyzstan, for example, there is a womans NGOs programme and innovative five year strategy on women's participation in political processes.[42] The women's rights groups are adopting various strategies to engage individual activists or smaller groups to work towards the common cause.[43] The Kyrgyz example is a case in its self as Kyrgyzstan is most democratic in nature due to more American influence, therefore, more women's campaign visible here.

The legal and constitutional provisions and the presence and effectiveness of civil societies vary from country to country. For instance, the 2008 Constitution of Turkmenistan recognises the right of citizens to form associations and the supremacy of international law. The Turkmen Civil Code envisions two legal organisational forms of non-entrepreneurial legal entities: public organisations and foundations. In Turkmenistan civic self-organisation remains extremely low. State financed institutions and organisations provide services in education, healthcare and social work. In Kazakhstan, Women's movement is building equal partnership with state for further engendering of governance at national and local levels.[44]

The NGOs in Central Asia have emerged as a sector for taking care of the issues which are often ignored by the governments. Their roles vary from policy advocacy to intervention for addressing social problems and for sustainable development. Among the significant policy changes, for example, was the inclusion of gender indices in the Perspective Plan of the Kazakhstan Government for 2001-2005 and the Strategic Plan for the Development of up till 2010. To address the problem of domestic violence, the President of Kazakhstan signed a law on domestic violence on 7 December 2009 and a new gender equality law that defines the terms gender, gender equality, sexual discrimination on 10 December 2009.[45]

The Kazakh President Nursultan Nazarbayev, in the Message to the nation, "Strategy Kazakhstan -2050" stressed that, "... women should be actively involved in state and public administration, especially at the local level and in the regions ... in practice to promote gender equality and equal opportunities for women as well as men".[46]

According to Myra Aisina, the curator of the expert group of Nur Otan party[47] ("Support for Women" subgroup) in Kazakhstan, "a woman who copes well both at home and with all life situations, can successfully offer a reasonable solution to problems on any state level".

> <<К примеру, по словам М. Айсиной, в казахстанском Парламенте 24,3 процента - это женщины, в местных представительных органах власти этот показатель составляет 24,6 процента, среди политических госслужащих - 12, а также 280 женщин - акимов городов, сельских округов. Доля прекрасной половины в малом и среднем бизнесе составляет 52 процента, в индивидуальном предпринимательстве - 66. Вклад женщин в ВВП страны - 40 процентов>>

(Kazakh Parliament in 2013 had 24.3 percent women and at the local levels 24.6 percent. There were 12 women among the political state officials and 280 women were *akim*s of cities and rural districts. The proportion of women in small and medium sized businesses accounted for 52 percent and 66 percent in individual entrepreneurship. Apart from this women's contribution to GDP in 2013 was 40 percent)[48] which was quite a lot.

Kazakhstan has not only successfully promulgated gender and development plan but also witnessed the results. For example, "Majority of the total state employees, are women" and there are measure and policy so that women's economic situations do not decline.[49] This was the case even as early as 2005, as literatures suggested that, close to sixty percent of the total state employees were women". Even in the micro loans disbursed under state sponsored programme on micro crediting for the poorest population two-thirds of the recipients were rural women.[50]

In Kazakhstan the NGO sector has experienced significant changes since its early stages of development. The NGOs in the country function in different areas including education, human rights, healthcare, environment, assistance to the disabled, and many others.[51]

In general, women movement in the region saw a rapid growth in the 1990s. However, there has been a decline in the women's movement in the region after reaching the peak in 2000.[52] Reasons are plenty which include from confusion; to constraint on functioning; to funding issues. Few countries allow international funding to women organisations, others do not allow at all. For instance, in Kyrgyzstan most NGOs are funded by West, whereas, in Turkmenistan, mostly, all women organisations and their activities are state funded.[53]

Kyrgyzstan has been relatively better than Tajikistan vis-à-vis women's participation in civil society, despite having similar economies and historical background. In Uzbekistan, during the 1990s, a large numbers of NGOs dealing with women's issues were established. The main reason was that, President Islam Karimov, on 2 March 1995, issued a decree on "Enhancing Women's role in the state and social development of Uzbekistan" and in 1999 specific measures on improving women's status was included in the state programme.[54] These steps spurred women's activities. Earlier, in 1991 there was only one women's NGO, the 'Business Women's Association' (BWA) however, by 2001, had grown to more than fifty NGOs. And most of these women's NGOs or the movements were led by a number of educated and professional women, who resisted the threatened loss of status for women due to the political and economic transitions or transformation. And many of these women turned their knowledge and experience to lead Uzbekistans growing women's NGO and women's movements.[55] And over the years the number had grown even more and due to their extensive grass-root networks.

Civil society groups are instrumental in realising UN Women programmes. Several women movements and self-help groups have found support from UN sponsored programmes in increasing their effectiveness, through sharing knowledge on women's rights and successful advocacy practices. The NGOs are providing support in building effective communication, leadership training and strengthening internal processes and other essential skills to influence political and governance processes.[56]

Women organisations and NGOs have also played a role in the peace-making and peace-building processes particularly in the wake of skirmishes between Kyrgyz and Uzbeks. These ethnic tensions are a threat to the peace and stability of the region. It was because of the women's movement that Kyrgyzstan could be pulled back from the brink. A lot of initiatives by women organisations have ensured women's safety, security, economic and basic rights particularly in Kyrgyzstan, Tajikistan, Uzbekistan and Kazakhstan. In Turkmenistan also women organisations have undertaken several initiatives though, they are in conjunction with the government. In fact, the growth of women's NGOs is one of the most positive achievements in terms of women's political participation in Uzbekistan. These women's NGOs provide assistance in areas central to women's economic, social and political status including business and vocational training, legal literacy, psychological counseling, health and domestic violence programmes, assistance to women with disabilities, etc.[57]

As mentioned earlier in Chapter 2, some women in Uzbekistan join social and economic saving networks such as *gaps* and *chernaya kassa.* Social networks like these represent a collective movement and action against economic dependency of women on men and the state micro-loan bank system. They function, as a mechanism for livelihood resilience and social and economic empowerment, in the post-socialist economy, in some villages. These are actually women's spaces of empowerment and these do not require external donor interventions and have been able to empower women for social justice, knowledge, redistribution of resources, and conflict resolution in ways that are vital to community development.[58] This is true in case of Kazakhstan and Kyrgyzstan and Uzbekistan and many other countries in the region.[59]

Conventions like CEDAW and UN initiatives like UNIFEM have laid down the foundation for gender equality. For instance, due to the international conventions and the women's movements within the country, Kyrgyzstan introduced a new Article 13 in the Constitution ensuring equal rights, freedom and opportunities to men and women in October 2007. While implementing the provisions of Article, the Election Code was revamped and a gender quota was introduced in the electoral lists of political parties that take part in the parliamentary elections[60] and this made way for increased female representation and has already been mentioned in Chapter 3. However, it is important to mention that several political parties have also contributed to women's cause and campaigns. The Women's Democratic Party (Formed in 1994, renamed as the Democratic Party of Women and Youth in 2005), *El Muras* (Peoples Heritage 2002), Agreement (2002) and the Communist Party of Kyrgyzstan (2000) and the Party of Women *El-Ene* (2000), which literally means mother of the people, are glaring examples of women's movements and political participation in Kyrgyzstan. The Women's Democratic Party won 2 seats in the Legislative Assembly during the parliamentary elections of 2000. Its leader Toktokan Borombaeva is an ardent advocate of gender equality. Two of the laws, namely, the 'Law on State Guarantees on Equal Rights and Opportunities of Men and Women', and the 'Law on Social and Legal Protection against Family Violence', could see the light of the day due to strong advocacy by these elected MPs. Finally Kyrgyz parliament approved these laws in 2003.[61]

Kyrgyz MP and Minister, Ms. Ainuru Altybaeva, together along with several NGOs, as part of the UN Secretary-Generals Campaign "UNiTE to End Violence against Women and Girls", organised a 'Bicycle March' in Bishkek with the participation of nearly 200 cyclists from across Kyrgyzstan. People from various walks of life came together to garner support to the call from the deputies of the *Jogorku Kenesh* (the Parliament), to students, fathers with their daughters, visitors like the Author (who was in Bishkek, then) in support of the Bill 155, which increases penalties for kidnapping a woman to marry against her will. Several football matches were also organised in support of non-violence as a follow on action (Image: 4.3).[62]

Image 4.3

Author at the Cycle March in support of article 155

Author with Minister, Ainuru Altybaeva, Kyrgyzstan and with Director of an NGO, Bishkek, Kyrgyzstan

In Central Asia, the civil societies working on gender equality are generally run through aids received from various multilateral organisations including the United Nations Children's Fund (UNICEF), the World Bank, and United Nations Development Programme (UNDP) and the Organisation for Security and Cooperation in Europe (OSCE). These international fundings helps the civil society movement to sustain themselves. This has in turn helped civil society to organise and bring about a positive change in the mindset of society in general and policy-makers in particular.[63]

In Kyrgyzstan, when Kurmanbek Bakiev was in power, there was an upsurge in direct action taken by informal groups within Kyrgyzstans society to promote the interests of their members. Many of these groups are not registered as non-governmental organisations and do not receive donor funding. However, they clearly fall within International NGO Training and Research Centres (INTRAC) working definition of civil society: "associations that exist outside of the state or market which maintain a degree of autonomy and independence and have the potential to provide alternative views, policies and actions to those promoted by the state and market".[64]

All across the former Soviet Union, and much of Eurasia, people celebrate every March 8th, the International Women's Day, a day to remember the accomplishments of women. Originally, this had started in 1909 during the women's suffrage and workers rights movements, the holiday was also promoted by the Soviets, and has continued in the post-independence as well and has become a popular day for congratulatory card giving and workplace parties. Even though few feminists are of the opinion that celebrating one day in a year for women doesn't address the way women are still pushed aside in other areas.[65] Many others are of the opinion that even though, it is just tokenism, atleast one day in a year women are getting appreciation for all their efforts.

Once drawn into the state sector in great numbers through political quotas during Soviet times, women's participation in politics has drastically declined since independence as men have come to dominate government positions. As a result of this development there is some sort of channelisation of women's political expression into NGOs and has resulted in the NGOisation of women's activism in the region. For example, in Kazakhstan due to the decline in the political representation and increase in violence against women and unemployment, several Women NGOs were formed.[66]

Kyrgyzstan and Kazakhstan have been influenced by the thought process of the Western funding agencies and even advocate promotion of liberal values such as the rights of sexual minorities and paid sex workers. On the contrary, WNGOs in Uzbekistan are still evolving.[67] In the last two and a half decades, most of the WNGOs have focused on almost common issues including gender politics; gender and media; the integration of gender research into science and education; and future directions for gender studies in the region.[68]

As mentioned earlier, both Kazakhstan and Kyrgyzstan are relatively more reform oriented than other Central Asian countries. Both have relatively independent media and multiparty political system. Several legislations and constitutional changes have helped NGOs and civil society to grow freely in the past decade or so.[69] Kazakhstan ratified a Presidential decree which states that this function is a domain for "political parties, local authorities, communities, labour unions, religious communities".[70] According to human rights expert Anki Wetterhall, the wife of the Swedish ambassador to Kazakhstan, "NGOs are playing a constructive and important role in helping foster the development of civil society in Kazakhstan".[71]

Turkmenistan on the other hand has negligible presence of NGOs, but for this Turkmenistan has reasons for it. Civil society in Turkmenistan is developing with a foundation rooted in centurys old collective traditions and distinctive Turkmen characteristics. One characteristic is that the people often do not create formal public associations as a legal form, but they collectively solve various socio-economic issues. The first "Law on Public Associations (Law on PAs) of Turkmenistan" was adopted on November 12, 1991, only 17 days after Turkmenistan declared independence on October 27, 1991.[72] And according to the Permanent Representative of Turkmenistan to the UN, Aksoltan Ataeva, "Women of Turkmenistan have played an active role in its economic development, notably in the realm of education and healthcare. The number of small businesses run by women was also growing".[73]

The ongoing civic engagements and volunteerism in the government funded organisations have the potential to mature into a 'civil society'. An officially recognised NGO and a private group have in 2009 attained Government Owned NGO (GONGO) status.[74] However, for instance as in case of Women organisations in Turkmenistan which are government funded, it is very less likely that they mature or fit into a category of 'civil society'. Eventhough, they are doing good work, the case was more or less similar even in November 2012, as it was evident during Author's interaction and interview session with the director/chairperson of 'Union of Women' in Ashgabat (Image: 4.4).[75]

Image 4.4
Author with Director/Chairperson,
'Union of Women', Ashgabat, Turkmenistan

Organisations and NGOs Working for Women's Issues

In contemporary Central Asia, considerably large numbers of NGOs are working on women issues having women workers/staff structures. NGOs have provided women platforms to voice their opinions and fight the odds arising due to the revival of traditionalism. In several instances these NGOs have been instrumental in implementing and monitoring international agreements. And many women have played very important role in women's campaign for change. (See, Appendix IV).

It is difficult to give the exact number of NGOs in each country. However, as per USAID a 2009, report, "In 2007, there were more than 15,000 registered non-profit organisations in Kyrgyzstan. The number of NGOs registered in Tajikistan is considerably fewer at only 2,300 in 2009. This, however, is a considerable increase from only 1,700 registered NGOs in 2008".[76]

Since 2000, the NGOs in Uzbekistan have been active through seminars and training programmes in educating legal professionals and also in conducting legal literacy programmes that train rural residents at community levels and setting up hot lines and providing free legal aid. However, such work has been neither systematic nor coordinated and has largely been limited in scope and outreach.[77] Women's NGOs are not protected by the government legally as well as materially, therefore, majority of NGOs face challenges in contributing singnificantly in the improvement of status of women. There are many women's organisation who have made a considerable change, few amongst them are being mentioned below:

The Women in Development (WID) Bureau is a quasi-governmental body which gets funding from the United Nations Development Program (UNDP). This body is mandated to encourage Tajik women's to get involved in civil society; support local NGOs in conceptualising and delivering women projects and provide an interface between local and international organisations. One of the modes of delivery is to provide credit to the women entrepreneurs to set up small enterprises. In this way, Association for Women's Rights in Development (AWID) has successfully helped several local NGOs to encourage women entrepreneurs.[78]

KARAT is a regional coalition of organisations and individuals that focuses on women's human rights and promotes gendered economic and social justice for the Central and Eastern European and Central Asian countries. Women and girls often miss out on the benefits of development because of politics, tradition, culture, patriarchy and violence. KARAT challenges women's exclusion by campaigning for women's leadership at all levels and by promoting their full political participation through campaign.[79]

The first NGOs that emergerd in the mid-1990s was by and for women. **Centre for Gender Studies** and **Feminist League** appeared more or less at the same time. Svetlana Shakirova was the Director, of Center for Gender Studies (NGO) (Almaty) from 1998-2011 and the President of Feminist League (NGO) (Almaty), from 1995- 2001. In fact, Svetlana Shakirova, who headed the Centre for Gender Studies, has played a pivotal role in creating awareness about gender issues and written a lot on women's issues. She feels that, gender is an issue in Kazakhstan, be it with respect to monument dedicated to women (in Almaty) or even in universities, where women are well represented in numeric terms, but seldom lead despite gender research being-on for close two decades. And with regard to gender related research in Kazakhstan, she opines, that the gender related research developed in Kazakhstan primarily for the purpose of providing and maintaining data and preparing annual report on the issues of women, mainly for the government.[80]

Feminist League is one of the women organisations in Kazakhstan with the primarily aim to promote equality of women and men in all spheres of life: economic, political, social, cultural and within the home. Among the prominent activities of the Feminist League are research and publication of reports on women's issues in Kazakhstan, informational support to women's NGOs and mass media, monitoring gender related legislation of the Republic of Kazakhstan, education on women's issues, informational electronic network FemLine and so on.[81] Under Svetlana Shakirovas leadership, the Feminist League did some phenomenal work related to women, sometime in collaboration with other agencies like UN, for example, for United Nations Secretary-Generals in-depth study on violence against women and Republic of Kazakhstan's Campaign on change of the criminal legislation.[82]

Forum of Women's NGOs of Kyrgyzstan (FWNGO) was set up in 1994. It was created to provide assistance to women's NGOs via development of a network as well as opportunities for mutual cooperation. On the 4th April 1996 the Forum was registered in the Ministry of Justice as a non-profit non-governmental organisation. It was re-registered on 10th October 2005 (required according to the new law on civil society organisations) in the Ministry of Justice of the Kyrgyz Republic. In 2005, FWNGO was given a special consultative status with United Nations Economic and Social Council (UN ECOSOC). Today the Forum of Women's NGOs of Kyrgyzstan unites more than 85 NGOs in Kyrgyzstan with various missions. It is a founder and regional coordinator of the Central Asian Forum of Women's NGOs and a member of Association for Women's Rights in Development (AWID), The Asia Pacific Women's Watch (APWW), Asia Pacific Forum on Women, Law and Development (APWLD), The Asia Pacific Research Network (APRN), Karat Coalition monitors network. The forums basic mission is the consolidation and strengthening of women's movement towards gender equality and women's empowerment, building partnership towards women's equality, increase of women's participation in public life through their organisations and NGOs. As part of this mission the Forum has contributed to women organisations capacity development, organisation of active networking in Kyrgyzstan and in Central Asia, promotion of integration of women's activism into the global trend of women's movement.[83]

The League of Women Lawyers of Republic of Tajikistan: The League of Women Lawyers of Republic of Tajikistan is a public organisation and the main objectives of the organisation are: to raise of legal awareness of citizens of the Republic of Tajikistan; the protection of civil, social, economic and cultural rights of women of Tajikistan; securing gender equality, improving women lawyers status in society, as well as assistance in training of legal personnel among young girls. League is designed to implement and protect the civil and social rights and freedoms of citizens, participate in the creation of a sovereign, democratic, rule of law and secular state of Tajikistan by coordinating and implementing programmes and projects aimed at achieving social development, equal access to opportunities for men and women in all spheres of activity, reduction of violence against women and providing assistance to vulnerable strata of population and risk groups in Tajikistan.[84]

The **Committee of Women of Uzbekistan** is a public organisation that unites women of Uzbekistan regardless of nationality, occupation, religion, and education on voluntary basis though. Committee actively works with other public groups, foundations for movements such as *Soglom avlod uchun (Healthy generation)* and on number of other programmes carried out nationwide. A special attention is paid towards promoting business activity amongst women. There is also a programme under way for supporting women in farming. The women's committee also successfully cooperates with organisations abroad and it is a member of Central Asian congress of women and International alliance of CIS countries.[85]

The Business Women's Association or *Tadbirkor Ayol* (Business Women) (BWA) is an NGO in Uzbekistan which over the years has helped women in many ways, right from imparting vocational education to young and new women who wanted to do small businesses, taught them basics of market economy, marketing, accounting and taxation, to embroidery and weaving. They also teach chain stitch and hand embroidery and basket weaving. The associations main goal is to help women achieve economic independence in unstable economic conditions. The centre for handicrafts, *Khamsa* which, is in Tashkent offers a great deal of support to craftswomen. In cooperation with representatives of German Trade Palace, the association offers courses in techniques of carpet weaving and gold embroidery in several Uzbek provinces. With the help of international organisations like United Nations Educational, Scientific and Cultural Organisation (UNESCO), Swiss Agency for Development and Cooperation (SDC)[86], etc., offer enormous aid to women wishing to work in craft production and to increase the income and social status of women and to revive traditional crafts. The Association of Business Women of Uzbekistan with the help from Jewellery school in Hanau (Germany), a jewellery school was established in Tashkent for young girls. This process has the support of the government, international organisations and women's organisations that are dedicated to help women adapt to new economic realities.[87]

The Women's Resource Centre, Tashkent, was organised as an informal group at the beginning of 1994, and later on got registered as a public society in 1995. The centers main activities focus on health, ecology and sustainable development, cultural development, human rights and the status of women.[88] The organisation also aims at strengthening women's independence, their spiritual, intellectual and professional potential. It encourages women's active attention to the realities of social life and supports initiatives to broaden and deepen women's awareness of their role in social, economic and political life and of their rights and opportunities to attain genuine equality in all spheres of life. There are various other NGOs as well, like the **women's society (merci)** which deals with educational programmes, reproductive health and legal literacy, the Centre of Confidence *Sabr*- has been honoured for its contribution to democracy and development of civic society.[89] And most of these NGOs, have been committed to enhancing the political and legal status of women.

Rural Women's NGO "Alga" exists since 1995. Mission of the organisation is to improve rural women's status and standards of living through stimulation of women's awareness of realities and develop their capabilities for self-actualisation, strengthening of the participation of rural women in development efforts and for the advocacy of their rights, development of empowering strategies and structures which promote the growth of economic and social status of women and communities.[90]

Image 4.5

Team of NGO "Alga"

Source: http://forumofwomenngos.kg

In Turkmenistan, the NGO ***Keik Okara*** is an officially registered NGO in Ashgabat headed by its director Roza Kuzakhmemedova. *Keik Okara* helps vulnerable categories of population under the social and economic conditions in Turkmenistan. It also provides legal and psychological counseling to individuals in need. A lawyer and a counsilor maintain offices where they meet people by appointment in privacy. Since these needs are sporadic, more of the organisations space is devoted to English and French classes in addition to community-building efforts. It established a Family Support Center and later on its activities expanded into areas of social, economic, psychological, and legal issues.[91]

Association of Parents of Disabled Children (ARDI) is an organisation in Kazakhstan that runs a daycare center for children with disabilities. The daycare center provides a place where the children can attend school, learn computer and English skills, as well as develop their creative talents in painting, sculpture, and theater.[92]

Institute of Equal Rights and Equal Opportunities of Kazakhstan works on programmes for social and psychological well-being of young girls and women. They also assist young women to find employment. They have a specific project on the issue of suicides amongst young girls. The organisation works in coordination with legal bodies, psychologists and social work specialists. They get some subsidy for this project from the government as well. So far they have saved many lives and assist in their well-being (Image: 4.6).[93]

In recent times civil society utilises the international funding for the promotion of economic reforms instead of the expansion of the society. As a result, NGOs in Central Asia rarely focus on political activity and policy

Image 4.6

Author with Bagayeva Katerina, Director of programmes for social and sychological well-being, Institute of equal rights and equal opportunities, Kazakhstan, Almaty, Kazakhstan

reform and instead focus on education, economic development, health, and awareness building. For example, the Aral Sea area has the Regional Environmental Center for Central Asia, supported by various international funding agencies and the Centre, that in turn implements NGO development, environmental management and education projects.[94]

It is evident that the NGOs and other organisations working for women's empowerment have done some significant work in creating awareness and building consensus with regards to education, employment and in some cases even politics as in case of India and Kyrgyzstan, though there are areas and issues which NGOs and other organisations have not made much headway. Reason being, things sometimes have not been really smooth for NGOs or other Organisations. They had to face and are still facing several challenges. These challenges are mostly indirect, though they hamper both directly and indirectly in the functioning and activities; for achieving goals and targets. For example, all the countries under study are signatory to the international convention, 'Beijing Platform for Action', which clearly mentions that, "Empowerment of women is a critical factor in the eradication of poverty and Equality in decision-making is essential for the empowerment of women; and Women's rights are human rights".[95] However, like many others, these countries also so far have not been able to tackle several critical issues related to women; Violence against women, Alcoholism etc.

Violence against women is one such obstacle or challenge to women's campaign for change as violence prevents the achievement of the objectives of equality, development and peace. Violence against women both violates and impairs or nullifies the enjoyment by women of their human rights and fundamental freedoms.[96] In India, violence in all its form, from domestic violence to sexual assault, rapes, human trafficking etc. is an issue for any government or organisation. These evils of society need to be dealt with, so as to make the environment conducive enough for not only women but for organisations to engage with women and work for their betterment. Though, there has been some good result due to women's campaign and stringent laws, specially, with regard to dowry deaths, and domestic violence, however, rape, and many other act of violence are still prevalent. Violence in Central Asia has yet another local association for example, bride kidnapping (mostly in Kyrgyzstan). Despite stringent law, it is still being practiced, sometime in the name of custom.

Violence comes in different forms and dimensions. the global or trans-regional dimension further pose challenge; for example, human trafficking and sometime women are used in drug and arms trafficking as well, which are local yet present a disturbing picture. And to these common but global issues, which both Indian and Central Asian women face, so far the governments, NGOs and women organisations have not been able to find permanent solution. In cases such as these which are not only local, national, trans-national, but regional and may turn out to be trans-regional as well, are very difficult to handle or manage as not one or two but many countries, are involved, hampering the work of organisations and poses new challenge for women's campaign for change and is also very discouraging and at times very frustrating for agencies.

In Central Asia, for example, human trafficking is one menace which neither the state nor women's organisations have been able to successfully deal with. In July of 2010, Turkmenistan government outlawed all forms of human trafficking through Article 129 of its criminal code.[97] Kazakhstan held from 24 to 28 February 2014, an operational and preventive action 'STOP traffic', in which measures were taken to prevent, combat, detect and solve crimes related to human trafficking.[98]

According to one report by Women Support Center, there were at least 11, 800 cases of forced abduction of girls every year in Kyrgyzstan, with more than 2000 girls being subject to rapes. Only one out of 700 cases is pursued indicating ineffective state control and occasional complicity of law enforcement and justice sector personnel in these crimes. Only one in 1,500 cases of abduction results in a judicial sentence.[99] Situation in India also, is more or less the same.

Even though, there is a law that prohibits trafficking in persons for all purposes, the practice remains a considerable problem. In case of Central Asia, internal trafficking is also a problem. Traffickers mostly targeted girls and young women in their teens and twenties for sexual exploitation.[100] NGOs on their part cooperate and assist the government officials in coordinating the assistance for trafficking victims. Though few NGOs reported a continued increase in the identification of victims, possibly reflecting greater awareness of the problem, however, the problem still persists.

There are several other impediments like problem of alcoholism. In India, alcoholism has been at the center of many violent activities. Men become alcoholics and then the salary goes for buying alcohol, thereby no income, leading to problems in the family, which further leads to wife beatings etc. The *Gulabi Gang*, and several other women organisations have been dealing with this issue. Alcoholism is also an issue in CARs and the government and women organisations have a tough time sorting out this problem.

To add on to these, there are several administrative issues like bribing and corruption, which force organisations to either abruptly leave the projects/ programmes or the entire thing gets delayed and thereby loses its importance or significance. As most of the time the programmes/projects are for particular time, funding becomes an issue.

So, for 'women's campaign for change' to be fully effective, proper implementation, monitoring and more funding are required. And above all, various stakeholders should work together towards the larger goal of women's overall empowerment including social, economic, political and cultural. Each organisation and institution working for women and women's issues along with government, should take proactive measures to ensure women's greater participation in social and political affairs including assuming leadership. Though, there have been some good and remarkable results, much more is needed.

IMAGES OF FIELD TRIP, CENTRAL ASIA OCTOBER 17 –14 DECEMBER, 2012

Image-1

(a) *(b)*

Author at the (a) Ministry of health, Astana (b) Ministry of Women, Labour & Social Development, Astana, Kazakhstan

Image-2

Author with Professor and students during a lecture by the Author at the Eurasian National University, Astana, Kazakhstan

Image-3

(a) *(b)*

(a) The Ministry of Economy and Trade of the Republic of Kazakhstan, Astana (b) Author with Ms. Akmaral Kainazarova very famous Kazakh National Artist of Kathak dance form in Almaty, Kazakhstan

Image-4

Author interacting with Students and Professors at The Al-Farabi National State University, Almaty, Kazakhstan

Image-5

Women selling and buying fruits at a shop in Almaty. Women making hot pancakes in Bazar *outside university, Almaty, Kazakhstan*

Image-6

Author with Bugayeva Katorina, Director of programs for social and psychological well-being, Institute of equal rights and equal opportunities, Kazakhstan, Almaty, Kazakhstan

Image-7

Author with students in the KAZGU hostel, Almaty, Kazakhstan

Image-8

Author with professors and other delegates for the UN conference at Al-Farabi National State University, Almaty, Kazakhstan

Image-9

(a) (b)

(a) Author with research scholars at the Eurasian National University, Astana, Kazakhstan (b) Author with Tatyana Zhdanova, Vice-president and Director of Foreign Economic Relations Department, Chamber of Commerce and Industry of the Republic of Kazakhstan; Director of Export Credit Insurance Corporation "Kazexport Garant", Almaty, Kazakhstan

Image-10

Kazakh students in tradional/National Dress, Almaty, Kazakhstan

Image-11

Author with Professor Roza Sarabayeva at KISI, Almaty, Kazakhstan

Author with professors at State University, Chimkent, Kazakhstan

Image-11

Author with Nazym Shedenova, Director, Center of Gender Studies Department of Philosophy and Politology. KAZNU. Almaty, Kazakhstan

Image-12

Author with Minister, Ainuru Altybaeva, Bishkek, Kyrgyzstan

Author at the Cycle March in support of article 155 with Director of an NGO, Bishkek, Kyrgyzstan

Image-13

(a) *(b)* *(c)*

(a) Author with Prof. and a newly wedded couple at, Kyrgyzstan (b) with a professor at Osh State University, Osh, Kyrgyzstan (c) Author with students at Ata-Beyit, Kyrgyzstan.

Image-14

(a) *(b)*

(c)

(a) woman at a chaikhana *on the way which the Author visited while travelling from Bishkek to Osh (b) woman in Osh* Bazzar; *(c) Author with Kyrgyz friend and her family at a* Kitti/Gaps *in Kyrgyz* Mohalla, *Osh.*

(d)

(d) Students from Jalalabad at Osh, Kyrgyzstan.

Image-15

(a) Author with Director, Centre for Gender Studies, Osh State University (b) With the director of NGO. (c) With Students at the centre for foriegn languages. (d) With the Director for India's study centre, Mr.Omorkulov Bakyt Kutubekovich, Faculty of Russian and Philology. (e) with Dean and Osh State University, Osh, Kyrgyzstan

Image-16

(a) Author with Director/chairperson, Maysa Meredovna azmuhammedova 'Union of Women'. Ashgabat, Turkmenistan (b) The author with Director, Institute of History, Academy of Sciences, Ashgabat, Turkmenistan

Image-17

(a) Author with professors at Turkmen National University, Ashgabat, Turkmenistan (b) Author with Director and professors National Institute of Democracy and Human Rights. Ashgabat, Turkmenistan

Image-18

Author in Russian Bazar *in Ashgabat, Turkmenistan Author with university students in Ashgabat, Turkmenistan*

Image-19

(a) Author with professors of Hindi at State University, Dushanbe, Tajikistan
(b) Author with The director and Research Consultant at the outskirt of Dushanbe Tajikistan

Image-20

(a) Author with members/students, (b) with the director, at Islamic Revival Party's office Dushanbe, Tajikistan Author with journalist Dushanbe. And the Prevent Domestic Violence (PDV) office, Tajikistan

Image-21

A Tajik woman making lipyoshka *in* Tandoor *at her house, Dushanbe, Tajikistan*

Author with the landlady's family, Dushanbe, Tajikistan

Women in traditional day- to-day attire, Dushanbe, Tajikistan

Image-22

Author at Barak-khan madrassah, *Tashkent, Uzbekistan*

Image-23

Author with bunch of students at Registan, *Samarkand, Uzbekistan*

Image-24

At the statue of Ex Indian PM Sri Lal Bahadur Shastri in Tashkent. Uzbekistan

Image-25

Image-26

(a) Author with a student who studies in Russian School and also learns English at Samarkand, Uzbekistan (b) Author with a successful business woman in Tashkent, Uzbekistan

Image-27

(a) The famous Registan, *Samarkand, Uzbekistan*
(b) Women at Samarkand Bazar, Uzbekistan

FIELD TRIP OBSERVATIONS AND HIGHLIGHT OF THE RESEARCH

As mentioned in the Introduction, the Author visited Central Asia-Kazakhstan, Kyrgyzstan, Tajikistan, Turkmenistan and Uzbekistan, between 17th October to 14 December 2012 for field research and a brief visit to Tajikistan and Kazakhstan in August 2014. As part of field work, the author visited Ministries, universities, institutes, head offices of organisations, libraries, pilgrimage sites, museums, archeological sites, Zilyoni bazaars, Tolkuchka bazaar, metro stations etc. and conducted interviews, interactions and discussion sessions, on "Women in Central Asian Society". In India, visits took place to as many cities possible during research, however, due to non-availability of funds, visits in India were not planned for the sake of Research rather, mostly, the conferences and workshops visits were also used for the purpose of research. Though, it was kept in mind that same methodology; similar questionnaire and list of questions were used as in case of Central Asia.

Data Sources and Methods of Data Collection

Key methods of information/data collection were; documents reviews, interviews, group interviews, group discussions, interactions, observations, and email correspondence.

During data and information collections, research ethics were duly followed. Prior appointments were taken, so as to have adequate time to talk and discuss things comfortably; keeping in mind the sensitivity of the theme particularly with reference to Central Asia (in Central Asia, people love to talk about culture, sports, environment, health, education, but when it comes to issues like politics, women and politics, everyone is not comfortable talking about it), the questions were at times asked indirectly. In comparison people in India were more forthcoming.

In Central Asia, the main thing, that was kept in mind during interviews, interactions and discussions was not to hurt their sentiment in any way. All interaction began with general introduction about India and Indian culture. Then, to know their understanding or knowledge about India; questions were asked regarding what they liked about India or if they would like to share something about their own culture, tradition, family, their occupation etc. when they were comfortable enough, only then questions pertaining to politics was discussed. In India, people were more than willing to discuss such matters; everyone had something to talk about politics and women's issues.

Questions

A questionnaire and a list of questions were prepared beforehand. The questions mainly revolved around women and their role in society. Questions pertaining to education, employment and other economic activities; what needs to be improved; in education, economic status, social security etc.? What do they think about the status of women post 1991? - In case of Central Asia, this question was modified to: what do they think about the status of women in soviet and post-Soviet society? - Improved, deteriorated, or not much change? Do they have more options and opportunity now? What do they think about themselves in terms of their role, importance in society? How can women contribute to the progress of nation? Is the government doing enough for women's welfare? - Their opinions, about women's role in politics. Do they think women can make a difference if they become ministers or in charge of certain office of importance? For details see appendix V.

Efforts were made to make sure that every age group, gender and profession was covered and people from all walks of life were interviewed, or interacted with. If not same strength in each category, at least some number from each category. Even discussions, in some cases group discussions were held: specially with college students; young and old women in markets and Bazaar's, library, museums, cinema halls, family get-together, *chaikhana*'s, bus, bus stand, metro, metro stations, polyclinics, parks, pilgrimage sites, etc. Even people from non-active employment (part time business; small business; self-employment) were part of this research, though, the participants were mostly women as men did not show much interest in talking about women.

Since, there was no uniformity in the time spent in each country including India; in terms of number of people interacted with or people interviewed in each place; no quantative data analysis has been done, rather the analysis is basically based on the review of all data, materials and information collected and through personal observations. The overall analysis and observations has been duly incorporated in the main text itself with footnoting. Some comments and special observation which were not directly related to the main research, but thought to be important in understanding the main issue have also been mentioned though, separately or in footnote.

Few Observations

It was observed that: in case of Central Asia, while social and cultural issues were of greater concern to both men and women, political issues took a back seat. However, more men were interested in political issues as compared to women. A greater proportion of women compared to men felt that disintegration had negatively impacted wages, health and security. Mostly, felt that the condition of women had either deteriorated or may be remained the same; very few, that too mostly men felt that the economic condition of women had improved since disintegration. Though, mostly, both men and women were of the opinion that there are many options and opportunities regarding career, employment, but at the same time the access is limited and only few are able to make use of such opportunities. However, almost everyone whom the author met or interacted in some way, were of the opinion that the disintegration did impact the status of women in society and off course women's movement as well. Discussion on politics, especially about women in politics is an alien subject or still a taboo. The Author found that the respondents, young and old, men and women alike were reluctant to discuss these issues and were very apprehensive about sharing their views regarding politics and women in politics and even if they shared they mostly said, politics is man's business, women should take care of family and home; if women will do politics then what will men do?; politics is not good for women as it consists of bad things like fraud, bribe, corruption and sometime also involves violence which, women cannot and should not do.

In case of India, all issues including politics was not only discussed but at times well-argued as well by both men and women. Of all the questions asked, majority of people, both men and women were of the opinion, that women were not playing an effective role in politics, which they are capable of. Only a few men and women thought that women were better than men, that is, they had a more balanced perspective, were more sincere and honest and were better decision makers than men. Very few and that too only women were of the opinion that participation of women in politics had increased to some level, and is good sign for Indian politics. While few, largely men were of the opinion that, women organisations were the most effective institution in improving the political participation of women; while few men and women were of the opinion that the government, political parties and women's organisations were all equally effective or non- effective.

Majority of women in India and Central Asia, whom the author interacted or interviewed, were of the opinion that the government was not doing enough to promote women's participation in all walks of life, however, there were few women who felt that the government was making efforts, even though, so far has not really succeeded. Amongst men, quite a number of them agreed that actually the government was not doing enough for women and even though women have more options and opportunities today, the respect and dignity for them in society have decreased.

Regarding education and employment mostly, in Central Asia were of the opinion that education and skill development amongst women has decreased considerably. Reasons are plenty, for example, due to no guarantee of employment, women start looking for jobs during college or sometime even immediately after schools. Also, women want to marry and settle down in life early, may be anytime after 18 years. Though, many young women do go for short vocational, diploma courses specially, in Computer application or English language. Also, worth noting is that many women preferred to work at two three places so as to earn more. And in case of India, the number of skilled women has increased considerably, as more and more women are moving out of home for higher education and pursuing vocational training etc. resulting in more women joining the labour force.

All the experiences, interactions, discussions and interviews that the author had, were very fruitful, informative, important, valuable and enriching for the research.

Few of such experience of Central Asia are being mentioned here

In all these countries, economy and issues relating to employment are the two main issues of concern, whereas, political issues and conflicts are the top non-economy related issues, which people do not shy away from talking about. In fact, people in few of these countries admitted the shortcomings of the state very openly.

Amongst the youth, in case of Central Asia, males were more vocal except in Kazakhstan and Kyrgyzstan, where the situation was opposite. Here mostly girls were vocal and very confident about their thought, responsibilities and also were conscious of their rights.

Two different but unique experiences worth a mention; is in Uzbekistan and Tajikistan, where, most of the interactions were unplanned and random. However, in both these countries the youth and adults male were very confident in terms of the development of the country and about leadership, governance, politics etc. however, women were confident and interested in issues which were of immediate concern to them like kids, education; kindergarten fee, facilities and what kids are taught there or things like 'today's young girls are more interested in clothes, style, fashion etc., and less concerned about etiquette's and manners and household and family responsibility'.

In Kazakhstan, Almaty was the place where author spent maximum time and got to see, observe, experience and explore the maximum. Visits to universities, Institutes and women organisations offices etc. all were very enriching. All interactions were also very helpful and experience of its kind. For example, Department of Philosophy and Politology on October, 22, 2012. The meeting was organised by Nazym Shedenova, Director, Centre of Gender Studies. See Image: 11c&d. The main points that emerged out of the interaction and discussion was that, "there is a new trend to understand the gender identity/issues; may be, due to inroad of western literature, interactions with western feminists etc. However, in general they opined that, 'women in Kazakhstan have had a very liberal mindset throughout its history' as there are folk songs and oral stories regarding games such as 'catch the girl' and images portraying; and narrations of women riding horses etc.".

Few other group discussions that was conducted with elderly women in Almaty, Astana and Chimkent were of the view that, "women enjoyed considerable high status in society during soviet times, at least all women had work and pay. Over the years post-independence the status of women has declined and today it is for majority of the population about sustaining themselves, their family and children's education etc., as now most of the social services have been done away with. However, women do have more options regarding work". They were sort of lamenting about "the future of youngsters and dilution of their culture and tradition".

In Bishkek, Kyrgyzstan, the author participated in the march which was being conducted as part of the UN Secretary-General Campaign "UNiTE to End Violence against Women and Girls". The first interview was during this event, with M P, Ainuru Altybaeva. She is a great advocator of women's issues, and has taken several initiatives with regard to women's issues. She was of the opinion that, the government is not doing enough for the well-being and safety and security of women and that is why she being a MP along with several other organisations are taking such initiatives like this 'March', so as to create awareness amongst the general public and somehow garner support to put pressure on the government to look into the issue of violence against women. That particular day she had inaugurated the 'bicycle march' that took place. For this event close to 200 cyclists from across Kyrgyzstan participated. See, Image: 12. People from various walks of life came together, to garner support to the call 'from the deputies of the Jogorku Kenesh' (the Parliament). Students, fathers with their daughters, activists and visitors like the Author (who was in Bishkek, then) came to the 'March' in support of the Bill 155 (which increases penalties for kidnapping a woman to marry against her will- 'Bride-Kidnapping' is very common in Kyrgyzstan). Several football matches were also organised in support of non-violence as a follow-on action.

There were also interactions with Ms. Alymkulova- Director, Women Support Centre and Red Crescent Society, which provides assistance to vulnerable women; Director, SEZIM Crisis Centre (1998), which works on the issue of 'bride kidnapping'. They all shared their concerns about the safety and security of women and women's issues.

Osh in Kyrgyzstan, was the next destination which, Author reached by road. Osh was altogether a new experience. Here the Author got the feel of the slow, 'take it easy' kind of place. The mixture of, both; the traditional and the modern, the rural yet urban outlook, the rusty and the sophisticated feel. Lot of interactions happened in Osh through visits to *mohallas*, monuments, museums, *Chaikhanas and Gaps*. The Author also attended a conference at the Institute of Gender Study and interacted with Faculty, Research scholars and staff. The author also visited the Osh University and met the dean. She visited the centre for foreign languages and had discussion with students and Faculty Dr. Gulzada Bilbaeva, Asstt. Prof. Russian Language at the Faculty of Russian and Philology and Prof. Omorkulov Bakyt Kutubekovich, the Director of the Centre for Indian Studies at the Faculty of Russian and Philology. See image: 15. The highlight of Osh was that, people in Osh are moderately religious and traditionally rooted, where, most marriages, at least a dozen of whom the Author met, were as a result of 'bride kidnapping' or 'arranged bride kidnapping'. Mostly, now as single mother, handling everything on their own, however, full of confidence of doing things very well. Common issues of concern, was education and marriage of children. Women were also engaged in the 'Committee' system; something similar to the practice in India ('Committee'-where each member of the Committee invests small/agreed amount every month and then each month somebody would get that collected amount either through lottery or according to the need).

The author also had the opportunity to deliver several lectures for the undergrad students in the Centre for Indian Studies in the department which turned out to be very enriching, as, there were lots of discussions regarding many important issues. In fact, the students were very confident and clear about the role 'they think, they can play' for the progress of society and development of their country. They were very conscious of the image of their country for example, one student pursuing medicine told the Author, "there are a lot of newspapers and journals and you might come across lot of literature which put the country in bad light. Please make sure you only write good things about my country". Youth here, sounded very ambitious and aspired to do something good for themselves, society and the country.

Another very striking feature to be noted is that in every discussion and interaction sessions, most of the people here aspired to visit America at some point of their life. And, visit India to see Taj Mahal and meet Bollywood Actors. They were of the impression that, the Author must have met most of them as she is an Indian.

Next destination, the Author travelled to was Dushanbe, Tajikistan by road. The Author had the 'at-home' feeling, as she stayed with a family in Dushanbe and the experience was amazing. The interview in Dushanbe was with Dr. Sofia R. Kasymova, Sociologist, Gender Education Center, and Prof. G.M. Maitdinova, Department of General History, Russian-Tajik (Slavic) University (RTSU) Dushanbe. They all shared vital information about the changing role and status of women in Tajikistan. In fact all the discussions and interactions in Dushanbe including the ones with the students at Islamic Revival Party's office gave a different perspective. The gender experts/academicians were of the view that, "women's role is changing very fast in Tajikistan and that too both for good and bad. For example, 'there are more options but at the same time, limited resources, economic hardship and revival of traditional roles which hampers the growth and overall development of women. The Author interacted with members/ students, at the Islamic Revival Party office and the director of the Islamic Revival Party, Dushanbe. The main points that came out could be divided into 3 category, i.e., (i) No major opposition Party present, which leads to bad governance; (ii) more corruption etc.; (iii) Women should be traditionally religious, and should know and learn to read Koran etc.". The Author interacted with many women whose source of income was from remittances including the landlady's (husband worked in Russia); Few young daughter-in-laws who were housewives, however, they had desire to study further and work in office; few of the young women, whose husband worked outside Tajikistan, mostly in Russia, were of the opinion, that their husbands have second wife and they don't care for them or their children enough anymore, adding to their economic misery and forcing them to go outside home, which they are not familiar hence faith discrimination and violence; young boys and girls had Indian names; the landlady's grand daughter's name was 'Suman'.

From Tajikistan, the author visited Astana, the capital city of Kazakhstan. Interview in Astana in the ministries, were very enriching.

Ministry of Health/ Healthcare on 19 November 2012. The interview was with Mrs. Bermaganbetova Gazima Nurashevna, the Head of Division for medical statistics and information. Important excerpts; "Government is taking a lot of measure to make sure that the population is healthy... Several awareness programmes through TV, Journal etc...'*Salamte* Kazakhstan', so as to have *salamat* population ... And several measures already exists for health of women, specially, pregnant women".

Interview in the Ministry of Economic Development and Trade was on 20 November 2012. The interview was with Ms. Zhuldyz Smagulova, Expert Social Policy Department. According to her, "there are measure and policy so that women's economic situations do not decline; to see that youth after university get involved in government work, 2011-20; unemployment less than 5.2 %. It was said that, the condition of women has become better in last five years (2007-12) and it is more visible. People seem to be happy. More measures are being taken for social protection, education etc. Right now there is free education up to 11 standard and provision for Grant for higher education".

Interview was in the 'Ministry of Women and Labour and social Development/ Ministry of Labour and Social Protection', on 20 November, 2012. The interview was with Mrs. Smagulova Alma Kurmetovna, Head of International Cooperation Department. According to her, "there are developments in agriculture. To encourage entrepreneurship there are provision of credit, 'to develop entrepreneurship'. Infrastructure in villages, are being increased so as to help women. Also the policy of '*Salamte* Kazakhstan' is being implemented so as to have *salamat* Kazakhstan".

From Astana, the Author went to Ashgabat, Turkmenistan. Lots of meetings and excursions took place. The interview with the Director of Women's Organisations, was on 27 November 2012; and Institute of Democracy and Human Rights on 28 November 2012; Institute of history, on 26 November 2012; Institute of Philology and Literature on 26 November 2012; National university- Institute of Culture and World Languages were all very valuable. The main outcome was the information regarding Turkmen society, since its history days. "Women in history were very intelligent and politically very active specially, in the Mary region". "People always listened to women". The summary of all interactions, discussions and interviews were that, "there has always been matriarchal society in Turkmen history and always there has been respect for women in society, even by kings and sultans". Therefore, there are many monuments dedicated to women. People always consult their mother and wife before they start important work.

"Every year on 8th March, International women's day, 40 *Mannat* is given to women as gift".

From Turkmenistan, the author went to Tashkent, Uzbekistan. Tashkent and Samarkand experiences, interviews and interactions were also very vital for this research work. All interactions and interviews in Tashkent and Samarkand was impromptu, however, went on very well. The most striking feature was the respect of people for their leadership and the trust the common man had in the leadership. Another very striking thing about people here was that, whatever, they said, it was with conviction; Academicians or be it a young school going students, college students, an old security guard, a group of old men in the park or young couples with children at monument sites, a woman in the bazaar or lady in the *chaikhana* or the land lady of the guest house. Even the taxi drivers were very confident of what they were talking, though they had very limited issues to talk about. Young and old had almost similar opinions regarding the state of affairs. However, when it came to other issues; like education system, employment, women's work, social security, there were varied opinions and answers. English language education, beauty and fashion were of interests to girls and English language education, fashion and foreign visits was of interests to boys. Young women were more inclined towards, career, job satisfaction and pay, whereas elderly women talked about the absence of social benefits, which was provided by the state during Soviet times and shared their worry about health and other issues related to women. Men mostly talked about the leadership and his wide-reach in terms of connects with the mass and other programmes and policy of the government, but mostly they sounded optimistic.

From Uzbekistan, Author went by road again to Kazakhstan but this time to the southern part of the country, Chimkent, Sairam, Turkistan and Taras which has rich history. Visits to these places were an experience in terms of understanding the society; the norms, customs and culture of these people; also people's attitude towards their leader and how the common man connects with Him. The time was perfect as it was 1st December, President Nursultan Nazarbayev's birthday. It was a holiday to celebrate their beloved leader's Birthday. This was a leisure experience for the author as well to enjoy the festivity. It was heartening to see the bond people share with the President and how they relate with him. Women here were very independent, confident and very active, at the same time culturally traditional and moderately religious as most places the Author visited in this leg had some connect with past and with strong religious link.

Highlight of the Research

Women in the countries under study have played and are expected to play a very pivotal role in shaping the society and nation. In fact, women have time and again had more responsibility bestowed upon themselves, with managing the age old traditional roles and crossing the boundaries and managing the other side of the fence too. It is important to note that women in the countries under study have experienced their share of privileges and shortcomings and their role and status in society has been changing. The governments in their respective countries have over the years taken steps to make sure that women have their share of opportunities in all programmes and policies for the welfare of society at large. Still, some level of disparity and discrimination exists. In India, women have added disadvantages in terms of access to education, which limit their chances of well-paid and productive work, and sometimes women do not even have choice to work. Though, this trend has been changing in last few years.

Sociocultural prejudices and stereotyping are still the main constraints to women's participation in the political and economic spheres in these countries. And with the traditional mindset prevailing over socioeconomic and political spheres, the space or scope for women to fully engage themselves in various roles has shrunk significantly. Women due to inequalities and gender disparities are finding it difficult to participate in the political and in some cases, to some extent even in socioeconomic activities.

Moreover, the impact of transition on women in Central Asia and the losses that they incurred are profoundly visible. Almost at once, the modernisation of the state was subsumed in the reestablishment of traditional Islam which immediately impacted the political, economic and social structure of the societies and, above all, the position of women in these societies. The transition from planned to market economy, from social engineering to an open and democratic space, have led to a religious revival of traditions that has had negative impact on women's status. As a result, these societies have witnessed increasing domestic and social violence. The transition also resulted in re-emergence of family and community values, along with traditional marriage practices. Women's role in society is defined purely in reproductive terms; education is seen in terms of equipping girls to be better wives and mothers, or increasing their chances of getting a suitable husband. These are legitimate aspirations, given the realities of the societies, however, they do little to equip girls and women to question the world around them, and the subordinate status assigned to them. In India, things are changing very fast and women do question these practices, though, there is still a long way to go.

Besides, despite the international conventions and agreements to safeguard, promote and ensure gender equality, differences and inequality is visible. Lower the country's literacy rate, the wider the gap, is likely between the two sexes. This clearly explains, why women and men alike in these Central Asian Republics are reluctant to accept that, there exists gender imbalance or gender gap. This is very much unlike India, where, majority of women are aware of gender disbalance and talk about it.

Noteworthy, with regard to Central Asian women is the portrayal of Central Asian women by the western authors which presents an incomplete picture. Western studies have ignored individual and different experiences of the Central Asian women in challenging the societal stereotypes. There is only a particular section of society in these countries who have had more opportunities to challenge patriarchal structures or stereotypes. Western concept of feminism and women's rights is not all together opposed; but hardly find takers in the society at large. Most people out-rightly disagree with the notion of inequality in Central Asia as projected by the West. Many people in these countries are of the opinion that Western perceptions are skewed. And they have a point, as there is definitely a need to see the gender issue in a different perspective. Specially, in terms of women in politics where, women themselves, do not have the desire to participate, irrespective of the fact whether there are challenges as reasons or not.

In countries under study, it is evident that NGOs have been instrumental in bringing more economic freedom to women specially, in the rural areas, but they have not been able to do much with regard to women's role in public sphere. There is no doubt that economic development and social modernisation have benefitted women and shrinking gender gaps in school and employment suggests that the status of women is improving. Yet, significant improvements in women's status require changes in attitudes that are embedded in centuries of traditional culture. High levels of education and economic activity not necessarily assure high status to women in societies with strong traditions of male domination. In some cases, relatively wealthy, educated women are more restricted within the household than poor, uneducated women who are forced to play a stronger, more independent role due to economic necessity.

In general, women's conditions have improved with economic development and social and political changes that favours equality and individual rights. At the same time, patriarchy and cultural traditions and practices, especially those related to family life, continue to have a strong influence on the status of women. However, the persistent gender gaps in access to education (in India); employment, political participation, lack of basic rights, and pervasive violence against women keep women from being fully productive members of the society.

These challenges seem dauntingly large for women to lessen the inequality gap. However, significant improvements in women's status require changes in attitudes that are embedded in centuries of traditional culture which indeed need immediate attention. Besides, programmes for women empowerment with the active participation of civil society and due patronage from the state governments, are required to be undertaken after properly analysing the factors that are responsible for the lack of women's interest, societal norms, economic vulnerability as well as participation. Since a balanced policy is indispensable for social change, modernisation and national development as well as growth of sociocultural and economic resources. Therefore, the present situation demands policy overhauling and institutional reforms so that more women can be given their due share and as a result, women play the role to their full potential.

So, what does the future hold for women in the countries under study?- Women are likely to occupy more space across the sectors and play more proactive role. With the increasing urbanisation and modernisation, it will be imperative to engage more and more women in economic activities. Social development for men and women in the form of education, media exposures, and opportunities to work outside the home, could provide access to new ideas, and with time, a transformation of cultural values. The government should take concrete measures in this direction, although it would be difficult to end gender discrimination and violence by government legislation alone. The role of civil society, NGOs and women organisation's would be equally important, as there have been examples of women's movements being instrumental in implementation of various international and domestic initiatives.

Notes

1. Lyn Norvell, "Gandhi And The Indian Women's Movement", http://www.bl.uk/eblj/1997articles/pdf/article2.pdf, accessed on 23 January 2014.
2. Sharon Smith, "Marxism, feminism and women's liberation", http://socialistworker.org/2013/01/31/marxism-feminism-and-women's-liberation, accessed on 23 February 2014.
3. Gaayathri Nair, "Its Time We Understood Intersectionality", *Forum News*, Nov, 2010, Vol. 23 No. 2, p. 5.
4. United Nations Office of the Special Adviser on Gender Issues and Advancement of Women http://www.un.org/womenwatch/osagi/pdf/factsheet1.pdf, accessed on 23 February 2014.

5. "Enhancing Women's Political Participation: A Policy Note for Europe and the Commonwealth of Independent States", UNDP Regional Bureau for Europe and the Commonwealth of Independent States, 2010, p. 8.
6. During Senate confirmation hearing, Secretary of State nominee Sen. Hillary Rodham Clinton (D- N.Y.) 'Laid out an ambitious agenda' for improving women's health worldwide as part of her comments on foreign policy, *National Politics & Policy* Senator, Clinton Pledges to Champion International Women's Rights as Secretary of State, Jan. 14, 2009, the New York Times, http://go.nationalpartnership.org/site/News2?abbr=daily2_&page=NewsArticle&id=14887, accessed on 23 February 2014.
7. The 2012 CSO Sustainability Index for Central and Eastern Europe and Eurasia 16th Edition, p. 238-240.
8. http://reports.weforum.org/global-gender-gap-report-2020/the-global-gender-gap-index- 2020/performance-by-subindex/. Accessed on 15 March 2020.
9. https://www.icnl.org/resources/research/global-trends-ngo-law/closing-civic-space-impact-on-development-and-humanitarian-csos. Accessed on 27 November 2019.
10. International IDEAs Strategy 2012–2017, https://eudevdays.eu/sites/default/files/Journeys-from-Exclusion-to-Inclusion-Marginalized-women-s-successes-in-overcoming-political-exclusion-PDF.pdf, accessed on 23 March 2014.
11. Women's Campaign International (WCI) empowers women to hold government accountable by mobilizing their communities and advocating for responsiveness to constituents. By working with men and women as equal partners, WCI broadens the civic engagement of all citizens. See http://www.women'scampaigninternational.org/what_we_do, accessed on 23 March 2014.
12. Kathleen M. Fallon, Liam Swiss, and Jocelyn Viternac, "Resolving the Democracy Paradox: Democratisation and Women's Legislative Representation in Developing Nations, 1975 to 2009", American Sociological Review, 77(3), 2012, pp. 380-408, p. 395.
13. Galiya Khassanova, "Women in Democratic Institutions in Kazakhstan", http://pdc.ceu.hu/archive/00001809/01/Khassanova.pdf, accessed on 23 March 2014.
14. "Reservation of Seats for Women in Legislative Bodies:Perspectives, Occasional Paper Series, 1/2008, Rajya Sabha Secretariat, New Delhi, July 2008, p. 2.

    http://rajyasabha.nic.in/rsnew/publication_electronic/reserv_women_pers2008.pdf, accessed on 23 March 2014.
15. Naila Kabeer, "Gender Equality and Women's Empowerment: A Critical Analysis of the Third Millennium Development Goal", *Gender and Development*, Vol. 13, No. 1, March, Millennium Development Goals 2005, pp. 13-24. Also see Niranjana, S., "Exploring Gender Inflections within Panchayat Raj institutions: Women's Politicisation in Andhra Pradesh", in K. Kapadia (ed.), The Violence of Development: The Politics of Identity, Gender and Social Inequalities in India, New Delhi: Kali for Women, 2002.
16. There have been many movements which have been successful even though here the Author mentions only few of them.

17. For details see http://gulabigangofficial.in/, accessed on 23 March 2014.
18. http://www.gulabigang.in/, accessed on 23 March 2014. Also read Amana Fontanella-Khan, " Pink Sari Revolution: A Tale of Women And Power in India", W W Norton & Company, NY, 2013. Also see http://www.thenational.ae/arts-culture/pink-sari-movement-in-india-fights-violence-against-women#ixzz2yAneEBNm, accessed on 23 March 2014.
19. For details http://gulabigangofficial.in/case-studies/, accessed on 23 March 2014.
20. The wedding industry in India is a huge and the rural market is an untapped source and provides for a potential opportunity in the field especially for women. Indian wedding industry surpasses others in terms of culture /traditions, especially in Uttar Pradesh where religious ceremonies and rituals are done with great devotion and for long hours. The services include tailoring bridal trousseau, catering for guests, flower arrangements, make-up and henna application. For details see http://gulabigangofficial.in/gulabi-services/, accessed on 23 March 2014.
21. The proposed legislation to reserve 33.3 percent seats in Parliament and state legislatures for women was drafted first by the H D Deve Gowda-led United Front government. http://timesofindia.indiatimes.com/india/Rajya-Sabha-passes-Women's-Reservation- Bill/articleshow/5663003.cms?referral=PM; http://www.rediff.com/news/2005/aug/24spec2.htm, accessed on 23 March 2014.
22. Pamela Philipose, "India -Battle for the Women's Bill: Bring in the Umbrellas", Alliance for 33%, Forum News,Vol. 23 No. 2, November 2010. http://apwld.org/wp- content/uploads/2013/09/APWLD-Forum-News-Vol.32,No.2-Web.pdf, accessed on 23 March 2014.
23. Pamela Philipose, "India -Battle for the Women's Bill: Bring in the Umbrellas", Alliance for 33%, Forum News,Vol. 23 No. 2, November 2010. http://apwld.org/wp-content/uploads/2013/09/APWLD-Forum-News-Vol.32,No.2-Web.pdf, accessed on 23 March 2014.
24. http://www.usaid.gov/where-we-work/asia, accessed on 23 March 2014.
25. www.cwds.ac.in/, accessed on 23 March 2014.
26. For details see http://www.csrindia.org/, accessed on 23 March 2014.
27. YMCA is affiliated to the world YWCA through the National Body, YWCA of India. The YWCA of Delhi over the years has emerged as a platform for the present generation of women to assume new responsibilities in contributing towards the growth of the nation and the society in large. https://www.ywcaofdelhi.org, accessed on 23 March 2014.
28. http://www.indianwomen.org.in/indian-women-ngos.htm, accessed on 23 March 2014.
29. http://www.indianwomen.org.in/indian-women-ngos.htm, accessed on 23 March 2014.
30. http://www.indianwomen.org.in/indian-women-ngos.htm, accessed on 23 March 2014.
31. http://www.indianwomen.org.in/indian-women-ngos.htm, accessed on 23 March 2014.

32. http://www.indianwomen.org.in/indian-women-ngos.htm, accessed on 23 March 2014.
33. http://www.indianwomen.org.in/indian-women-ngos.htm, accessed on 23 March 2014.
34. http://www.indianwomen.org.in/indian-women-ngos.htm, accessed on 23 March 2014.
35. Akiner, Shirin. "Between Tradition and Modernity: the Dilemma Facing Contemporary Central Asian Women." In Post-Soviet Women: from the Baltic to Central Asia, edited by Mary Buckley. New York: Cambridge University Press, 1997. p. 284. Also see Rebecca Anne Blackburn, "Women Of Kyrgyzstan And Tajikistan:Historical Legacies Impacting Contemporary Involvement", MA Thesis, College of the University of Illinois at Urbana-Champaign, 2011, Urbana, Illinois, p. 20.
36. Ondjik Musayev "Democratic Party of Turkmenistan", First Secretary, International Department of Central Committee of CPC, 3rd international conference of Asian political parties, Beijing China 2004-09-05, 2004. http://www.idcpc.org.cn/icapp3/2004-09/05/content_2809095.htm; http://www.un.org/News/Press/docs/2006/wom1558.doc.htm, accessed on 23 March 2014.
37. Saniya Edelbay, "The Islamic Situation in Kazakhstan", *International Journal of Humanities and Social Science,* Vol. 2, No. 21; November 2012, p. 217.
38. Saniya Edelbay, "The Islamic Situation in Kazakhstan", *International Journal of Humanities and Social Science,* Vol. 2, No. 21; November 2012, p. 208.
39. Marfua Tokhtakhodjaeva (center) speaks at the exhibits opening Nov. 19 at the National Art Gallery of Uzbekistan, Photo Exhibition Documents on Uzbek Women throughout 20th Century, 12/02/2009 http://uzbekistan.usembassy.gov/pe120209_2.html, accessed on 23 March 2014.
40. Kamala Kumari, "Identifying women's issues in Central Asia: Problems and Prospects" *Contemporary Central Asia*, Vol.xiv, No. I, March 2010, pp. 45-62,
41. Jay Cooper, "The Real Work: Sustaining NGO Growth in Central Asia", in M. Holt Ruffin and Daniel Waugh eds, "Civil Society in Central Asia", Seattle: University of Washington Press, 1999, p. 214.
42. Forum of women's NGOs of Kyrgyzstan held its side event "Women's empowerment in Central Asia and movement building", 2 March 2010, http://forumofwomenngos.kg/about-us-2/, accessed on 23 March 2014.
43. Forum of women's NGOs of Kyrgyzstan held its side event "Women's empowerment in Central Asia and movement building", 2 March 2010, http://forumofwomenngos.kg/about-us-2/, accessed on 23 March 2014.
44. Svetlana Shakirova, "Gender Policy and Nation Building in Kazakhstan: Parallel of Conflicting Processes", in Mondira Dutta ed., "Gender and Human Development in Central and South Asia, Delhi: Pentagon Press, pp. 253-262.
45. This law criminalises rape with severe punishment ranging from three to 15 years and ensures equal opportunity, and prohibits gender based discrimination; Violence against women, trafficking in persons, and discrimination against persons with disabilities, etc. The law defines for the first time domestic violence

and victim; identifies various types of violence, such as physical, psychological, sexual, and economic; and outlines the responsibilities of the local and national governments and NGOs in providing support to domestic violence victims. The criminal procedure code sets the maximum sentence for spousal assault and battery at 10 years in prison, which is the same as for any beating (website OECD-SIGI; US Dept of State 2009, 2010). Maarten van Klaveren, Kea Tijdens, Melanie Hughie-Williams, Nuria Ramos, Netherlands, March, "An Overview of Women's Work and Employment in Kazakhstan, Decisions for Life", MDG3 Project, Country Report No. 10, University of Amsterdam /Amsterdam Institute for Advanced Labour Studies (AIAS) 2010, www.uva.nl/aias,accessed on 23 March 2014. Also see http://www.wageindicator.org/documents/publicationslist/publications-2010/An-Overview-of-Women's-Work-and-Employment-in-Kazakhstan.pdf, accessed on 23 March 2014.

46. For more see http://e-history.kz/en/contents/view/764, accessed on 23 March 2014, accessed on 23 March 2014.

    http://e-history.kz/media/upload/728/2013/11/14/355dcbc74f1022ed36c56c005d6bfe4a.pdf, accessed on 23 March 2014.

47. *Nur Otan* (Light of the Fatherland) Party is the Democratic Peoples Party. Since 2007 it is headed by President of Kazakhstan, Nursultan Nazarbayev. Myra Aisina represents Kazakhstan at the Forum.

48. Myra Aisina, who is a deputat (MP) in Kazakh parliament, 25.11.2013.

    http://www.zakon.kz/4588325-v-kazakhstanskom-parlamente-243.html, accessed on 23 March 2014; http://kzopengov.com/in-the-kazakh-parliament-24-3-percent-of-deputies-are-women/, accessed on 23 March 2014.

49. During an interview in Astana in the Ministry of Economic Development and Trade on 20 November 2012 with Ms. Zhuldyz Smagulova, Expert Social Policy Department.

50. Kazakhstan, Answers to the Questions on Implementation of Beijing Platform of Actions (1995) and Resolutions of the 23d Special Session of the UN General Assembly (2000), 2005, p. 3. http://www.un.org/womenwatch/daw/Review/responses/KAZAKHSTAN-English.pdf, accessed on 23 March 2014.

51. Aliya Kabdiyeva, "Developing Sustainable NGOs in Kazakhstan", http://ccsenet.org/journal/index.php/ass/article/viewFile/27954/16874, accessed on 23 March 2014.

52. During interaction and interview with Svetlana Shakirova, Centre for Gender Studies, Almaty, Kazakhstan, October 21, 2012.

53. During interaction and interview with Maysa Meredovna Yazmuhammedova, Director/chairperson, Union of Women, 27 November 2012, Ashgabat, Turkmenistan, see, Images of Author in Central Asia (Image: 16). The author was in Turkmenistan from 24-28 November 2012. Also see. https://www genderindex.org/wp-content/uploads/files/datasheets/2019/TM.pdf; The Women's Movement in Central Asia. http://www.awid.org/Library/The-Women s-Movement-in-Central-Asia, accessed on 23 March 2020.

54. Lyudmilla Kim, "Mass Perception of Gender roles in Modern Uzbekistan: an Empirical Study" in Christa Hammerle, Nikola Langreiter, Magreth Lanzinger,

Edith Saurer ed., Gender and politics in Central Asia, Vienna, Austria: Bohlau Verlag Koln, 2008a, pp. 133-144.

55. Wendy Mee, "Women in the Republic of Uzbekistan", Country Briefing Paper, 2001, p. x.

56 http://www.unwomen.org/en/what-we-do/leadership-and-political-participation/women's-movements, accessed on 23 March 2014;

http://www.unesco.kz/new/en/social-and-human-sciences/news/1449, accessed on 23 March 2014.

57. Wendy Mee, "Women in the Republic of Uzbekistan", Country Briefing Paper, 2001, p. 20.

58. Zulfiya Tursunova, "Women's Lives and Livelihoods in Post-Soviet Uzbekistan: Ceremonies of Empowerment and Peacebuilding", Lexington Books, 2014, pp. 115-16.

59. During the authors stay in Central Asia, she came across such similar get-togethers in Almaty, Tashkent and Osh. In fact, in Osh, she attended two such *Gaps,* one in Uzbek *Mohalla* and another in Kyrgyz, see, Images of Author in Central Asia, (Image 14B). The author was in Osh from 2- 8 November 2012.

60. UN Committee for the Elimination of Discrimination of Women, CEDAW General Recommendation No. 23 (16th session, 1997), http://www.un.org/womenwatch/daw/cedaw/recommendations/recomm.htm#recom23. Also see "Enhancing Women's Political Participation: A Policy Note for Europe and the Commonwealth of Independent States", UNDP Regional Bureau for Europe and the Commonwealth of Independent.

States, 2010 p. 27. Also see UN Committee for the Elimination of Discrimination of Women, Concluding Comments: Kyrgyzstan, http://www.un.org/womenwatch/daw/cedaw/cedaw30/KyrgyzstanCC.PDF, accessed on 23 March 2014.

61. "Enhancing Women's Political Participation: A Policy Note for Europe and the Commonwealth of Independent States", UNDP Regional Bureau for Europe and the Commonwealth of Independent States, 2010, p. 38.

62. During field research the author had participated in a March in support of "Women non-violence action in Kyrgyzstan" on 28.10.2012, A march in support of draft law 155 of the Kyrgyz Republic - advocacy within the framework of the UN Secretary-General Campaign "UNiTE to End Violence against Women and Girls". The author was in Bishkek, Kyrgyzstan from 27 October-1November 2012, see Images of Author in Central Asia during her Field Work (Image:12). Also see http://un.org.kg/en/news-center/news-releases/list/News%20Center/74-UNIFEM?start=10, accessed on 23 March 2014.

63. http://www.intrac.org/docs.php/2991/Social%20Movements%20case%20studies%20March%202008.pdf, accessed on 23 March 2014.

64. Matthew Naumann and Burul Usmanalieva, INTRAC Central Asia: social movements case studies, 2008, p. 1. http://www.intrac.org/data/files/resources/645/Social-Movements-and-Conflict-in-Post-Revolution-Kyrgyzstan.pdf., accessed on 23 March 2014.

65. During discussions with Research Scholars in Bishkek on 29 October, 2012. The author was in Bishkek, Kyrgyzstan from 27 October-1November 2012.

66. Elise Helen LoBue, "Kazakhstans Soviet Past, Globalised Present, and 'Emancipated Women': A Case For A New Gender And Development Domain", The University of Iowa, 2007. 3301725.
67. Erica Marat, (book review), "Lost Voices: Central Asian Women: Confronting Transition" by Yvonne Corcoran-Nantes, London and New York: Zed Books, 2005, Central Asia - Caucasus Institute and Silk Road Studies Program, University of Uppsala/The Johns Hopkins University, Uppsala, Sweden. See more in Resolution adopted by the General Assembly on 19 December 2011 66/130. Women And Political Participation, (http://www.un.org/ga/search/view_doc.asp?symbol=A/RES/66/130, accessed on 23 March 2014.
68. http://www.unesco.kz/new/en/social-and-human-sciences/news/1449, accessed on 23 March 2014.
69. USAIDs Assistance Strategy for Central Asia 2001-2005.
70. Zauresh Galimzhanovna Saktaganova and Dinara Kenesovna Ospanova, "Non-Governmental Organisations in the Republic of Kazakhstan: Principle Stages of Formation and Development", *Middle-East Journal of Scientific Research* 15 (9): 1277-1284, 2013, p. 1277.
71. Manshuk Bekentayeva, "NGOs Helping Build Civil Society in Kazakhstan", *People* on 24 April, 2013. See, http://www.astanatimes.com/2013/04/ngos-helping-build-civil-society-in-kazakhstan-swedish-expert-says/, accessed on 23 March 2014.
72. See http://www.icnl.org/research/monitor/turkmenistan.html, accessed on 23 March 2014.
73. Aksoltan Ataeva was representing her country at the meeting was the Permanent Representative of Turkmenistan to UN. For details see, WOM/1558, 17 May 2006, Concluding Consideration of Turkmenistans Report, Women's Anti-Discrimination Committee Highlights Difficulties in Assessing Progress, Discrimination against Women, 2006, http://www.un.org/News/Press/docs/2006/wom1558.doc.htm, accessed on 23 March 2014.
74. Government Organised Non-Governmental Program, http://www.ucis.pitt.edu/nceeer/2009_824- 02h_Clement.pdf, accessed on 23 March 2014.
75. During the authors interaction and interview with Maysa Meredovna Yazmuhammedova, Director/Chairperson, 'Union of Women NGO' on 27 November 2012 in Ashgabat, See (Images of Author in Central Asia during her Field Work October 17 –14 December, 2012, Image: 16a). The Author was in Ashgabat, Turkmenistan from 24-28 November, 2012.
76. USAID report, 2009, pp. 129, 205.
77. Saud Joseph, Encyclopedia of Women and Islamic Cultures, Economics, Education, Mobility and Space, Brill Leiden-Boston, 2007, Vol. IV, p. 374.
78. AWIDs Young Feminist Activism programme is aimed at forming a multi-generational movement with an emphasis on highlighting young women's experiences and voices to strategise, plan and execute several assertive and women friendly initiatives. Strategic Initiatives of AWID have been running for many years and have spread across areas including consultations and surveys, primary research and dialogues with policy makers, regional networking and

information dissemination. Besides, AWID also strategises to reduce the adverse impact of religious fundamentalism on women's rights organisations and movements. For details see Jane Falkingham, "Women in Tajikistan", Asian Development Bank Country Briefing Paper, Asian Development Bank, 2000, pp. 29-30.

79. See http://www.karat.org/, accessed on 23 March 2014.
80. During several discussion sessions, between 17th October to 14 December 2012 for field research to field trip to Kazakhstan.
81. http://www.igpn.net/download/igpn_regional_report_(interviews_with_political_parties).pdf, accessed on 23 March 2014.
82. Republic of Kazakhstan. Campania on change of the criminal legislation. https://www.un.org/womenwatch/daw/vaw/ngocontribute/Feminist%20League.pdf. Accessed on 23 March, 2014.
83. Dr. Nurgul Djanaeva is the president of the Forum. http://forumofwomenngos.kg/about-us-2/, accessed on 23 March 2014.
84. http://www.deathpenaltyabolition.tj/en/about-usl, accessed on 23 March 2014.
85. For details see, http://wcu.uz/ and http://ich.uz/en/ich-of-uzbekistan/ich-organisations/114- women's-committee. Also see http://www.uzbekistanitalia.org/home/uzbekistan/fondi-in-uzbekistan. Accessed on 27 March 2014.
86. The Swiss Agency for Development and Cooperation (SDC) is Switzerlands international cooperation agency within the Federal Department of Foreign Affairs (FDFA). SDC- Uzbekistan aims at poverty alleviation, facilitation of sustainable, private sector-led growth, equitable access to good quality public services and transition towards a pluralistic and economically viable state by supporting the implementation of national development strategies in cooperation with other donors. The organisation is also concerned with the professional training system in selected vocational-technical schools and the strengthening of the national identity concept at the cultural level. SDC also funded the study on Central Asia Energy-Water Development Programme (CAEWDP).
87. Suad Joseph, Encyclopedia of Women and Islamic Cultures, Vol. IV, Brill-Leiden-Boston, 2007, pp. 161-162.
88. Marfua Tokhtakhodjaeva is the director. for details see http://www.friends-partners.org/ccsi/nisorgs/uzbek/wmrsrctr.htm, accessed on 23 March 2014.
89. Zulfiya Tursunova, Nodira Azizova, "Women's progress in Uzbekistan: Political Particiption", in ed. Christa Hammerle, Nikola Langreiter, Magreth Lanzinger and Edith Saurer, Gender and Politics in Central Asia,Vienna, Austria: Bohlau Verlag Koln, 2008a, pp. 113-32.
90. The main aim is to improve rural women's status and standard of living via stimulation of women's awareness of their realities, develop their capacity for personal development, strengthen their participation in development activities, and advocate for their rights. Olga Janaeva, Founder and Director of Alga, sees a source of leadership in these women which needs only to be tapped. The Alga organisation has three main programmes: prevention of violence against women; training in leadership development and women's rights; and reproductive health

and family planning - all part of the rural women's empowerment programme. In addition, Alga created an information-consultation educational center where women can access services that were not available before. It is not exaggerated to say that *Alga* radically transformed the life of many rural people. In addition to these numerous activities, it has helped bring attention to this region, and shows that a wealth of motivated people awaits the chance to take control of their lives. http://www.wmgd.net/symposium/2007/report/olgadjanaeva.htm, accessed on 23 March 2014.

91. Kamala Kumari, "Women and Development in Turkmenistan", *Contemporary Central Asia,* Vol. XVIII, No. 2&3, May-December, 2014, pp. 47-56.

92. The Association receives funding through a contract with the city of Almaty to provide social services. As Kazakhstans Social Contracting Law does not permit contracts to last longer than one year, the Association often had to close its doors to disabled children and their families during the interim period between contracts. Promoting Civic Space, International Center For Not-For-Profit Law, Annual Report 2011-2012, p. 9. http://www.icnl.org/about/reports/ICNL_AR_2011-2012.pdf, accessed on 23 March 2014.

93. During authors discussion and interview with Bagayeva Katerina, Director Institute of equal rights and equal opportunities, Kazakhstan, on 11 December 2012.

94. http://www.fpif.org/briefs/vol5/v5n06aral_body.html. Accessed on 23 March 2014.

95. Beijing Platform for Action Document, 1995. https://www.unsystem.org/content/beijing-declaration-and-platform-action-september-1995. Accessed on 23 March, 2014.

96. Women organisations have been working hard for peace and improvement of women's environment in society, but not succeeded even if it has the government support and the laws in place, as there are several lapses in the implementation process. http://www.un.org/womenwatch/directory/critical_areas_of_concern_30.htm, accessed on 23 March 2014.

97. United States Department of State, Report 2012, on trafficking in Persons, supra note 16. Also see, http://www.stopvaw.org/turkmenistan, accessed on 23 March 2014.

98. http://mvd.gov.kz/, accessed on 23 March 2014; http://mvd.gov.kz/portal/page/portal/mvd/mvd page/mvd_president/.htm, accessed on 23 March 2014; http://mvd.gov.kz/portal/page/portal/mvd/mvd_page/mvd_kidnapping/F45DDEDCF0C03757E044002655122E6A, accessed on 23 March 2014.

99. During, discussion with Rimma Sultanova, Bishkek, 30 October, 2012. The author was in Bishkek from 27 October-1 November 2012. For details also see http://www.unwomen.org/en/news/stories/2013/2/new-law-in-kyrgyzstan-toughens-penalties-for-bride-kidnapping, accessed on 23 March 2014.

100. Interview with Elina Schröder. She works with UN agency, on 29th October 2012 in Bishkek. The author was in Bishkek from 27 October-1 November 2012.

Chapter 5

Conclusion

With India and Central Asia having innumerable similarities like, great and rich cultural heritage and common values like democracy and rule of law and also, sharing cultural and civilisational links, the study has managed to explore many interesting facets of the similarities and dissimilarities. India is the biggest practicing democracy in the world, whereas, Central Asian Republics are young and evolving democracies, however, the 1990s, has been a point of reference for both India and Central Asian Republics, as there were fundamental changes; the economic liberalisation in India and the disintegration of USSR and independence of these Central Asian Republics.

The economic liberalisation in India and the disintegration of USSR impacted the entire population in India and Central Asia, particularly women. The economic reforms along with globalisation brought a lot of opportunities for women in India, something like never before, but along with it brought several challenges as well. Similarly Central Asia also had its own unique situation. While independence opened new opportunities for social mobility and cultural expression, political and economic dynamics also imposed severe hardships. Today, India has become one of the fastest growing economies of the world following the market based economic reforms in 1991. Similarly the CARs have also come a long way in terms of development; economic and political. However, despite economic growth, societal transition and globalisation, women continue to face several socioeconomic problems based on the traditional mindset dominated by patriarchy and gender discrimination.

Historically, women in India have had their share of ups and downs in their status, role and identity at different times. There have been many scholarly and learned women in Indian history; often enjoyed prominent roles in public sphere; as administrators, rulers and warrior queens. At the same time issues like patriarchy, caste systems and several other prejudices against women did affect their overall position in society at large. Though, second half of nineteenth century and the early years of the twentieth century witnessed several socio-religious reform movements which helped in breaking many of these taboos and gave added impetus to the awakening against prejudices and practices. Later, Gandhiji played very important role in bringing women and their issues to the forefront. Women played very important role in India's freedom struggle. Even Independent India has had many powerful women.

Women in Central Asia also had different experiences at different times. Central Asian people prior to 1917 had Islamic culture and practices as the vast majority of Central Asians were Muslims. These people observed Islamic practices in accordance with Quranic percepts. The combination of formal laws of *Sharia* and the local customary laws of *Adat* were intimately related to the social structures and dominant forms of social life in these societies. Women though made important contribution to the family income, but their most important duty was child bearing. Society in the pre-Soviet era was in general very patriarchal and sanctified by religion; host of traditions and customs generally confined women to home. Men were the breadwinners while women carried out all the domestic chores. Though, in few of these countries which had nomadic culture; women were believed to have played a very important role in the nomadic group as the economic structure of the nomadic organisation could not be sustained without women.

However, with the Soviet rule in Central Asia, the situations changed drastically for Muslims, especially women. And the most striking thing was that, the traditional customs and gender stereotyping; women's confinement to reproduction and housekeeping were abandoned and women participated in public sphere. Women in Soviet-Central Asia clearly gained some degree of gender equality, as they had free access to education and employment. Also the system provided them with sufficient social benefits. Equal political rights and women's emancipation programmes in Muslim Central Asia were the biggest achievements of the Soviet era. During Soviet times, these countries had good literacy and employment rate and social security measures. However, in the post-Independent Central Asia, resurgence of traditionalism and Islam has had a profound impact on the role and status of women. As a result, traditional role, status and dress code of women were quickly embraced by large sections of the female population.

Contemporary India and CARs, have come a long way in terms of development and so women's status and role in society has also changed over time. There has been a remarkable change with regards to education, employment and women's role in public sphere. The progress India has made with regard to education is worth mentioning. There have been tremendous changes taking place in this regard as several new policies and measures have been taken. The progress is visible and women have shown remarkably good improvement in terms of enrollment, performance or successful completion of course. And in cases, where girls have not completed studies, it is societal pressure that is to be blamed. Enrollment of girls and women in tertiary education has increased considerably.

In case of Central Asia, with regard to education there are continuities of the Soviet times, as well as changes. Two decades of post-socialist transformations, reveals that education systems in Central Asia, has responded to the rapidly changing political, economic, and social environment in profoundly, new and unique ways. Some countries moved towards western models, some went backwards, and some followed entirely new courses. Though, certain elements of the old system remains. It had close to 100% literacy rate during Soviet times, even now there is not much change in literacy rate, though, in comparison, there seems to be decline in terms of enrollment, completion or performance of girls. And reasons range from traditional to economic issues.

What is worth noting is that, both in India and Central Asia, the situation of women and girls to some degree depends on public opinion, traditions and life style and not education alone. Specially, in rural areas as it depends on the life style, where family links the welfare of the house with male members. So, given a choice, the preference is given to boys. The belief that 'Girls in any case will get married and will go to live in another family' and sons have to support parents in future, holds a lot of weightage. The situation earlier was same in India too, however, there has been a remarkable change in this thinking and attitude towards women's role and girl's education in the last few years. Governments on its part in India and Central Asia are making all efforts for improvement in education system and access to education.

The economic activity of women has also gone through transformation both in India and Central Asia. In India, in the post-liberalisation period, women are increasingly occupying relatively larger space in almost all the spheres of economic activities. Female employment in India grew considerably. However, there exists gender gap, as men still make up the majority of people employed in agriculture, industry and services, but the gender gap is biggest in industry. Many service jobs, such as nursing and social and clerical work, are considered 'feminine' because of a perceived similarity to women's traditional roles. Sometimes, women often do not receive the training needed to take advantage of changing employment opportunities. And the greater availability of part time work in service industries lures women more.

In case of Central Asia, in the initial years post-Independence, each of these countries apart of having some similar traits had their own unique problems related to women's work or employment. With the introduction of market principles into the economy and the revision of the extensive social protection system etc. women had more opportunities and exciting options but there were uncertainties and challenges as well. For example, economic problems decreased the state's ability to provide social security and welfare schemes, as they were either withdrawn or became non-operational. And with the reemergence of Islamic traditions, family and community values, and the absence of subsidised social services, women were further burdened with extra responsibility. Even though, women in these countries are more actively pursuing opportunities to contribute to the economy of the family, the pressures for women to return to more traditional roles in few countries has resulted in considerably fewer opportunities for female involvement in the economic sphere.

So, there are different levels of female involvement in the economy in these countries. But the most important thing about women in these countries is that they are involved in some economic activities; some women who are not into salaried employment have some sort of business, big or small. At times women sit on the roadside with fruits or vegetables plucked right from their garden to earn some money. In India, women are either into salaried employment indicating women's economic role or are housewives and the household chores that they do, are not considered in terms of economy hence, never get acknowledged. Though, the trend has been changing slowly and women in India have also started actively in small businesses like *Dabba, Tiffin* system etc. and it has started giving good results as well.

The impact of sociopolitical changes in the countries under study has been tremendous. The transition and transformation gave the opportunity to challenge the gender stereotypes and helped change visible and invisible discriminatory practices and structures. At the same time it is also true that not much has happened in terms of women participation as well as representations in political affairs. The prevalent conditions are still far from equal, and progress toward goals set in the 1995 Beijing Platform for Action and the 2000 MDGs remains slow. However, the last two decades have seen an increase in women's political participation worldwide, likewise there have been improvement in these countries as well. In case of India, due to Panchayati Raj Institution, women seems to have made a good progress at the local level, but at the national level there isn't much to talk about. In case of Central Asia too, the scene is more or less the same, in spite of the fact that, women in Central Asia, have had a history of women's important role in public sphere at least during soviet period, the current situation is not very appealing.

There are several but varied reasons for this low or non-remarkable progress. The stereotype that politics is not a woman's place; and politics is a hostile environment for women, makes it difficult for women to take up political positions and sometime family demands and responsibilities hinder their participation. Even when they participate, they mostly remain traditionally concentrated at lower level of decision-making as well as at lower levels of state administration. This is besides the fact that, even when women are as educated as their male counterparts, they do not make to the seat of power. The reasons for this are not to be found in education and economic independence alone. Rather, it is simply because of the stereotyped and traditional mindset and structure of society. To add on to these there several other obstacles like violence, patriarchal mindset, traditional prejudices etc. In India, in spite of more awareness and mature political environment and vibrant political culture women have not really succeeded in bridging the political gap. And in the case of Central Asia, despite, a long tradition of active participation in the workforce by a vast majority of women, both women and men see motherhood and marriage as the most important goals in a woman's life. In case of Central Asia, a common standpoint is that 'politics is a man's business,' and that women are too emotional to deal with affairs of the state.

Recognising the need for making the position of women better, safer and stronger, several measures have been taken by governments in all these countries including India in recent years to empower women socially, economically and politically. Though, so far there have been some visible change or improvement in education and economic sectors but politics so far remains with least improvement. And, in case of Central Asia, it is interesting to note that women themselves do not show any inclination towards politics.

As mentioned earlier, several governmental initiatives have been launched in all these countries since the 1990s, to enhance gender equality. And women activism and movements have remained instrumental in pushing governments to carry out policy reforms in these countries. Civil society specially, women NGOs have remained at the center-stage to influence governmental decisions as per the provisions of international conventions. Women, through women's movements and different campaigns for change have been working hard to make women realise their potential and also making them aware of their political and social rights and responsibilities.

The organisations have done some significant work, though, the journey has not been very smooth for NGOs or Women Organisations as there have been many challenges. These challenges are mostly indirect, however, they hamper both directly and indirectly; the functioning and activities in achieving goals and targets. For example, violence in all its form, from domestic violence to sexual assault, rapes, human trafficking, are an issue for any government or organisations. These evils of society need to be dealt with, so as to make the environment conducive enough for organisations to engage with women and work for their betterment. There are several other impediments like problem of alcoholism, dowry deaths etc. specially, in case of India. These, indirectly create hindrances in the women's empowerment programmes and projects. Then there are several governance issues like bribe, corruption, etc. which force organisations to either abruptly leave the projects/ programmes or the entire things gets delayed and thereby loses its importance or significance. Also other issues like human trafficking which is trans-regional and transnational, is very difficult to handle or manage. So it is evident that, directly or indirectly these issues hinder women's campaign for change and prevent the achievement of the objectives of equality, development and peace.

To sum up, this study shows that, economic development and social modernisation have benefitted women in India improving their status to some extent. The study also suggests that, due to availability of more options and opportunities, the role of women in India and Central Asia are changing. More and more women are taking the center stage and this is expected to expand further in the future and the social, political and economic achievements of women and their role in the development of the society and nation is praiseworthy. However, much more is needed to be done for women to play their role to full potential. And the onus lies with the government and civil society to make sure that the changing role of women is always in favour of women so as to make their future less challenging. And to begin with; facilitating women's well-being and overall growth; and acknowledging women's role and contribution in peace and prosperity of the nation.

Select Bibliography

Primary Sources

*Turkmen

In Russian

Zhenshini v SSSR 1991, Statisticheskie Materialy, Moskva, "Finansi I Statistika", 1991.

Zhenshini I mushini kazakhstana, gendernaya statistika- almati: Agenstvo RK Po statistike, 2012.

Zhenshina, Simiya, obshestvo, Ashgabat, Turkmenistan, 2011, st. 137, 139-154.

Demokratiya i Pravo, Turkmensnkii natsionalnii institut demokratii u prav cheloveka pri prezidente turkmenistana, 2, 2012.st.-156.

*Medeniyet, 4,(yul-avfgust) 2012, Ministriterestva kulturi Turkmenistana, Ashkhabad, Turkmenistan, p-55.

*Medeniyet, 3,(may-jyun) 2012, Ministriterestva kulturi Turkmenistana, Ashkhabad, Turkmenistan.

*Medeniyet, 2,(mart-apriel) 2012, Ministriterestva kulturi Turkmenistana, Ashkhabad, Turkmenistan.

**Prava* Zhenshin v Turkmenistane, seriya, "Prava Cheloveka", No. 20, *Turkmensnkii natsionalnii institut demokratii u prav cheloveka pri prezidente Turkmenistana, Turkmen Dowlet Nesiryat gullugy, Ashgabat, 2012.*

*Zenan 7, 2012, Hatiya Begim, pp. 23, 29.

In English

Documents and Materials, Reports and Speeches before the 19th All Union Conference of the CPSU Moscow, (1988).

Speech of Kazakh President, "Calls For More Women in Politics", at the first women's congress, 05/03/2011, http://en.ria.ru/world/20110305/162871147.html, accessed on 14 March 2014.

Address by Statement By H.E. Mrs. Aitkul B. Samakova, Minister of the Republic of Kazakhstan, Chairperson of the National Commission on Family and Women's Affairs Under the President of the Republic of Kazakhstan, to the 23rd Special Session of the United Nations General Assembly, "Women 2000: Gender Equality, Development, and Peace for the Twenty-First Century.", New York, June 8, 2000, Permanent Mission of the Republic of Kazakhstan to the United Nations, http://www.un.org

CEDAW document, http://www2.ohchr.org/english/bodies/cedaw/docs/CEDAW-C-50-4.pdf

Millennium Development Goals Report 2012, p. 24.

Asian Development Bank Report, Uzbekistan, Philippines, 2005.

UN Committee for the Elimination of Discrimination of Women, CEDAW General Recommendation No. 23 (UN Committee for the Elimination of Discrimination of Women, CEDAW General Recommendation No. 23 16th session, 1997). http://www.un.org/womenwatch/daw/cedaw/recommendations/recomm.htm#recom23.

Clinton Pledges to Champion International Women's Rights as Secretary of State, Jan. 14, 2009, the New York Times, Reports. http://go.nationalpartnership.org/site/News2?abbr=daily2_&page=NewsArticle&id=14887

CSO Sustainability Index for Central and Eastern Europe and Eurasia, 16th Edition - June, 2013.

International IDEA's Strategy 2012–2017, https://eudevdays.eu/sites/default/files/Journeys-from-Exclusion-to-Inclusion-Marginalized-women-s-successes-in-overcoming-political-exclusion-PDF.pdf

Report of the Fourth World Conference on Women, Beijing, 4-15 September 1995, http://www.un.org/documents/ga/conf177/aconf177-20en.ht

Myra Aisina, who is a deputat (MP) in Kazakh parliament, 25.11.2013, http://www.zakon.kz/4588325-v-kazakhstanskom-parlamente-243.html

USAID's Assistance Strategy for Central Asia 2001-2005, Report, USAID.

UGC report, 2013-14, p. 58.

UNDP Report, Report on the Status of Official Statistics Related to Gender Equality in Eastern Europe and the CIS Countries, Geneva, October 2004.

UNDP Report, Programme to Improve Gender Statistics in Uzbekistan, New York, December, 2006.

UNDP Report, 2008.

UNECE, Countries in Figures, June 2009, http://www.unece.org/stats/profiles2009/Welcome.html

United Nations Office of the Special Adviser on Gender Issues and Advancement of Women. http://www.un.org/womenwatch/osagi/pdf/factsheet1.pdf

United Nations (UN) Millenium Development Goals (MDG), March, 2010, http://mdgs.un.org/unsd/mdg/Default.aspx

United States Department of State, Report 2012, on trafficking in Persons, supra note 16, http://www.stopvaw.org/turkmenistan

World Bank Report, 2011.

World Bank 1998, Tajikistan Poverty Note, Washington, DC: World Bank. 1998.

World Bank 2000, Republic of Tajikistan Poverty Assessment, Washington, DC: World Bank.

World Bank 2006, Republic of Tajikistan Poverty Assessment, Washington, DC: World Bank.

Secondary Sources

Books/ Articles

in Russian

Gosudarstvennia programma razvitija obrazov, http://www.edu.gov.kz/.../gosudarstvennia_programma_razvitija_obrazov

"Razvitiye matiryalnoi i dukhovnoi kulturi crednebekobovo Merva" v matiryali mejhdunarodnoi nayuchnoi konferentsii na Srednebekobiye goroda turkmenistana v sisteme evraziiskoi tsivilizatsii, 28-30 Marta, 2012, p. 547-48.

Saidbayev, T., "Islam i obshchestvo", (Nauka, Moscow, 1984), p. 79.

in English

Abalova, Nazgul and Almeiiz Abalov, "Women as apolitical Resource: Kyrgyzstan and India, in Mondira Dutta ed., *Gender and Human Development in Central and South Asia*, Delhi: Pentagon Press, pp. 235- 252.

Abaraham, E., *Violence against Women: Enduring Questions and Civic Concerns, Women's Link*, 10(4), 2004, 2-6.

Abraham, Taisha (ed.), *Women and the Politics of Violence*, New Delhi: Har-Anand Publications, 2002.

Abazov, Rafis, *Culture and Customs of Central Asia*, London: Greenwood, 2007.

Abdullaeva, Marifat, Background paper prepared for the "Education for All", Global Monitoring Report 2006, Literacy for Life, 2006, Review of Central Asian countries, UNESCO, 2006. http://unesdoc.unesco.org/images/0014/001459/145934e.pdf

Abdullaeva Marifat, "Education For All And Literacy: Review of Central Asian Countries", *Adult Education and Development*, Number 66, DVV Publications, http://www.dvv-international.de/index.php?article_id=207&clang=1

Abdurazakova, Dono, "Political-Social Movements: Unions and Workers' Movements", in Suad Joseph ed. *Encyclopedia of Women & Islamic Cultures: Family, Law and Politics*, Vol. II, brill Leiden - Boston, 2005, p. 680.

Afshar, Haleh (ed), *Women and Politics in the Third World*, London: Routledge, 1996.

Aggrawal, Chandra Mohan, *Yugyugin Bhartiya Nari*, New Delhi: Indian Publishers Distributers, 2000.

Agrew, Vijay, *Elite Women in Indian Politics*, New Delhi: Vikas Publishing House, 1979.

Akiner, Shirin, "Islam, the State and Ethnicity in Central Asia in Historical Perspective", *Religion, State & Society*, Vol. 24, Nos. 2/3, 1996 p. 108. http://www.biblicalstudies.org.uk/pdf/rss/24_2-3_091.pdf.

Akiner, Shirin. "Between Tradition and Modernity: the Dilemma Facing Contemporary Central Asian Women." in Mary Buckley ed., *Post-Soviet Women: from the Baltic to Central Asia*, New York: Cambridge University Press, 1997, p. 288.

"An Overview of Women's Work and Employment in Kazakhstan. Decisions for Life", MDG3 Project, Country Report No. 10, University of Amsterdam / Amsterdam Institute for Advanced Labour Studies (AIAS)www.uva.nl/aias

Andal N, *Women and Indian Society: Options and Constraints*, New Delhi: Rawat Publications, 2002.

Ayse, Günes-Ayata, Ayça Ergun. "Gender Politics in Transitional Societies: A Comparative Perspective on Azerbaijan, Kazakhstan, Kyrgyzstan, and Uzbekistan" in Gender Politics, 2009, p. 211.

Ballington, Julie and Azza Karam, eds., *Increasing Women's Political Representation: New Trends in Gender Quotas*, International IDEA, 2005.

Ballington, Julie and Azza Karam eds., *Women in Parliament: Beyond Numbers*, (revised edition), International IDEA, 2005.

Banakar, Reza, "The Politics of Legal Cultures", 53, Scandinavian Studies in Law, 2008. p. 40. http://www.retfaerd.org/gamle_pdf/2008/4/Retfaerd_123_2008_4_s37_60.pdf. Accessed on 6 May, 2014.

Banerjee, Mukulika, Democracy, http://www.lse.ac.uk/IDEAS/publications/reports/pdf/SR010/banerjee.pdf, accessed on 14 March 2014.

"Beijing Platform for Action". Chapter IV. B. *Education and training of women*. p. 69. http://www.un.org/esa/gopher-data/conf/fwcw/off/a—20.en

Bekentayeva, Manshuk, "NGOs Helping Build Civil Society in Kazakhstan", *PEOPLE* on 24 April, 2013. See, http://www.astanatimes.com/2013/04/ngos-helping-build-civil-society-in-kazakhstan-swedish-expert-says/

Bennigsen, A and C Lemercier-Quelquejay, *Islam in the Soviet Union*, London, 1967, p.78.

Bethmann, Erich W., *The Fate of Muslims under Soviet Rule*, http://www.bjpa.org/Publications/downloadFile.cfm?FileID=16761

Bhatt, Yashoda, and C N Mangala (eds.), *Beyond the Threshold: Indian Women on the Move*, New Delhi: B R Publishing Corporation, 1995.

Bick, Megan, "EU- Central Asia Civil Society Seminar on Women's Rights", Brussels 21-24 June 2010, FINAL REPORT, September 2010, http://eeas.europa.eu/human_rights/civil_society/docs/2010_ca_final_report_en.pdf, accessed on 14 March 2014.

Browning, Genia K., *Women & Politics in the U.S.S.R: Consciousness Raising and Soviet Women's Groups*, Sussex: Wheatsheaf Books, 1987, p. 34.

LoBue, Elise Helen, "Kazakhstan's Soviet Past, Globalised Present, And 'Emancipated Women': A Case For A New Gender And Development Domain", The University Of Iowa, 2007. 3301725.

Bug, Amy, "Has Feminism Changed Physics?", *Signs*, 28.3 (2003), pp. 881–99. http://books.openedition.org/obp/1239. accessed on 14 March, 2013.

Buskirk, Linda, "The Silk Road", Quest Paper, Presented on October 31, 2008, p. 2. http://www.fwquestclub.com/welcome_files/papers/the_silk_road.pdf

Bystydzienski, Jill M., *Women in Electoral Politics: Lessons from Norway,* Praeger. 1995.

Chakrapani C., and S Vijaya Kumar (eds), *Changing Status and Role of Women in Indian Society*, New Delhi: M D Publications Private Ltd., 1994.

Chen, Lincoln C, et al., "Health Crisis in Central Asian Republics," *Economic and Political Weekly,* Vol. 27, No. 23, June 6, 1992, pp. 1197-1202.

Chenoy, Anuradha M, "Islam, Women and Identity in Contemporary Central Asia," *Economic and Political Weekly*, Vol. 31, No. 9, March 2, 1996, pp. 516-518.

Chowdhury, Najma, "Bangladesh: Gender Issues and Politics in a Patriarchy", in Barbara J. Nelson and Najma Chowdhury, eds., *Women and Politics Worldwide* (New Haven: Yale University Press, 1994), p. 94.

Chowdhury, Najma et al, "Redefining Politics: Patterns of Women's Political Engagement from a Global Perspective," in Barbara J Nelson and Najma Chowdhury, *Women and Politics Worldwide*, (New Haven: Yale University Press, 1997).

Coleman, Isobel, May/June issue, 2010., http://www.foreignaffairs.com/articles/66206/isobel-coleman/the-global-glass-ceiling

Collins, Kathleen, *Clan Politics and Regime Transition in Central Asia*, Cambridge University Press, 2006, p. 74.

Consolidated response from the E-Discussion on Violence Against women in politics, *iKNOW Politics*, http://www.iknowpolitics.org/files/Consolidatedreply_violenceagainstwomen in politics_.pdf

Consolidated Response on Women's Party Sections, *iKNOW Politics*, http://www.iknowpolitics.org/files/consolidatedresponsewomen'spartysection iknowpolitics.pdf

Complete edition of Lenin's works in Russian (2nd ed., Moscow 1928) Vol. 25, p. 64.

Cooper, Jay, "The Real Work: Sustaining NGO Growth in Central Asia", in M. Holt Ruffin and Daniel Waugh eds, *Civil Society in Central Asia*, Seattle: University of Washington Press, 1999, p. 214.

Corcoran-Nantes, Yvonne, *Lost Voices: Central Asian Women: Confronting Transition*, London and New York: Zed Books, 2005. 208 pages, p. 63.

Crouch, Dave, "The Bolsheviks and Islam", Issue: 110, April 2006, http://isj.org.uk/the-bolsheviks-and-islam/

Curtis, Glenn E., ed., *Kazakstan, Kyrgyzstan, Tajikistan, Turkmenistan, and Uzbekistan country studies*, Federal Research Division, Library of Congress, 1997, p. xxxii. https://ia601903.us.archive.org/18/items/kazakstankyrgyzs00curt_0/kazakstankyrgyzs00curt_0.pdf

Curtis, Glenn E., Ed., *Kazakstan, Kyrgystan, Tajikistan, Turkmenistan, And Uzbekistan, Country Studies*, Area Handbook Series, 1997, p. xix. http://www.marines.mil/Portals/59/Publications/Kazakstan,%20Kyrgystan,%20Tajikistan,%20Turkmenistan,%20and%20Uzbekistan%20Study_1.pdf

Dahlerup, Drude, ed., *Women, Quotas and Politics*, Routledge, 2006.

Dahlerup, Drude, Monique Leyenaar, (eds), *Breaking Male Dominance in Old Democracies*, Oxford University Press, 2013.

Data from Women in Muslim Countries (WIMC) http://www.unescap.org/Rural/doc/women/index.htm

Datta, Prabhat, Payel Sen, "Women in Urban Local Governance: Empowerment Through Participation", *Journal* of *Governance and Public Policy*, Vol. 4, Nos. 3 & 4, October 9, 2009, pp. 48-61.

Democracy and Gender Equality: The Role of the UN, Discussion Paper September 2013, https://eudevdays.eu/sites/default/files/Democracy-and-Gender-Equality-The-Role-of-the-UN-PDF.pdf

Deth, Jan W. Van, José Ramón Montero, Anders Westholm, (eds), *Citizenship and Involvement in European Democracies: A Comparative Analysis*, Routledge Research in Comparative Politics, 2007, p. 343-387.

DISE Report 2011-12, Flash Statistics National University of Educational Planning and Administration, Delhi, 2013.

Djanaeva, Nurgul, "The Systemic Crisis′ Impact On Women: Sub Regional Perspectives, AWID: Women's Rights, Brief 5, p. 5, http://www.awid.org

Douglas, Northrop, *Veiled Empire: Gender and Power in Stalinist Central Asia*, 1st edn. Ithaca: Cornell University Press, 2004, p. 11.

Edgar, Adrienne, "Bolshevism, Patriarchy and the Nation: The Soviet Emancipation of Muslim women in Pan-Islamic Perspective", *Slavic Review*, Vol.65, no. 2, Summer, 2006.

Edgar, Adrienne, "Emancipation of the Unveiled: Turkmen Women under Soviet Rule, 1924-1929," *Russian Review*, Vol. 62, No. 1, January, 2003, 132-49.

Edelbay, Saniya, "The Islamic Situation in Kazakhstan", *International Journal of Humanities and Social Science,* Vol. 2, No. 21; November 2012, p. 217.

Education in Uzbekistan Country Profile, UNICEF, p. 4, http://www.unicef.org/ceecis/Uzbekistan.pdf

Ekman, Joakim, Erik Amnå, "Political Participation And Civic Engagement: Towards A New Typology", *Human Affairs* 22, 283–300, 2012, pp. 286-92, http://www.degruyter.com/downloadpdf/j/humaff.2012.22.issue-3/s13374-012-0024-1/s13374-012-0024-1.xml, accessed on 14 March 2014.

Fallon, Kathleen M., Liam Swiss, and Jocelyn Viternac, "Resolving the Democracy Paradox:Democratisation and Women's Legislative Representation in Developing Nations, 1975 to 2009", *American Sociological Review*, 77(3), 2012, pp. 380–408, p. 395.

Feddersen,Gustavo Henrique, Giovanna Esther Zucatto, "Infrastructure in Central Asia: Energy and Transportation Controversies", UFRGSMUN/UFRGS Model United Nation Journal, Vol.1, 20013, p. 159-181, p. 159.

Fontanella- Khan, Amana, *Pink Sari Revolution: A Tale of Women And Power in India*, W W Norton & Company, NY, 2013.

Fried, Susana T, "Violence against Women," *Health and Human Rights*, Vol. 6, No. 2, 2003, pp. 88-111.

Fuszara, Malgorzata, "*Kobicty w polityce*" [Women in Politics], Warszawa 2007.

"Gender Equality and Women's Empowerment in India", Ministry of Health and Family Welfare, Government of India, National Family Health Survey (NFHS-3), India, 2005-06. http://www.rchiips.org/nfhs/a_subject_report_gender_for_website.pdf

Ghadially, Rehana (ed), *Urban Women in Contemporary India: A Reader*, London: Sage Publications, 2007.

Ghosal, Anupam, "Gender and Poverty: A Case Study of India", *Jadavpur Journal of International Relations*, 11(12), 2008, 302-316.

Giri, Mohini, "Women and Politics," in Yashoda Bhat, (ed.), *Beyond the Threshold: Indian Women on the Move*, New Delhi: B R Publishing Corporation (1995).

"Global Employment Trends for Women", March, 2009, *International Labour Organisation* 2009. p. 19.

Gokak, V.K., *India and World Culture*, Sahitya Akademi, New Delhi, 1994.

Government Organised Non-Governmental Program, http://www.ucis.pitt.edu/nceeer/2009_824- 02h_Clement.pdf

Green, Duncan, *From Poverty to Power: How active citizens and effective states can change the world*, 2nd ed. Rugby, UK: Practical Action Publishing and Oxford: Oxfam International, 2012, p. ix.

Grown, C. A. and J. Sebstad, "Towards a wider perspective on women's employment," *World Development* Vol. 17, No. 1, 1989, pp. 937-952.

Harris, C. "Coping With Daily Life in Post-Soviet Tajikistan: The Gharmi Villages of Khatlon Province," *Central Asian Survey*, Vol. 17, No. 4, 1998, pp. 655-671.

Harris, Colette, "Identity Politics: Central Asia" in Suad Joseph, Afsāna Nag mābādī, ed., *Encyclopedia of Women and Islamic Cultures: Family, Law and Politics*, 2004, p. 283-284.

Heer, D M, Youssef, N., "Female status among soviet central Asian nationalities: The melding of Islam and Marxism and its implications for population increase", *Population Studies*, Mar, 31(1), 1977, pp. 155-73.

Hornbeck, Stephen, "Educational Attainment and its Impact on Women's Status in Central Asia", March, 2012. http://www.d3systems.com/wp-content/uploads/2010/09/WIMC-Educational-Attainment-in-Central-Asia-Final1.pdf. Accessed on 23 May 2014.

IOM International Organisation for migration, "Fertile Field: Trafficking in Persons in Central Asia", Vienna, April 2005.

Inter-Parliamentary Union (IPU), *Politics: Women's Insight,* Geneva, Switzerland: Inter-Parliamentary Union, 2000a, p. 23.

Ishkanian, Armine, "Gendered Transitions: The Impact of the Post-Soviet Transition on Women in Central Asia and the Caucasus", *Perspectives on Global Development and Technology*, Vol. 2, no. 3-4, 2003, pp. 475-496, http://booksandjournals.brillonline.com/content/journals/15691497/2/3

Jain, Devaki, *The Vocabulary of Women's Politics*, New Delhi: Friedrich-Ebert-Stifiting, 2000.

Joseph, Suad, Afsana Nagmabad,eds, *Encyclopedia of Women and Islamic Cultures: Family, Law and Politics*, p. 50.

Joseph, Suad ed., *Encyclopedia of Women & Islamic Cultures: Family, Law and Politics*, Vol. II, brill leiden - boston, 2005, p. 680.

Joseph, Ammu, and Kalpana Sharma (eds), *Whose News? The Media and Women's Issues*, New Delhi: Sage Publications, 1994.

Joshi, Kishore M, "Higher Education, Social Demand and Social Equity in India", in Simon Schwartzman, Rómulo Pinheiro, Pundy Pillay, eds., *Higher Education in the BRICS Countries: Investigating the Pact between Higher Education and Society*, Higher Education Dynamics, Volume 44, 2015, p. 125-142.

Kabeer, Naila, "Gender Equality And Women's Empowerment: A Critical Analysis of the Third Millennium Development Goal", *Gender And Development* Vol. 13, No. 1, March 2005, pp. 13-24.

Kabdiyeva, Aliya, "Developing Sustainable NGOs in Kazakhstan", http://ccsenet.org/journal/index.php/ass/article/viewFile/27954/16874.

Khalid, Adeeb, *The Politics of Muslim Cultural Reform: Jadidism in Central Asia*, Berkeley: University of California Press, 1998, p. 190.

Kamat, Jyotsna K, "Perspectives in Education", Sadashiva Wodeyar's 50th Birthday Felicitation Volume, Dharwad 1980.

Kandiyoti, D, "Poverty in transition: An Ethnographic Critique of Household Surveys in Post-Soviet Asia," *Development and Change*, Vol. 30, No. 3, pp. 499-524.

Kandiyoti, Deniz, " The politics of Gender and the Soviet paradox: Neither Colonized, nor Modern?", Volume 26, 2007 - Issue 4, pp. 601-623 http://www.tandfonline.com/doi/abs/10.1080/02634930802018521

Kandiyoti, D. and R. Mandel, "Editor's Preface", *Central Asian Survey*, Vol. 17 No. 4, 1998, pp. 533-537.

Kane, Danielle, Ksenia O. Gorbenko. "States and Women's Rights in Central Asia." Paper presented at the American Sociological Association. Las Vegas, NV, 22 August 2011.

Kanji, Nazneen, "Trading and Trade-Offs: Women's Livelihoods in Gorno-Badakhshan, Tajikistan", *Development in Practice*, Vol. 12, No. 2 (May, 2002), pp. 138-152.

Kapsos, S. and A. Silberman, "Female Labour Force Participation in India", ILO, Geneva, 2013.

Kapsos, Steven, Evangelia Bourmpoula, Andrea Silberman, "Why is female labour force participation declining so sharply in India?",ILO Research Paper No. 10, 2014, p. 31http://www.ilo.org/wcmsp5/groups/public/—dgreports/—inst/documents/publication/wcms_250977.pdf

Karam, Azza (ed.), *Women in Parliament: Beyond Numbers*, Stockholm: International IDEA, 1998.

Kassam, Tazim R, "Those who Sing pray Twice", *American Academy of Religion,* Vol. 16, No. 2, 2001, https://www.aarweb.org/sites/default/files/pdfs/Spotlight/Teaching/Issues/2001-02SPRING.pdf

Kaushik, Susheela, (ed.), *Women's Participation in Politics*, New Delhi: Vikas Publishing House Pvt. Ltd., 1993.

Kelleher, Fatimah, "Women and the Teaching Profession: Exploring the Feminisation Debate", Commonwealth Secretariat and UNESCO 2011, p. 26, http://www.ungei.org/files/212200e.pdf.

Khassanova, Galiya, "On the Way to Democracy: Women's Activism in Kazakhstan". http://www.gwu.edu/~ieresgwu/assets/docs/demokratizatsiya%20archive/08-3_Khassanova.PDF

Kidayator, G., "Uzbekistan: Between the Past and Future", *Contemporary Central Asia*, 1 (1), 12-25, 1997, p. 15.

Klaveren, Maarten van, Kea Tijdens,Melanie Hughie-Williams, Nuria Ramos, "An Overview of Women's Work and Employment in Kazakhstan. Decisions for Life", MDG3 Project, Country Report No. 10, University of Amsterdam /Amsterdam Institute for Advanced Labour Studies (AIAS), Netherlands, March 2010, p. 41 www.uva.nl/aias.

Kocaoglu, Timur, "The Past as Prologue? Challenging the Myth of the Subordinated, Docile Woman in Muslim Central Eurasia", in Linda Racioppi and Katherine O'Sullivan See eds., *Gender politics in post-communist Eurasia*, East Lansing: Michigan State University Press, 2009, pp. 169-208.

Kocaoglu, Timur, *The Past as Prologue? Challenging the Myth of the Subordinated, Docile Woman in Muslim Central Eurasia*, p. 177. http://www.iccrimea.org/scholarly/kocaoglu-gender.pdf

Kochar, Soonu, "Geo-Political Diversity" in Kurt April & Marylou Shockley, eds, "*Diversity New Realities in a Changing World*", Palgrave, N Y, 2007, p. 154.

Kollontai, Alexandra, "V.I. Lenin and the First Congress of Women Workers", https://www.marxists.org/archive/kollonta/1918/congress.htm.

Krook, Mona Lena, "Electoral Gender Quotas: A Conceptual Analysis", *Comparative Political Studies,* Vol. 47(9), 2014, 1268–1293.

Kuehnast, Kathleen R., Carol Nechemias, Eds., "Post-Soviet Women Encountering Transition: Nation Building, Economic Survival, And Civic Activism", Woodrow Wilson Center Press, 2004, p. 4.

Kumar, Arvind, "Privatisation of School Education: A Social Welfare Program or Industry for Profit", *European Academic Research*, Vol. II, Issue 1, April 2014, p. 1552.

Kumari, Kamala, *Women in New Russia*, 2012, p. 15.

Kumari, Kamala, "Political Participation of Women in India", in Alok Kumar Gupta and Asha Bhandari, Eds, *Women and Political Participation in Indian Democratic System*, Author's Press, 2010, p. 6.

Kumari, Kamala, "Identifying women's issues in Central Asia: Problems and Prospects" *Contemporary Central Asia*, Vol.xiv, No. I, March 2010, pp.45-62.

Kumari, Kamala, "Globalisation and Women in India", Tuesday, 27 July 2010, paxindica.in/

Kumari, R. Letha, *Women in Politics: Participation and Governance*, Delhi: Authorspress, 2006.

Kunjan Raja, C., *Vedic Culture, The Cultural Heritage of India*, Vol. I, The Ramakrishna Mission, Calcutta, 1975.

Landman, Todd, Marco Larizza, *EU Policy Discourse: Democracy, Governance, and Human Rights*, International IDEA, Stockholm, Sweden, 2010, p. 8.

Lapidus, Gail W., *Women in Soviet Society*, Berkeley: University of California Press, 1978, p. 205.

Lenin, "Soviet Power and the Status of Women 1919", in Lenin, V. I., *On the Emancipation of Women*. Moscow: Progress Publishers, 1974. http://icl-fi.org/english/ssa/5/women.html. Accessed on 14 March 2012.

Lenin, Selected Works (New York 1935-38) Vol. 9, pp. 494-9.

Lenin, Vladimir Ilyich, "*Reminiscences: 1900-1922*", Moscow, 1963, pp. 221-223.

Lokar, Sonja, in replyviolence against women in politics, http://www.iknowpolitics.org/files/Consolidate.pdf

Jinee Lokeneela, "Women Empowerment: Redefining Agenda" in Kiran Saxena, (ed.), *Women and Politics*, New Delhi: Gyan Publishing House, 2000.

Maghadam, Valentine M (ed.), *Identity Politics and Women: Cultural Reassertations and Feminisms in International Perspective*, Oxford: Westview Press, 1994.

Mahadevan, T.M.P., *The Religio-Philosophic Culture of India, The Cultural Heritage of India*, Vol. I, The Rama Krishna Mission, Calcutta, 1975.

Majumdar, Ramesh Chandra, *Ancient India*, Motilal Banarsidass, 1977, ISBN 978-81-208-0436-4.

Majumdar R. C., A. D. Pusalker (editors): *The history and culture of the Indian people*. Volume I, The Vedic Age, Bombay: Bharatiya Vidya Bhavan, 1951, p. 394.

Malashenko, A V, "The Eighties: A New Political Start for Islam", *Russian Social Science Review*, March, 1993.

Marat Erica, (book review), "Lost Voices: Central Asian Women: Confronting Transition" by Yvonne Corcoran-Nantes, London and New York: Zed Books, 2005, Central Asia - Caucasus Institute and Silk Road Studies Program, University of Uppsala/The Johns Hopkins University, Uppsala, Sweden.

Mathai, Raichel, "Political status of Indian Women: Progress since Independence", *Mainstream*, Xliv (1), 2006, pp. 83-86.

McAuley, Alastair, "Development Strategy, Welfare Regime and Poverty Reduction in the Former Soviet Union", United Nations Research Institute for Social Development (UNRISD), 2008, p-11, http://www.unrisd.org/80256B3C005BB128/%28httpAuxPages%29/61A3639B57518A12C125773D004A78AA/$file/USSRweb-3.pdf

McBride, Dorothy E. (Review), Ann E. Towns, "Women and States: Norms and Hierarchies in International Society", New York: Cambridge University Press, 2010, in *Politics & Gender*, 7 (2011), Florida Atlantic University, 605–613.

Mee, Wendy, "Women in the Republic of Uzbekistan", Country Briefing Paper, 2001, p. x.

Mehra, Vikash, "Women in India: Status, Position and Condition of Women in India", February 17, 2014.

Mendikulova, Gulnara, "Kazakh Women: the Impact of Three Different Socio political Systems within Two Centuries", in Christa Hämmerle, ed. *Gender Politics in Central Asia: Historical Perspectives and Current Living Conditions of Women*, Germany: Böhlau Verlag Köln Weimar, 2008, p. 21-34.

Menon, Nivedita, (ed.), *Themes in Politics: Gender and Politics in India*, New Delhi: Oxford University Press, 1999.

Ministry of Human Resource Development Dept of School Education & Literacy, GOI. http://wcddel.in/ksy.html

Mirsaidov, Negmatullo, 20.07.2012, http://centralasiaonline.com/en_GB/articles/caii/features/main/2012/07/20/feature-01, accessed on 23 January 2014.

Moldosheva, Anara, "Kyrgyzstan National Report on Women & Governance", Bishkek, November 2008.

Musayev, Ondjik, "Democratic Party of Turkmenistan", First Secretary, International Department of Central Committee of CPC, 3rd international conference of Asian political parties, Beijing China 2004-09-05, 2004, http://www.idcpc.org.cn/icapp3/2004-09/05/content_2809095.htm

Nair, Gaayathri, "It's Time We Understood Intersectionality", *Forum News*, Nov, 2010, Vol. 23, No. 2, p. 5.

Nair, Janaki, "Women and Law in Colonial India: A Social History," in Kiran Saxena (ed), *Women and Politics*, New Delhi: Gyan Publishing House, 2000.

Najafizadeh, Mehrangiz, "Women's Empowering Carework in Post-Soviet Azerbaijan," *Gender and Society*, Vol. 17, No. 2, April, 2003, pp. 293-304.

Naumann, Matthew and Burul Usmanalieva, "Central Asia: social movements case studies", INTRAC, 2008, p. 1. http://www.intrac.org/data/files/resources/645/Social-Movements-and-Conflict-in-Post-Revolution-Kyrgyzstan.pdf

Nehru, Jawaharlal, *The Discovery of India*, Centenary Edition, (Delhi: Oxford University Press, 1989), p. 562.

Niranjana, S., 'Exploring Gender Inflections within Panchayat Raj institutions: Women's Politicisation in Andhra Pradesh", in K. Kapadia (ed.), *The Violence of Development: The Politics of Identity, Gender and Social Inequalities in India*, New Delhi: Kali for Women, 2002.

Norris, Pippa, *Driving Democracy Do Power-Sharing Institutions Work?,* Cambridge: Cambridge University Press, 2008, p. xi.

Norvell, Lyn, "Gandhi And The Indian Women's Movement", http://www.bl.uk/eblj/1997articles/pdf/article2.pdf

Pande, Rohini, Petia Topalova, "Women in Charge", Finance & Development, June 2013, https://www.imf.org/external/pubs/ft/fandd/2013/06/pdf/pande.pdf. Accessed on 6 May, 2014.

Pandey, Sumana, *Women in Politics*, Jaipur: Rawat Publications, 1990.

Pargunan, M., "Political Empowerment of women: An Illusion", *Kurukshetra*, 55(5), 2007, pp. 12-18.

Patnaik, Ajay, *Perestroika and Women Labour Force in Soviet Central Asia*, New Delhi: New Literature, 1989.

Patnaik, Ajay, "Democracy Debate in Central Asia: Missing the Social Dimension", *Contemporary Central Asia*, Vol. XVII, No. 3, 2013, pp. 2-3.

Patrick, Olivelle, (Trans), Upanishads, Oxford University Press, 1998, ISBN: 978-0-19-283576-5.

Paxton, Pamela, Sheri Kunovich, "Women's Political Representation: The Importance of Ideology", *Social Forces*, Volume 82, Number 1, September 2003, pp. 87-113.

Pearson, R., "All Change? Men, Women And Reproductive Work In The Global Economy," *European Journal of Development Research*, Vol. 12, No. 2, 2000, pp. 219-237.

Philip, G ., Altbach, Patti Mcgill Peterson Eds, "Higher Education In The 21st Century: Global Challenge And National Response", April 1999. www.iie.org/.../Research-Report-029.

Philipose, Pamela, "India -Battle for the Women's Bill: Bring in the Umbrellas", Alliance for 33%, *Forum News*,Vol. 23 No. 2, NOVEMBER 2010. http://apwld.org/wp-content/uploads/2013/09/APWLD-Forum-News-Vol32No2-Web.pdf

Pipes, Daniel, "The Third World Peoples of Soviet Central Asia", in W. Scott Thompson Ed., *The Third World: Premises of U.S. Foreign Policy*, San Francisco: Institute for Contemporary Studies, 1983, pp. 183-203.

Pipes, R, *The Formation of the Soviet Union*, New York, 1954, p. 77.

Presentation on 'Women's Participation in Politics in the Asia Region-A Case Study of Local Governance' for the use of Indian Parliamentary Delegation at the 10th Commonwealth Women Affairs Ministers Meeting to be held in Dhaka, 17-19 June 2013.

Promoting Civic Space, International Center For Not-For-Profit Law, Annual Report 2011-2012, p. 9 http://www.icnl.org/about/reports/ICNL_AR_2011-2012.pdf

Pujari, Premalala, and Vijay Kumar Kaushik, Women Power in India, Vol. 1,2&3, Delhi: Kanishka Publishers, 1994.

Purushothaman, Sangeetha, *The Empowerment of Women in India: Grassroots Women's Network and the State*, New Delhi: Sage Publications, 1998.

Rai, Sihirin M. (ed.), International Perspectives on Gender and Democratisation, London: Macmillan Press, 2000.

Rajan, Rajeswari Sunder, *The Scandal of the State: Women, Law, and Citizenship in Postcolonial India*, Durham: Duke University Press, 2003.

"Reservation of Seats For Women in Legislative Bodies:Perspectives, Occasional Paper Series, 1/2008, Rajya Sabha Secretariat, New Delhi, July 2008, p. 2. http://rajyasabha.nic.in/rsnew/publication_electronic/reserv_women_pers2008.pdf

Resolution adopted by the General Assembly on 19 December 2011 66/130. Women and Political Participation, (http://www.un.org/ga/search/view_doc.asp?symbol= A/RES/66/130

Richter, Linda K, "Exploring Theories of Female Leadership in South and Southeast Asia," *Pacific Affairs*, No. 4, Winter 1990-1991.

Rifkatovna, Ismagilova Nuria, "Women in Politics and Gender-Based Corruption in Central Asia: Realities and Responses", http://www.10iacc.org/download/t1-05.pdf, accessed on 14 March 2014.

Roberts, Andrew, Jason Seawright, Jennifer Cyr "Do Electoral Laws Affect Women's Representation?", Comparative Political Studies, 46: 1555, November, Sage Publications, 2013. p. 1. http://www.sagepublications.com

Rokicka, Magdalena, "Gender Gap in the CIS…", *Center for Social and Economic Research (CASE) Network Studies & Analyses*, No. 376, Warsaw, 2008, p. 48.

Rossabi Morris, "Central Asia: A Historical Overview", http://asiasociety.org/central-asia-historical-overview?page=0,0. Accessed on 6 May, 2014.

Roy, Rushoti, "The Changing Roles of Women- An Overview into the Perception of Women Over Time in India", The Institute of Chartered Accountants of India, Jan 2010, p. 1103.

Rudenko, Yelena I., "Public Issues and Social Initiatives for the differently abled people of Kazakhstan", in Mondira Dutta ed., *Gender and Human Development in Central and South Asia*, Delhi: Pentagon Press, p. 87-98.

Rysalieva, Zainura, " Kyrgyzstan: Culture and Identity in the process of Globalisation", in Mondira Dutta ed., Gender and Human Development in Central and South Asia, Delhi: Pentagon Press, 131-139, p. 135.

Saktaganova, Zauresh Galimzhanovna and Dinara Kenesovna Ospanova, "Non-Governmental Organisations in the Republic of Kazakhstan: Principle Stages of Formation and Development", *Middle-East Journal of Scientific Research* 15 (9): 1277-1284, 2013, p. 1277.

Santos, Lean Alfred, "How Central Asia can improve governance for development", 9 October 2013, https://www.devex.com/en/news/how-central-asia-can-improve-governance-for/82046, accessed on 14 March 2014.

Saxena Kiran (ed), *Women and Politics*, New Delhi: Gyan Publishing House, 2000.

Shakirova, Svetlana, "Gender Policy And Nation Building In Kazakhstan: Parallel of Conflicting Processes", in Mondira Dutta ed., *Gender and Human Development in Central and South Asia*, Delhi: Pentagon Press, pp. 253-262.

Saktaganova, Zauresh Galimzhanovna and Dinara Kenesovna Ospanova, "Non-Governmental Organisations in the Republic of Kazakhstan: Principle Stages of Formation and Development", *Middle-East Journal of Scientific Research* 15 (9): 1277-1284, 2013, p. 1277.

Sharipova, Muborak, "One More War Against Women: Historical And Socio-Cultural Aspects Of Violence Against Women In Tajikistan", In Hämmerle, Christa, Nikola Langreiter, Margareth Lanzinger, And Edith Saurer, Eds., *Gender Politics In Central Asia: Historical Perspectives And Current Living Conditions Of Women*. Germany: Behlau, 2008, pp. 67-94.

Sharma Sandeep Kumar, *International Journal for Research* in *Education*, Vol. 2, Issue: 9, October- Nov. 2013. http://raijmr.com/wp-content/uploads/2014/01/4, accessed 14 March 2013.

Shaw George Bernard, in the preface to his play "Major Barbara", 1907, https://archive.org/details/BernardShawsMajorBarbaraTheCompletePreface

Silova, Iveta, Mark S. Johnson, And Stephen P. Heyneman, "Education and the Crisis of Social Cohesion in Azerbaijan and Central Asia", May 2007 p. 176, http://www.vanderbilt.edu/peabody/heyneman/PUBLICATIONS/Ed.%20and%20the%20Crisis%20of%20Social%20Cohesion%20in%20Azerbaijan%20and%20Central%20Asia.pdf, accessed on 23 March 2014.

Singh, Upinder, *A History of Ancient and Early Mediaeval India: From the Stone Age to the 12th Century*, Pearson Education India, 2008, ISBN: 978-81-317-1120-0.

Sinha, Niroj, (ed.), *Women in Indian Politics: Empowerment of women through Political Particpation*, New Delhi: Gyan Publishing House, 2000.

Sinor, D., *The Cambridge History of Early Inner Asia*, London: Cambridge University Press, 1990, p. 344.

Smith, Sharon, "Marxism, feminism and women's liberation", http://socialistworker.org/2013/01/31/marxism-feminism-and-women's-liberation

Speech at Women's Conference, Sojitra, Gujrat, in *Collected works of Mahatma Gandhi*, Vol. 30, 27 December 1924, 21 March (1925), p. 108.

Sperl, Louise, "The Crisis and its Consequences for Women, in Development and Transition", Newsletter, 2/2009, http://www.developmentandtransition.net/index.cfm?module=ActiveWeb&page=WebPage&DocumentID=728

State Statistical Agency of the Government of the Republic of Tajikistan: Women in Development Bureau, 1999.

Stobaugh, James P., *World History: Observations and Assessments from Creation to Today*, New Leaf Publishing Group, 01-Mar-2012, p. 129.

Sultanova, Razia, "From Shamanism to Sufism: Women, Islam and Culture in Central Asia", *International Library of Central Asia Studies,* N Y, 2011.

Surkov, Vladislav, "Vladislav Surkov Divides Democracy", June 29, 2006, http://www.kommersant.com/p686274/r_1/Vladislav_Surkov_Divides_Democracy/, accessed on 14 March 2014.

Sweetman Caroline, "Gender and the Millennium Development Goals", Oxfam, 2005, p. 17.

Tadjbakhsh, S, "Between Lenin and Allah: Women and Ideology in Tajikistan," in H. L. Bodman and N. Tohidi (eds.), *Women in Muslim Societies*, London: Lynne Reinner. UNDP (2000).

The Condition of Higher Education in Turkmenistan, http://www.silkproject.org/highereducationinturkmenistan.htm

"The World's Women", United Nations, New York, 2010. http://unstats.un.org/unsd/demographic/products/Worldswomen/WW_full report_color.pdf

The Women's Movement in Central Asia, http://www.awid.org/Library/The-Women-s-Movement-in-Central-Asia

"The Woman Question: Selections from the Writings of Karl Marx, Frederick Engels, V. I. Lenin, Joseph Stalin", Printed in 1951 in the United States of America.

Tajikistan Human Development Report 2006, Dushanbe, Tajikistan: UNDP, 2006.

Tan Netina, Ethnic Quota and Unintended Effects on Women's Political Representation in Singapore, p. 3-4, http://www.cpsa-acsp.ca/papers-2013/Tan1.pdf, accessed on 14 March 2014.

Teplova, Tatyana, Welfare State Transformation, childcare and women's work in Russia, The Author 2007, Oxford: Oxford University Press, 2007.

Thompson, Mark R., "Female Leadership of Democratic Transitions in Asia", *Pacific Affairs*, Vol. 75, No. 4, Winter, 2002-2003, pp. 535-555.

Tokhtakhodzhaeva, Marfua, "The Re-Islamisation of Society and the Position of Women in Post-Soviet Uzbekistan", 2008, E-ISBN: 9789004213241, http://booksandjournals.brillonline.com/books/9789004213241

Tokhtakhodjaeva, Marfua, Balchin, Cassandra and Shirkat Gah, "Between the Slogans of Communism and the Laws of Islam", Shirkat Gah Women's Resource Centre, Lahore, Pakistan, 1995. p. 21.

Tokhtakhodjaeva, Marfua, "Uzbek Women throughout 20th Century", Photo Exhibition Documents, 12/02/2009 http://uzbekistan.usembassy.gov/pe120209_2.html

Verveer, Melanne, "The Political and Economic Power of Women", 2011 http://www.cipe.org/sites/default/files/publication-docs/071511.pdf

Waris, Amtul, B. C. Viraktamath, "Gender Gaps and Women's Empowerment in India: Issues And Strategies", *International Journal of Scientific and Research Publications*, Volume 3, Issue 9, September 2013. http://www.ijsrp.org/research-paper-0913/ijsrp-p21116.pdf

What is Good Governance?, United Nations Economic and Social Commission for Asia and the Pacific, July 10, 2009, http://www.unescap.org/pdd/prs/ProjectActivities/Ongoing/gg/governance.asp

World Economic Forum's (WEF) Gender Gap Report 2013.

"Women And Economy In Central Asia", http://editorials.voa.gov.

"Women and Men in Decision-Making", Analysis of the Situation and Trends, European Commission 2007. http://ec.europa.eu/employment_social/publications/ 2008/ke8108186_en.pdf

"Women and Labour Markets in Asia: Rebalancing for Gender Equality", http://www.indianexpress.com/news/asia-needs-to-improve-employment-options-for-women-adb/783426/, Accessed on 23 March 2014.

Women in National Parliaments, World and Regional Averages, http://www.ipu.org/wmn-e/world.htm

Women's Access to Justice in Central and Eastern Europe and Central Asia, KARAT, Coalition with Partners, 2012. http://www.karat.org/wp-content/uploads/2012/01/Women_Access_To_Justice_ENG_final_version.pdf.

Zhakenov, G., "The National Report on the Development of the System of Higher Education of the Republic of Kazakhstan", 2008.
http://www.unesco.kz/education/he/kazakh/kazakh_ru.htm

Web sites

http://censusindia.gov.in/Census_And_You/literacy_and_level_of_education.aspx

http://rajyasabha.nic.in/rsnew/publication_electronic/reserv_women_pers2008.pdf

www.ipu.org

http://www.vedicsanskriti.com/2016/04/manusmriti-in-hindi-pdf.html

https://docs.google.com/file/d/0Bz1OumJznV7ucmwyelNvQy1CcUU/edit

http://pdf.usaid.gov/pdf_docs/pdabu135.pdf.

http://www.marines.mil/Portals/59/Publications/Kazakstan,%20Kyrgystan,%20Tajikistan,%20Turkmenistan,%20and%20Uzbekistan%20Study_4.pdf. http://data.mongabay.com/reference/country_studies/tajikistan/all.html

http://www.un.org/womenwatch/directory/women_and_poverty_3001.htm

http://www.ucis.pitt.edu/nceeer/2009_824-02h_Clement.pdf http://www.nuepa.org/Download/Publications/UnPriced/NUEPA_SAsia%20models_Final_Full.pdf

https://www.scribd.com/document/233313295/India-Education-Report-January-2012

http://shodhganga.inflibnet.ac.in/bitstream/10603/40092/9/09_chapter1.pdf

http://shodhganga.inflibnet.ac.in/bitstream/10603/37480/7/07_chapter%201.pdf

http://mhrd.gov.in/statistics_data.

http://unesdoc.unesco.org/images/0014/001459/145934e.pdf

http://www.silkproject.org/highereducation.htm

http://www.unesco.org/new/en/education/themes/leading-the-international-agenda/education-for-all/the-efa-movement/dakar-2000/

http://www.marines.mil/Portals/59/Publications/Kazakstan, Kyrgystan, Tajikistan, Turkmenistan, and UzbekistanStudy_4.pdf

http://www.dvv-international.de/index.php?article_id=207&clang=1

http://pdf.usaid.gov/pdf_docs/pdabu135.pdf.

http://www.gsleducation.com/news-28-UN-Millennium-Development-Goals-and-Education—.html

http://www.un.org/millenniumgoals/education.shtml

http://www.oitbrasil.org.br/sites/default/files/topic/gender/doc/getwomen2012_963.pdf; http://databank.worldbank.org/data/views/reports/tableview.aspx?isshared=true https://www.scribd.com/doc/17512075/World-Development-Indicators-2008

http://databank.worldbank.org/data/views/reports/tableview.aspx?isshared=true

http://www.unescap.org/rural/doc/women/index.htm

http://www.ucentralasia.org/news.asp?Nid=415

www.fao.org/sofa/gender/en/

http://www.un.org/womenwatch/directory/women_and_poverty_3001.htm

www.fao.org/gender/infographic/en.

http://www.un.org/womenwatch/directory/women_and_poverty_3001.htm

http://www.un.org/documents/ga/conf177/aconf177-20en.htm

http://www.oitbrasil.org.br/sites/default/files/topic/gender/doc/getwomen2012_963.pdf

http://www.unfpa.org/modules/6billion/populationissues/empower.htm http://genderindex.org/country/india/kazakhstan/kyrgyzsatn/tajikistan/turkmenisatn/uzbekistan

http://www.intrac.org/data/files/resources/412/Praxis-Paper-15-Organisational-Capacity-Building-in-Central-Asia.pdf

http://www.unescap.org/pdd/prs/ProjectActivities/Ongoing/gg/governance.asp

http://www.idea.int/

http://www.un.org/womenwatch/daw/cedaw/history.htm

http://www.ipu.org/english/surveys.htm

http://www.unece.org/stats/gender/genpols/keyinds/genpols-2work.htm http://europeandcis.undp.org/gender/gendermainstreaming/show/66F1EDBD-F203-1EE9-B3F12FEA5C87F079

http: www.parlam.kz/ru/legislative-act/1666

www.quotaproject.org

http://www.stopvaw.org

http://eci.nic.in/

http://www.ipu.org/pdf/publications/wmnmap14_en.pdf

www.worldbank.org/opendata/women-ministerial-positions-worldwide-looking-data-close

http://www.wilpf.int.ch/publications/CEDAW_Report_Jan_2004.html

http://daccessdds.un.org/doc/UNDOC/GEN/N07/264/90/PDF/N0726490.pdf

http://www.nationsencyclopedia.com/World-Leaders-2003/Uzbekistan-domestic-policy.html

http://www.unhcr.org/publ/PUBL/3eaff4422.html

www.bti-project.org.

http://www.usaid.gov/sites/default/files/documents/1863/2012CSOSI_0.pdf

http://www.icnl.org/research/resources/regional/NGOSICEE2009.pdf

http://www.women'scampaigninternational.org/what_we_do

http://gulabigangofficial.in/

http://www.gulabigang.in/

http://www.thenational.ae/arts-culture/pink-sari-movement-in-india-fights-violence-against-women#ixzz2yAneEBNm

http://gulabigangofficial.in/case-studies/

http://gulabigangofficial.in/gulabi-services/

http://timesofindia.indiatimes.com/india/Rajya-Sabha-passes-Women's-Reservation-http://bill/articleshow/5663003.cms?referral=PM

http://www.rediff.com/news/2005/aug/24spec2.htm

http://www.usaid.gov/where-we-work/asia

www.cwds.ac.in/

http://www.csrindia.org/

https://www.ywcaofdelhi.org

http://www.indianwomen.org.in/indian-women-ngos.htm

http://www.un.org/News/Press/docs/2006/wom1558.doc.htm

http://forumofwomenngos.kg/about-us-2/

http://www.wageindicator.org/documents/publicationslist/publications-2010/An-Overview-of-Women's-Work-and-Employment-in-Kazakhstan.pdf

http://e-history.kz/en/contents/view/764

http://e-history.kz/media/upload/728/2013/11/14/355dcbc74f1022ed36c56c005d6bfe4a.pdf

http://kzopengov.com/in-the-kazakh-parliament-24-3-percent-of-deputies-are-women/

http://www.un.org/womenwatch/daw/Review/responses/KAZAKHSTAN-English.pdf

http://www.unwomen.org/en/what-we-do/leadership-and-political-participation/women's-movements;

http://www.unesco.kz/new/en/social-and-human-sciences/news/1449

http://www.un.org/womenwatch/daw/cedaw/recommendations/recomm.htm#recom23

http://un.org.kg/en/news-center/news-releases/list/News%20Center/74-UNIFEM?start=10

http://www.intrac.org/docs.php/2991/Social%20Movements%20case%20studies%20March%202008.pdf

http://www.un.org/ga/search/view_doc.asp?symbol=A/RES/66/130

http://www.unesco.kz/new/en/social-and-human-sciences/news/1449

http://www.icnl.org/research/monitor/turkmenistan.html

http://www.un.org/News/Press/docs/2006/wom1558.doc.htm

http://www.karat.org/ http://www.igpn.net/download/igpn_regional_report_(interviews_with_political_parties).pdf

http://www.deathpenaltyabolition.tj/en/about-usl

http://www.friends-partners.org/ccsi/nisorgs/uzbek/wmrsrctr.htm

http://www.wmgd.net/symposium/2007/report/olgadjanaeva.htm

http://www.icnl.org/about/reports/ICNL_AR_2011-2012.pdf

http://www.fpif.org/briefs/vol5/v5n06aral_body.html

http://www.stopvaw.org/turkmenistan

http://mvd.gov.kz/

http://mvd.gov.kz/portal/page/portal/mvd/mvd_page/mvd_president/.htm

http://mvd.gov.kz/portal/page/portal/mvd/mvd_page/mvd_kidnapping/F45DDEDCF0C03757E044002655122E6A

http://www.unwomen.org/en/news/stories/2013/2/new-law-in-kyrgyzstan-toughens-penalties-for-bride-kidnapping

http://www.un.org/womenwatch/directory/critical_areas_of_concern_30.htm

Appendices

APPENDIX 1.A THE CONSTITUTION OF THE REPUBLIC OF KAZAKHSTAN

Adopted by the all-nation referendum on August 30, 1995

Decree of the President of the Republic of Kazakhstan

On the Constitution of the Republic of Kazakhstan The President of the Republic of Kazakhstan proposed, and the people of Kazakhstan, at the republican referendum on August 30, 1995, adopted the New Constitution of the Republic of Kazakhstan. In view of the results of the republican referendum having been officially published, and the New Constitution having come into force since September 5, 1995, I RESOLVE:

1. To publish the Constitution of the Republic of Kazakhstan.
2. To stipulate that the original text of the Constitution of the Republic of Kazakhstan, adopted at the republican referendum on August 30, 1995, shall be kept by the President of the Republic of Kazakhstan.
3. The original text of the Constitution of the Republic of Kazakhstan, adopted at the ninth session of the Supreme Soviet of the Republic of Kazakhstan of the twelfth convocation on January 28, 1993, shall be placed for eternal custody with the Central State Archives of the Republic of Kazakhstan.
4. The present Decree comes into effect on the day it is published.

The President of the Republic of Kazakhstan N. NAZARBAYEV Almaty, September 6, 1995

No. 2454

We, the people of Kazakhstan, united by a common historic fate, creating a state on the indigenous Kazakh land, considering ourselves a peaceloving and civil society, dedicated to the ideals of freedom, equality and concord, wishing to take a worthy place in the world community, realizing our high responsibility before the present and future generations, proceeding from our sovereign right, accept this Constitution.

Section - I

General Provisions

Article 1

1. The Republic of Kazakhstan proclaims itself a democratic, secular, legal and social state whose highest values are an individual, his life, rights and freedoms.
2. The fundamental principles of the activity of the Republic are public concord and political stability; economic development for the benefit of all the nation; Kazakhstan patriotism and resolution of the most important issues of the affairs of state by democratic methods including voting at an all-nation referendum or in the Parliament.

Article 2

1. The Republic of Kazakhstan is a unitary state with a presidential form of government.

2. The sovereignty of the Republic extends to its entire territory. The state ensures the integrity, inviolability and inalienability of its territory.
3. The administrative-territorial division of the Republic of Kazakhstan, location and status of its capital are determined by law.
4. The names "Republic of Kazakhstan" and "Kazakhstan" have the same meaning.

Article 3

1. The people shall be the only source of state power.
2. The people shall exercise power directly through an all-nation referendum and free elections as well as delegate the execution of their power to state institutions.
3. Nobody shall have the right to appropriate power in the Republic of Kazakhstan. Appropriation of power shall be persecuted by law. The right to act on behalf of the people and the state shall belong to the President as well as to Parliament of the Republic within the limits of the constitutional powers. The government and other state bodies shall act on behalf of the state only within the limits of their delegated authorities.
4. The state power in the Republic of Kazakhstan is unified and executed on the basis of the Constitution and laws in accordance with the principle of its division into the legislative, executive and judicial branches and a system of checks and balances that governs their interaction.

Article 4

1. The provisions of the Constitution, the laws corresponding to it, other regulatory legal acts, international treaty and other commitments of the Republic as well as regulatory resolutions of Constitutional Council and the Supreme Court of the Republic shall be the functioning law in the Republic of Kazakhstan.
2. The Constitution shall have the highest juridical force and direct effect on the entire territory of the Republic.
3. International treaties ratified by the Republic shall have priority over its laws and be directly implemented except in cases when the application of an international treaty shall require the promulgation of a law.
4. All laws, international treaties of which the Republic is a party shall be published. Official publication of regulatory legal acts dealing with the rights, freedoms and responsibilities of citizens shall be a necessary condition for their application.

Article 5

1. The Republic of Kazakhstan shall recognize ideological and political diversity. The merging of public and state institutions, and the formation of political party organisations in state bodies shall not be permitted.
2. Public associations shall be equal before the law. Illegal interference of the state in the affairs of public associations and of public associations in the

affairs of the state, imposing the functions of state institutions on public associations, and financing of public associations by the state shall not be permitted.

3. Formation and functioning of public associations pursuing the goals or actions directed toward a violent change of the constitutional system, violation of the integrity of the Republic, undermining the security of the state, inciting social, racial, national, religious, class and tribal enmity, as well as formation of unauthorised paramilitary units shall be prohibited.
4. Activities of political parties and trade unions of other states, religious parties as well as financing political parties and trade unions by foreign legal entities and citizens, foreign states and international organisations shall not be permitted in the Republic.
5. Activities of foreign religious associations on the territory of the Republic as well as appointment of heads of religious associations in the Republic by foreign religious centers shall be carried out in coordination with the respective state institutions of the Republic.

Article 6

1. The Republic of Kazakhstan shall recognize and by the same token protect state and private property.
2. Property shall impose obligations, and its use must simultaneously benefit the society. Subjects and objects of ownership, the scope and limits of the rights of proprietors, and guarantees of their protection shall be determined by law.
3. The land and underground resources, waters, flora and fauna, other natural resources shall be owned by the state. The land may also be privately owned on terms, conditions and within the limits established by legislation.

Article 7

1. The state language of the Republic of Kazakhstan shall be the Kazakh language.
2. In state institutions and local self-administrative bodies the Russian language shall be officially used on equal grounds along with the Kazakh language.
3. The state shall promote conditions for the study and development of the languages of the people of Kazakhstan.

Article 8

The Republic of Kazakhstan shall respect principles and norms of international law, pursue the policy of cooperation and good-neighbourly relations between states, their equality and noninterference in each other's domestic affairs, peaceful settlement of international disputes and renounce the first use of the military force.

Article 9

The Republic of Kazakhstan shall have its state symbols - the flag, emblem and anthem. Their description and order of official use shall be established by the constitutional law.

Section - II

The Individual and Citizen

Article 10

1. Citizenship of the Republic of Kazakhstan shall be acquired and terminated as prescribed by law, shall be indivisible and equal regardless of the grounds of its acquisition.
2. A citizen of the Republic of Kazakhstan under no circumstances may be deprived of citizenship of the right to change his citizenship, and may not be exiled from the territory of Kazakhstan.
3. Foreign citizenship of a citizen of the Republic shall not be recognised.

Article 11

1. A citizen of the Republic of Kazakhstan may not be extradicted to a foreign state unless otherwise stipulated by international treaties of the Republic.
2. The Republic shall guarantee its citizens protection and patronage outside its boundaries.

Article 12

1. Human rights and freedoms in the Republic of Kazakhstan shall be recognised and guaranteed in accordance with this Constitution.
2. Human rights and freedoms shall belong to everyone by virtue of birth, be recognised as absolute and inalienable, and define the contents and implementation of laws and other regulatory legal acts.
3. Every citizen of the Republic shall have rights and bear responsibilities owing to his citizenship.
4. Foreigners and stateless persons in the Republic shall enjoy rights and freedoms as well as bear responsibilities established for the citizens unless otherwise stipulated by the Constitution, laws and international treaties.
5. Exercise of a citizen's human rights and freedoms must not violate rights and freedoms of other persons, infringe on the constitutional system and public morals.

Article 13

1. Everyone shall have the right to be recognised as subject of the law and protect his rights and freedoms with all means not contradicting the law including self-defence.
2. Everyone shall have the right to judicial defence of his rights and freedoms.
3. Everyone shall have the right to qualified legal assistance. In cases stipulated by law, legal assistance shall be provided free of charge.

Article 14

1. Everyone shall be equal before the law and court.
2. No one shall be subject to any discrimination for reasons of origin, social, property status, occupation, sex, race, nationality, language, attitude towards religion, convictions, place of residence or any other circumstances.

Article 15

1. Everyone shall have the right to life.
2. No one shall have the right to arbitrarily deprive a person of life. The law shall establish the death penalty as an extraordinary measure of punishment for especially grave crimes and grant the sentenced person the right to appeal for pardon.

Article 16

1. Everyone shall have the right to personal freedom.
2. Arrest and detention shall be allowed only in cases stipulated by law and only with the sanction of a court or prosecutor of law. The detained person shall be provided with the right to appeal. Without the sanction of a procurator, a person may be detained for a period no more than seventytwo hours.
3. Every person detained, arrested and accused of committing a crime shall have the right to the assistance of a defense lawyer (defender) from the moment of detention, arrest or accusation.

Article 17

1. A person's dignity shall be inviolable.
2. No one must be subject to torture, violence or other treatment and punishment that is cruel or humiliating to human dignity.

Article 18

1. Everyone shall have the right to inviolability of private life, personal or family secrets, protection of honour and dignity.
2. Everyone shall have the right to confidentiality of personal deposits and savings, correspondence, telephone conversations, postal, telegraph and other messages. Limitation of this right shall be permitted only in the cases and according to the procedure directly established by law.
3. State bodies, public associations, officials, and the mass media must provide every citizen with the possibility to obtain access to documents, decisions and other sources of information concerning his rights and interests.

Article 19

1. Everyone shall have the right to determine and indicate or not to indicate his national, party and religious affiliation.
2. Everyone shall have the right to use his native language and culture, to freely choose the language of communication, education, instruction and creative activities.

Article 20

1. The freedom of speech and creative activities shall be guaranteed. Censorship shall be prohibited.
2. Everyone shall have the right to freely receive and disseminate information by any means not prohibited by law. The list of items constituting state secrets of the Republic of Kazakhstan shall be determined by law.

3. Propaganda of or agitation for the forcible change of the constitutional system, violation of the integrity of the Republic, undermining of state security, and advocating war, social, racial, national, religious, class and clannish superiority as well as the cult of cruelty and violence shall not be allowed.

Article 21

1. Everyone who has a legal right to stay on the territory of the Republic of Kazakhstan shall have the right to freely move about its territory and freely choose a place of residence except in cases stipulated by law.
2. Everyone shall have the right to leave the territory of the Republic. Citizens of the Republic shall have the right to freely return to the Republic.

Article 22

1. Everyone shall have the right to freedom of conscience.
2. The right to freedom of conscience must not specify or limit universal human and civil rights and responsibilities before the state.

Article 23

1. Citizens of the Republic of Kazakhstan shall have the right to freedom of forming associations. The activities of public associations shall be regulated by law.
2. The military, employees of national security, law-enforcement bodies and judges must abstain from membership in political parties, trade unions, and actions in support of any political party.

Article 24

1. Everyone shall have the right to freedom of labour, and the free choice of occupation and profession. Involuntary labour shall be permitted only on a sentence of court or in the conditions of a state of emergency or martial law.
2. Everyone shall have the right to safe and hygienic working conditions, to just remuneration for labour without discrimination, as well as to social protection against unemployment.
3. The right to individual and collective labour disputes with the use of methods for resolving them, stipulated by law including the right to strike, shall be recognized.
4. Everyone shall have the right to rest. Working labour agreements stipulating the length of working time, days-off and holidays, and paid annual leave shall be guaranteed by law.

Article 25

1. Housing shall be inviolable. Deprivation of housing shall not be permitted unless otherwise stipulated by a court decision. Penetration into housing, its inspection and search shall be permitted only in cases and according to the procedure stipulated by law.

2. Conditions shall be created in the Republic of Kazakhstan to provide citizens with housing. Citizens in need of housing shall be categorised in a manner to be prescribed by law and provided with housing at an affordable price from the state housing funds in accordance with the norms stipulated by law.

Article 26

1. Citizens of the Republic of Kazakhstan may privately own any legally acquired property.
2. Property, including the right of inheritance, shall be guaranteed by law.
3. No one may be deprived of his property unless otherwise stipulated by a court decision. Forcible alienation of property for the public use in extraordinary cases stipulated by law may be exercised on condition of its equivalent compensation.
4. Everyone shall have the right to freedom of entrepreneurial activity, and free use of his property for any legal entrepreneurial activity. Monopolistic activity shall be regulated and limited by law.

Unfair competition shall be prohibited.

Article 27

1. Marriage and family, motherhood, fatherhood and childhood shall be under the protection of the state.
2. Care of children and their upbringing shall be a natural right and responsibility of parents.
3. Able-bodied children of age must take care of their disabled parents.

Article 28

1. A citizen of the Republic of Kazakhstan shall be guaranteed a minimum wage and pension, and guaranteed social security in old age, in case of disease, disability or loss of a breadwinner and other legal grounds.
2. Voluntary social insurance, creation of additional forms of social security, and charity shall be encouraged.

Article 29

1. Citizens of the Republic of Kazakhstan shall have the right to protection of health.
2. Citizens of the Republic shall be entitled to free, guaranteed, extensive medical assistance established by law.
3. Paid medical treatment shall be provided by state and private medical institutions as well as by persons engaged in private medical practice on the terms and according to the procedures stipulated by law.

Article 30

1. The citizens shall be guaranteed free secondary education in state educational establishments. Secondary education shall be obligatory.

2. A citizen shall have the right to receive on a competitive basis a higher education in a state higher educational establishment.
3. The citizens shall have the right to pay and receive an education in private educational establishments on the basis and terms established by law.
4. The state shall set uniform compulsory standards in education. The activity of any educational establishment must comply with these standards.

Article 31

1. The state shall set an objective to protect the environment favourable for the life and health of the person.
2. Officials shall be held accountable for the concealment of facts and circumstances endangering the life and health of the people in accordance with law.

Article 32

Citizens of the Republic of Kazakhstan shall have the right to peacefully and without arms assemble, hold meetings, rallies and demonstrations, street processions and pickets. The use of this right may be restricted by law in the interests of state security, public order, protection of health, rights and freedoms of other persons.

Article 33

1. Citizens of the Republic of Kazakhstan shall have the right to participate in the government of the state's affairs directly and through their representatives, to address personally as well as to direct individual and collective appeals to public and local self-administrative bodies.
2. Citizens of the Republic shall have the right to elect and be elected into public and local self-administrations as well as to participate in an all-nation referendum.
3. The right to elect and be elected, to participate in the all-nation referendum shall not extend to the citizens judged incapable by a court as well as those held in places of confinement on a court's sentence.
4. Citizens of the Republic shall have the equal right to serve in a public office. The requirements for candidates for public offices shall be conditioned only by the character of the office duties and shall be established by law.

'Paragraph 4 of Article 33 is given in a wording of the Law of the Republic of Kazakhstan of October 7, 1998 No. *284-1 of* LRK.

Article 34

1. Everyone must observe the Constitution, legislation of the Republic of Kazakhstan and respect the rights, freedoms, honour and dignity of other persons.
2. Everyone must respect the state symbols of the Republic.

Article 35

Payment of legally established taxes, fees and other obligatory payments shall be a duty and responsibility of everyone.

Article 36

1. Defence of the Republic of Kazakhstan shall be a sacred duty and responsibility of its every citizen.
2. Citizens of the Republic shall perform military service according to the procedure and in the forms established by law.

Article 37

Citizens of the Republic of Kazakhstan must care for the protection of historical and cultural heritage, and preserve monuments of history and culture.

Article 38

Citizens of the Republic of Kazakhstan must preserve nature and protect natural resources.

Article 39

1. Rights and freedoms of an individual and citizen may be limited only by laws and only to the extent necessary for protection of the constitutional system, defence of the public order, human rights and freedoms, health and morality of the population.
2. Any actions capable of upsetting interethnic concord shall be deemed unconstitutional.
3. Any form of restrictions to the rights and freedoms of the citizens on political grounds shall not be permitted. Rights and freedoms stipulated by articles 10-11; 13-15 paragraph 1 of article 16; article 17; article 19; article 22; paragraph 2 of article 26 of the Constitution shall not be restricted in any event.

Section - III

The President

Article 40

1. The President of the Republic of Kazakhstan shall be the head of state, its highest official determining the main directions of the domestic and foreign policy of the state and representing Kazakhstan within the country and in international relations.
2. The President of the Republic shall be the symbol and guarantor of the unity of the people and the state power, inviolability of the Constitution, rights and freedoms of an individual and citizen.
3. The President of the Republic shall ensure by his arbitration concerted functioning of all branches of state power and responsibility of the institutions of power before the people.

Article 41

1. The President of the Republic shall be elected by universal, equal and direct suffrage under a secret ballot for a seven-year term in accordance with the constitutional law by the citizens of the Republic who have come of age.

2. A citizen of the Republic shall be eligible for the office of the President of the Republic of Kazakhstan if he is by birth not younger than forty and has a perfect command of the state language and has lived in Kazakhstan for not less than fifteen years.
3. Regular elections of the President of the Republic shall be held on the first Sunday of December and shall not coincide with the election of a new Parliament of the Republic.
4. Excluded.
5. The candidate who receives more than 50 percent of the votes of the constituents that took part in the election shall be deemed elected. If none of the candidates receives the above number of votes, a second round of elections shall be held between the two candidates who obtained the largest number of votes. The candidate who receives the larger number of votes of the constituents who take part in the second round of elections shall be deemed elected.

Article 42

1. The President of the Republic of Kazakhstan shall take office from the moment of swearing to the people the following oath: "I solemnly swear that I will faithfully serve the people of Kazakhstan, strictly observe the Constitution and the laws of the Republic of Kazakhstan, guarantee the rights and freedoms of the citizens, honestly perform the high duties of the President of the Republic of Kazakhstan entrusted to me."
2. The oath shall be taken on the second Wednesday of January in a ceremonial atmosphere in the presence of the deputies of Parliament, the members of the Constitutional Council, the judges of the Supreme Court as well as all former Presidents of the Republic. In case, stipulated by Article 48 of the Constitution, the oath shall be taken by a person who has taken the powers of the President of the Republic of Kazakhstan within one month since taking the powers of the President of the Republic.
3. The powers of the President of the Republic shall terminate from the moment the newly elected President of the Republic takes office as well as in the case of premature release from office, resignation or death. All former Presidents of the Republic except those who were discharged from office shall have the title of ex-President of the Republic of Kazakhstan.
4. Excluded.

   'Paragraphs 2,4,5 of Article 41, paragraphs 2 and 4 of Article 42 are given in a wording of the Law of the Republic of Kazakhstan of October 7, 1998 No. 284-1 of LRK.

5. One and the same person may not be elected the President of the Republic more than two times in a row.

Article 43

1. The President of the Republic of Kazakhstan shall not have the right to be a deputy of a representative body, hold other paid offices and engage in entrepreneurial-activity.

2. The President of the Republic snail suspend activity in any political party for the period he exercises his powers.

Article 44

The President of the Republic of Kazakhstan shall:

(1) annually address the people of Kazakhstan with a message on the state of the country and main directions of the domestic and foreign policy of the Republic of Kazakhstan;

(2) appoint regular and extraordinary elections to the Parliament of the Republic; convene the first session of Parliament and accept the oath of its members to the people of Kazakhstan; call extraordinary joint sessions of the Chambers of Parliament; sign laws submitted by the Senate of Parliament within fifteen working days, promulgate the law or return the law or its separate articles for a second discussion and vote;

(3) appoint a Prime Minister of the Republic with the Parliament's consent; release him from office; determine the structure of the Government of the Republic at the proposal of the Prime Minister, appoint to and release from office its members, as well as form, abolish and reorganize central executive bodies of the Republic which are not included into the Government; accept the oath of the members of the Government; preside at the meetings of the Government on especially important issues; charge the Government with bringing a bill into the Majilis of Parliament; annul or suspend completely or partially the effect of the Government's acts and those of the akims of the oblasts, major cities and the capital;

(4) appoint the Chairperson of the National Bank of the Republic of Kazakhstan with the Parliament's consent; release him from office;

(5) appoint the Procurator General and Chairperson of the Committee of National Security of the Republic with the consent of the Senate of Parliament; release them from office;

(6) appoint and recall heads of diplomatic representative offices of the Republic;

(7) appoint the Chairperson and two members of the Estimation Committee for control over Implementation of the Republican Budget for a five-year term;

(8) approve state programmes of the Republic;

(9) approve a unified system of financing and labour payment for all bodies financed by the state budget of the Republic at the proposal of the Prime Minister of the Republic;

(10) adopt a resolution on conducting the all-nation referendum;

(11) conduct negotiations and sign international treaties of the Republic; sign ratification instruments; receive letters of credentials and recall from diplomatic and other representatives of foreign states accredited to him;

(12) act as the Commander-in-Chief of the Armed Forces of the Republic, appoint and replace the highest command of the Armed Forces;

(13) award state decorations of the Republic and confer-honorary, highest military and other ranks, ranked positions, diplomatic ranks and qualification degrees;

(14) resolve issues of citizenship of the Republic, and political asylum;

(15) exercise pardon of citizens;

(16) in the event of a serious and immediate threat to the democratic institutions of the Republic, its independence and territorial integrity, political stability of the Republic, security of its citizens and the disruption of normal functioning of the Constitutional bodies of the state, the President snail have official consultation with Prime Minister and Chairpersons of the Parliamentary Chambers of the Republic and take measures, caused by a state of emergency on the entire territory or in particular areas of Kazakhstan, and immediately inform the Parliament of the use of the Armed Forces of the Republic;

(17) in the case of aggression against the Republic or immediate external threat to its security, the President shall impose martial law on the entire territory of the Republic or in particular areas, declare a partial or total mobilisation and immediately inform the Parliament of the Republic to the effect;

(18) form the Republican Guard as well as the Presidential Guard subordinated to the President;

(19) appoint to and release from office the State Secretary of the Republic of Kazakhstan, define his status and powers; form the administration of the President of the Republic;

(20) form the Security Council, the Higher Judicial Council and other consultative and advisory bodies;

(21) exercise other powers in accordance with the Constitution and the laws of the Republic.

Article 45

1. The President of the Republic of Kazakhstan, on the basis of and with the exercise of the Constitution and the laws, shall issue decrees and resolutions which are binding on the entire territory of the Republic.
2. In the case envisioned by subparagraph 4 of Article 53 of the Constitution the President of the Republic shall issue laws, and in the case envisioned by subparagraph 2 of Article 61 of the Constitution, - the President or the Republic shall issue decrees having the force of laws in the Republic.
3. The acts of Parliament signed by the President of the Republic as well as the acts of the President issued on the initiative of the Government shall be preliminary signed respectively by the Chairperson of each Parliaments Chambers or the Prime Minister on whom bear juridical responsibility for the legality of these acts.

Article 46

1. The President of the Republic of Kazakhstan, his honour and dignity shall be inviolable.
2. Provision, service, and guard of the President of the Republic and his family shall be carried out at the state's expense.
3. The provisions of this article shall extend to ex-Presidents of the Republic.

'Subparagraph (7) of Article 44 is given in a wording of the Law of the Republic of Kazakhstan of October 7, 1998, No. 284-1 of LRK.

Article 47

1. The President of the Republic of Kazakhstan may be prematurely released from office in the case of continued incapacity to perform his duties due to illness. In this case the Parliament shall form a commission consisting of equal numbers of deputies from each Chamber and specialists of the respective areas of medicine. The decision of premature release based on the conclusion of the commission and that of the Constitutional Council confirming observance of the established constitutional procedures shall be adopted at a joint sitting of the Parliament's Chambers by the majority of no less than three-fourths from the total number of deputies of each Chamber.
2. The President of the Republic shall bear responsibility for the actions performed while exercising his duties and only in the case of high treason may be discharged from office by Parliament. The decision to bring an accusation and conduct its investigation may be adopted by the majority of the deputies of the Majilis at the initiative of no less than one-third of the total number of its deputies. Investigation of the accusation shall be organised by the Senate and by the majority of votes of the total number of the deputies of the Senate its results are transferred for consideration at a joint session of the Parliament's Chambers. The final decision of this issue shall be adopted at a joint session of the Parliament's Chambers by the majority of no less than three-fourths of the total number of the deputies of each Chamber, provided the Supreme Court concludes the validity of the accusation and conclusion by the Constitutional Council that the established constitutional procedures were observed. The failure to arrive at a final decision within two months from the moment of the accusation shall result in the recognition that the accusation against the President of the Republic is rejected. Rejection of the accusation of the President of the Republic in perpetration of high treason at any stage shall result in premature termination of the powers of the deputies of the Majilis who initiated the consideration of this issue.
3. The issue of discharge of the President of the Republic from office may not be initiated in the period when the President is considering premature termination of the powers of the Parliament of the Republic.

Article 48

1. In case of premature release or discharge of the President of the Republic of Kazakstan from office as well as in case of his death the powers of the President of the Republic shall be transmitted to the Chairperson of the Senate of the Parliament for the rest of the term; if the Chairperson of the Senate is unable to assume the powers of the President they shall be transmitted to the Chairperson of the Majilis of the Parliament; if the Chairperson of the Majilis is unable to assume the powers of the President they shall be transmitted to the Prime Minister of the Republic. A person who has taken the powers of the President of the Republic shall correspondingly withdraw his powers of the Chairperson of the Senate, the Majilis, the Prime Minister. In this case filling of those state positions shall be carried out in the order, stipulated by the Constitution.

2. A person who has taken the powers of the President of the Republic of Kazakhstan, on the basis and in the order stipulated by Paragraph 1 of the present Article, has no right to initiate amendments and additions to the Constitution of the Republic of Kazakhstan'.

Section - IV
Parliament

Article 49

1. Parliament of the Republic of Kazakhstan is the highest representative body of the Republic performing legislative functions.
2. Parliament's powers shall begin from the opening of its first session and terminate with the first session of a new convocation.
3. The powers of Parliament may be prematurely terminated in cases and according to the procedure stipulated by the Constitution.
4. The organisation and activities of Parliament, the legal status of its deputies shall be determined by constitutional law'.

Article 50

1. Parliament shall consist of two Chambers acting on a permanent basis: the Senate and the Majilis.
2. The Senate shall be composed of deputies elected in twos from each oblast, major city and the capital of the Republic of Kazakhstan, at a joint session of the deputies of all representative bodies of, correspondingly, the oblast, major city and the capital of the Republic. Seven deputies of the Senate shall be appointed by the President of the Republic for the term of the Senate.
3. The Majilis shall consist of seventy-seven deputies. Sixty-seven deputies shall be elected in constituencies having one mandate and formed according to the administrative-territorial division of the Republic with an approximately equal number of constituents. Ten deputies shall be elected on the basis of the Party Lists according to the system of proportional representation and in the territory of a unified national constituency.
4. A deputy of Parliament may not be a member of both Chambers simultaneously.
5. Term of the powers of Senate deputies shall be six years, term of the powers of the Majilis deputies shall be five years'.

Article 51

1. Elections of the deputies of the Majilis shall be carried out on the basis of the universal, equal and direct right under secret ballot. Regular elections of the deputies of the Majilis shall be held no later than two months before the termination of the powers of current Parliament.

'Article 48 is given in a wording of the Law of the Republic of Kazakhstan of October 7, 1998, No. *284-1 of LRK.*

'Paragraph 2 of Article 49 is given in a wording of the Law of the Republic of Kazakhstan of October 7, 1998, No. *284 of LRK.*

'Paragraphs 2,3,5 of Article 50 are given in a wording of the Law of the Republic of Kazakhstan of October 7, 1998 No. 284-1 of LRK.

2. The elections of the deputies of the Senate shall be carried out on the basis of indirect electoral right under secret ballot. Half of the elected deputies of the Senate shall be re-elected every three years. In this case, their regular elections shall be held no later than two months before the end of their term in office.
3. Extraordinary elections of the deputies of Parliament shall be held within two months from the moment of premature termination of Parliament's powers.
4. A deputy of the Senate may be a citizen of the Republic of Kazakhstan who has been a citizen of the Republic for not less than five years and who has reached thirty years of age, has a higher education and length of service of not less than five years, and has been a permanent resident for not less than three years on the territory of the respective oblast, major city or the capital of the Republic. A deputy of the Majilis may be a citizen of the Republic of Kazakhstan who has reached twenty-five years of age.
5. A candidate shall be deemed elected if he receives more than fifty percent of the votes of constituents or electors who took part in the voting in a constituency having one mandate, at the joint session of deputies of all the representative bodies correspondingly of the oblasts, the city of republican significance and the capital of the Republic. If none of the candidates receives the above numbers of votes, a second round of elections shall be held between the two candidates who obtained the largest number of votes. The candidate who receives the larger number of votes of the constituents or electors who took part in the second round of elections shall be deemed elected. Only those political parties which received not less than seven percent of votes of constituents who took part in the elections, shall be admitted to distribution of deputy mandates in accordance with the results of elections to the Majilis on the basis of Party Lists. Elections to the Senate shall be deemed valid in case more than fifty percent of electors took part in the voting. Procedure of elections of the deputies of the Parliament of the Republic shall be determined by constitutional law.
6. A deputy shall take an oath before the people of Kazakhstan'.

Article 52

1. A deputy of Parliament shall not be bound by any imperative mandate.
2. The deputies of Parliament must take part in its work. The deputies shall only vote in person in Parliament. Absence of a deputy at sittings of the Chambers and their bodies without a good reason for more than three times as well as transferring the right to vote shall cause the imposition of penalties established by law.
3. A deputy of Parliament shall have no right to be a deputy of another representative body, hold other paid offices, except teaching, research and creative activities, engage in entrepreneurial activity, enter a managing body or a supervisory board of a commercial organisation. Violation of this rule shall result in the termination of a deputy's powers.

'Paragraphs 2 and 5 of Article 51 are given in a wording of the Law of the Republic of Kazakhstan of October 7, 1998, No. 284-1 of LRK.

4. A deputy of Parliament during the term of his office may not be arrested, subject to detention, measures of administrative punishment imposed by a court of law, arraigned on a criminal charge without the consent of a respective Chamber except for the cases of being apprehended on the scene of a crime or committing grave crimes.
5. The powers of the deputies of Parliament shall be terminated in cases of resignation, being recognised as incapable, dissolution of Parliament and in other cases stipulated by the Constitution. A deputy of Parliament shall be deprived of his mandate in cases being duly convicted in a court of law, establishing permanent residency beyond the boundaries of the Republic of Kazakhstan.
6. Preparation of questions concerning the imposition of penalties on the deputies, their observance of the requirements of paragraph 3 of this article, principles of the deputies' ethics, as well as termination of the deputies' powers and deprivation of their powers and deputy immunity, shall be delegated to the Central Election Commission of the Republic of Kazakhstan.'

Article 53

Parliament at a joint session of the Chambers shall:

(1) introduce amendments and make additions to the Constitution; adopt constitutional laws, introduce amendments and make additions to the Constitution at the proposal of the President of the Republic of Kazakhstan;

(2) approve the republican budget, the reports of the Government, and Estimation Committee about its implementation, and introduce changes into the budget;

(3) conduct a second round of discussion and voting on the laws or articles of the law that caused objections of the President of the Republic within a month's term from the moment the objections were presented. Non-observance of this term denotes the acceptance of the President's objections. If Parliament by the majority of two-thirds of votes from the total number of deputies from each Chamber confirms the decision adopted earlier, the President shall sign the law within seven days. If the President's objections are not overruled, the law shall be deemed not adopted or adopted in the version proposed by the President;

(4) have the right to delegate legislative Powers for a term not exceeding one year to the President by two-thirds of the votes from the total number of deputies of each Chamber at the initiative of the President;

(5) give consent to the appointment of the Prime Minister of the Republic and the Chairperson of the National Bank of the Republic by the President of the Republic;

(6) hear the report of the Prime Minister on the Government's programme and approve or reject the programme. A second rejection of the programme brought about by the majority of two-thirds of votes from the total number of deputies of each Chamber denotes a vote of no confidence in the Government.

The absence of such a majority implies the approval of the Government's programme;

(7) express a vote of no confidence in the Government by the majority of two-thirds of votes from the total number of deputies of each Chamber at the initiative of no less than one-fifth of the total number of the Parliament's deputies and in cases established by this Constitution;

'Paragraph 3 of Article 52 is given in a wording of the Law of the Republic of Kazakhstan of October 7, 1998, No. 284 of LRK.

(8) decide issues of war and peace;

(9) adopt a decision concerning the use of the Armed Forces of the Republic to fulfill international obligations in support of peace and security at the proposal of the President of the Republic;

(10) put forward an initiative calling for an all-nation referendum;

(11) hear annual messages of the Constitutional Council of the Republic on the state of the constitutional legality in the Republic;

(12) form joint commissions of the Chambers; elect and release from office their chairpersons; hear reports on the activity of the commissions;

(13) exercise other powers assigned to Parliament by the Constitution.

Article 54

Parliament at separate sessions of the Chambers through consecutive consideration of issues first in the Majilis and then in the Senate shall:

(1) adopt laws;

(2) discuss the republican budget and reports about its implementation, changes and additions in the budget, establish and annul state taxes and fees;

(3) establish the procedure for resolving the issues of the administrative-territorial division of the Republic of Kazakhstan;

(4) establish state awards, honorary, military and other titles, ranked positions, diplomatic ranks of the Republic of Kazakhstan, and define state symbols of the Republic;

(5) decide issues of state loans and rendering of economic and other assistance by the Republic;

(6) issue acts of amnesty to citizens;

(7) ratify and denounce international treaties of the Republic.

Article 55

The following shall belong to exclusive jurisdiction of the Senate:

(1) election and discharge from office, the Chairperson of the Supreme Court, the Chairpersons of the Collegium of Justice, and judges of the Supreme Court of the Republic at the proposal of the President of the Republic of Kazakhstan, and swearing them into office;

(2) approval of the appointment of the Procurator General and the Chairperson of the Committee of National Security by the President of the Republic of Kazakhstan;

(3) deprivation of inviolability of the Procurator General, the Chairperson and judges of the Supreme Court of the Republic;

(4) premature termination of the powers of local representative administrative bodies in accordance with the legislation of the Republic;

(5) delegation of two deputies to the Highest Judicial Council of the Republic of Kazakhstan;

(6) consideration of the issue raised by the Majilis about the discharge from office of the President of the Republic and submitting the results for consideration at a joint session of the Chambers.

Article 56

The following belongs to exclusive jurisdiction of the Majilis:

(1) accepting drafts of laws for consideration and consideration of the drafts of laws;

(2) preparation of suggestions concerning the objections of the President of the Republic of Kazakhstan to laws adopted by Parliament of the Republic;

(3) election and discharge from office of the Chairperson, Deputy Chairperson, Secretary and members of the Central Election Commission of the Republic at the proposal of the President of the Republic of Kazakhstan;

(4) announcing regular elections of the President of the Republic;

(5) delegation of two deputies to the Qualification Collegium of Justice;

(6) bringing an accusation of high treason against the President of the Republic'.

Article 57

Each Chamber of the Parliament independently, without participation of the other Chamber shall:

(1) appoint three members for a five-year term to the Estimation Committee for control over implementation of the republican budget;

(2) delegate half of the members of the commission formed by Parliament in the case envisaged by paragraph I of Article 47 of the Constitution;

(3) elect half of the members of joint commissions of the Chambers;

(4) terminate powers of the deputies of the Chambers, as well as resolve the issues of depriving deputies of their deputy immunity at the proposal of the Procurator General of the Republic of Kazakhstan;

(5) hold Parliamentary hearings on the issues of its jurisdiction;

(6) have the right to hear reports of the members of the Government of the Republic on the issues of their activities, at the initiative of no less than one-third from the total number of the deputies of the Chambers, and adopt an appeal by a majority of two-thirds of the total number of the deputies of the Chambers to the President of the Republic of Kazakhstan to discharge a member of the Government from office in the case of nonobservance of the laws of the Republic, if the President of the Republic refuses such appeal, then the deputies, by majority of not less than two-thirds of votes of the total number of deputies of the Chamber, shall possess the right to put a question to the President anew on release from the position of a member of the Government

on expiration of six months since the first appeal. In this case the President of the Republic shall release from the position of a member of the Government.

(7) form coordinating and working bodies of the Chambers;

(8) adopt procedural orders of their activities and other decisions on the issues connected with organisation and the internal routine of the Chambers".

'Subparagraph (4) of Article 56 is given in a wording of the Law of the Republic of Kazakhstan of October 7, 1998 No. 284-1 of LRK.

'Subparagraphs (1) and (6) of Article 57 are given in a wording of the Law of the Republic of Kazakhstan of October 7, 1998, No. 284-1 of LRK.

Article 58

1. The Chambers shall be headed by their chairpersons who are elected by the Senate and the Majilis from among the deputies who have a perfect command of the state language, under secret ballot by a majority of votes from the total number of the deputies of the Chambers. The candidacy for the Chairperson of the Senate shall be nominated by the President of the Republic of Kazakhstan. The candidacy for the Chairperson of the Majilis shall be nominated by the deputies of the Chamber.
2. The Chairpersons of the Chambers may be recalled from office and also have the right to submit their resignation if the majority of the total number of the deputies of the Chambers have voted against them.
3. The Chairpersons of Parliament's Chambers shall:
   (1) convene sessions of the Chambers and preside over them;
   (2) exercise general supervision in preparation of the issues under consideration by the Chambers;
   (3) nominate the candidacies of Deputy Chairpersons to the Chambers;
   (4) ensure the observance of the procedural orders in the activities of the Chambers;
   (5) supervise the activities of the coordinating bodies of the Chambers;
   (6) sign acts issued by the Chambers;
   (7) each appoint two members to the Constitutional Council of the Republic of Kazakhstan;
   (8) fulfill other duties assigned to them by the procedural orders of Parliament.
4. The Chairperson of the Majilis shall:
   (1) open sessions of Parliament;
   (2) convene regular joint sessions of the Chambers, preside at regular and extraordinary joint sessions of the Chambers.
5. The chairpersons of the Chambers shall issue instructions on the items of their jurisdiction.

Article 59

1. Parliament's sessions shall proceed in the form of joint and separate sessions of its chambers.

2. The first session of Parliament shall be convened by the President of the Republic of Kazakhstan no later than thirty days from the day of publishing of the election results.
3. Regular sessions of the Parliament shall be held once a year from the first working day of September to the last working day of June.
4. Session of Parliament shall be opened by the President of the Republic and closed at joint sessions of the Senate and Majilis. In the period between Parliament's sessions, the President of the Republic of Kazakhstan may call an extraordinary joint session of the Chambers on his own initiative, at the suggestion of the chairpersons of the Chambers or no less than one-third from the total number of the deputies of Parliament. Only the issues that were the reason for convocation shall be reviewed at this session.
5. Joint and separate sessions of the Chambers shall be held on condition that no less than two-thirds from the total number of the deputies of each Chamber are present.
6. Joint and separate sessions of the Chambers shall be open. In cases stipulated by the procedural orders, sessions may be closed. The President of the Republic, the Prime Minister and members of the Government, the Chairperson of National Bank, the Procurator General, the Chairperson of the Committee of National Security shall have the right to be present at any session and be heard.

Article 60

1. The Chambers shall form standing committees, the number of which shall not exceed seven in each Chamber.
2. The Senate and Majilis shall have the right to form joint commissions on a parity basis for solution of issues dealing with the joint activity of the Chambers.
3. The committees and commissions shall issue resolutions on items of their jurisdictions.
4. The procedure of formation, the powers and organisation of the activities of the committees and commissions shall be determined by law.

Article 61

1. The right of a legislative initiative shall belong to the deputies of Parliament of the Republic of Kazakhstan, the Government of the Republic and shall be realised exclusively in the Majilis.
2. The President of the Republic of Kazakhstan shall have the right to determine priority consideration of draft of laws as well as to declare consideration of a draft of law urgent signifying that Parliament must consider this draft within a month from the day of its submission. If the Parliament does not meet this requirement, the President of the Republic shall have the right to issue a decree having the force of law which shall be in effect until Parliament adopts a new law as established by the Constitution.
3. Parliament shall have the right to issue laws that regulate the most important public relations, establish fundamental principles and standards dealing with:

(1) legal capacity of individuals and legal entities, civil freedoms and rights, obligations and responsibility of individuals and legal entities;

(2) conditions of ownership and other rights of property;

(3) foundations of organisation and activity of state bodies and bodies of local self-administration, state and military service;

(4) taxation, establishment and levying of duties and other obligatory payments;

(5) the republican budget;

(6) issues of the judicial system and legal proceedings;

(7) education, healthcare and social provision;

(8) privatisation of enterprises and their property;

(9) environmental protection;

(10) administrative-territorial structure of the Republic;

(11) ensuring defense and security of the state. All other relations shall be regulated by legislative acts.

4. A draft of law considered and approved by the majority of votes from the total number of the deputies of the Majilis shall be transmitted to the Senate where it shall be considered for no more than sixty days. A draft of law approved by the majority of votes of the total number of deputies of the Senate shall become the law and shall be submitted to the President to be signed within ten days. A draft of law rejected as a whole by the majority of votes from the total number of the Senate's deputies shall be returned to the Majilis. If the Majilis approves the draft of law again by the majority of two-thirds of votes from the total number of its deputies, it shall be transferred to the Senate for a second discussion and voting. A twice -rejected draft may not be submitted again during the same session.

5. Amendments and additions to a draft of law proposed by the majority of votes from the total number of the Senate's deputies shall be sent to the Majilis. If the Majilis by the majority of votes from the total number of its deputies agrees with the proposed amendments and additions, the law shall be deemed to be adopted. If the Majilis by the same majority of votes objects to the amendments and additions proposed by the Senate, the disagreement between the Chambers shall be resolved through conciliatory procedures.

6. Drafts of law envisioning reduction of state revenues or increase in state expenditures may be submitted only when supplied with the positive resolution of the Government of the Republic.

7. In the case when of a draft of law submitted by the Government is not adopted, the Prime Minister shall have the right to raise an issue of nonconfidence in the Government at a joint session of the Chambers. Voting on this issue shall be held not earlier than within forty-eight hours from the moment of calling for a vote of confidence. If the call for a vote of no confidence does not receive the necessary number of votes established by this Constitution, a draft of law shall be deemed adopted without voting. However, the Government may not use this right more than twice a year.

Article 62

1. The Parliament shall adopt legislative acts in the form of laws of the Republic of Kazakhstan, resolutions of the Parliament, resolutions of the Senate and the Majilis having obligatory force on the entire territory of the Republic.
2. Laws of the Republic shall come into effect after they are signed by the President of the Republic.
3. Amendments and additions to the Constitution shall be introduced by the majority of no less than three-fourths of votes from the total number of the deputies of each chamber.
4. Constitutional laws shall be adopted on the issues stipulated by the Constitution by the majority of no less than two-thirds of votes from the total number of the deputies of each Chamber.
5. Legislative acts of the Parliament and its Chambers shall be adopted by the majority of votes from the total number of the deputies of the Chambers unless otherwise stipulated by the Constitution.
6. No less than two readings introducing amendments and additions to the Constitution, adopting constitutional laws or introducing of changes and additions into them shall be obligatory.
7. Laws of the Republic, resolutions of the Parliament and its Chambers must not contradict the Constitution. Resolutions of the Parliament and its Chambers must not contradict laws.
8. The procedure for development, submission, discussion, bringing into effect and promulgation of legislative and other regulatory legal acts of the Republic shall be regulated by a special law and the procedural orders of Parliament and its Chambers.

Article 63

1. The President of the Republic of Kazakhstan may dissolve Parliament in cases: expressing by Parliament of a vote of no confidence in the Government, twice refusal of Parliament to give consent to the appointment of the Prime Minister, political crisis resulting from of insurmountable differences between the Chambers of Parliament or Parliament and other branches of state power.
2. The Parliament may not be dissolved in the period of a state of emergency or martial law, during the last six months of the President's term, as well as within a year after a previous dissolution.

Section - V
Government

Article 64

1. The Government shall implement the executive power of the Republic of Kazakhstan, head the system of executive bodies and exercise supervision of their activity.
2. The Government in its entire activity shall be responsible before the President of the Republic as well as accountable to the Parliament of the Republic in the case stipulated by paragraph 6 of Article 53 of the Constitution.

3. Members of the Government shall be accountable to the Chambers of Parliament in the case stipulated by paragraph 6 of Article 57 of the Constitution.
4. The jurisdiction, the procedure of organisation and activity of the Government shall be determined by constitutional law.

Article 65

1. The Government shall be formed by the President of the Republic of Kazakhstan according to the procedure stipulated by this Constitution.
2. Suggestions about the structure and composition of the Government shall be submitted to the President of the Republic of Kazakhstan by the Prime Minister of the Republic within ten days after his appointment.
3. The members of the Government shall take an oath to the people and President of Kazakhstan.

Article 66

The Government shall:

(1) develop the main directions of the social-economic policy of the state, its defence capability, security, guarantee of public order and organise their realisation;

(2) present to the Parliament the republican budget and a report about its performance, ensure implementation of the budget;

(3) introduce draft of laws into the Majilis and ensure enforcement of laws;

(4) organise management of state property;

(5) develop measures for the conduct of the foreign policy of the Republic of Kazakhstan;

(6) manage the activity of ministries, state committees, other central and local executive bodies;

(7) annul or suspend completely or partially, the effect of acts of ministries, state committees, other central and local executive bodies of the Republic;

(8) appoint to and release from office heads of central executive bodies not encompassed by the Government;

(9) excluded;

(10) perform other functions assigned to it by this Constitution, laws and acts of the President

Article 67

The Prime Minister of the Republic of Kazakhstan shall:

(1) organize and supervise the work of the Government, personally answer for its work;

(2) within a month after his appointment, present to the Parliament a report about the Programme of the Government and in the event of its rejection, present a new report about the Programme within two months;

(3) sign resolutions of the Government;

(4) report the main directions of the Government's activity and all of its important decisions to the President;

(5) perform other functions connected with organisation and supervision of the Government's activity.

Article 68

1. Members of the Government shall be independent in making decisions within their competence and bear personal responsibility before the Prime Minister for the activity of bodies subordinated to them. A member of the Government who does not agree with the policy, pursued by the Government, or who does not pursue it shall resign or subjected to release from his office.
2. Members of the Government shall not have right to be deputies of a representative body, hold other paid offices except teaching, scientific and other creative activities, engage in entrepreneurial activity, enter governing body or a supervisory board of a commercial organisation.

Article 69

1. The Government of the Republic of Kazakhstan shall issue resolutions on the items of its jurisdiction having obligatory force on the entire territory of the Republic.
2. The Prime Minister of the Republic shall issue directions having mandatory force on the entire territory of the Republic.

   'Subparagraphs (2) and (9) of Article 66 are given in a wording of the Law of the Republic of Kazakhstan of October 7, 1998, No. 284-1 of LRK. 2 Paragraph I of Article 68 is given in a wording of the Law of the Republic of Kazakhstan of October 7, 1998, No. 284-1 of LRK.
3. Resolutions of the Government and directions of the Prime Minister must not contradict the Constitution, legislative acts, decrees and resolutions of the President of the Republic.

Article 70

1. The Government shall resign its powers to the newly elected President of the Republic of Kazakhstan.
2. The Government and any of its members shall have the right to submit a resignation to the President of the Republic of Kazakhstan if they consider further performance of the functions assigned to them to be impossible.
3. The Government shall submit its resignation to the President of the Republic of Kazakhstan in the event that Parliament passes a vote of no confidence in the Government.
4. The President of the Republic within a period often days shall consider the issue of accepting or declining the resignation.
5. Acceptance of the resignation shall denote the termination of the powers of the Government or a respective member. Acceptance of the resignation of the Prime Minister shall denote the termination of the powers of the entire Government.

6. In the event that the resignation of the Government or its member is declined, the President shall charge the Government or its member with continued performance of their responsibilities. In the event that the resignation of the Government owing to the passage of a vote of no confidence is declined, the President shall have the right to dissolve Parliament.
7. The President of the Republic shall have the right on his own initiative to adopt a decision to terminate the powers of the Government and to release any of its members from their offices. The release of the Prime Minister from office shall denote the termination of the powers of the entire Government.

Section - VI
The Constitutional Council

Article 71

1. The Constitutional Council of the Republic of Kazakhstan shall consist of seven members whose powers shall last for six years. The ex-Presidents of the Republic shall have the right to be life-long members of the Constitutional Council.
2. The Chairperson of the Constitutional Council shall be appointed by the President of the Republic, and in case the votes are equally divided, his vote shall be decisive.
3. Two members of the Constitutional Council shall be appointed by the President of the Republic, two - by the Chairperson of Senate, and two - by the Chairperson of the Majilis. Half of the members of the Constitutional Council shall be renewed every three years.
4. The Chairperson and members of the Constitutional Council shall not be deputies, hold paid offices except teaching, scientific or other creative activities, engage in entrepreneurial activity, enter a governing body or a supervisory board of a commercial organisation.
5. The Chairperson and members of the Constitutional Council during their term in office may not be arrested, subject to detention, measures of administrative punishment imposed by a court of law, arraigned on a criminal charge without the consent of Parliament, except in cases of being apprehended on the scene of a crime or committing grave crimes.
6. Organisation and activity of the Constitutional Council shall be regulated by Constitutional Law.

Article 72

1. The Constitutional Council by appeal of the President of the Republic of Kazakhstan, the Chairperson of the Senate, the Chairperson of Majilis, not less than one-fifth of the total number of deputies of Parliament, the Prime Minister shall:
   (1) decide on the correctness of conducting the elections of the President of the Republic, deputies of Parliament, and conducting an all-nation referendum in case of dispute;

(2) consider the laws adopted by Parliament with respect to their compliance with the Constitution of the Republic, before they are signed by the President;

(3) consider the international treaties of the Republic with respect to their compliance with the constitution, before they are ratified;

(4) officially interpret the standards of the Constitution;

(5) conclude in cases stipulated by paragraphs 1 and 2 of Article 47 of the Constitution.

2. The Constitutional Council shall consider the appeals of courts of law in cases stipulated by Article 78 of the Constitution.

Article 73

1. The inauguration of the President, registration of the elected deputies of Parliament or results of all-nation referendum shall be suspended in cases of appeal to the Constitutional Council on issues mentioned in subparagraph (1) of paragraph 1 of Article 72 of the Constitution.
2. The term of signing or ratifying of the corresponding acts shall be suspended in case of appeal to the Constitutional Council on issues mentioned in subparagraphs 2 and 3 of paragraph 1 of Article 72 of the Constitution.
3. The constitutional Council shall pass a resolution within one month from the day of appeal. This period of time, at the demand of the President or the Republic, may be shortened by 10 days if the issue is urgent.
4. The President of the Republic may object, as a whole or in part to the resolutions of the Constitutional Council. These objection shall be overruled by two-thirds of the votes of the total number of the members of the Constitutional Council. If the objections of the President are not overruled, the resolution of the Constitutional Council shall be considered not adopted.

Article 74

1. Laws and international treaties recognised not to be in compliance with the Constitution of the Republic of Kazakhstan, may not be signed or, accordingly, ratified and brought into effect.
2. Laws and other regulatory legal acts, recognised as infringing on the rights and freedoms of an individual and citizen secured by the Constitution, shall be cancelled and shall not be in effect.
3. Resolutions of the Constitutional Council shall come into effect from the day they are adopted, shall be binding on the entire territory of the Republic, final and not subject to appeal.

Section - VII

Court and Justice

Article 75

1. Justice in the Republic of Kazakhstan shall be exercised only by the court.
2. Judicial power shall be exercised through the constitutional, civil, administrative, criminal and other forms of judicial procedure as established

by law. In cases, stipulated by law, criminal procedure shall be carried out with participation of jurymen.

3. The courts of the Republic shall be the Supreme Court of the Republic and local courts of the Republic established by law.
4. The judicial system of the Republic shall be established by the Constitution of the Republic and the constitutional law. The establishment of special and extraordinary courts under any name shall not be allowed'.

Article 76

1. Judicial power shall be exercised on behalf of the Republic of Kazakhstan and shall be intended to protect the rights, freedoms, and legal interests of the citizens and organisations for ensuring the observance of the Constitution, laws, other regulatory legal acts, and shall ensure international treaties of the Republic.
2. Judicial power shall be extended to all cases and disputes arising on the basis of this Constitution, laws, other regulatory legal acts, international treaties of the Republic.
3. Decisions, sentences and other judgments of courts shall have an obligatory force in the entire territory of the Republic.

Article 77

1. A judge when executing justice shall be independent and subordinate only to the Constitution and the law.
2. Any interference in the activity of the court in the exercise of justice shall be inadmissible and accountable by the law. Judges shall not be held accountable with regard to specific cases.
3. In application of law a judge must be guided by the following principles:
   (1) a person shall be considered to be innocent of committing a crime until his guilt is established by a court's sentence that has come into force;
   (2) no one may be subject twice to criminal or administrative prosecution for one and the same offence;
   (3) no one may have his jurisdiction, as stipulated by law changed without his consent;
   (4) everyone shall have the right to be heard in court;
   Paragraph 2 of Article 75 is given in a wording of the Law of the Republic of Kazakhstan of October 1, 1998, No. *284-LRK.*'
   (5) the laws establishing or intensifying liability, imposing new responsibilities on the citizens or deteriorating their conditions shall have no retroactive force. If after the commitment of an offence accountability for it is canceled by law or reduced, the new law shall be applied;
   (6) the accused shall not be obligated to prove his innocence;
   (7) no person shall be compelled to give testimony against oneself, one's spouse and close relatives whose circle is determined by law. The clergy

shall not be obligated to testify against those who confided in them with some information at a confession;

(8) any doubts of a person's guilt shall be interpreted in the favour of the accused;

(9) evidence obtained by illegal means shall have no juridical force. No person may be sentenced on the basis of his own admission of guilt;

(10) application of the criminal law by analogy shall not be allowed.

4. The principles of justice established by the Constitution shall be common and uniform for all courts and judges in the Republic.

Article 78

1. The courts shall have no right to apply laws and other regulatory legal acts infringing on the rights and liberties of an individual and a citizen established by the Constitution. If a court finds that a law or other regulatory legal act subject to application infringes on the rights and liberties of an individual and a citizen it shall suspend legal proceedings and address the Constitutional Council with a proposal to declare that law unconstitutional.

Article 79

1. Courts shall consist of permanent judges whose independence shall be protected by the Constitution and law. A judge's powers may be terminated or suspended exclusively on the grounds established by law.
2. A judge may not be arrested, subject to detention, measures of administrative punishment, imposed by a court of law, arraigned on a criminal charge without the consent of the President of the Republic of Kazakhstan based on a conclusion of the Highest Judicial Council of the Republic or in a case stipulated by paragraph 3 of Article 55 of the Constitution; without the consent of Senate except for the cases of being apprehended on the scene of a crime or committing grave crimes.
3. Judges may be citizens of the Republic who have reached twenty-five years of age, have a higher juridical education, length of service of not less than two years in the legal profession and who have passed a qualification examination. Additional requirements to the judges of the courts of the Republic may be established by law.
4. The office of a judge shall be incompatible with a deputy's mandate, holding other paid offices except teaching, research or other creative activity engaging in other entrepreneurial activity, or being a member of a managing body or supervisory board of a commercial enterprise.

Article 80

Financing of courts, provision of judges with housing shall be performed from the republican budget and must ensure the possibility of complete and free exercise of justice.

Article 81

The Supreme Court of the Republic of Kazakhstan shall be the highest judicial body for civil, criminal and other cases which are under the courts of general jurisdiction; exercises the supervision over their activities in the forms of juridical procedure stipulated by law, and provide interpretation on the issues of judicial practice.

Article 82

1. The Chairperson of the Supreme Court, the Chairpersons of the Collegiums and judges of the Supreme Court of the Republic of Kazakhstan shall be elected by the Senate at the proposal of the President of the Republic based on a recommendation of the Highest Judicial Council of the Republic.
2. The Chairpersons of oblast and equivalent courts, the Chairpersons of the Collegiums and judges of the oblast and equivalent courts shall be appointed by the President of the Republic at the recommendation of the Highest Judicial Court of the Republic.
3. The Chairperson and judges of other courts of the Republic shall be appointed by the President of the Republic at the proposal of the Minister of Justice based on a recommendation of the Qualification Collegium of Justice.
4. The Highest Judicial Council shall be headed by the Chairperson who is appointed by the President of the Republic and consist of the Chairperson of the Constitutional Council, the Chairperson of the Supreme Court, the Procurator General, the Minister of Justice, deputies of the Senate, judges and other persons appointed by the President of the Republic. The Qualification Collegium of Justice shall be an autonomous, independent institution formed from deputies of the Majilis, judges, public prosecutors, teachers and scholars of law and workers of the bodies of justice.
5. The status of the Highest Judicial Council and the Qualification Collegium of Justice, and their procedure of formation and organisation of their work shall be determined by law'.

Article 83

1. The procurator's office on behalf of the state shall exercise the highest supervision over exact and uniform application of law, the decrees of the President of the Republic of Kazakhstan and other regulatory legal acts on the territory of the Republic, legality of preliminary investigation, inquest and inspection, administrative and executive legal procedure; and take measures for exposure and elimination of any violations of the law, the independence of courts as well as the appeal of laws and other regulatory legal acts contradicting the Constitution and laws of the Republic. The Procurator's office of the Republic shall represent interest of the state in court as well as conduct criminal prosecution in cases using procedures and within the limits, stipulated by law.

   'Paragraph 4 of Article 82 is given in a wording of the Law of the Republic of Kazakhstan of October 7, 1998, No. 284 of LRK.

2. The procurator's office of the Republic shall be a unified centralised system with subordination of junior procurators to their seniors and the Procurator General of the Republic. It shall exercise its authorities independently of other state bodies and officials and be accountable only to the President of the Republic.

3. The Procurator General of the Republic during the term of his office may not be arrested, subject to detention, measures of administrative punishment imposed by a court of law, arraigned on a criminal charge without the consent of the Senate except for the cases of being apprehended on the scene of a crime or committing grave crimes. The term of the Procurator General shall be five years.
4. The jurisdiction, organisation and procedure of the activity of the procurator's office of the Republic shall be determined by law.

Article 84

1. Inquiry and preliminary investigation of criminal cases shall be carried out by special bodies and be separated from the court and the procurator's office.
2. The powers, organisation and procedure of the activity of the inquest and investigation bodies, other questions of preliminary investigation in the Republic of Kazakhstan shall be regulated by law.

Section - VIII

Local Public Administration and Self-administration

Article 85

Local public administration shall be exercised by local representative and executive bodies which are responsible for the state of affairs of the respective territory.

Article 86

1. Local representative bodies - maslikhats - shall express the will of the population of corresponding administrative-territorial units and with regard to the common public interests shall determine the measures needed for its realisation, and control their implementation.
2. Maslikhats shall be elected by the population on the basis of universal, equal suffrage under secret ballot for a four-year term.
3. A deputy of a maslikhat may be a citizen of the Republic of Kazakhstan who has reached twenty years of age. A citizen of the Republic may be a deputy of only one maslikhat.
4. The jurisdiction of maslikhats shall include:
   (1) approval of plans, economic and social programmes for development of the territory, local budget and reports of their performance;
   (2) decision of issues of local administrative-territorial organisation in their jurisdiction;
   (3) consideration of reports by heads of local executive bodies on the issues delegated by law to the jurisdiction of a maslikhat;
   (4) formation of standing commissions and other working bodies of a maslikhat, nearing reports about their activity, decision of other issues connected with organisation of the work of a maslikhat;
   (5) exercise other authorities for insuring of the rights and legitimate interests of citizens in accordance with the legislation of the Republic.

5. The powers of a maslikhat shall be prematurely terminated by the Senate on the grounds and according to the procedure established by law as well as in the case of adoption of a decision about self-dissolution.
6. The jurisdiction of maslikhats, procedure of their organisation and activity, and legal status of their deputies shall be established by law.

Article 87

1. Local executive bodies shall be a part of a unified system of the executive bodies of the Republic of Kazakhstan, and ensure conduct of the general state policy of the executive power in conjunction with the interests and development needs of the corresponding territory.
2. The jurisdiction of local executive bodies shall include:
   (1) development of drafts of plans, economic and social programmes for development of the territory, local budget and provision of their realisation;
   (2) management of public property;
   (3) appointment to and release from office the heads of local executive bodies, resolution of other issues connected with organisation of the work of local executive bodies;
   (4) exercise other powers delegated to local executive bodies by the legislation of the Republic in the interests of local public administration.
3. A local executive body shall be headed by an akim of the corresponding administrative territorial unit who is a representative of the President and the Government of the Republic.
4. Akims of the oblasts, the major city and the capital shall be appointed to office by the President of the Republic on the recommendation of the Prime Minister. Akims of other administrative-territorial units shall be appointed or elected to office in the order, determined by the President of the Republic of Kazakhstan. The President of the Republic shall have the right to release akims from office at his own discretion.
5. A maslikhat shall have the right by two-thirds of votes from the total number of its deputies to express non-confidence in the akim and raise the issue of his release from office correspondingly before the President of the Republic or a senior akim. The powers of akims of the oblasts, the major cities and the capital shall terminate when a newly elected President assumes office.
6. The jurisdiction of local executive bodies, organisation and procedure of their activity shall be established by law'.

Article 88

1. Maslikhats shall adopt decisions on the issues of their jurisdiction, akims shall adopt decisions and resolutions which are binding on the territory of the corresponding administrative-territorial unit.

'Paragraph 4 of Article 87 is given in a wording of the Law of the Republic of Kazakhstan of October 7, 1998, No. 284 of LRK.

2. Drafts of decisions of maslikhats envisioning a reduction of local budgetary revenues or an increase of local budgetary expenditures may be submitted for consideration only with a positive resolution of the akim.
3. Decisions of maslikhats not corresponding to the Constitution and the laws of the Republic of Kazakhstan may be annulled by a legal process.
4. Decisions and resolutions of akims may be correspondingly annulled by the President, the Government of the Republic of Kazakhstan or a senior akim, as well as by a legal process.

Article 89

1. In the Republic of Kazakhstan, local self-administration which ensures that the issues of local significance shall be resolved independently by the population, shall be recognised.
2. Local self-administration shall be exercised by the population directly through elections as well as through elective and other bodies of local self-administration in rural and urban local communities covering the territories on which groups of the population live compactly.
3. The procedure or organisation and activity of the bodies of local self-administration shall be determined by citizens themselves within the limits of their powers established by law.
4. The independence of the bodies of local self-administration shall be guaranteed within the limits of their powers established by law.

Section - IX
Concluding and Transitional Provisions

Article 90

1. The Constitution of the Republic of Kazakhstan adopted at an all-nation referendum shall come into effect from the day of official publication of the results of the referendum with the simultaneous termination of the functioning of the previously adopted Constitution of the Republic of Kazakhstan.
2. The day of adoption of the Constitution at the all-nation referendum shall be proclaimed a national holiday - the Constitution Day of the Republic of Kazakhstan.

Article 91

1. Amendments and additions to the Constitution of the Republic of Kazakhstan may be introduced only by an all-nation referendum held by the decision of the President of the Republic made on his own initiative, at the recommendation of Parliament or the Government. The draft of amendments and additions to the Constitution shall not be submitted to an all-nation referendum if the President decides to pass it to the consideration of Parliament. In this case, Parliament's decision shall be adopted according to the procedure established by this Constitution. In case the President of the Republic refuses the proposal of the Parliament on submission of amendments and additions to the Constitution for the consideration of the Republican referendum, the Parliament has the right by majority of not less than four-fifths of votes of the total

number of deputies of each Chamber of the Parliament to adopt the law on making of these amendments and additions to the Constitution. In such case the President of the Republic shall sign this law or submit it for the consideration of the Republican referendum which shall be deemed valid if more than half of the Republican citizens, possessing the right to participate in the Republican referendum, take part in it. Amendments and additions to the Constitution, which are submitted for the consideration of the Republican referendum, shall be deemed adopted, if more than half of citizens, taking part in it, vote for it.

2. The unitary status and territorial integrity of the Republic, the forms of government may not be changed'.

Article 92

1. The constitutional laws must be adopted within a year from the day of enactment of the Constitution. If the laws called constitutional in the Constitution or the acts having the force thereof have been adopted by the moment of enactment of the Constitution, they are brought into accordance with the Constitution and deemed to be the constitutional laws of the Republic of Kazakhstan.
2. Other laws named in the Constitution must be adopted according to the procedure and within the terms determined by the Parliament but no later than two years after the enactment of the Constitution.
3. The decrees of the President of the Republic published within the term of his exercise of additional powers in accordance with the law of the Republic of Kazakhstan from December 10, 1993 "On Temporary Delegation of Additional Powers to the President of the Republic of Kazakhstan and Heads of Local Administration" and having the force of law shall attain the force of law and may be altered, amended or annulled according to the procedure stipulated for alteration, amendment or annulment of the laws of the Republic. The decrees of the President of the Republic published within a term he exercises additional powers on the issues stipulated by paragraphs 12-15, 18 and 20 of Article 64 of the Constitution of the Republic of Kazakhstan adopted on January 28, 1993 shall not be subject to approval by Parliament of the Republic.
4. The legislation of the Republic of Kazakhstan functioning at the moment of enactment of this Constitution shall be applied in the part that does not contradict it and within two years from the day of the adoption of the Constitution must be brought into accordance with it.

Article 93

With the purpose of implementation of Article 7 of the Constitution, the Government, local representative and executive bodies must create all necessary organisational, material and technical conditions for fluent and free-of-charge mastery of the state language by all citizens of the Republic of Kazakhstan in accordance with a special law.

'Paragraph 1 of Article 91 is given in a wording of the Law of the Republic of Kazakhstan of October 7, 1998, No. 284 of LRK.

Article 94

1. The President of the Republic of Kazakhstan elected in accordance with the legislation of the Republic of Kazakhstan functioning at the moment of enactment of this Constitution shall acquire the powers of the President of the Republic of Kazakhstan stipulated by it and exercise them during the term established by the decision adopted at the all-nation referendum of April 29, 1995. By consent of the President of the Republic of Kazakhstan the present term of the powers of the President of the Republic may be reduced by resolution of the Parliament of the Republic, adopted at the joint session of its Chambers by the majority of votes of the total number of deputies of each Chamber. In such case the Majilis of the Parliament within one month shall order elections of the President of the Republic of Kazakhstan. The President of the Republic, elected according to the results of these elections, shall take the oath within one month since the day of publication of the results of elections and exercise his duties before taking office of the President of the Republic, elected in regular Presidential elections, which shall be held after the expiration of a seven-year term on the first Sunday of December.
2. The Vice-President of the Republic of Kazakhstan elected in accordance with the legislation of the Republic of Kazakhstan functioning at the moment of enactment of this Constitution shall preserve his powers until the expiration of the term for which he was elected'.

Article 95

One half of the deputies of the Senate of the first convocation shall be elected for a four-year term, the other half of the deputies shall be elected for a two-year term in the procedure, established by Constitutional Law. 2. Provisions of the Constitution of the Republic of Kazakhstan on elections of deputies of the Majilis of the Parliament on the basis of Party Lists shall be applied from the beginning of elections of deputies of the Majilis of the Parliament of the second convocation.

Article 96

The Cabinet of Ministers of the Republic of Kazakstan from the day of enactment of this Constitution shall acquire the rights, obligations and responsibility of the Government of the Republic of Kazakhstan.

Article 97

The first composition of the Constitutional Council of the Republic of Kazakhstan shall be formed in the following manner: the President of the Republic, the Chairperson of the Senate of Parliament, the Chairperson of the Majilis of Parliament shall each appoint one member to the Constitutional Council for a three-year term and shall each appoint one member to the Constitutional Council for a six-year term. The Chairperson of the Constitutional Council shall be appointed by the President of the Republic for a six-year term.

'Paragraph 1 of Article 94 is given in a wording of the Law of the Republic of Kazakhstan of October 7, 1998, No. 284 of LRK.

2 Paragraph 2 of Article 95 is given in a wording of the Law of the Republic of Kazakhstan of October 7, 1998, No. 284 of LRK.

Article 98

1. The justice and investigation bodies stipulated by this Constitution shall be formed according to the procedure and within the terms stipulated by the respective laws. The functioning juridical and inquiry bodies shall retain their powers until new bodies are formed.
2. Judges of the Supreme Court and the Highest Arbitration Court and local courts of the Republic of Kazakhstan shall retain their powers until the formation of courts, as stipulated by the Constitution. Vacant offices of judges shall be filled according to the procedure, established by the Constitution.

APPENDIX 1.B
CONSTITUTION OF THE KYRGYZ REPUBLIC

(As amended October 21, 1998 by the Law of the Kyrgyz Republic, N134)

We, the People of the Kyrgyz Republic, aspiring to secure the national revival of the Kyrgyz, the protection and development of interests of representatives of all nationalities, who together with the Kyrgyz form the people of Kyrgyzstan, following our ancestors precepts to live in unity, peace and concord; confirming our adherence to human rights and freedoms and the idea of national statehood; filled with a determination to develop an economy, political and legal institutions and a culture which provide appropriate living standards for everyone; proclaiming our adherence to national ethnic traditions and to moral principles common to all mankind; desiring to establish ourselves among peoples of the world as a free and democratic civil society; through our authorised representatives, hereby adopt this Constitution.

CHAPTER ONE
THE KYRGYZ REPUBLIC

Section One
General Principles

Article 1

1. The Kyrgyz Republic (Kyrgyzstan) is a sovereign, unitary, democratic Republic, constructed on the basis of a legal secular state.
2. The sovereignty of the Kyrgyz Republic is not limited and shall extend throughout its territory.
3. The people of Kyrgyzstan are the holders of sovereignty and are the single source of state power in the Kyrgyz Republic.
4. The people of the Kyrgyz Republic exercise their power directly and through a system of state bodies on the basis of this Constitution and laws of the Kyrgyz Republic.

   Only the Jogorku Kenesh and the President of the Kyrgyz Republic elected by the People of the Kyrgyz Republic have the right to act on behalf of the People of the Kyrgyz Republic.
5. Amendments and supplements to the Constitution of the Kyrgyz Republic, the Laws of the Kyrgyz Republic, and other important matters of state life

may be referred for a referendum (national vote). The grounds and procedure for holding a referendum shall be established by constitutional law.

6. Citizens of the Kyrgyz Republic elect the President, deputies of the Legislative Assembly of the Jogorku Kenesh and the Assembly of Peoples' Representatives of the Jogorku Kenesh and their representatives to bodies of local self-government.

   Elections shall be free and shall be held on the basis of universal equal and direct suffrage by secret ballot. Citizens who have attained the age of 18 are allowed to participate in elections.

Article 2

1. The State and its bodies shall serve the whole society, and not a particular group.
2. No separate group of people, no association, nor any individual person shall have the right to usurp power of the State. The usurpation of State Power shall be the gravest crime.

Article 3

1. The territory of the Kyrgyz Republic, within its existing boundaries, is inviolable and indivisible.
2. For purposes of governmental management, the territory of the Kyrgyz Republic is divided into administrative territorial units determined by law.

Article 4

1. In the Kyrgyz Republic, state, communal, private, and other forms of property shall be recognised and protected.

   The Kyrgyz Republic guarantees diversity of forms of property and their equal legal protection.
2. The land, its underlying resources, air space, forests, flora and fauna, and other natural resources in the Kyrgyz Republic shall be used as the basis of life and activity of people of Kyrgyztan and shall have special protection of the state.
3. The land may be in state, communal, private, or other type of property.

   Limits to and procedure for execution of rights by land owners and guarantees of their protection shall be set forth in law.
4. The Kyrgyz Republic shall protect the rights of ownership of its citizens and juridical persons to property, and also their property and ownership located within territories of other governments.

Article 5

1. The state language of the Kyrgyz Republic is the Kyrgyz language.
2. The Kyrgyz Republic guarantees the preservation, equal and free development and functioning of the Russian language and all the other languages used by the population of the Republic.

3. Infringement upon citizens= rights and freedoms based upon lack of knowledge or command of the state language is not permitted.

Article 6

The Kyrgyz Republic has state symbols - the State Flag, Emblem, and Anthem. The Capital of the Kyrgyz Republic is the City of Bishkek. The unit of currency of the Kyrgyz Republic is the Som.

Section two

The Structure and Activities of the State

Article 7

1. State power in the Kyrgyz Republic is based on the following principles: the supremacy of the power of the people, represented and ensured by the nationally elected head of the state, the President of the Kyrgyz Republic; division of state power into legislative, executive, and judicial branches, and their coordinated functions and interaction; the responsibility of state bodies to the people and execution by them of their authority on behalf of the people; differentiation between functions of state power and local self-government.
2. Within the bounds of authority created by this Constitution, the following represent and carry out state power in the Kyrgyz Republic: the President of the Kyrgyz Republic; the Jogorku Kenesh of the Kyrgyz Republic, comprised of two chambers: the Legislative Assembly of the Jogorku Kenesh and the Assembly of People's Representatives of the Jogorku Kenesh; the Pravitel'stvo of the Kyrgyz Republic and local state Administrations; the Constitutional Court, the Supreme Court, the Supreme Arbitration Court and the courts and judges of the justice system;

Article 8

1. In the Kyrgyz Republic political parties, trade unions and other public associations may be organised on the basis of free will and common interests. The State ensures the observation of rights and legal interests of public associations.
2. Political parties may participate in State affairs only in the following ways: by nominating their candidates for election to the Jogorku Kenesh, for state positions and for bodies of local self-government; by forming fractions in representative bodies;
3. Religion, all faiths, shall be separated from the State.
4. In the Kyrgyz Republic the following are not allowed:
   - the merger of State and party institutions, as well as subordination of State activity to party programmes and decisions;
   - the formation and activity of party organisations within state institutions and organisations; civil servants shall have the right to conduct party activities unrelated to their work activity;
   - membership in parties and rendering support to any political party by those serving in the military, and by officials working in bodies of internal affairs, national security, justice, the procuracy and the courts;

- the creation of political parties on a religious basis. Religious organisations shall not pursue political goals and tasks;
- interference by members of religious organisations and sects with the activity of state bodies;
- activities of political parties of other governments.

Article 9

1. The Kyrgyz Republic has no goals of expansion, aggression and territorial claims, which are to be resolved by military force. It rejects militarisation of state life, the subordination of the state and its activity to purposes of war. The Armed Forces of the Kyrgyz Republic shall be formed in accordance with principles of self-defence and defencive sufficiency.
2. The right to initiate war shall not be acknowledged except in cases of aggression against Kyrgyzstan and other states bound by responsibilities for collective defence. In each instance, permission for military units of the Armed Forces to cross the borders of the Kyrgyz Republic shall be granted by decision of the Legislative Assembly to be adopted by no less than by two-thirds of the total number of deputies.
3. The use of Armed Forces to resolve internal State political issues is prohibited. Military forces may be used to liquidate the aftermath of natural disasters and in other similar circumstances directly provided by the law.
4. The Kyrgyz Republic strives toward universal and just peace, mutually beneficial cooperation, resolution of global and regional problems by peaceful means, and shall observe the universally recognised principles of international law.

   Activities directed at disturbing the peaceful communal life of the people, propagandising and igniting international strife are unconstitutional.

Article 10

1. A state of emergency in Kyrgyzstan may be imposed only in cases of natural disaster, direct threat to the constitutional structure, mass disorder accompanied by violence and threat to human life, according to circumstances and subject to time limits established by constitutional law.
2. A state of emergency throughout the Kyrgyz Republic may be imposed only by the Legislative Assembly, but for particular localities where circumstances demand urgent measures, by the President of the Kyrgyz Republic, with immediate, same day notification to the Legislative Assembly which must confirm the act of the President within three days. In absence of such confirmation, the state of emergency is canceled.
3. Martial law in Kyrgyzstan may be introduced by the Legislative Assembly only in case of aggression against the Kyrgyz Republic.
4. Recess of a session of the Legislative Assembly is not allowed during a state of emergency or martial law. In the event that the Legislative Assembly is not in session, and a state of emergency already has been imposed by the President, the Legislative Assembly shall assemble without notice not later than the day after the state of emergency has been imposed.

5. During a period of a state of emergency or martial law, referenda or elections to state bodies and any changes in the structure, functions and authority of state bodies established by the Constitution are not permitted.

Article 11

1. The state budget of the Kyrgyz Republic consists of republican and local budgets and includes all expenditures and income of the state. The republican budget shall be approved by the Assembly of People's Representatives upon presentation by the Pravitel'stvo.
2. Income of the republican budget shall be raised from taxes established by law, other obligatory payments, revenue from state property and other receipts.

   A single tax system applies on the territory of the Kyrgyz Republic. The Jogorku Kenesh of the Kyrgyz Republic has the right to establish taxes. Laws establishing new taxes and negatively affecting the condition of taxpayers shall not have retroactive force.
3. The Jogorku Kenesh has the right to establish non-budgetary targeted funds. Sources for contributions into non-budgetary funds may be attracted.
4. A report on implementation of the republican budget and extra-budgetary funds is to be approved by the Jogorku Kenesh.

Article 12

1. The Constitution shall have supreme legal force and direct application in the Kyrgyz Republic.
2. Laws and other normative acts are to be adopted on the basis of the Constitution.
3. Interstate treaties and other normatives of international law ratified by the Kyrgyz Republic are a constituent and directly effective part of the Legislation of the Kyrgyz Republic.

CHAPTER TWO
CITIZENS

Section One
Citizenship

Article 13

1. The affiliation of an individual to the Kyrgyz Republic and his status is determined by citizenship. A citizen of the Kyrgyz Republic must observe the Constitution and the laws of the republic, and must respect the rights, freedom, honour and dignity of other people.
2. Citizens of the Kyrgyz Republic shall not be recognised as citizens of other states.
3. No citizen of the Kyrgyz Republic can be deprived of his/her citizenship or of his right to change his/her citizenship.
4. The Kyrgyz Republic guarantees the defence and protection of its citizens beyond its borders.

Article 14

1. Every citizen of the Kyrgyz Republic by virtue of his/her citizenship enjoys rights and bears responsibilities.
2. In the Kyrgyz Republic, foreigners and persons without citizenship enjoy the rights and freedoms of citizens, and also bear responsibilities on the grounds, terms and according to procedures, provided by laws, international treaties and agreements.

Article 15

1. The dignity of individuals in the Kyrgyz Republic is absolute and inviolable.
2. Every person from birth is entitled to basic human rights and freedoms. These rights shall be recognised as absolute, inalienable, and protected by law and the courts from infringement by any other person.
3. All persons in the Kyrgyz Republic shall be equal before the law and the court.

   No one shall be subject to any type of discrimination, violation of his rights and freedoms, on the grounds of ethnic origin, sex, race, nationality, language, religious belief, or other conditions or circumstances of a personal or social nature.
4. Human rights and freedoms are valid in the Kyrgyz Republic. As such, they determine, the meaning, content and application of laws, and obligate legislative and executive powers, local self-government and are guaranteed by the judiciary.
5. In the Kyrgyz Republic, folk customs and traditions which do not contradict human rights and freedoms are supported by the state.

Article 16

1. In the Kyrgyz Republic, basic human rights and freedoms are recognised and guaranteed in accordance with universally accepted norms and principles of international law, international treaties and agreements concerning human rights which are ratified by the Kyrgyz Republic.
2. Every person in the Kyrgyz Republic has the right:
   - to life, to physical and moral inviolability;
   - to personal freedom and safety;
   - to free development of his individuality;
   - to freedom of religious belief, spiritual freedom and freedom of worship;
   - to free expression and dissemination of thoughts, ideas and opinions, freedom of literary, artistic, scientific and technical creativity, freedom of press, transmission and dissemination of information;
   - to freedom of movement, choice of destination and residence throughout the territory of Kyrgyzstan, and the right to travel freely abroad and to return home without hindrance;
   - to associate;

- to assemble peacefully and without arms, to freely conduct meetings and demonstrations;
- to the inviolability of residence;
- to the freedom and secrecy of correspondence;
- to honour and freedom of private life, to private and family secrets;
- to secrecy of postal, telephonic and telegraphic communications;
- to own property and to possess, use and dispose of it at one's own discretion;
- to economic freedom, free use of one's abilities and property for any economic activity;
- to freedom of labour, free choice of activity and profession.

The enumeration of rights and freedoms in the Constitution should not be interpreted as negating or diminishing other universally recognised human rights and freedoms

Article 17

1. In the Kyrgyz Republic, no laws shall be issued which abolish or infringe upon human rights and freedoms.
2. Restrictions to the exercise of rights and freedoms is allowed by the Constitution and laws of the Kyrgyz Republic only for the purposes of protecting the rights and freedoms of other persons, public safety and the protection of the constitutional structure. But in doing so, the essence of constitutional rights and freedoms shall not be affected.

Article 18

1. Limitations which affect the physical and moral inviolability of an individual are allowed only on the basis of law by the decision of a court as punishment for the commission of a crime. No one may be tortured, subjected to mistreatment or inhuman, degrading punishments.
2. Medical, biological, and psychological experiments on people are prohibited without the properly expressed and verified voluntary agreement of the person participating in the experiment.
3. No one may be subjected to arrest or detention except on the basis of law. Any actions aimed at imposing responsibility for a crime on a person before a decision has been made by a court are not allowed, and are grounds for compensation to the victim through the court for the material and moral harm suffered.
4. Capital punishment may be imposed only in exceptional cases by court order. Any person sentenced to capital punishment shall have the right to seek a pardon.

Article 19

1. Private ownership in the Kyrgyz Republic is recognised and guaranteed as an inalienable human right, as a natural source of one's welfare, business and creative activity, and as a guarantor of one's economic and personal independence.

2. Property is inviolable. No person can be deprived of his/her property arbitrarily; Confiscation against the will of the owner is allowed by decision of a court.
3. In the Kyrgyz Republic the right of inheritance is guaranteed and protected by law.

Article 20

The Kyrgyz Republic may grant political asylum to foreign citizens and persons without citizenship on the basis of violation of human rights.

Section Three
Rights and Duties of a Citizen

Article 21

1. Citizens of the Kyrgyz Republic and their associations shall be allowed to engage in any act or activity, except those prohibited or restricted by this Constitution and laws of the Kyrgyz Republic.
2. The exercise of rights and freedoms by a citizen of the Kyrgyz Republic shall be inseparable from his/her duties which must be performed for the security of personal and national interests.

Article 22

Laws of the Kyrgyz Republic concerning the rights and duties of citizens are to be applied equally to all citizens and do not bestow on anyone advantages and privileges, except those provided by the Constitution and by laws for the social protection of citizens.

Article 23

Citizens of the Kyrgyz Republic participate in state governance directly and through their representatives in the discussion and adoption of laws and decisions of republican and local significance, and they have equal access to governmental services.

Article 24

Citizens of the Kyrgyz Republic have the right and duty to defend the Motherland. Citizens perform military service within the limits and in the forms established by law.

Article 25

Citizens of the Kyrgyz Republic are obliged to pay taxes and fees in accordance with legislation.

Article 26

1. The family shall be the primary unit of society; family, fatherhood, motherhood, and childhood are the concern of the whole society and preferential protection by law; childcare and upbringing is a natural right and civic duty of parents. Able-bodied, legal aged children are obligated to care for their parents.
2. The state provides maintenance, up-bringing, education for orphans and children without parental support.

3. Respect for the elderly and caring for relatives and friends are sacred traditions of the people of Kyrgyzstan.

Article 27

1. In the Kyrgyz Republic social security at the expense of the state is guaranteed in old age, in sickness and in the event of work disability or loss of the main provider.
2. Pensions and social security in accordance with economic resources of the society shall provide a standard of living not below the minimum wage established by law.
3. Voluntary social insurance and the establishment of additional forms of security and charity are encouraged.

Article 28

1. A citizen of the Kyrgyz Republic has the right to job protection in all its forms and appearances, and to working conditions which comply with requirements of security and hygiene, as well as the right to social protection against unemployment.
2. The state will concern itself with professional training and improvement of professional qualification of citizens, and encourages and promotes international agreements and international organisations, which have the aim of strengthening and securing the right to work.
3. Forced labour of citizens is prohibited, except in cases of war, natural disaster, epidemic, or in other extraordinary circumstances, as well as in accordance with execution of punishment per order of court.

Article 29

Citizens of the Kyrgyz Republic, working under a labour agreement (contract), shall have the right to remuneration not less than the minimum wage established by the state.

Article 30

Citizens of the Kyrgyz Republic shall have the right to strike.

The procedure and conditions for holding strikes shall be prescribed by law.

Article 31

1. Citizens of the Kyrgyz Republic have the right to time off.
2. The maximum duration of working hours, the minimum weekly time off and annual paid leave, as well as other conditions for exercising of the right to time off, shall be prescribed by law.

Article 32

1. Every citizen of the Kyrgyz Republic has the right to education.
2. Basic education shall be compulsory and free of charge; everyone shall have the right to receive it at state educational institutions. In state educational institutions every citizen has the right to a free education.

3. The state provides every person in accordance with individual aptitude access to vocational, special secondary and higher education.
4. Paid education of citizens in state and other educational institutions is allowed on the basis and in the procedure established by legislation.
5. The state exercises control over the activity of educational institutions.

Article 33

Citizens of the Kyrgyz Republic have the right to housing. The state facilitates the fulfillment of the right to housing by supplying and selling housing from the state-owned housing fund and by encouraging construction of individual dwellings.

Article 34

1. Citizens of the Kyrgyz Republic have the right to the protection of health and to free use of the network of state public health institutions.
2. Paid medical service shall be allowed on the basis and in the procedure established by law.

Article 35

1. Citizens of the Kyrgyz Republic have the right to a healthy, safe environment and to compensation for damage caused to one's health or property by activities utilizing nature.
2. The protection of the environment, natural resources and historical monuments is the sacred duty of every citizen.

Article 36

1. Culture, art, literature, science and the mass media are free [uncontrolled].
2. The state protects historical monuments, cares for and creates necessary conditions for the development of literature, art, science, mass media and sports.
3. Citizens have the right of access to cultural treasures and to be involved in artistic and scientific activities.

Article 37

Social activity of the State shall not lead to the substitution of state guardianship over a citizen's own economic freedom, activity and the opportunity of the citizen to achieve economic welfare for himself/herself and his/her own family.

Article 38

1. It is the duty of the state, all its bodies and state officials to provide for full, absolute and immediate protection of the rights and freedoms of citizens, to prevent the infringement upon rights in this area and to restore a violated status.
2. The Kyrgyz Republic guarantees judicial defence of all rights and freedoms of citizens fixed by the Constitution and the laws.

Article 39

1. A citizen is presumed innocent of committing a criminal offence until determined guilty by an order of court in force.
2. The state guarantees everyone protection from arbitrary and unlawful interference into one's private and family life, infringement upon one's honour and dignity, and violation of secrecy of correspondence and telephone conversations.
3. No one shall have the right to enter a dwelling except in cases when it is necessary to conduct a sanctioned search or seizure of property, to secure public order, to arrest a criminal or to save the life, health or property of an individual.

Article 40

Every citizen in the Kyrgyz Republic shall be provided qualified legal assistance and defence of the rights and freedoms guaranteed by the Constitution.

Article 41

The publication of laws and other normative legal acts concerning the rights, freedoms and duties of an individual and a citizen is a prerequisite for their utilisation.

CHAPTER THREE
THE PRESIDENT

Article 42

1. The President of the Kyrgyz Republic is the head of state and the highest official of the Kyrgyz Republic.
2. The President of the Kyrgyz Republic is the symbol of the unity of the people and state power, the guarantor of the Constitution of the Kyrgyz Republic, and of rights and freedoms of the person and citizen.
3. The President of the Kyrgyz Republic defines the fundamental directions of internal and external policy of the state, represents the Kyrgyz Republic within the country and in international relations, adopts measures to protect the sovereignty and territorial integrity of the Kyrgyz Republic, and ensures the unity and continuity of state power and the coordinated functioning and interaction of state bodies and their responsibility to the people.

Section One
Election

Article 43

1. The President of the Kyrgyz Republic shall be elected for a term of five years.
2. The same person cannot be elected President for more than two consecutive terms.
3. A citizen of the Kyrgyz Republic who has command of the state language and who has been a resident of the republic for not less than 15 years before the nomination of his candidature to the office of the President, may be elected

President of the Kyrgyz Republic if he is not less than 35 years of age and not older than 65 years of age.

4. The President of the Kyrgyz Republic cannot be a deputy of the Jogorku Kenesh, hold any other posts or engage in entrepreneurial activity.
5. The President of the Kyrgyz Republic must suspend his activity in political parties and organisations during the term of office until the beginning of a new presidential election in the Kyrgyz Republic.

Article 44

1. A new presidential election in the Kyrgyz Republic is held two months before the date on which the powers of the President of the Kyrgyz Republic expire.
2. The President of the Kyrgyz Republic is elected by citizens of the Kyrgyz Republic by a majority of actual votes cast; elections shall be held on the basis of universal, equal and direct suffrage, and by secret ballot.
3. The number of candidates for the office of the President of the Kyrgyz Republic is not limited. A person, who has registered and who has collected not less than 50,000 voters' signatures may be a candidate for the President of the Kyrgyz Republic.
4. The election of the President of the Kyrgyz Republic is considered valid if more than fifty percent of all voters in the republic shall have taken part in the elections.

   In the first ballot, a candidate is considered elected to the office of the President if he/she obtains more than a half of the votes of voters who have taken part in the elections.

   If no candidate receives more than half of the votes cast in the first ballot, only the two candidates who received the most votes shall appear on the second ballot. In the second ballot, a candidate who receives more than half of the votes cast shall be considered elected if not less than fifty percent of all voters participate.

Article 45

1. The results of the election for the President of the Kyrgyz Republic must be confirmed by the Constitutional Court of the Kyrgyz Republic within 7 days after their completion.
2. After the Chairman of the Constitutional Court of the Kyrgyz Republic announces the results of voting, the President takes the oath of office within 30 days in the presence of the deputies of the Legislative Assembly and the Assembly of People's Representatives.
3. Upon entering office, the President of the Kyrgyz Republic takes an oath to the people of Kyrgyzstan:

   "I, ..., assuming the office of the President of the Kyrgyz Republic, before my People and the Sacred homeland Ala-Too do swear: to sacredly observe and defend the Constitution and laws of the Kyrgyz Republic; to defend the sovereignty and independence of the Kyrgyz State; to respect and guarantee the rights and freedoms of all citizens of the Kyrgyz Republic; with honour and tirelessly to perform the great responsibility of the President of the Kyrgyz Republic entrusted to me by the confidence of all the People!"

4. The term of the Presidential mandate begins from the moment of taking the oath of office. The powers of the President terminate upon the moment when the newly elected President takes office.

Section Two
Powers of the President

Article 46

1. The President of the Kyrgyz Republic:
   (a) determines the structure of the Pravitel'stvo of the Kyrgyz Republic;
   (b) appoints the Prime Minister of the Kyrgyz Republic with the approval of the Assembly of People's Representatives;
   (c) appoints in consultation with the Prime Minister of the Kyrgyz Republic, the members of the Pravitel'stvo of the Kyrgyz Republic and also the heads of administrative departments, and relieves them of their offices;
   (d) accepts requests by the Prime Minister, the Pravitel'stvo, or an individual member of the Pravitel'stvo to resign; adopts decisions on his own initiative regarding dismissal of the Prime Minister or Pravitel'stvo;
   (e) appoints with the consent of the appropriate local keneshes the heads of state administration of oblasts, rayons and cities; and relieves them of their offices;
   (f) appoints the State Secretary of the Kyrgyz Republic and determines his status and powers; forms the Administration of the President of the Kyrgyz Republic;
   (g) forms and abolishes executive organs not included in the composition of the Pravitel'stvo;
   (h) forms and heads the Security Council of the Kyrgyz Republic and other coordinated organs;
   (i) forms services of Government defence and the National Guard, which are under his purview;
   (j) confirms, in consultation with the Prime Minister, a unified system of training and selection of personnel for bodies maintained at the expense of the state budget, and of the financing of state bodies and payment of those working in the service of the state.
2. The President of the Kyrgyz Republic:
   (a) appoints, with the consent of the Assembly of People's Representatives, the Procurator General of the Kyrgyz Republic; appoints the deputy of the Procurator General, procurators of oblasts, the City of Bishkek and the military procurator of the Kyrgyz Republic; and relieves them of office;
   (b) appoints with the approval of the Assembly of the People's Representatives, the Chairman of the Board of the National Bank of the Kyrgyz Republic, and relieves him of office;

(c) presents to the Legislative Assembly and to the Assembly of People's Representatives candidates for election to the offices of Chairman of the Constitutional Court of the Kyrgyz Republic, his deputy, and judges of the Constitutional Court of the Kyrgyz Republic;

(d) presents to the Assembly of People's Representatives candidates for election to the offices of Chairman of the Supreme Court of the Kyrgyz Republic and of the Supreme Arbitration Court of the Kyrgyz Republic, their deputies, and judges of the Supreme Court of the Kyrgyz Republic and of the Supreme Arbitration Court of the Kyrgyz Republic;

(e) appoints the chairmen, their deputies, and judges of the courts of oblasts, the city of Bishkek, rayons, cities, arbitration courts of the oblasts and the city of Bishkek, and also of the military courts of the Kyrgyz Republic, and relieves them of office under circumstances prescribed by the Constitution and laws.

3. The President of the Kyrgyz Republic:

(a) directs the foreign policy of the Kyrgyz Republic;

(b) conducts negotiations and signs international treaties of the Kyrgyz Republic;

(c) signs instruments of ratification;

(d) appoints and recalls diplomatic representatives of the Kyrgyz Republic in foreign states and international organisations; accepts the credentials and letters of recall of the heads of diplomatic missions of foreign states and representatives of international organisations accredited to the President of the Kyrgyz Republic;

(e) decides questions of acceptance and forfeiture of citizenship in the Kyrgyz Republic and of granting political asylum.

4. The President of the Kyrgyz Republic:

(1) confers state awards of the Kyrgyz Republic;

(2) confers honorary titles of the Kyrgyz Republic;

(3) confers higher military ranks, diplomatic ranks, class ranks, and other special titles;

(4) grants pardons.

5. The President of the Kyrgyz Republic:

(a) presents draft laws to the Jogorku Kenesh;

(b) signs laws or returns them with his objections to the appropriate chamber of the Jogorku Kenesh for further consideration; publishes laws; has the right to protest laws and international treaties ratified by the Kyrgyz Republic to the Constitutional Court of the Kyrgyz Republic;

(c) speaks to the people in yearly messages on the state of affairs in the country, to be delivered at a joint sitting of both Chambers of the Jogorku Kenesh;

(d) has the right to suspend or annul the effectiveness of acts of the Pravitel'stvo of the Kyrgyz Republic and acts of other bodies of executive power;

(e) has the right to decide issues of financing urgent matters at state expense; and establishes funds;

(f) exercises legislative power under the circumstances and in accordance with the procedure set forth in Article 68 of this Constitution.

6. The President of the Kyrgyz Republic:

   (1) has the right to call early meetings of the Legislative Assembly and early sessions of the Assembly of People's Represen-tatives and to determine issues subject to consideration;

   (2) designates referenda on his own initiative, or decides to call referenda upon the initiative of no less than 300,000 voters or a majority of the total number of deputies of both Chambers of the Jogorku Kenesh;

   (3) calls elections to the Legislative Assembly and the Assembly of People's Representatives, carries out early dissolution of the Legislative Assembly and Assembly of People's Representatives under the circumstances set forth in this Constitution;

   (4) calls elections to local Keneshes and carries out their early dissolution under the circumstances set forth in the laws of the Kyrgyz Republic;

   (5) appoints the Chairman of the Central Commission on Elections and the Conducting of Referenda and one-third of its members;

   (6) appoints the Chairman of the Chamber of Auditors and one-third of its auditors.

7. The President of the Kyrgyz Republic upon grounds specified by law, warns of the possibility of introducing a state of emergency, and when necessary introduces a state of emergency in specific localities without prior declaration, of which action he promptly informs the Legislative Assembly.

8. The President of the Kyrgyz Republic declares universal or partial mobilisation; announces a state of war in the event of aggression or direct threat of aggression to the Kyrgyz Republic, promptly submits the issue for consideration of the Legislative Assembly; declares a state of war in the interests of the defense of the country and the safety of its citizens, and promptly submits the issue for consideration of the Legislative Assembly.

9. The President of the Kyrgyz Republic is the Commander-in-Chief of the Armed Forces, and appoints and dismisses commanders of the Armed Forces of the Kyrgyz Republic.

Article 47

1. The President of the Kyrgyz Republic issues decrees and orders.
2. Decrees and orders of the President of the Kyrgyz Republic must be executed within the entire territory of the Kyrgyz Republic.
3. Decrees issued by the President of the Kyrgyz Republic while executing legislative powers in accordance with subpoint 6 of point 5 of Article 46 of the Constitution have the force of law.

Article 48

The President of the Kyrgyz Republic has the right to transfer powers specified in subpoint 2 of point 3 of Article 46 of the Constitution to the Prime Minister, members of the Pravitel'stvo, and other officials; and also has the right to ratify international financial contracts and credit agreements signed by them.

Article 49

1. The President of the Kyrgyz Republic enjoys the right of immunity. The honour and dignity of the President of the Kyrgyz Republic is protected by law.
2. The support, service and protection of the President of the Kyrgyz Republic, as well as his family, is provided at state expense.

Article 50

1. The powers of the President may be terminated as a result of resignation on his own petition made by him at a joint session of the Chambers of the Jogorku Kenesh or upon his dismissal from office in accordance with the procedure specified in this Constitution or also upon inability to execute his powers due to illness or as a result of his death.
2. If the President of the Kyrgyz Republic is unable to carry out his duties due to illness, both Chambers of the Jogorku Kenesh are to adopt a decision on early dismissal of the President of the Kyrgyz Republic from office based upon the conclusion of a State Medical Commission created by them upon a vote of no less than two-thirds of the total number of the deputies of each of the Chambers.

Article 51

1. The President of the Kyrgyz Republic may be dismissed from office by the Assembly of Peoples' Representatives only on the basis of a charge made by the Legislative Assembly of high treason or commission of another grievous crime confirmed by a ruling of the Constitutional Court of the Kyrgyz Republic.
2. The decision by the Legislative Assembly to bring a charge against the President of the Kyrgyz Republic for dismissal of him from office must be made by a vote of not less than two-thirds of the total number of deputies of the Legislative Assembly upon the initiative of a majority of the total number of deputies of that chamber, and is to be accompanied by a ruling by a special commission formed by the Legislative Assembly.
3. A negative ruling by the Constitutional Court of the Kyrgyz Republic on a charge made by the Legislative Assembly shall result in the dissolution of the Legislative Assembly.
4. A resolution of the Assembly of People's Representatives on dismissal of the President of the Kyrgyz Republic from office must be adopted by a majority vote of no fewer than two-thirds of the total number of deputies of that chamber, no later than two months after the bringing of the charge against the President by the Legislative Assembly. If a decision shall not be reached by the Assembly within this period, the charge shall be considered refuted.

Article 52

1. If the President of the Kyrgyz Republic is unable to carry out his duties for reasons stated in Article 50 of the this Constitution, the Prime Minister thereafter shall carry out his duties until the election of a new President of the Kyrgyz Republic. Elections for a new President of the Kyrgyz Republic must in this case be conducted within three months of the termination of the term of office of the President of the Kyrgyz Republic.
2. The Prime Minister, while executing the duties of the President of the Kyrgyz Republic, does not have the right to dissolve the Legislative Assembly or the Assembly of People's Representatives, to call a referendum, to terminate the authority of the Pravitel'stvo, or to make proposals for introducing amendments and supplements to the Constitution of the Kyrgyz Republic.

Article 53

1. All former Presidents of the Kyrgyz Republic, except those who have been dismissed from office by the procedure established in Article 51 of the Constitution, shall have the title of ex-President of the Kyrgyz Republic.
2. Provision, maintenance, and protection of an ex-President of the Kyrgyz Republic shall be made at state expense by a procedure established by law.

CHAPTER FOUR
THE JOGORKU KENESH

Article 54

1. The Jogorku Kenesh, the Parliament of the Kyrgyz Republic, is the representative body which has legislative power.
2. The Jogorku Kenesh consists of two chambers:

   The Legislative Assembly, with 60 deputies, which acts continuously and is elected on the basis of representation of the interests of the total population of the republic;

   The Assembly of People's Representatives, with 45 deputies, which shall work in sessions and shall be elected on the basis of representing territorial interests.
3. Deputies of the Legislative Assembly and the Assembly of People's Representatives are elected for five years. Procedure for election of deputies of the Legislative Assembly and Assembly of People's Representatives shall be stipulated by law.

Article 55

1. Each chamber of the Jogorku Kenesh shall assemble for its first sitting after election with no fewer than two-thirds of the members of the given chamber and no later than 30 days after the publication of the results of the election.
2. The eldest deputy of each chamber of the Jogorku Kenesh shall open the first session of that chamber.
3. The Legislative Assembly and the Assembly of People's Representatives shall meet separately. The Chambers shall meet jointly for taking oaths of judges of

the Constitutional Court of the Kyrgyz Republic, for hearing addresses and declarations of the President of the Kyrgyz Republic, and addresses of leaders of foreign states, and also in other cases envisaged by regulations of the chambers of the Jogorku Kenesh.

4. From the day work of the newly convened Legislative Assembly and the Assembly of People's Representatives begins, the powers of the prior sessions of the Legislative Assembly and the Assembly of People's Representatives end.

Article 56

1. A citizen of the Kyrgyz Republic who has reached 25 years of age by the day of the elections, has the right to participate in the elections, and has permanently resided in the Republic for not less than 5 years prior to nomination as a Deputy, may be elected a Deputy of the Legislative Assembly of the Jogorku Kenesh.

   A citizen of the Kyrgyz Republic who has reached 25 years of age by the day of the elections, has the right to participate in the elections, and has permanently resided in the Republic for not less than 5 years prior to nomination as a Deputy, of which not than 3 years have been within the territory of the respective region or city of Bishkek, may be elected a Deputy of the Assembly of People's Representatives of the Jogorku Kenesh.

2. Deputies of the Legislative Assembly of the Jogorku Kenesh and deputies of the Assembly of People's Representatives of the Jogorku Kenesh are representatives of the people of Kyrgyzstan, and are subordinate to the Constitution and to their conscience.

3. A Deputy of the Legislative Assembly and a Deputy of the Assembly of People's Representatives within the entire term of powers may not be prosecuted or held liable for opinion expressed or for voting in the course of execution of their powers as a Deputy.

4. One and the same person may not simultaneously be a deputy of the Legislative Assembly and of the Assembly of People's Representatives. A deputy of the Legislative Assembly or Assembly of People's Representatives can not simultaneously be a deputy of a local Kenesh.

   A deputy of the Legislative Assembly can not work in other state service and can not engage in entrepreneurial activity. A deputy of the Legislative Assembly has the right to engage in teaching, scientific, or other creative activity, if such activity does not interfere with the performance of his duties as deputy.

   A deputy of the Assembly of People's Representatives can not simultaneously be employed as a member of the Pravitel'stvo, a procurator, a judge, or another office of state service specified by law. A deputy of the Assembly of People's Representatives working in state service may be relieved from an occupied position without the consent of the chamber.

5. A deputy of the Legislative Assembly or Assembly of People's Representatives who has not warranted the trust of the voters may be dismissed by decision of a majority of voters in the procedure established by law.

6. Powers of a Deputy of the Legislative Assembly or a Deputy of the Assembly of People's Representatives may be terminated early in the event of submission of resignation in writing, a court decision that the Deputy is not legally capable, dissolution of their chamber, entry into force of a court decision on announcing the Deputy deceased, and death of a Deputy.

   A Deputy of the Legislative Assembly or a Deputy of the Assembly of People's Representatives shall be deprived of his powers in the event of his recall by voters, entry into force of a guilty verdict against him by court, acceptance of a job or failure to quit a job not compatible with fulfilment of his duties as a Deputy, annulment of the election, change of permanent residents beyond the borders of the Kyrgyz Republic, renunciation of citizenship of the Kyrgyz Republic, or loss of Kyrgyz citizenship.

   Early termination of powers of a Deputy of the Legislative Assembly and a Deputy of the Assembly of People's Representatives, and their deprivation of powers, shall be executed based on a Resolution of the Central Committee on Elections and Referenda.

Article 57

A deputy of the Legislative Assembly and the Assembly of People's Representatives has the right of inquiry to bodies of executive power and their officials, who are obliged to answer the inquiry within 10 days.

Section One

Powers of the Legislative Assembly and Assembly of People's Representatives

Article 58

1. The work of the Legislative Assembly of the Jogorku Kenesh includes:
   (a) introduction of amendments and supplements to the Constitution of the Kyrgyz Republic in the procedure established by the Constitution;
   (b) adoption of laws of the Kyrgyz Republic;
   (c) official interpretation of the Constitution and of laws adopted by it;
   (d) alteration of the borders of the Kyrgyz Republic;
   (e) approval of laws adopted by the Assembly of the People's Representatives;
   (f) election, upon nomination by the President of the Kyrgyz Republic, of the Chairman of the Constitutional Court of the Kyrgyz Republic, his deputy, and judges of the Constitutional Court of the Kyrgyz Republic; determining issues of dismissing them from their positions under the circumstances and according to the procedures set forth in this Constitution;
   (g) election of one third of the members of the Central Commission on Elections and Conduct of Referenda;
   (h) appointment of one-third of the auditors of the Accounting Chamber;
   (i) ratification and denunciation of international treaties, except cases envisaged in Article 48 of this Constitution;

(j) introduction of states of emergency, authorisation of annulment of decrees of the President of the Kyrgyz Republic concerning this issue;

(k) deciding matters of war and peace; introducing the state of war; and authorisation or annulment of decrees of the President of the Kyrgyz Republic about these issues;

(l) deciding matters about the possibility of using the Armed Forces of the Kyrgyz Republic beyond its borders when necessary to fulfill International treaty obligations in support of peace and security;

(m) establishing of military ranks, diplomatic ranks, class categories and other special titles of the Kyrgyz Republic;

(n) establishment of state awards and honorary titles of the Kyrgyz Republic;

(o) issuing acts of amnesty;

(p) hearing annual reports of the Prime Minister as well as of bodies and officials appointed and elected by it, with account taken of the rules of autonomy and independence of such bodies and officials established in this Constitution;

(q) bringing charges against the President of the Republic for dismissal from office.

2. The Legislative Assembly adopts resolutions on issues envisaged in sub-points 5-8, 16, and 17 of point 1 of this Article.

3. The work of the Assembly of People's Representatives of the Jogorku Kenesh includes:

(a) introduction of amendments and supplements to the Constitution of the Kyrgyz Republic; adoption of laws in cases envisaged by the Constitution;

(b) approval of the laws adopted by the Legislative Assembly in cases set forth by the Constitution;

(c) official interpretation of the Constitution and of laws adopted by it;

(d) authorisation of the republican budget and of reports on its implementation;

(e) alteration of the borders of the Kyrgyz Republic;

(f) deciding matters of the administrative and territorial structure of the Kyrgyz Republic;

(g) calling elections for President of the Kyrgyz Republic;

(h) approval of appointments of the Prime Minister of the Kyrgyz Republic;

(i) approval of appointments of the Procurator General of the Kyrgyz Republic;

(j) approval of appointments of the Chairman of the Board of the National Bank of the Kyrgyz Republic;

(k) election, upon nomination by the President of the Kyrgyz Republic, of the Chairman of the Constitutional Court of the Kyrgyz Republic, his deputy, and the judges of the Constitutional Court of the Kyrgyz Republic;

(l) election, upon nomination by the President of the Kyrgyz Republic, of the Chairmen of the Supreme Court and Supreme Arbitration Court of the Kyrgyz Republic, their deputies, and the judges of the Supreme Court and Supreme Arbitration Court of the Kyrgyz Republic;

(m) election of one-third of the members of the Central Commission on Elections and Conduct of Referenda;

(n) deciding issue about dismissing judges in cases according to the procedure set forth in this Constitution;

(o) appointing one-third of the auditors of the Chamber of Auditors;

(p) dismissal of the President of the Kyrgyz Republic from office;

(q) hearing reports of the Prime Minister as well as of bodies and officials appointed or elected by the Assembly of People's Deputies, with consideration taken of the rules of autonomy and independence of such bodies and officials established in this Constitution;

(r) expression of a no confidence vote to the Prime Minister;

(s) hearing of the reports of the Procurator General and the Chairman of the Board of the National Bank.

4. The Assembly of People's Representatives adopts resolutions on issues described in subpoints 2 and 7-19 of point 3 of this Article.

Article 59

1. Laws on the introduction of amendments and supplements to the Constitution, constitutional laws, laws on the alteration of the borders of the Kyrgyz Republic, and on interpretation of the Constitution and constitutional laws, are adopted by both Chambers of the Jogorku Kenesh by majority vote of no less than two-thirds of the total number of deputies of each Chamber.

2. Laws adopted by the Legislative Assembly on matters of taxes and fees, financial and customs regulations, banking activities, the ratification or denunciation of international treaties of the Kyrgyz Republic, and amnesty, are subject to consideration by the Assembly of People's Representatives and are considered approved if they receive yes votes from no fewer than half the total number of deputies of the Assembly of People's Representatives. In the event the Assembly of People's Representatives disapproves a decision taken by the Legislative Assembly, the decision on the matter under consideration may be approved by majority vote of no fewer than two-thirds of the total number of deputies of the Legislative Assembly.

3. Laws adopted by the Assembly of People's Representatives on matters stated in subpoints 4 and 6 of point 3 of Article 58 of this Constitution, are subject to consideration by the Legislative Assembly and shall be considered approved if they receive yes votes from no fewer than half of the total number of deputies of the Legislative Assembly. In the event the Legislative Assembly disapproves a law, the decision on the matter under consideration may be approved by a majority vote of no fewer than two-thirds of the total number of deputies of the Assembly of People's Representatives.

4. Laws described in the first paragraph of point 2 and the first paragraph of point 3 of this Article are deemed approved if not reviewed by the respective chamber of the Jogorku Kenesh within 60 days of adoption.

Article 60

1. Each chamber of the Jogorku Kenesh shall elect from among its members a Toraga of the Chamber and his deputy, and shall form committees and commissions.
2. The Toraga of each Chamber shall be elected by secret vote. He shall be accountable to the appropriate chamber and may be removed from his office by a decision of such chamber adopted by a vote of no fewer than two-thirds of the total number of deputies.
3. The Toraga of the Legislative Assembly and the Assembly of People's Representatives conduct the sessions of their respective chambers, generally carry out the preparation of issues for consideration during sessions of the chambers, manage internal routine, and sign resolutions adopted by their respective Chambers.
4. The Deputy Toraga of the respective Chamber of the Jogorku Kenesh is elected by secret vote, fulfills specific functions of the Toraga as authorised by him, and substitutes for the Toraga in his absence.

Article 61

Committees and temporary commissions of the chambers of the Jogorku Kenesh perform law drafting work, preliminarily review issues referred to their competency, and control implementation of the adopted laws and resolutions.

Article 62

1. The Legislative Assembly conducts its business during conventions. The Legislative Assembly convenes once per year; the convention begins the first work day of September and ends the last work day of June.
2. The Assembly of People's Representatives conducts its business during sessions. Sessions of the Assembly of People's Representatives are called no fewer than two times a year.
3. A convention of the Legislative Assembly or session of the Assembly of People's Representatives is legally valid upon the attendance of no fewer than two-thirds of the total number of deputies of the given Chamber. The procedure for conducting business of the Chambers of the Jogorku Kenesh shall be defined by their Regulations.

Article 63

1. The Legislative Assembly and the Assembly of People's Representatives may be dissolved early by a decision adopted by a majority vote of no fewer than two-thirds of the total number of deputies of the respective Chamber.
2. The Legislative Assembly or the Assembly of People's Represen-tatives, or both chambers of the Jogorku Kenesh simultaneously, may be dissolved early by the President of the Kyrgyz Republic as the result of a referendum in the

event of three refusals to approve the appointment of a Prime Minister or in the event of another crisis caused by insurmountable differences between the chambers of the Jogorku Kenesh or between one or both chambers of the Jogorku Kenesh and other branches of state power.

3. In the case foreseen under point 3 of Article 51 of this Constitution, the Legislative Assembly is considered dissolved from the moment of issuance of a resolution by the Constitutional Court of the Kyrgyz Republic.
4. The chambers of the Jogorku Kenesh may not be dissolved in time of a state emergency or war, during consideration by the chambers of the Jogorku Kenesh of the issue of dismissing the President of the Kyrgyz Republic from office or when there shall be fewer than six months remaining until the end of the term of office of the President of the Kyrgyz Republic.
5. In the event of dissolution of the Legislative Assembly, the Assembly of People's Representatives, or both chambers of the Jogorku Kenesh, the President of the Kyrgyz Republic designates the date for elections of deputies of the given chamber or chambers, so that the newly elected chamber or chambers convene their first session no later than six months after the moment of dissolution.

Section Two
Legislative Activities

Article 64

The right to initiate legislative belongs to:

30.000 voters (a popular initiative);

the President of the Kyrgyz Republic;

deputies of the Legislative Assembly;

deputies of the Assembly of the People's Representatives;

the Pravitel'stvo of the Kyrgyz Republic;

the Supreme Court of the Kyrgyz Republic, and the Supreme Arbitration Court of the Kyrgyz Republic, on matters within their jurisdiction.

Article 65

1. Draft laws are introduced in both chambers of the Jogorku Kenesh. Upon introduction the respective chamber of the Jogorku Kenesh is obligated to decide within one month the issue of introducing the draft law for review by that chamber, and either to determine the order of priority of review or to state a reason for rejection.
2. Amendments to a draft law on the republican budget may be introduced with the consent of the Pravitel'stvo.
3. Amendments to the Law on national budget, draft laws on introducing or lifting taxes, providing tax exemptions, on changes in financial obligations of the state, and other draft law providing for increased costs to be covered from the national budget or for decreases in revenues of the budget, may only be adopted with consent of the Government.

4. A draft law shall be considered adopted if a majority of the total number of deputies of a chamber vote for it.
5. A draft law which has been adopted by one chamber, on a matter which in accordance with the Constitution, requires approval from the other chamber, shall be presented to that chamber no later than five working days after its adoption by the first chamber. Such draft laws are considered adopted from the moment of approval by the other chamber, or in cases when such approval is not obtained, from the moment of confirmation in accordance with points 2 and 3 of Article 59 of this Constitution.
6. Drafts of laws introducing amendments and supplements to the Constitution, of Constitutional laws, of laws altering the borders of the Kyrgyz Republic, and of laws interpreting of the Constitution and constitutional laws, are considered adopted after no fewer than two readings if no fewer than two-thirds of the total number of deputies of each chamber of the Jogorku Kenesh have voted for them. The date of adoption of the draft law is considered to be the day when the vote on adopting the draft was held in both chambers. If the chambers voted on different days then the date of adoption of the law is the day when the second chamber voted for its adoption.
7. Introduction of amendments and supplements to the Constitution and constitutional laws during states of emergency is not allowed.
8. No laws restricting freedom of speech and freedom of the press may be adopted.

Article 66

1. An adopted law shall be sent within five days to the President of the Kyrgyz Republic for signing.
2. The President of the Kyrgyz Republic, no later than 15 working days after receiving the law, shall sign it or return it with his objections. The given law is subject to reconsideration in the chamber which adopted it. If upon reconsideration the law is approved in the earlier adopted wording by majority vote of no less than two-thirds of the total number of deputies, then the law is to be signed by the President of the Kyrgyz Republic within seven working days.
3. A law rejected by the President which, in accordance with this Constitution, has been adopted by a majority vote of no fewer than two-thirds of the total number of deputies of each chamber of the Jogorku Kenesh, is to be signed by the President within the period established in point 2 of this Article if upon reconsideration it is approved in the earlier adopted wording by a majority vote of no fewer than three-fourths of the total number of deputies of each of the chambers of the Jogorku Kenesh.

Article 67

A law enters into effect ten days from the moment of its publication if no other stipulation is made in the law itself or in a law on the procedure for its entering into force.

Article 68

1. The chambers of the Jogorku Kenesh may delegate their legislative powers to the President of the Kyrgyz Republic for a period of no more than one year.
2. Legislative powers transfer to the President of the Kyrgyz Republic in the event of dissolution of chambers of the Jogorku Kenesh.
3. Legislative powers are carried out by the President of the Kyrgyz Republic by the adoption of decrees, which have the force of law.
4. In the event of dissolution of one of the chambers of the Jogorku Kenesh, the President of the Kyrgyz Republic carries out the legislative powers of that chamber only.

CHAPTER FIVE
EXECUTIVE POWER

Article 69

Executive power in the Kyrgyz Republic is carried out by the Pravitel'stvo of the Kyrgyz Republic, by ministries accountable to it, by state committees, administrative departments and local state administration.

Section One
The Pravitel'stvo

Article 70

1. The Pravitel'stvo of the Kyrgyz Republic is the highest body of state executive power in the Kyrgyz Republic.
2. The activity of the Pravitel'stvo of the Kyrgyz Republic is headed by the Prime Minister of the Kyrgyz Republic. The Pravitel'stvo of the Kyrgyz Republic consists of the Prime Minister of the Kyrgyz Republic, Vice Prime Ministers, Ministers and Chairmen of State Committees of the Kyrgyz Republic.
3. Entry into office of the newly elected President of the Kyrgyz Republic results in resignation from power of the Pravitel'stvo of the Kyrgyz Republic.
4. The Prime Minister, the Pravitel'stvo of the Kyrgyz Republic or an individual member of it has the right to submit his resignation, which shall be accepted or declined by the President of the Kyrgyz Republic.
5. Acceptance of the resignation of the Prime Minister of the Kyrgyz Republic results in the resignation of all members of the Pravitel'stvo. In the event of acceptance of the resignation, the Pravitel'stvo may continue to act upon authorisation from the President of the Kyrgyz Republic, until the formation of a new Pravitel'stvo of the Kyrgyz Republic.

Article 71

1. The Prime Minister shall be appointed by the President of the Kyrgyz Republic with the consent of the Assembly of People's Representatives.
2. A nomination of a candidate for Prime Minister is submitted to the Assembly of People's Representatives no later than two weeks after entry into office of

the newly elected President of the Kyrgyz Republic, or after resignation of the Prime Minister or Pravitel'stvo, or within one week from the day of rejection of a nominee by the Assembly of People's Representatives.

3. The Assembly of People's Representatives shall make its decision concerning the giving of consent to the appointment of a Prime Minister no later than seven days from the day of submission of the nominee.
4. After three refusals by the Assembly of People's Representatives of nominees for Prime Minister, the President of the Kyrgyz Republic appoints a Prime Minister and dissolves the Assembly of People's Representatives.
5. The Assembly of Peoples' Representatives may express lack of confidence in the Prime Minister. A resolution of no confidence in the Prime Minister is adopted by a majority vote of no fewer than two-thirds of the total number of deputies of the Assembly of People's Representatives. After an expression of no confidence in the Prime Minister by the Assembly of People's Representatives, the President of the Kyrgyz Republic shall have the right either to announce the resignation of the Prime Minister or to reject the decision of the Assembly of People's Representatives. In the event that the Assembly of People's Representatives expresses no confidence in the Prime Minister a second time within three months, the President of the Kyrgyz Republic shall either announce the resignation of the Prime Minister or dissolve the Assembly of People's Representatives.
6. The Prime Minister, in accordance with the Constitution of the Kyrgyz Republic, laws and decrees of the President of the Kyrgyz Republic, determines the fundamental directions of the activities of the Pravitel'stvo, organizes its work, and is personally responsible for its activities.

Article 72

1. The President of the Kyrgyz Republic exercises control over the Pravitel'stvo of the Kyrgyz Republic.
2. The Prime Minister presents a report on the work of the Pravitel'stvo to the Legislative Assembly and the Assembly of People's Representatives annually.

Article 73

1. The Pravitel'stvo of the Kyrgyz Republic shall decide all issues about state administration, excluding the powers relegated by the Constitution to the competency of the President of the Kyrgyz Republic and to the Jogorku Kenesh.
2. The Pravitel'stvo of the Kyrgyz Republic:

   prepares the republican budget and submits it to the Assembly of People's Representatives, and ensures its implementation;

   exercises budgetary-financial, tax and price policy;

   organizes and exercises management over state property;

   takes measures to secure the defence of the country, state security, and the realisation of foreign policy of the Kyrgyz Republic;

carries out measures to guarantee lawful activity, rights and freedoms of citizens, the protection of property and public order, the fighting of crime.

3. The Pravitel'stvo of the Kyrgyz Republic and the National Bank of Kyrgyzstan ensure the provision of a unitary monetary - credit and hard currency policy.

Article 74

The Pravitel'stvo of the Kyrgyz Republic issues decrees and instructions binding throughout the territory of the Kyrgyz Republic for all bodies, organisations, officials and citizens and organises, supervises and secures their fulfillment.

Article 75

1. The Pravitel'stvo of the Kyrgyz Republic oversees the activity of all ministries, government committees, administrative agencies and state organs of local administration.
2. Ministries, state committees, and administrative departments, within the limits of their competency, issue orders and instructions on the basis of and as part of implementing of the Constitution, laws of the Kyrgyz Republic, resolutions of the chambers of the Jogorku Kenesh, acts of the President, resolutions and instructions of the Pravitel'stvo of the Kyrgyz Republic, and organise, check and ensure their implementation.
3. The Pravitel'stvo of the Kyrgyz Republic hears reports of the heads of the ministries, state committees administrative agencies and also heads of the local state administrations and annuls their acts which contradict the legislation of the Kyrgyz Republic.

Section Two
Local State Administration

Article 76

Executive power in oblasts, rayons and cities is carried out by the local state administration.

Article 77

1. Local state administrations act on the basis of this Constitution and the laws of the Kyrgyz Republic.
2. Implementation of decisions of a local state administration adopted within the bounds of its competency is mandatory on the respective territory.

Section Three
The Procurator General's Office

Article 78

Auditing accurate and uniform implementation of legislative is performed by the Procuracy of the Kyrgyz Republic within the bounds of its competency.

Bodies of the procuracy conduct criminal investigations and participate in trials of cases in circumstances and procedures set forth by law.

CHAPTER SIX
COURTS AND JUSTICE

Article 79

1. Justice in the Kyrgyz Republic is administered only by the court.
2. The Courts of the Kyrgyz Republic are the Constitutional Court of the Kyrgyz Republic, the Supreme Court of the Kyrgyz Republic, the Supreme Arbitration Court of the Kyrgyz Republic, local courts (oblast courts, courts of the City of Bishkek, courts of rayons, cities, arbitration courts of oblasts and the city of Bishkek, military courts). The creation and founding of extraordinary, special courts and the position of judges is not allowed.
3. The status of courts and judges in the Kyrgyz Republic is specified by Constitutional laws. The organisation and procedure for activity of the courts is specified by law.
4. A Judge is subordinated only to the Constitution and to the law. Judges shall enjoy the right of inviolability and immunity; a judge, in accordance with his status, is ensured social, material and other guarantees of his independence.

Article 80

1. A citizen of the Kyrgyz Republic who is not younger than 35 years of age and no older 70 years of age and who has an advanced legal education and no less than 10 years of experience in the legal profession may be a judge of the Constitutional Court, the Supreme Court or the Supreme Arbitration Court of the Kyrgyz Republic. Judges of the Constitutional Court of the Kyrgyz Republic are elected by the Legislative Assembly and the Assembly of People's Representatives upon nomination by the President of the Kyrgyz Republic for a term of 15 years. Judges of the Supreme Court and the Supreme Arbitration Court of the Kyrgyz Republic are elected by the Assembly of People's Representatives upon nomination by the President of the Kyrgyz Republic for a term of 10 years.
2. A citizen of the Kyrgyz Republic not older than 65 years of age who has a higher legal education and a record of service in his specialty for no less than 5 years may serve as a judge of a local court. Judges of local courts are appointed by the President of the Kyrgyz Republic the first time for a term of 3 years, and the next time for a term of 7 years.

Article 81

1. Judges are removed from office on the basis of health, by their own request, for commission of a crime where there is a conviction of a court in force and for other reasons specified by law. Judges of local courts also may be relieved from their offices of the basis of results of attestation.
2. Judges of the Constitutional Court of the Kyrgyz Republic may be dismissed from their office upon the petition of the President of the Kyrgyz Republic by a majority vote of no fewer than two-thirds of the total number of deputies of each of the chambers of the Jogorku Kenesh of the Kyrgyz Republic.
3. Judges of the Supreme Court and the Supreme Arbitration Courts may be relieved from their office on the petition of the President of the Kyrgyz

Republic by a majority vote of no fewer than two-thirds of the total number of deputies of the Assembly of People's Representatives.

Article 82

1. The Constitutional Court is the highest body of judicial power for protection of the Constitution of the Kyrgyz Republic.
2. The Constitutional Court consists of the Chairman, the Deputy Chairman and seven judges of the Constitutional Court.
3. The Constitutional Court:
   (a) declares laws and other normative legal acts unconstitutional if they contradict the Constitution;
   (b) decides disputes concerning the effect, use and interpretation of the Constitution;
   (c) determines the validity of elections of the President of the Kyrgyz Republic;
   (d) issues a determination concerning the removal from office of the President of the Kyrgyz Republic as well as judges of the Constitutional Court, the Supreme Court and the Supreme Arbitration Court of the Kyrgyz Republic;
   (e) gives its consent to the criminal prosecution of judges of local courts;
   (f) issues a determination concerning issues about amendments and alterations to the Constitution of the Kyrgyz Republic;
   (g) annuls the decisions of bodies of local self-government which contradict the Constitution of the Kyrgyz Republic;
   (h) renders a decision concerning the constitutionality of practices concerning the application of laws which affect the constitutional rights of citizens.
4. The decision of the Constitutional Court is final and no appeal is allowed. The determination of the unconstitutionality of laws and other acts by the Constitutional Court annuls their application on the territory of the Kyrgyz Republic and also cancels the effect of other normative and other acts based on the act determined to be unconstitutional.

Article 83

1. The Supreme Court of the Kyrgyz Republic is the highest body of judicial power in the sphere of civil, criminal and administrative legal proceedings.
2. The Supreme Court of the Kyrgyz Republic oversees the judicial activity of the oblast, City of Bishkek, rayon, municipal and military courts of the Kyrgyz Republic.

Article 84

1. The Supreme Arbitration Court of the Kyrgyz Republic and arbitration courts of oblasts and the City of Bishkek form a unified system of arbitration courts of the Kyrgyz Republic.

2. Arbitration courts settle economic disputes arising in the economic sphere and in the process of its management of disputes between business entities based on different forms of ownership.
3. The Supreme Arbitration Court of the Kyrgyz Republic oversees judicial activities of arbitration courts in oblasts and in the City of Bishkek.

Article 85

1. Pursuant to a decision of a gathering of citizens, local keneshes, or other representative body of local self-government in villages, settlements and towns, aksakal courts (courts of elders) may be organised from elders or other citizens who enjoy respect and authority.
2. Courts of elders consider property, family disputes and any other matters allowed by law which are submitted to them for review by agreement of the parties with the aim of reaching reconciliation by the parties and delivery of a just verdict which does not contradict law.
3. Decisions of courts of elders and courts of arbitration may be appealed to the corresponding rayon and municipal courts of the Kyrgyz Republic.

Article 86

1. Decisions of the courts of the Kyrgyz Republic which are in effects are binding for all state bodies, entities conducting economic activities, public associations, state officials and citizens and are enforceable throughout of the Kyrgyz Republic.
2. Failure to implement a court decision in legal force and also interference with the activities of courts results in the responsibility established by Law.

Article 87

1. The court does not have the right to apply a normative act which contradicts the Constitution of the Kyrgyz Republic.
2. If during consideration of a case in any court matter there arises an issue about the constitutionality of the law or other act, on which determination of the case rests, the court shall send an inquiry to the Constitutional Court of the Kyrgyz Republic.

Article 88

1. In the event of a public or other accusation, a citizen has the right to defend his dignity and right in court; under no circumstance shall he be denied such court protection.
2. [The right of] Defence is an inalienable right of a person at any stage of review of a judicial matter. In case of a citizen's lack of a financial means, legal assistance and defence is ensured to him at the expense of the State.
3. In court, every participant in the legal process shall have the right to be heard.

Article 89

1. The burden of proving guilt in criminal and administrative cases is on the accuser.

2. Evidence obtained in violation of the law shall be considered non-existent and reference to it in court is not allowed.

Article 90

Principles of justice established by this Constitution are general and unified for all courts and judges of the Kyrgyz Republic.

CHAPTER SEVEN
LOCAL SELF-ADMINISTRATION

Article 91

Local self-government in the Kyrgyz Republic is carried out by local associations which manage affairs of a local character within the bounds of the law and under their own responsibility.

Article 92

Local self-government is exercised through the local keneshes and other bodies, which may be formed by the population itself in the procedure established by law. Bodies of local self-government may have communal property in their own possession and at their own use and disposal.

Article 93

The basis for organisation and the activities of bodies of local self-government is established by the laws of the Kyrgyz Republic, which also regulate their mutual relations with bodies of state power.

Article 94

Bodies of local self-government may be endowed with separate governmental powers, accompanied by transfer [to them] of the material, financial, and other means necessary for their execution. Bodies of local self-government are accountable to state bodies concerning transferred power.

Article 95

1. Local keneshes: approve and control programmes of social-economical development of the territory and social protection of the population; approve the local budget and report on its implementation and also hear information on the use of extra-budgetary funds;
2. Local keneshes of rayons, towns and oblasts have the right to express by majority vote of two-thirds of the total number of deputies, no confidence in the head of the local state administration of the corresponding territorial unit.
3. Local keneshes act independently from local state administration.
4 Local keneshes, within the limits of their powers adopt acts binding for implementation on their territory.
5. Local keneshes and other bodies of local self-government are responsible before the state for observation and implementation of laws and before local society for the results of their activities.

CHAPTER EIGHT

PROCEDURE FOR AMENDMENTS AND SUPPLEMENTS TO THE CONSTITUTION OF THE KYRGYZ REPUBLIC

Article 96

1. Amendments and supplements to this Constitution are adopted by referendum called by the President of the Kyrgyz Republic.
2. Amendments and supplements may be adopted in the Chambers of the Jogorku Kenesh after a proposal by the President of the Kyrgyz Republic by a majority of the total number of deputies of the Legislative Assembly and Assembly of People's Representatives, or by no fewer than 300,000 voters.
3. Proposals to introduce amendments and supplements to the Constitution of the Kyrgyz Republic are considered by the Legislative Assembly and Assembly of People's Representatives, taking into account the ruling of the Constitutional Court of the Kyrgyz Republic, no earlier than three months and no later than six months from the day of submission of the proposal to the Legislative Assembly and the Assembly of People's Representatives.
4. The text of a draft law on introducing amendments and supplements to the Constitution of the Kyrgyz Republic may not be altered during discussion on it in the Legislative Assembly and Assembly of People's Representatives.

Article 97

1. Amendments and supplements to this Constitution are considered adopted by the Jogorku Kenesh if no fewer than two-thirds of the total number of deputies of each of its chambers have voted for them.
2. A rejected proposal may be re-submitted to the Jogorku Kenesh no earlier than after one year.

President of the Kyrgyz Republic A. Akaev

APPENDIX 1.C

CONSTITUTION OF THE REPUBLIC OF TAJIKISTAN

Dushanbe 1994

We, the people of Tajikistan, being an integral part of the world community, appreciating our duty and our responsibility before past, present, and future generations, understanding the necessity of securing sovereignty and the development of our state, acknowledging the unwavering freedoms and rights of the person, respecting the equal rights and friendship of all nations and peoples, setting as our goal the creation of a just society, adopt and announce this Constitution.

CHAPTER ONE

FOUNDATIONS OF THE CONSTITUTIONAL SYSTEM

Article 1: The Republic of Tajikistan is a sovereign democratic, rule of law, secular, and united state. Tajikistan is a social state whose policies are directed towards creating conditions to ensure a worthwhile life and the free development of the person. "Republic of Tajikistan" and "Tajikistan" are equal in meaning.

Article 2: The state language of Tajikistan is Tajik. Russian is a language of inter-ethnic communication. All nations and peoples residing on the territory of the republic have the right to use freely their native languages.

Article 3: The state symbols of the Republic of Tajikistan are its Flag, Coat of Arms, and Anthem.

Article 4: The capital of Tajikistan is the city of Dushanbe.

Article 5: Life, honour, dignity, and other natural human rights are inviolable. The rights and liberties of the person and citizen are recognized, observed, and protected by the state.

Article 6: In Tajikistan, the people are the possessors of the sovereignty and are the only source of state power, which is exercised both directly and also through the people's representatives. The people of Tajikistan are the citizens of the Republic of Tajikistan regardless of their ethnicity. No social organisation, group of people, or individual has the right to arrogate state power. Usurpation of power is a very serious crime. The right to speak in the name of all the people of Tajikistan belongs only to the President and Parliament (Majlisi Oli).

Article 7: The territory of Tajikistan is indivisible and inviolable. Tajikistan consists of Gorno-Badakhshan Autonomous Region, regions, cities, districts, towns, and villages. The state ensures the sovereignty, independence, and territorial integrity of the republic. Propaganda and acts directed towards division of state unity are prohibited. The procedures for forming and altering administrative territorial units are regulated by constitutional law.

Article 8: In Tajikistan, social life develops on the basis of political and ideological pluralism. No state ideology or religion may be established. Social associations are formed and operate within the framework of the Constitution and laws. The state provides them with equal possibilities in their operations. Religious organisations are separate from the state and may not interfere in governmental affairs. The formation and operation of social associations which advocate racial, ethnic, social, or religious animosity or which incite violent overthrow of the constitutional system, as well as the organisation of armed groups, are forbidden.

Article 9: Governmental power is based upon its division into legislative, executive, and judicial powers.

Article 10: The Constitution of Tajikistan possesses supreme legal power, and its norms have direct application. Laws and other legal acts that are contrary to the Constitution do not have legal force. The government and all its organs, officials, citizens, and citizens' associations are obligated to comply with and execute the Constitution and laws of the republic. International legal acts recognised by Tajikistan are a constituent part of the legal system of the republic. In the case of a discrepancy between the laws of the republic and recognised international legal acts, the norms of the international legal acts are applied. Laws and international legal acts recognised by Tajikistan enter into force after their official publication.

Article 11: Tajikistan, conducting peace loving policies, respects the sovereignty and independence of other states and determines its foreign policy on the basis of international norms. War propaganda is prohibited. Tajikistan, controlled by the higher interests of the people, may enter into commonwealths and other international organisations, and, likewise, exit from them, as well as establish relations with foreign countries. The government cooperates with fellow countrymen in other countries.

Article 12: The economic foundations of Tajikistan are comprised of various forms of property. The government guarantees freedom of economic and business activity, as well as equal rights and legal protection for all forms of property, including private property.

Article 13: The earth, its resources, water, the atmosphere, flora, fauna, and other natural resources are the exclusive property of the state, and the government guarantees their effective utilisation in the interests of the people.

CHAPTER TWO

THE RIGHTS, FREEDOMS, AND BASIC OBLIGATIONS OF THE PERSON AND THE CITIZEN

Article 14: The rights and freedoms of the person and the citizen are regulated and protected by the Constitution and laws of the republic, as well as by international legal acts recognised by Tajikistan. Limitations of the rights and freedoms of citizens are only allowed for the purposes of ensuring the rights and freedoms of other citizens, ensuring social order, and protecting the constitutional system and territorial integrity of the republic.

Article 15: A person who on the day the Constitution is adopted is a citizen of the Republic of Tajikistan is considered a citizen of Tajikistan. A citizen of Tajikistan is not allowed to be a citizen of another state, except in the cases anticipated by the laws and interstate treaties of Tajikistan. The procedures for acquisition and loss of citizenship are determined by constitutional law.

Article 16: A citizen of Tajikistan located in another country enjoys the protection of the state. No citizen of the republic may be extradited to a foreign state. Extradition of a criminal to a foreign state is permitted on the grounds of a bilateral agreement. Foreign citizens and stateless persons enjoy these announced rights and freedoms, and have obligations and responsibilities equal to those of citizens of Tajikistan, except in cases anticipated by law. Tajikistan may offer political asylum to foreign citizens who have been victims of human rights violations.

Article 17: All persons are equal before the law and the courts. The government guarantees the rights and freedoms of every person regardless of ethnicity, race, sex, language, faith, political beliefs, education, or social or property status. Men and women have equal rights.

Article 18: Every person has the right to life. No person may be deprived of life except by the verdict of a court for a very serious crime. The inviolability of the individual is guaranteed by the government. No one may be subjected to torture or cruel and inhuman treatment. Forced medical and scientific experiments on people are prohibited.

Article 19: Every person is guaranteed judicial protection. Every person has the right to demand review of her or his case by a competent and non-partisan court. Without lawful grounds, no one may be subjected to detainment, arrest, or deportation. From the moment of detainment, a person has the right to employ the services of a lawyer.

Article 20: No one may be considered guilty of commission of a crime until the verdict of a court enters into legal force. No one may be brought to trial after expiration of the time limit on criminal prosecution or for an act which at the moment of its commission was not considered a crime. No one may be tried twice for one and the same crime. A law that is adopted after a person's commission of an illegal act and that increases punishment for that act does not have ex post facto force. If after a person's commission of an illegal act, liability for that act is repealed or reduced, the new law is applied. Full confiscation of a convicted person's property is not allowed.

Article 21: The law protects the rights of victims. The government guarantees the victim judicial protection and compensation for harms suffered by him or her.

Article 22: The home is inviolable. Invading the home and depriving a person of his or her home are not permitted, except in cases anticipated by law.

Article 23: The privacy of correspondence, telephone conversations, and telegraphic and other communications are ensured, except in cases anticipated by law. The collection, keeping, use, or dissemination of information about the private life of a person without her or his permission to do so is forbidden.

Article 24: Each citizen has the right to free movement, choice of location of residence, departure beyond the borders of the republic, and return to the republic.

Article 25: Governmental organs, social associations, and officials are obligated to provide each person with the possibility of receiving and becoming acquainted with documents that affect her or his rights and interests, except in cases anticipated by law.

Article 26: Each person has the right independently to determine her or his religious preference, to practice any religion alone or in association with others or to practice no religion, and to participate in the performance of religious cults, rituals, and ceremonies.

Article 27: Each citizen has the right, directly or through representatives, to participate in political life and in the governing of the state. Each citizen has equal rights to government service. Each citizen, upon reaching 18 years of age, has the right to elect and be elected. Persons who are declared by a court to be incompetent or who are being detained in prison by the verdict of a court do not have the right to participate in elections or referenda. Elections and referenda are carried out on the basis of general, equal, and direct voting rights by secret ballot.

Article 28: Citizens have the right of association. Each citizen has the right to participate in the formation of political parties, trade unions, and other social associations, as well as voluntarily to join them and resign from them.

Article 29: Each citizen has the right to participate in lawfully established meetings, protests, demonstrations, and peaceful marches. No one may be forced to participate in these activities.

Article 30: Each person is guaranteed the freedoms of speech and the press, as well as the right to use information media. Governmental censorship and prosecution for criticism are forbidden. A list of information considered secrets of the state is determined by law.

Article 31: Citizens have the right personally or in association with others to appeal to governmental organs.

Article 32: Each person has the right to own property and the right to inherit. No one has the right to deprive or limit a citizen's property rights. Seizure of personal property by the government for social needs is permissible only on the grounds provided by law and with the assent of the owner and her or his full compensation for the value of the property. Material and moral harms incurred by individuals as the result of the unlawful activities of governmental organs, social associations, or individual persons are compensated at the expense of the perpetrators in accordance with the law.

Article 33: As the foundation of society, the family is under the protection of the government. Each person has the right to start a family. Men and women who have reached the age of marriage have the right to enter freely into marriage. In familial relations and in the event of abrogation of a marriage, spouses have equal rights. Polygamy is forbidden.

Article 34: Mothers and children are under the special protection and patronage of the government. Parents are responsible for raising children, and adult children who are able to work are obligated to care for their parents. The government takes care to protect orphans and the disabled, as well as their upbringing and education.

Article 35: Each person has the right to employment, to choose a profession and job, to have their job protected, and to social protection against unemployment. Salaries should not be lower than the minimum working wage. Any kind of limitation in employment relations is forbidden. Equal work is equally compensated. No one may be subjected to forced labour, except in cases anticipated by law. The use of the labour of women and minors in heavy or underground work, as well as for work in dangerous work conditions, is forbidden.

Article 36: Each person has the right to housing. This right is ensured through the provision of governmental, social, cooperative, and individual housing construction.

Article 37: Each person has the right to relaxation. This right is ensured through establishment of the length of the working day and week, the provision of an annual paid vacation, weekly days of rest, and through other conditions anticipated by law.

Article 38: Each person has the right to healthcare. This right is ensured through free medical assistance in governmental healthcare institutions, measures to improve the condition of the environment, formation and development of mass athletics, physical fitness, and other sports. Other forms of medical assistance to be provided are determined by law.

Article 39: Each person is guaranteed social assistance in old age, in the case of illness, disability, or loss of ability to work, in the case of loss of a provider, or in other cases determined by law.

Article 40: Each person has the right freely to participate in the cultural life of society, as well as in artistic, scientific, and technical creation and make use of their achievements. Cultural and spiritual valuables are protected by the government. Intellectual property is under the protection of the law.

Article 41: Each person has the right to education. General basic education is obligatory. The government guarantees free high school, trade, and, in accordance with ability and on a competitive basis, specialised high school and university education. Other forms of education to be provided are determined by law.

Article 42: On the territory of Tajikistan, each person is obligated to comply with Tajikistan's Constitution and laws, as well as to respect the rights, freedoms, honour, and dignity of other people. Ignorance of the law does not free a person from liability.

Article 43: Defence of the homeland, protection of the interests of the state, and strengthening the state's independence, security, and defence forces are the sacred duty of the citizen. The procedures for completing military service are determined by law.

Article 44: Every person is obligated to protect nature and historic and cultural monuments.

Article 45: Every person is obligated to pay those taxes and tariffs that are established by law.

Article 46: If, as the result of a natural disaster or a real threat to the rights and freedoms of citizens, to the independence of the state, or to the state's territorial integrity, the constitutional organs of the republic cannot function normally, as a temporary measure in order to ensure the safety of citizens and the state, a state of emergency may be declared. A state of emergency may be established for no longer than a three month period. In cases of necessity, this time limit may be extended by the President of the Republic of Tajikistan.

Article 47: In the case of a state of emergency, the rights and freedoms anticipated in articles 16, 17, 18, 19, 20, 22, 25, and 28 of the Constitution may not be limited. Over the time period for which a state of emergency is declared, Parliament does not disband. The legal regime during a state of emergency is determined by constitutional law.

CHAPTER THREE
PARLIAMENT

Article 48: Parliament is the highest representative and legislative organ of the Republic of Tajikistan. Parliament is elected for a five-year term. Citizens not younger than 25 years of age may be elected to Parliament. The organisation and operations of Parliament are determined by constitutional law.

Article 49: The powers of Parliament:

(1) adopting, amending, and repealing laws and resolutions;

(2) interpreting the Constitution and laws;

(3) determining the basic directions of domestic and foreign governmental policies;

(4) forming the Central Elections and Referenda Commission;

(5) scheduling referenda;

(6) introducing draft legislation and other important governmental and social issues for popular discussion;

(7) scheduling elections for the President of the Republic;

(8) scheduling elections for higher and local representative organs;

(9) giving consent to the formation and abolition of ministries and governmental committees;

(10) approving decrees of the President concerning the appointment or dismissal of the Prime Minister and other members of the Government;

(11) approving decrees of the President concerning the appointment or dismissal of the Chair of the National Bank and her or his assistants;

(12) on the petition of the President of the Republic, electing and recalling the chair, assistant chairs, and judges of the Constitutional Court, the Supreme Court, and the High Economic Court;

(13) giving consent to the appointment and dismissal of the Procurator General and her or his assistants;

(14) approving the socio-economic programme, and giving consent to the provision of economic assistance to other states;

(15) approving the state budget, determining the possible amount of the state budget deficit and sources to cover this deficit, monitoring implementation of the budget, determining tax policies, and giving permission for the extension and receipt of governmental credit;

(16) determining the monetary system;

(17) determining the structure of, formation of, abolition of, and changes in administrative territorial units. In necessary cases at its own discretion, also independently changes the borders of administrative territorial units;

(18) ratifying and denouncing international treaties;

(19) forming courts;

(20) approving decrees of the President concerning martial law and states of emergency;

(21) approving state awards;

(22) establishing military, diplomatic, and other specialised ranks;

(23) approving the state symbols;

(24) declaring general amnesties;

(25) repealing resolutions of the Presidium of Parliament in the event that they are contrary to the Constitution and laws;

(26) exercising other powers determined by the Constitution and laws.

Article 50: The basic form of operations for Parliament is the session. A session of Parliament is convened by the Presidium of Parliament no less frequently than two times each year. A session of Parliament is competent if no less than two-thirds of the total number people's deputies participate in it. The first session of Parliament is convened by the Central Elections and Referenda Commission within one month after elections for people's deputies.

Article 51: In order to organize the work of Parliament and exercise powers anticipated in the Constitution and laws, a Presidium of Parliament is formed which is headed by the Chair of Parliament. The composition of the Presidium of Parliament consists of the Chair of Parliament, her or his First Assistant and assistants, and the chairs of the committees and permanent commissions of Parliament. Parliament may also elect other people's deputies to membership in the Presidium of Parliament.

Article 52: The powers of the Presidium of Parliament:

(1) convening Parliament;

(2) organising preparations for sessions of Parliament;

(3) coordinating the activities of the committees and permanent commissions of Parliament;

(4) organising inter-parliamentary connections;

(5) managing the press organs of Parliament, and appointing and dismissing their chief editors;

(6) giving consent to the appointment or recalling of the heads of diplomatic missions of Tajikistan in foreign states and representatives of the republic in international organisations;

(7) exercising other powers determined by the Constitution and laws. Without exceeding its powers, the Presidium of Parliament adopts resolutions.

Article 53: From among the people's deputies, Parliament elects a Chair of Parliament, her or his First Assistant and assistants, and the chairs of the committees and permanent commissions of Parliament. One of the assistants to the Chair of Parliament must be a people's deputy from Gorno-Badakhshan Autonomous Region. The Chair of

Parliament is elected by secret ballot and must have a majority of the votes of the total number of people's deputies.

Article 54: The powers of the Chair of Parliament:

(1) managing the preparation of issues subject to review during sessions;

(2) chairing sessions of Parliament and meetings of its Presidium;

(3) presenting Parliament with candidates for the First Assistant and assistants to the Chair of Parliament, and for the chairs of the committees and permanent commissions of Parliament;

(4) signing resolutions of Parliament and resolutions of its Presidium;

(5) representing Parliament both within the country and abroad;

(6) signing inter-parliamentary agreements;

(7) managing the administrative machinery of Parliament, and issuing orders;

(8) exercising other powers determined by the Constitution and laws.

Article 55: The First Assistant and assistants to the Chair of Parliament, when authorised to do so by the Chair, fulfill certain functions of the Chair. In the event of the absence of the Chair of Parliament, her or his obligations are carried out by the First Assistant.

Article 56: From among the people's deputies, Parliament elects committees and permanent commissions to draft legislation, exercise monitoring functions, and conduct preliminary review and preparation of issues. Parliament may, when necessary, form investigatory, audit, and other temporary commissions.

Article 57: An official is obligated to provide a people's deputy with information that is necessary so that that deputy can fulfill her or his functions, except in cases determined by law. A people's deputy has the right freely to express her or his opinion and to vote according to her or his beliefs.

Article 58: A people's deputy who is working in Parliament on a full-time basis may not occupy another position or engage in entrepreneurial activity aside from scientific or creative activities. A citizen of Tajikistan may not simultaneously be a deputy in more than two representative organs.

Article 59: A people's deputy enjoys the right of immunity. She or he may not be subjected to any kind of arrest, administrative penalty imposed through judicial proceedings, or criminal trial without the consent of Parliament. Without the consent of Parliament, a people's deputy may not be detained, except when apprehended at the scene of a crime. The powers of a people's deputy terminate upon resignation, a declaration by a court of incompetence, or by a well-founded decision of Parliament to that effect. The legal status of people's deputies is determined by constitutional law.

Article 60: The right to introduce draft legislation belongs to people's deputies, the President, the Government, the Constitutional Court, the Supreme Court, the High Economic Court, and the Parliament of People's Deputies of Gorno-Badakhshan Autonomous Region.

Article 61: The laws of Tajikistan and resolutions of Parliament are adopted by a majority of the votes of the total number of people's deputies. Constitutional laws are adopted by the positive vote of no less than two-thirds of the total number of people's deputies.

Article 62: Laws of Tajikistan are presented to the President for her or his signature. If the President does not agree with the law, then she or he returns the laws with her or his objections to the Parliament within fifteen days. If two-thirds of Parliament votes to affirm Parliament's previously adopted decision, the President signs the law. If the President does not return a law within the established time period, then she or he is required to sign that law.

Article 63: Parliament may prematurely disband itself with the consent of not less than two-thirds of the people's deputies. In any case, the powers of the people's deputies of Tajikistan are terminated on the day that the first session of a new Parliament is convened.

CHAPTER FOUR

THE PRESIDENT

Article 64: The President of the Republic of Tajikistan is the head of state and of the executive power (Government). The President is the guarantor of the Constitution and laws, of the rights and freedoms of the person and citizen, of national independence, unity, and territorial integrity, of the continuity and longevity of the state, of the coordinated functioning and cooperation of governmental organs, and of compliance with the international treaties of Tajikistan.

Article 65: The President is elected for a term of five years by the citizens of Tajikistan on the basis of general, equal, and direct voting rights by secret ballot. Any citizen who is age 35 to 65, is fluent in the state language, and has been resident on the territory of Tajikistan for at least the previous ten years may be nominated as a candidate for the office of President of the Republic. A candidate for the office of President of the Republic is any person who has so registered and has collected the signatures of nomination of no less than five percent of the voters. No one may be President for more than two consecutive terms.

Article 66: An election for President is considered official when more than half of the voters participate in it. A candidate for the office of President who receives more than half the votes of the voters who participate in an election is considered elected. The procedures for Presidential elections are determined by constitutional law.

Article 67: Before assuming office, the President takes the following oath at a meeting of Parliament:

> *"As President, I swear to defend the Constitution and laws of the Republic, to guarantee the rights, freedoms, honour, and integrity of citizens, to defend the territorial integrity and political, economic, and cultural independence of Tajikistan, and to serve the people with devotion."*

The powers of the President are terminated at the moment a newly elected President takes this oath.

Article 68: The President does not have the right to occupy another office, be a deputy in a representative organ, or engage in entrepreneurial activity. The salary of the President is established by Parliament.

Article 69: The President of the Republic of Tajikistan:

(1) represents Tajikistan both within the country and in international relations;

(2) with the consent of Parliament, forms and abolishes ministries and governmental committees;

(3) appoints and dismisses the Prime Minister and other members of the Government, and presents decrees to this effect to Parliament for approval;

(4) appoints and dismisses the Chair of the National Bank and her or his assistants, and presents decrees to this effect to Parliament for approval;

(5) creates the executive administration of the President;

(6) appoints and dismisses the chairs of the Gorno-Badakhshan Autonomous Region, regions, the city of Dushanbe, cities, and districts, and presents them to the corresponding parliament of people's deputies for approval;

(7) presents Parliament with candidates for election to or removal from positions as chair, assistant chairs, and judges of the Constitutional Court, the Supreme Court, and the High Economic Court;

(8) with the consent of Parliament, appoints and dismisses the Procurator General and her or his assistants;

(9) on the petition of the Minister of Justice, appoints and dismisses the judges of military courts, the court of the Gorno-Badakhshan Autonomous Region, and regional, Dushanbe city, city, and district courts;

(10) manages the reserve fund and informs Parliament of its expenditures;

(11) introduces proposals in Parliament regarding determination of the monetary system;

(12) signs laws;

(13) repeals or suspends the force of acts of organs of state government in the event that they are contrary to the Constitution and laws;

(14) manages the implementation of foreign policy, signs international treaties, and presents them to Parliament for approval;

(15) with the consent of the Presidium of Parliament, appoints the heads of diplomatic missions of Tajikistan in foreign states and representatives of the republic in international organisations;

(16) accepts the credentials of heads of the diplomatic missions of foreign states;

(17) is the Supreme Commander-in-Chief of the Armed Forces of Tajikistan; appoints and dismisses the commanders of the troops of the Armed Forces of Tajikistan;

(18) in case of a real threat to the security of the state, declares martial law and issues a decree to that effect for approval by Parliament;

(19) declares states of emergency over the entire territory of the republic or in separate localities, and immediately issues a decree to that effect for approval by Parliament and notifies the United Nations;

(20) forms and manages a Security Council;

(21) extends political asylum;

(22) decides issues of acquisition and loss of citizenship;

(23) decides issues of pardoning the convicted;

(24) confers high military, diplomatic, and other specialised ranks;

(25) awards citizens with state awards and confers state prizes and honorary titles of Tajikistan;

(26) fulfills other powers anticipated by the Constitution and laws.

Article 70: The President issues decrees and orders without exceeding her or his authority, informs Parliament about conditions in the country, and introduces important and essential issues for consideration in Parliament.

Article 71: In the event of the President's death, resignation, or dismissal, or if the President is declared incompetent, until a newly elected President assumes office, the President's obligations are transferred to the Chair of Parliament, and the obligations of the Chair of Parliament are transferred to the First Assistant. In these circumstances, elections for President are held within three months. A question concerning the premature termination of the President's powers is decided by a majority vote of the people's deputies of Parliament, except in the circumstances anticipated in Article 72.

Article 72: The President enjoys the right of immunity. In the event that the President violates her or his oath or commits a crime, Parliament, taking into consideration the findings of the Constitutional Court and a special Parliamentary commission, by the positive vote of no less than two-thirds of the people's deputies, dismisses the President from office. A question concerning charging the President of the Republic with violation of his or her oath or committing a crime is raised on the petition of no less than one-third of the people's deputies. In this event, the Chair of the Supreme Court is assigned to chair a special session of Parliament. The people's deputies swear an oath to the effect that in reviewing this issue, they will be motivated by their own conscience, the law, and justice. After the President is dismissed from office, the investigation of her or his case continues, she or he is charged, and the case is transferred to a court.

CHAPTER FIVE
THE GOVERNMENT

Article 73: The Government of the Republic consists of the Prime Minister, her or his First Assistant and assistants, ministers, and the chairs of governmental committees. The Government ensures the effective management and functioning of the economy and the social and spiritual spheres, as well as of compliance with laws, decisions of Parliament, and decrees and orders of the President of Tajikistan. The members of the Government do not have the right to occupy another office, be deputies in representative organs, or engage in entrepreneurial activity.

Article 74: In accordance with the Constitution and laws of the republic, the Government issues resolutions and orders, the execution of which is obligatory over the entirety of the territory of the republic. The Government relinquishes its powers before a newly elected President. In the event that the Government declares that it is unable to function normally, it may present its resignation to the President. Each member of Parliament has the right to resign. The organisation, operations, and powers of the Government are determined by constitutional law.

Article 75: The government presents socio-economic programs and issues of extension and receipt of governmental credit, the provision of economic assistance to other states, draft state budgets, the possible amount of the state budget deficit, and sources to cover this deficit to Parliament for review.

CHAPTER SIX
LOCAL POWER

Article 76: Local power consists of representative and legislative organs that operate within exceeding their powers. They ensure execution of the Constitution, laws, and acts of Parliament and the President.

Article 77: Managed by a chair, parliaments of people's deputies are organs of local representative power in regions, cities, and districts. Deputies of local parliaments are elected for five year terms. A parliament of people's deputies approves the local budget and the report of its implementation, determines paths of local socio-economic development, determines local taxes and payments in accordance with the law, determines means of management and possession of communal property, and exercises other powers determined by the Constitution and laws.

Article 78: Local executive power is exercised by representatives of the President: chairs of regions, cities, and districts. Local representative and executive organs of corresponding administrative territorial units are headed by the chair. The chairs of Gorno-Badakhshan Autonomous Region, regions, the city of Dushanbe, cities, and districts are appointed and dismissed by the President, having presented her or his candidates for approval by the corresponding parliament of people's deputies. The chair is responsible before higher executive organs and the corresponding parliament of people's deputies. The council (jamoat) is the self-government organ of towns and villages. The formation, powers, and operations of organs of local power are regulated by constitutional law.

Article 79: Representative organs and their chairs, without exceeding their powers, adopt legal acts, compliance with which is obligatory over the corresponding territory. In the event that acts of representative organs and chairs are contrary to the Constitution and laws, they are repealed by higher organs and courts.

Article 80: In the event that a parliament of people's deputies of Gorno-Badakhshan Autonomous Region, a region, the city of Dushanbe, a city, or a district systematically fails to comply with the Constitution and laws, Parliament has the right to disband that local parliament and schedule new elections.

CHAPTER SEVEN
GORNO-BADAKHSHAN AUTONOMOUS REGION

Article 81: Gorno-Badakhshan Autonomous Region is a component and indivisible part of the Republic of Tajikistan. Without the permission of the local parliament of people's deputies, it is not permissible to alter the borders of the territory of Gorno-Badakhshan Autonomous Region.

Article 82: People's deputies of Tajikistan from Gorno-Badakhshan Autonomous Region are elected in accordance with established legal norms, regardless of the size of the population.

Article 83: The powers of Gorno-Badakhshan Autonomous Region in the social, economic, and cultural spheres of life, as well as other powers of the region, are determined by constitutional law.

CHAPTER EIGHT
COURTS

Article 84: The judicial power is independent and protects the rights and freedoms of individuals, the interests of the state, organisations, and institutions, and legality and justice. Judicial power is exercised by the Constitutional Court, the Supreme Court, the High Economic Court, the Military Court, the court of Gorno-Badakhshan Autonomous Region, and regional, Dushanbe city, city, and district courts. The organisation of and work procedures of courts are determined by constitutional law. Judges have terms of five years. The creation of emergency courts is forbidden.

Article 85: Lawyers not younger than 30 years of age and not older than 60 years of age who have worked as judges for not less than 5 years, may be elected or appointed to office as a judge of the Supreme Court, the High Economic Court, the Military Court, a regional court, or Dushanbe City Court. Persons not younger than 25 years of age and not older than 60 years of age who have at least 3 years of work experience in the legal profession may be appointed to office as a judge of a city or district court.

Article 86: Judges of the Military Court, the court of Gorno-Badakhshan Autonomous Region, and regional, Dushanbe city, city, and district courts are appointed and dismissed by the President on the petition of the Minister of Justice.

Article 87: In their work, judges are independent and subordinate only to the Constitution and law. Interference in their work is forbidden.

Article 88: Judges review cases both on panels and individually. The judicial process is exercised on the basis of the principle of the adversarial nature and equality of parties. Hearings in all courts are open, except in cases anticipated by law. Judicial proceedings are carried out in either the state language or in the language of the majority of the people of a given locality. Persons who do not speak the language of the judicial proceedings are provided with the services of an interpreter.

Article 89: The Constitutional Court consists of seven people, one of whom is a representative of Gorno-Badakhshan Autonomous Region. The judges of the Constitutional Court are elected from among all lawyers not younger than 30 years of age and not older than 60 years of age who have at least ten years of experience working in the legal profession. The powers of the Constitutional Court:

(1) determining whether laws and legal acts of Parliament, the President, the Government, the Supreme Court, the High Economic Court, and other governmental and social organs, as well as treaties of Tajikistan that have not yet entered into legal force, are in accordance with the Constitution;

(2) resolving conflicts between governmental organs regarding their competencies;

(3) fulfilling other powers determined by the Constitution and laws. Decisions of the Constitutional Court are final.

Article 90: Judges may not occupy other positions, be deputies in representative organs, be members of political parties or associations, or engage in entrepreneurial activity besides scientific, creative, and teaching activities.

Article 91: Judges enjoy the right of immunity. Without the consent of the organ which elected or appointed her or him, a judge is not subject to arrest or criminal trial. A judge is not subject to detention, except when she or he is detained at the scene of a crime.

Article 92: Legal assistance is guaranteed at all stages of investigation and trial. The organisation or and work procedures of the bar and other forms of legal assistance to be provided are determined by constitutional law.

CHAPTER NINE
THE PROCURACY

Article 93: Oversight for exact and uniform compliance with the law on the territory of Tajikistan is exercised by the Procurator General and procurators subordinate to her or him.

Article 94: The Procurator General heads a unified, centralised system of organs of the procuracy of Tajikistan. The Procurator General is accountable to Parliament and the President.

Article 95: The Procurator General of Tajikistan is appointed for a term of five years. The Procurator General appoints and dismisses procurators subordinate to her or him. The term of office of procurators is five years. The operations, powers, and structure of the organs of the procuracy are regulated by law.

Article 96: The Procurator General and procurators subordinate to her or him exercise their powers independently of other governmental organs and officials and are subordinate only to the law.

Article 97: A procurator may not occupy another position, be a deputy in a representative organ, be a members of a political parties or association, or engage in entrepreneurial activity besides scientific, creative, and teaching activities.

CHAPTER TEN
PROCEDURES FOR AMENDING THE CONSTITUTION

Article 98: Amendments and additions to the Constitution are introduced through general referenda. A referendum is held if two-thirds of the people's deputies vote for it to be held. The procedures for holding a referendum are determined by constitutional law.

Article 99: Proposals to amend or add to the Constitution are introduced by the President or on the petition of no less than one-third of the people's deputies of Tajikistan. Proposals to amend or add to the Constitution are published in the press three months before the referendum.

Article 100: The republican form of government of, the territorial integrity of, and the democratic, rule of law, secular, and social natures of the state may not be changed.

APPENDIX 1.D
THE CONSTITUTION OF TURKMENISTAN

Adopted by Khalk Maslahaty on 26 September 2008 in Ashgabat

Unofficial English language translation and official text in the Russian language

***Disclaimer**: This is unofficial, slightly paraphrased, translation of the Constitution of Turkmenistan. It has no legal force. nCa is not responsible for any problems or complications arising from the use of this text. Only the Turkmen and Russian versions issued by the government of Turkmenistan are legally valid. The Russian version is included in this document for reference purpose. All the nuances of the original text may not have been reflected fully in this translation.*

We, the people of Turkmenistan, based on our inalienable right to determine our destiny;

Proceeding from the responsibility for present and future of the Motherland;

Expressing loyalty to the covenant of ancestors to live in unity, peace and harmony;

With the aim of protecting the national values and interests, strengthening the independence, sovereignty, the status of permanent neutrality of Turkmenistan;

Guaranteeing the rights and freedoms of each person and citizen, and seeking to ensure civil peace and national accord in the society, to substantiate the foundations of democracy and democratic, legal, secular state, we adopt the present Constitution – the Basic Law of Turkmenistan.

Section I: Fundamentals of the Constitutional System of Turkmenistan

Article 1: Turkmenistan is a democratic, legal and secular state in which the government takes the form of presidential republic.

Turkmenistan exercises the complete power and complete authority on its territory, and independently conducts the internal and foreign policy. The state sovereignty and territory of Turkmenistan are homogeneous and indivisible.

The State protects the independence, territorial integrity of Turkmenistan, and constitutional system, and provides law and order.

Turkmenistan, by law, has the status of permanent neutrality. The United Nations General Assembly resolution "Permanent Neutrality of Turkmenistan" dated 12 December 1995: "1. Recognizes and supports the declared status of permanent neutrality of Turkmenistan; 2. Calls upon the member states of the United Nations to respect and support this status of Turkmenistan and also to respect its independence, sovereignty and territorial integrity." The permanent neutrality of Turkmenistan, recognised by the world community, is the basis of its domestic and foreign policy.

Article 2: The people are the bearer of and the sole source of the state power in Turkmenistan. The people of Turkmenistan exercise their power directly or through representative bodies.

No part (group) of the people, organisation or individuals, have the right to abrogate the state power.

Article 3: In Turkmenistan, the people are the highest value of the society and the state.

The state is responsible for every citizen and creates conditions for free development of the individual, protects the life, honour, dignity and freedom, personal integrity, natural and inalienable rights of the citizen.

Every citizen is responsible before the State for the responsibilities entrusted to him by the Constitution and laws.

Article 4: State power is based on the principle of separation of powers between the legislative, executive and judicial branches, which operate independently, balancing each other.

Article 5: The state and all of its organs and officials are linked by law and constitutional order.

The Constitution of Turkmenistan is the Basic Law of the State. Rules and regulations laid down in it are unswervingly applicable. The laws and other legal acts that contradict the Constitution are null and void.

The normative-legal acts of the government and administration, and the local self-government, are published for general information or made available through other means, except when they contain state or other secrets protected by law. The normative legal acts affecting the rights and freedom of the individual and citizen, if not brought to the general information of the public, are invalid from the time of their adoption.

Article 6: Turkmenistan, being a full subject of the global community, has the foreign policy of permanent neutrality, non-interference in the internal affairs of other countries, refrains from the use of force and participation in military blocs and alliances, promotes peaceful, friendly and mutually beneficial relations with countries in the region and states of the whole world.

Turkmenistan recognises the priority of the universally accepted norms of international law. If an international treaty (contract) of Turkmenistan establishes rules other than those stipulated by the laws of Turkmenistan, the rules of international treaty will apply.

Article 7: Turkmenistan has its own citizenship. The citizenship is acquired, retained and lost in accordance with the law.

Citizenship of another state is not recognised for the citizens of Turkmenistan.

No one can be deprived of citizenship or the right to change citizenship. A citizen of Turkmenistan cannot be extradited to another state or expelled from the limits of Turkmenistan, or restricted in the right to return to the homeland.

The citizens of Turkmenistan are guaranteed the protection and patronage of the state in the territory of Turkmenistan and beyond its borders.

Article 8: Foreign nationals and stateless persons enjoy the rights and freedoms, and bear the responsibilities, of citizens of Turkmenistan in accordance with law and international treaties of Turkmenistan.

Turkmenistan, in accordance with universally recognised norms of international right and in the order established by the law, gives refuge to foreign citizens and stateless persons.

Article 9: The property is inviolable. Turkmenistan approves the right to private ownership of the means of production, land and other material and intellectual values. They can also belong to the associations of citizens and the state. The law establishes objects that are exclusive property of the state. The state guarantees equal protection and creation of equal conditions for development of all forms of ownership.

Confiscation of property is prohibited, except for the property acquired by means prohibited by law.

Forced confiscation of property is permissible only in cases stipulated by law.

Article 10: The economy of Turkmenistan is based on the principles of market relations. The state encourages and supports entrepreneurship, promotes development of small and medium enterprises.

Article 11: The state is responsible for safeguarding the national historical and cultural heritage, natural environment, ensuring equality between social and ethnic communities. The state encourages scientific and artistic creativity and distribution of its positive results, promotes development of international relations in the fields of science, culture, education and training, sports and tourism.

Article 12: The state guarantees freedom of religion and worship, and equality before the law. Religious organisations are separate from the state, cannot interfere in the state affairs and carry out state functions. The public education system is separate from religious organisations and is secular.

Each person independently determines his attitude toward religion, has the right to, individually or jointly with others, profess any religion or none, to express and disseminate beliefs related to attitude toward religion, to participate in religious observances, rituals, and ceremonies.

Article 13: In order to protect the state sovereignty and security, Turkmenistan has its own armed forces.

Article 14: Turkmen is the state [official] language of Turkmenistan. The use of their native language is guaranteed to all citizens of Turkmenistan.

Article 15: The State Flag, the State Emblem, and the National Anthem are the Symbols of Turkmenistan.

The flag, national emblem and national anthem are established and protected by law.

Article 16: The administrative-territorial structure of Turkmenistan consists of: Velayats (provinces), cities with right of Velayat, Etraps (districts), cities with right of district, cities (towns) in district, settlements, Gengeshlyk.

The territory of one or more villages forms a Gengeshlyk.

Article 17: Ashgabat is the capital of Turkmenistan.

Section II: Rights, Freedoms and Duties of the citizens of Turkmenistan

Article 18: The rights and freedoms of the individual are inviolable and inalienable.

No one can be deprived of their rights and freedoms, or restrictions on their rights and freedoms, except in accordance with the Constitution and laws.

The enumeration in the Constitution and laws of certain rights and freedoms can not be used to deny or diminish the rights and freedoms of others.

Article 19: Turkmenistan guarantees the equality of rights and freedoms of individual and citizen, and also the equality of the individual and citizen before the law regardless of their nationality, race, gender, origin, property and official status, place of residence, language, religion, political beliefs, party affiliation or lack of affiliation to any party.

Article 20: Men and Women in Turkmenistan have equal civil rights. Violation of equality on the basis of gender is punishable by law.

Article 21: The exercise of rights and freedoms must not violate the rights and freedoms of others, as well as the requirements of morality, law, public order, [or] cause damage to national security.

Article 22: Each individual has the right to life and liberty and the exercise (of this right). No one can be deprived of the right to life. The right of each person to free life is protected by the state on the basis of law.

The death penalty has been abolished in Turkmenistan.

Article 23: A person cannot be restrict in or deprived of rights, convicted or punished, except in strict accordance with the law.

No one can be subjected to torture, cruel, inhuman or degrading treatment, or punishment, and without his consent to medical (medicinal or medical) or other experiments. A person can be arrested by the court or with the approval of the prosecutor only on the grounds precisely specified by the law. In urgent cases, precisely specified by the law, the state authorities have the right to detain the citizens temporarily.

Article 24: Every citizen has the right to support of state in obtaining or acquiring a comfortable living accommodation, and construction of individual housing. The home is inviolable. No one has the right to enter a home or otherwise violate the sanctity of the home against the wishes of people living there without any legal grounds. Protecting the home against unlawful assault (encroachment) is the right of the individual and citizen.

No one can be deprived of their living accommodation except on the grounds established by law.

Article 25: Everyone has the right to protection from arbitrary interference in their privacy, as well as infringement of the rules of secrecy of correspondence, telephone and other (means of) communication, attacks on their honour and reputation.

Article 26: Every citizen has the right to move freely and choose their place of residence in Turkmenistan.

Restrictions on entry into separate territories, and movement in those territories, can only be set by law.

Article 27: Men and women having reached the marriageable age have the right, by mutual consent, to marry and create families. Spouses have equal rights in family relations.

Parents and substitute parents have the right and obligation to raise the children, care for their health, development, education, prepare them for work, and impart to them the culture of respect for the law, historical and national traditions. Adult children are obliged to take care of their parents and to extend help (support) to them.

Article 28: Citizens of Turkmenistan have the right to freedom of opinion and expression, as well as to receive information if it is not a state or other secret protected by law.

Article 29: Citizens are guaranteed freedom of assembly, rallies and demonstrations in the manner prescribed by law.

Article 30: Citizens have the right to form political parties and other public associations operating within the framework of the Constitution and laws.

Prohibited is the establishment and activity of political parties, other public, paramilitary associations, aimed at bringing violent change to the constitutional order, introducing violence in their activity, opposing the constitutional rights and freedoms of citizens, advocating war, racial, national or religious hatred, encroaching on the health and morals of the people, as well as the political parties with ethnic or religious attributes.

Article 31: Every citizen has the right to participate in managing the affairs of the society and state, either directly or through freely elected representatives.

Article 32: Citizens have the right to elect and be elected to the bodies of state authority.

Citizens of Turkmenistan, in accordance with their abilities and professional training, have equal right to access to public service.

Article 33: Citizens have the right to work, choice of profession at their own discretion, sort of employment and place of work, to safe and healthy working conditions.

Wage earners are entitled to compensation, appropriate to amount and quality of work. This compensation cannot be less than the subsistence minimum established by the state.

Article 34: Citizens have the right to rest, as expressed in establishment of limits of work week, grant of annual paid holidays, and days of weekly rest.

The State creates favourable conditions for recreation and use of leisure time.

Article 35: Citizens have the right to healthcare, including free use of the network of public health institutions. Paid medical and non-traditional healthcare is permitted under, and in accordance with, the procedure established by law.

Article 36: Everyone has the right to favourable environment.

The State supervises the management of natural resources in order to protect and improve living conditions, as well as environmental protection and regeneration.

Article 37: Citizens have the right to social security in old age, sickness, disability, loss of ability to work, loss of breadwinner, unemployment.

Families with large number of children, orphans, veterans, people who lost their health while protecting the state or public interests, are provided additional support and privileges from state and public funds.

Article 38: Every citizen has the right to education.

Secondary education is compulsory; everyone is entitled to receive it in public schools free of charge.

The state ensures availability of vocational education for each person according to their abilities.

On the basis and in the manner prescribed by the legislation of Turkmenistan, governmental and non-governmental organisations, citizens have the right to engage in paid work activity.

The State sets educational standards, mandatory for all educational institutions.

Article 39: Citizens of Turkmenistan have the right to freedom of artistic, scientific and technical creativity. All rights (copyrights) and interests of citizens in the area of scientific, technical, creative, artistic, literary and cultural activities are protected by law.

The State contributes to the development of science, culture, arts, folk arts, sports and tourism.

Article 40: The exercise of the rights and freedoms is inseparable from the performance by the individual and citizen their responsibilities toward the society and the state.

Everyone, living or staying temporarily in the territory of Turkmenistan, is obliged to abide by the Constitution, the laws, and respect the national traditions.

Article 41: Protection of Turkmenistan is the sacred duty of every citizen. General conscription is compulsory for the male citizens of Turkmenistan.

Article 42: Everyone is required to pay state taxes and other payments in the manner and extent established by law.

Article 43: Citizens are guaranteed judicial protection of honour and dignity, personal and political rights and freedoms of individual and citizen [as stipulated] by the Constitution and laws.

Citizens have the right to appeal in the court against the decisions and actions of the state bodies, public associations and officials.

Article 44: Citizens have the right to seek redress in courts for material and moral damage caused to them by unlawful actions of state bodies, other organisations and their employees, as well as private individuals.

Article 45: A person cannot be compelled to testify and give evidence against self and close relatives.

Evidence obtained as a result of mental or physical influence, as well as through other illegal methods, has no legal force.

Article 46: A law, aggravating the situation of citizens, shall not be retroactive. No one can be held responsible for actions that, at the time of their commission, were not recognised by law as offence.

Article 47: The implementation of the rights and freedoms of citizens may be suspended only in a state of emergency or martial law in a manner and within the limits established by the Constitution and laws.

Section III: The System of Government and Administration in Turkmenistan

Chapter I: General Provisions

Article 48: The highest state authority and government in Turkmenistan is exercised by the President of Turkmenistan, the Mejlis (parliament) of Turkmenistan, the Cabinet of Ministers of Turkmenistan, and the Supreme Court of Turkmenistan.

Article 49: Local district representatives and executives bodies are the local authority in Velayats, cities with the right of Velayat, districts, and districts with rights of city, and in towns of Etraps, settlements, and the Gengeshlyks the local authority are Gengeshes.

Chapter II: President of Turkmenistan

Article 50: The President of Turkmenistan is the head of the state and executive power, the highest official of Turkmenistan, acting as guarantor of the state independence and the status of neutrality of Turkmenistan, its territorial integrity, respect for the Constitution and fulfillment of international obligations.

Article 51: A citizen of Turkmenistan, born in Turkmenistan, not younger than 45 years and not older than 70 years, who speaks the national language, has been living constantly in Turkmenistan and working in the state bodies, public associations, enterprise, institutions, organisations, for the past 15 years, can be elected as President of Turkmenistan.

Article 52: The President of Turkmenistan is elected directly by the people for a period of five years, and enters office on taking the oath.

The procedures for electing the President of Turkmenistan and his assumption of office are established by law.

Article 53: The President of Turkmenistan:

(1) Implements the Constitution and laws;

(2) Supervises the execution of foreign policy, represents Turkmenistan in relations with other nations, appoints and dismisses ambassadors and other diplomatic representatives of Turkmenistan to foreign countries, with interstate and international organisations, accepts the credentials and letters of recall of diplomatic representatives of foreign countries;

(3) Is the Supreme Commander of the Armed Forces of Turkmenistan, orders general or partial mobilisation, use of armed forces and their military [readiness] status, appoints the top command of the Armed Forces of Turkmenistan.

(4) Forms and presides over the National Security Council of Turkmenistan, the status of which is determined by law;

(5) Approves the programme and basic directions of the political, economic and social development of the country;

(6) Sends for consideration and approval of the Mejlis of Turkmenistan the state budget and reports on performance of the budget;

(7) Signs the laws, is entitled to, no later than two weeks, using the right of suspensive veto, return the law with his objections to the parliament for a second hearing and vote. If the parliament, with at least two-thirds of the established number of deputies, confirms the decision earlier expected of him, the President of Turkmenistan signs the law. The President of Turkmenistan does not have the right of suspensive veto concerning the laws on amendments and additions to the Constitution;

(8) Forms the Central Commission for Elections and Referendums in Turkmenistan, makes changes in its composition;

(9) Designates the date of the referendum, has the right to convene an early session of the Mejlis;

(10) Decides questions related to grant of citizenship and removal from citizenship, grant of asylum;

(11) Awards honours and other state awards of Turkmenistan and grants military and other special state titles and distinctions;

(12) With the consent of the Mejlis, appoints and dismisses the Chairman of the Supreme Court, the Prosecutor General, the Minister of Internal Affairs, the Minister of Justice;

(13) Grants pardon and amnesty;

(14) In order to ensure the safety of citizens, orders the state of emergency throughout the national territory or in certain areas of Turkmenistan. Use of the state of emergency is governed by the law of Turkmenistan.

(15) Decides other questions, referred to his competence by the Constitution and the laws.

Article 54: The President of Turkmenistan issues decrees, decisions and orders, binding on the entire territory of Turkmenistan.

Article 55: The President of Turkmenistan cannot be the deputy [member] of the Mejlis [Parliament].

Article 56: The President of Turkmenistan has the right to immunity. His honour and dignity are protected by law.

Maintenance and security of the President of Turkmenistan and his family are carried out by the state.

Article 57: The President of Turkmenistan may be prematurely released from his duty in case of his inability to fulfill his duties because of illness. The Mejlis, on the recommendation of an independent medical board created by it, may decide to release the President from the office. Such decision is taken by at least two-third vote of the established members of the Mejlis.

In case of violation of the Constitution and laws of Turkmenistan by the President of Turkmenistan, the parliament may express no-confidence in him. The issue of no-confidence can be considered at the request of no less than two-thirds of the established members of the Mejlis. The decision of no-confidence is adopted by at least three-fourth of the established members of the Mejlis. The question for removal of President of Turkmenistan from the office is put on national referendum.

Article 58: The President of Turkmenistan is not entitled to transfer his authority to other public authorities or officials except for powers stipulated by paragraphs 2, 11, 13 of the Article 53 of the Constitution.

If the President of Turkmenistan, for whatever reason, is unable to perform his duties, pending the election of the new interim President the duties of the President of Turkmenistan, by a decision of the Security Council of Turkmenistan, can be assigned to a deputy chairman of the cabinet of ministers. Election of the President of Turkmenistan, in this case, should be held no later than 60 days from the day of transfer of powers temporarily to the Acting President of Turkmenistan. A person, who is temporarily acting as President of Turkmenistan, cannot run for the presidency.

Chapter III: Mejlis of Turkmenistan

Article 59: Turkmenistan's Mejlis (parliament) is the highest representative body, exercising the legislative authority.

Article 60: The Parliament consists of 125 deputies, elected from geographical constituencies with approximately equal number of voters, for five years.

Article 61: Parliament can be dissolved prematurely in the following cases:

(1) On the basis of a decision through national referendum.

(2) On the basis of a resolution of the Mejlis, accepted by no less than two-third of the votes of established number of deputies of the Mejlis (self dissolution).

(3) By the President of Turkmenistan in case the formation of Mejlis office bearers [chairman, deputy chairmen etc.] is not done within six months.

Article 62: The parliament independently establishes the powers of the deputies, elects from among the deputies, the chairman of the Mejlis, his deputy, forms committees and commissions.

The deputies of the Mejlis of the previous convocation remain in office until the first session of the Mejlis of the new convocation.

Article 63: Mejlis:

(1) Enacts laws, makes amendments and additions to the Constitution and laws, monitors their performance and their interpretation;

(2) Considers for approval the programme activities of the Cabinet of Ministers;

(3) Examines questions related to approval of the state budget of Turkmenistan and reports on its implementation;

(4) Considers the basic directions and programmes of political, economic and social development of the country;

(5) Determines whether to hold national referendums;

(6) Appoints [decides for] the election of the President of Turkmenistan, deputies of the Mejlis, members of the velayat, district, municipal representative bodies and the Gengeshes;

(7) Considers the recommendations of the President of Turkmenistan on the issues related to the appointment and dismissal of the Chairman of the Supreme Court, the Prosecutor General, the minister for Internal Affairs, the minister for Justice;

(8) Establishes state awards, awards state decorations to the President of Turkmenistan, assigns him the military ranks and distinctions;

(9) Determines conformity to or divergence from the Constitution and the normative legal Acts by the state authorities and administration (government);

(10) Ratifies and denounces international treaties;

(11) Considers questions related to change of state borders and administrative and territorial division of Turkmenistan;

(12) Examines the issues related to peace and security;

(13) Decides other questions in the competence of the Mejlis under the Constitution and laws.

Article 64: The Mejlis can transfer the right to issue laws on certain matters to the President of Turkmenistan, with subsequent consideration by the parliament for their approval.

The Mejlis cannot transfer to anyone the right to legislate on:

(1) Changes in the Constitution;

(2) Criminal and administrative law;

(3) Legal proceedings.

Article 65: The right of legislative initiative belongs to the President of Turkmenistan, the deputies of the Mejlis, the Cabinet of Ministers, and the Supreme Court.

Article 66: The Mejlis deputies have the right to enquiry, by oral and written questions, to the Cabinet of Ministers, ministers, and chiefs of other state bodies.

Article 67: The state guarantees to each deputy of the Mejlis the creation of conditions for smooth and effective implementation of their powers, protection of their rights and freedom, life, honour and dignity and personal inviolability.

Article 68: A deputy can be deprived of his parliamentary powers only by the Mejlis. The decision should be taken by at least two-third vote of the established members of the Mejlis.

A deputy cannot be held criminally liable, detained, or otherwise deprived of liberty, without the consent of the Mejlis.

Article 69: A deputy of the Mejlis cannot concurrently hold the post of a cabinet member, Hyakim (governor), Archyn (village leader), judge, and prosecutor.

Article 70: The chairman of the Mejlis shall be elected by secret ballot. He reports to the Mejlis and may be relieved of his post by a decision of the Mejlis, voted by at least two-third majority of the established members of the Mejlis.

Vice chairman of the Mejlis shall be elected by open ballot, performs functions on behalf of the chairman, and acts as chairman of the Mejlis in the absence of the chairman or his inability to exercise his powers.

Article 71: The order of activity of the Mejlis and its committees and commissions, deputies, their function and powers, are established by law.

Chapter IV: The Cabinet of Ministers of Turkmenistan

Article 72: The Cabinet of Ministers (Government) is an executive and administrative body. The President of Turkmenistan is the Chairman of the Cabinet of Ministers of Turkmenistan.

Article 73: The Cabinet of Ministers is composed of Vice-Chairmen, and ministers. The President of Turkmenistan can introduce other persons into the Cabinet of Ministers who are heads of central bodies of the executive authority.

The Cabinet is formed by the President of Turkmenistan within one month of assuming office and resigns its powers to the newly elected President.

Article 74: The meetings of the Cabinet of Ministers are held (called/chaired) by the President of Turkmenistan, or on his behalf, one of the vice-chairman of the Cabinet.

The Cabinet of Ministers, within its competence, adopts resolutions and issues binding orders.

Article 75: The Cabinet of Ministers:

(1) Arranges execution of the laws of Turkmenistan, Acts of the President and the Mejlis of Turkmenistan;

(2) Carries out measures to ensure and protect the rights and freedoms of citizens, protection of property rights and public order, national security;

(3) Develops and sends for the consideration of the Mejlis proposals on basic directions of the internal and foreign policy, economic and social development;

(4) Carries out management of economic and social development; organises management of public enterprises, institutions and organisations; ensures rational use and conservation of natural resources;

(5) Takes measures to strengthen monetary and credit system;

(6) Forms, where necessary, committees, senior management and other departments under the Cabinet of Ministers;

(7) Carries out foreign economic activities, ensures development of cultural and other relations with foreign countries;

(8) Directs the activities of government agencies, state enterprise and organisations; has the right to revoke the legal acts of ministries and departments and the bodies of local executive authority;

(9) Decides on other issues falling under its competence by the Constitution, laws and other normative-legal Acts of Turkmenistan.

Article 76: The powers of the Cabinet of Ministers, the order of its activity, and the manner of its relations with other state bodies are defined by law.

Chapter V: Local Authorities

Article 77: The local authority consists of the representatives and executive bodies that operate within their jurisdiction.

Article 78: In Velayats, cities with stats of velayat, etrap, cities with status of etrap, local bodies – Peoples Council – are formed by members elected by the citizens of administrative-territorial units for a period of four years in the manner prescribed by law.

Article 79: Peoples Council (Khalk Maslahaty), within its powers, participates in the decision of issues related to economic, social and cultural development.

Functions and powers of the Peoples Council and its members, conduct of its activities and its relationship with other government and state bodies is determined by law.

Article 80: Executive power is exercises in places: in Velayat – Hyakim (governor), in cities – Hyakim city (city governor), in districts – Hyakim etrap (district governor).

Article 81: Hyakims are representatives of the President of Turkmenistan in their areas, appointed and dismissed by the President, and accountable to him.

Article 82: Hyakims manage activities of on-ground executive authority, ensure execution of the Constitution and laws of Turkmenistan, Acts of the President and the Cabinet of Ministers, and decisions of Mejlis [in their areas of jurisdiction]. Hyakims, within the limits of their competence, take necessary decisions for management in their subordinated territory.

Article 83: Functions and powers of Hyakims, their activities and relationship with other bodies of authority and government, are determined by law.

Section IV: Local Self-Government

Article 84: The system of local self-government is formed by the Gengeshes and the bodies of territorial public self-government.

Gengeshes are representative bodies of people's power in etrap, settlement and Gengeshlyk. Members of the Gengesh are elected directly by citizens for a period of three years.

Article: 85: Gengeshes are independent in their activity. Mutual relations with the bodies of authority and government are dealt with in accordance with the laws of Turkmenistan.

Article 86: Gengeshes:

(1) Determine the basic directions of economic, social and cultural development of their territories;

(2) Create and approve the budget and report on its performance;

(3) Establish local taxes and the manner of their charging;

(4) Define measures for rational use of natural resources and environmental protection;

(5) Deal with other issues assigned by law to them.

The decisions taken by Gengeshes within the limits of their competence are binding in their territory.

Article 87: Gengesh elects Archyn (Gengesh Head) from its members, who supervises the work of the Gengesh and is accountable to it.

Archyn enforces the decisions of the Gengesh, Acts of the state and government authorities, and addresses the issues of local importance.

Article 88: The order of the activity of Gengesh, and other bodies of local self-government, is defined by law.

Section V: Election System, Referendum

Article 89: Elections of the President of Turkmenistan, deputies of Mejlis, members of the Peoples Council and Gengesh are universal and equal. The citizens of Turkmenistan, having reached the age of 18, have the right to vote; each voter has one vote.

Citizens recognised by the court as incompetent, persons serving sentence in prisons, do not participate in elections. Limiting the electoral rights of citizens in other cases is not acceptable, and is punishable by law.

Article 90: A citizen of Turkmenistan who has attained the age of 25 and has lived [continuously] in Turkmenistan for the past ten years, can be elected as deputy of Mejlis. The requirements for candidates for membership of Mejlis, Peoples Council and Gengesh are defined by the laws of Turkmenistan.

Article 91: Elections are direct; the elected persons are elected directly by the citizens.

Article 92: Voting in elections is by secret ballot, manipulation of the will of the voters during voting is not permitted.

Article 93: The right to nominate candidates belongs to political parties, public associations and citizens' groups, exercised in accordance with laws of Turkmenistan.

Article 94: National and local referendums can be carried out for decision of major questions of state and public life.

Decisions adopted by referendums may be repealed or amended only through referendum.

Article 95: The right to conduct national referendum belongs to the Mejlis of Turkmenistan on proposal of at least two-third of its established deputies, or on the petition of no less than 250000 eligible voters.

Article 96: The right to conduct local referendum belongs to Gengesh on its territory, or at the suggestion of no less than one quarter of voters residing in that territory.

Article 97: Referendums are held through universal, equal, direct and secret vote.

Citizens of Turkmenistan with electoral rights can participate in referendums.

Article 98: Conduct of elections, national and local referendums, is determined by law. The elections and referendums are not held during a state of emergency.

Section VI: Judiciary

Article 99: The judicial authority in Turkmenistan belongs only to the courts.

The judiciary is intended to guard the citizens' rights and freedoms, protected under the state laws and public interests.

Article 100: The judicial power is exercised by the Supreme Court of Turkmenistan and other courts, established by law.

The establishment of emergency courts and other structures, empowered as court, is not permitted.

Article 101: Judges are independent; they are subject only to law and are guided by inner belief. Interference in the work of judges, by whichever side, is unacceptable and punishable by law. The immunity of judges is guaranteed by law.

Article 102: Judges are appointed by the President of Turkmenistan. The order of appointment and dismissal, and the terms of their office, are determined by law.

Judges can be removed from office prior to the expiration of their term only on grounds specified by law.

Article 103: Judges cannot hold any other paid post, except for teaching and research.

Article 104: Cases in the court are dealt with collectively [bench], and in cases stipulated by law, by a single judge.

Article 105: The trials are held in open court. Hearing in closed session is permitted only in cases specified by law, in compliance with all the rules of the procedure.

Article 106: Judicial proceedings are conducted in the state language. Those involved in the case and not speaking the language of the proceedings, have the right to get familiar with the case material and the judicial proceedings through an interpreter, as well as the right to speak in the court in their native language.

Article 107: Justice is dispensed on the basis of equality and rights of defence.

The parties have the right to appeal the decisions, sentences and other verdicts of the courts of Turkmenistan.

Article 108: The right to professional legal assistance is recognised at any stage of the legal proceedings.

The legal aid to citizens and organisations is rendered by lawyers, and other individuals and organisations.

Article 109: The competence, formation and procedures of the court are defined by law.

Section VII: The Prosecutor's Office

Article 110: The supervision of precise and uniform enforcement of the laws of Turkmenistan, Acts of the President of Turkmenistan and the Cabinet of Ministers, decisions of the Mejlis, is vested in the Prosecutor General of Turkmenistan, and his subordinate prosecutors.

The public prosecutor participates in the disposal of legal cases in the court on the basis of and in the order established by law.

Article 111: The Prosecutor General's office oversees the legality of operational and investigative activities, and investigation of criminal cases.

Article 112: The uniform, centralised, system of prosecutors' offices is headed by the Prosecutor General of Turkmenistan.

The order of appointment to and dismissal from office, the terms of the office of prosecutors, are determined by law.

Article 113: The Prosecutor General of Turkmenistan and his subordinate prosecutors, in exercising their powers, are guided by law only.

Article 114: The competence, order of formation, and activity of the bodies of the offices of the prosecutors are defined by law.

Section VIII: Final Provisions

Article 115: The laws and other legal Acts of state bodies and officials are issued on the basis of and in accordance with the Constitution.

In case of divergence between the rules specified in the Constitution and the laws, the provisions of the Constitution will apply.

Article 116: The constitutional provisions on the form of governance as a presidential republic cannot be changed.

Article 117: The Acts to amend the Constitution shall be considered adopted if voted for by at least two-third of the established deputies of Mejlis, or in case of a national referendum, if supported by more than half of the participating citizens of Turkmenistan.

APPENDIX 1.E

CONSTITUTION OF THE REPUBLIC OF UZBEKISTAN

Preamble

The people of Uzbekistan, solemnly declaring their adherence to human rights and principles of state sovereignty, aware of their ultimate responsibility to the present and the future generations, relying on historical experience in the development of Uzbek statehood, affirming their commitment to the ideals of democracy and social justice, recognising priority of the generally accepted norms of the international law, aspiring to a worthy life for the citizens of the Republic, setting forth the task of creating a humane and democratic rule of law, aiming to ensure civil peace and national accord, represented by their plenipotentiary deputies adopt the present Constitution of the Republic of Uzbekistan.

Part one: Fundamental principles

Chapter 1: State Sovereignty

Article 1. Uzbekistan is a sovereign democratic republic. Both names of the state - the Republic of Uzbekistan and Uzbekistan - shall be equivalent.

Article 2. The state shall express the will of the people and serve their interests. State bodies and officials shall be accountable to the society and the citizens.

Article 3. The Republic of Uzbekistan shall determine its national-state and administrative-territorial structure, its structure of state authority and administration, and shall pursue independent home and foreign policies. The state frontier and the territory of Uzbekistan shall be inviolable and indivisible.

Article 4. The state language of the Republic of Uzbekistan shall be Uzbek. The Republic of Uzbekistan shall ensure a respectful attitude toward the languages, customs and traditions of all nationalities and ethnic groups living on its territory, and create the conditions necessary for their development.

Article 5. The Republic of Uzbekistan shall have its state symbols - the flag, the emblem, and the anthem sanctioned by the law.

Article 6. The capital of the Republic of Uzbekistan shall be the city of Tashkent.

Chapter 2: Democracy

Article 7. The people are the sole source of state power. State power in the Republic of Uzbekistan shall be exercised in the interests of the people and solely by the bodies empowered therefore by the Constitution of the Republic of Uzbekistan and the laws passed on its basis. Any seizure of powers belonging to state authority, suspension or termination of activity of the bodies of state authority contrary to the procedure prescribed by the Constitution, as well as the formation of any new or parallel bodies of state authority shall be regarded as unconstitutional and punishable by law.

Article 8. All citizens of the Republic of Uzbekistan, regardless of their nationality, constitute the people of Uzbekistan.

Article 9. Major matters of public and state life shall be submitted for a nation-wide discussion and put to a direct vote of the people (a referendum). The procedure for holding referendums shall be specified by law.

Article 10. The Oily Majlis (Supreme Assembly) and President of the Republic, elected by the people, shall have the exclusive right to act on behalf of the people. No section of society, political party, public association, movement or individual shall have the right to act on behalf of the people of Uzbekistan.

Article 11. The principle of the separation of power between the legislative, executive and judicial authorities shall underlie the system of state authority in the Republic of Uzbekistan.

Article 12. In the Republic of Uzbekistan, public life shall develop on the basis of a diversity of political institutions, ideologies and opinions. No ideology shall be granted the status of state ideology. The principle of the separation of power between the legislative, executive and judicial authorities shall underlie the system of state authority in the Republic of Uzbekistan.

Article 13. Democracy in the Republic of Uzbekistan shall rest on the principles common to all mankind, according to which the ultimate value is the human being, his life, freedom, honour, dignity and other inalienable rights. Democratic rights and freedoms shall be protected by the Constitution and the laws.

Article 14. The state shall function on the principles of social justice and legality in the interests of the people and society.

Chapter 3: Supremacy of the Constitution and the Law

Article 15. The Constitution and the laws of the Republic of Uzbekistan shall have absolute supremacy in the Republic of Uzbekistan. The state, its bodies, officials, public associations and citizens shall act in accordance with the Constitution and the laws.

Article 16. None of the provisions of the present Constitution shall be interpreted in a way detrimental to the rights and interests of the Republic of Uzbekistan. None of the laws or normative legal acts shall run counter to the norms and principles established by the Constitution.

Chapter 4: Foreign Policy

Article 17. The Republic of Uzbekistan shall have full rights in international relations. Its foreign policy shall be based on the principles of sovereign equality of the states, non-use of force or threat of its use, inviolability of frontiers, peaceful settlement of disputes, non-interference in the internal affairs of other states, and other universally recognised norms of international law.

The Republic may form alliances, join or withdraw from unions and other inter-state organisations proceeding from the ultimate interests of the state and the people, their well-being and security.

Part two: Basic human and civil rights, freedoms and duties

Chapter 5: General Provisions

Article 18. All citizens of the Republic of Uzbekistan shall have equal rights and freedoms, and shall be equal before the law, without discrimination by sex, race, nationality, language, religion, social origin, convictions, individual and social status.

Any privileges may be granted solely by the law and shall conform to the principles of social justice.

Article 19. Both citizens of the Republic of Uzbekistan and the state shall be bound by mutual rights and mutual responsibility. Citizens' rights and freedoms, established by the Constitution and the laws, shall be inalienable. No one shall have the power to deny a citizen his rights and freedoms, or to infringe on them except by the sentence of a court.

Article 20. The exercise of rights and freedoms by a citizen shall not encroach on the lawful interests, rights and freedoms of other citizens, the state or society.

Chapter 6: Citizenship

Article 21. In the Republic of Uzbekistan, uniform citizenship shall be established throughout its territory.

Citizenship in the Republic of Uzbekistan shall be equal for all regardless of the grounds of its acquisition.

Every citizen of the Republic of Karakalpakstan shall be a citizen of the Republic of Uzbekistan.

The grounds and procedure for acquiring and forfeiting citizenship shall be defined by law.

Article 22. The Republic of Uzbekistan shall guarantee legal protection to all its citizens both on the territory of the republic and abroad.

Article 23. Foreign citizens and stateless persons, during their stay on the territory of the Republic of Uzbekistan, shall be guaranteed the rights and freedoms in accordance with the norms of international law.

They shall perform the duties established by the Constitution, laws, and international agreements signed by the Republic of Uzbekistan.

Chapter 7: Personal Rights and Freedoms

Article 24. The right to exist is the inalienable right of every human being. Attempts on anyone's life shall be regarded as the gravest crime.

Article 25. Everyone shall have the right to freedom and inviolability of the person. No one may be arrested or taken into custody except on lawful grounds.

Article 26. No one may be adjudged guilty of a crime except by the sentence of a court and in conformity with the law. Such a person shall be guaranteed the right to legal defence during open court proceedings.

No one may be subject to torture, violence or any other cruel or humiliating treatment. No one may be subject to any medical or scientific experiments without his consent.

Article 27. Everyone shall be entitled to protection against encroachments on his honour, dignity, and interference in his private life, and shall be guaranteed inviolability of the home.

No one may enter a home, carry out a search or an examination, or violate the privacy of correspondence and telephone conversations, except on lawful grounds and in accordance with the procedure prescribed by law.

Article 28. Any citizen of the Republic of Uzbekistan shall have the right to freedom of movement on the territory of the Republic, as well as a free entry to and exit from it, except in the events specified by law.

Article 29. Everyone shall be guaranteed freedom of thought, speech and convictions. Everyone shall have the right to seek, obtain and disseminate any information, except that which is directed against the existing constitutional system and in some other instances specified by law.

Freedom of opinion and its expression may be restricted by law if any state or other secret is involved.

Article 30. All state bodies, public associations and officials in the Republic of Uzbekistan shall allow any citizen access to documents, resolutions and other materials, relating to their rights and interests.

Article 31. Freedom of conscience is guaranteed to all. Everyone shall have the right to profess or not to profess any religion. Any compulsory imposition of religion shall be impermissible.

Chapter 8: Political Rights

Article 32. All citizens of the Republic of Uzbekistan shall have the right to participate in the management and administration of public and state affairs, both directly and through representation. They may exercise this right by way of self-government, referendums and democratic formation of state bodies.

Article 33. All citizens shall have the right to engage in public life by holding rallies, meetings and demonstrations in accordance with the legislation of the Republic of Uzbekistan. The bodies of authority shall have the right to suspend or ban such undertakings exclusively on the grounds of security.

Article 34. All citizens of the republic of Uzbekistan shall have the right to form trade unions, political parties and any other public associations, and to participate in mass movements.

Article 35. Everyone shall have the right, both individually and collectively, to submit applications and proposals, and to lodge complaints with competent state bodies, institutions and public representatives.

Such applications, proposals and complaints shall be considered in accordance with the procedure and within the time-limit specified by law.

Chapter 9: Economic and Social Rights

Article 36. Everyone shall have the right to own property.

The privacy of bank deposits and the right to inheritance shall be guaranteed by law.

Article 37. Everyone shall have the right to work, including the right to choose their occupation. Every citizen shall be entitled to fair conditions of labour and protection against unemployment in accordance with the procedure prescribed by law.

Any forced labour shall be prohibited, except as punishment under the sentence of a court, or in some other instances specified by law.

Article 38. Citizens working on hire shall be entitled to a paid rest. The number of working hours and the duration of paid leave shall be specified by law.

Article 39. Everyone shall have the right to social security in old age, in the event of disability and loss of the breadwinner as well as in some other cases specified by law.

Pensions, allowances and other kinds of welfare may not be lower than the officially fixed minimum subsistence wage.

Article 40. Everyone shall have the right to receive skilled medical care.

Article 41. Everyone shall have the right to education. The state shall guarantee free secondary education. Schooling shall be under state supervision.

Article 42. Everyone shall be guaranteed the freedom of scientific research and engineering work, as well as the right to enjoy cultural benefits. The state shall promote the cultural, scientific and technical development of society.

Chapter 10: Guarantees of Human Rights and Freedoms

Article 43. The state shall safeguard the rights and freedoms of citizens proclaimed by the Constitution and laws.

Article 44. Everyone shall be entitled to legally defend his rights and freedoms, and shall have the right to appeal any unlawful action of state bodies, officials and public associations.

Article 45. The rights of minors, the disabled, and the elderly shall be protected by the state.

Article 46. Women and men shall have equal rights.

Chapter 11: Duties of Citizens

Article 47. All citizens shall perform the duties established by the Constitution.

Article 48. All citizens shall be obliged to observe the Constitution and laws, and to respect the rights, freedoms, honour and dignity of others.

Article 49. It is the duty of every citizen to protect the historical, spiritual and cultural heritage of the people of Uzbekistan.

Cultural monuments shall have protection by the state.

Article 50. All citizens shall protect the environment.

Article 51. All citizens shall be obliged to pay taxes and local fees established by law.

Article 52. Defence of the Republic of Uzbekistan is the duty of every citizen of the Republic of Uzbekistan. Citizens will be obliged to perform military or alternative service in accordance with the procedure prescribed by law.

Part three: Society and the individual

Chapter 12: The Economic Foundation of Society

Article 53. The economy of Uzbekistan, evolving towards market relations, is based on various forms of ownership. The state shall guarantee freedom of economic activity, entrepreneurship and labour with due regard for the priority of consumers' rights, as well as equality and legal protection of all forms of ownership.

Private property, along with the other types of property, shall be inviolable and protected by the state. An owner may be deprived of his property solely in the cases and in accordance with the procedure prescribed by law.

Article 54. An owner shall possess, use and dispose of his property. The use of any property must not be harmful to the ecological environment, nor shall it infringe on the rights and legally protected interests of citizens, juridical entities or the state.

Article 55. The land, its minerals, fauna and flora, as well as other natural resources shall constitute the national wealth, and shall be rationally used and protected by the state.

Chapter 13: Public Associations

Article 56. Trade unions, political parties, and scientific societies, as well as women's, veterans' and youth leagues, professional associations, mass movements and other organisations registered in accordance with the procedure prescribed by law, shall have the status of public associations in the Republic of Uzbekistan.

Article 57. The formation and functioning of political parties and public associations aiming to do the following shall be prohibited: changing the existing constitutional system by force; coming out against the sovereignty, territorial integrity and security of the Republic, as well as the constitutional rights and freedoms of its citizens; advocating war and social, national, racial and religious hostility, and encroaching on the health and morality of the people, as well as of any armed associations and political parties based on the national or religious principles.

All secret societies and associations shall be banned.

Article 58. The state shall safeguard the rights and lawful interests of public associations and provide them with equal legal possibilities for participating in public life.

Interference by state bodies and officials in the activity of public associations, as well as interference by public associations in the activity of state bodies and officials is impermissible.

Article 59. Trade unions shall express and protect the socio-economic rights and interests of the working people. Membership in trade unions is optional.

Article 60. Political parties shall express the political will of various sections and groups of the population, and through their democratically elected representatives shall participate in the formation of state authority. Political parties shall submit public reports on their financial sources to the Oily Majlis or their plenipotentiary body in a prescribed manner.

Article 61. Religious organisations and associations shall be separated from the state and equal before law. The state shall not interfere with the activity of religious associations.

Article 62. Public associations may be dissolved or banned, or subject to restricted activity solely by the sentence of a court.

Chapter 14: Family

Article 63. The family is the primary unit of society and shall have the right to state and societal protection. Marriage shall be based on the willing consent and equality of both parties.

Article 64. Parents shall be obliged to support and care for their children until the latter are of age.

The state and society shall support, care for and educate orphaned children, as well as children deprived of parental guardianship, and encourage charity in their favour.

Article 65. All children shall be equal before the law regardless of their origin and the civic status of their parents. Motherhood and childhood shall be protected by the state.

Article 66. Able-bodied children who are of age shall be obliged to care for their parents.

Chapter 15: Mass Media

Article 67. The mass media shall be free and act in accordance with the law. It shall bear responsibility for trustworthiness of information in a prescribed manner. Censorship is impermissible.

Part four: Administrative and territorial structure and State system

Chapter 16: Administrative and Territorial Structure of the Republic of Uzbekistan

Article 68. The Republic of Uzbekistan shall consist of regions, districts, cities, towns, settlements, kishlaks and auls (villages) in Uzbekistan and the Republic of Karakalpakstan.

Article 69. Any alteration of the boundaries of the Republic of Karakalpakstan, regions, the city of Tashkent, as well as the formation and annulment of regions, cities, towns and districts shall be sanctioned by the Oliy Majlis of the Republic of Uzbekistan.

Chapter 17: Republic of Karakalpakstan

Article 70. The sovereign Republic of Karakalpakstan is part of the Republic of Uzbekistan. The sovereignty of the Republic of Karakalpakstan shall be protected by the republic of Uzbekistan.

Article 71. The republic of Karakalpakstan shall have its own Constitution.

The Constitution of the Republic of Karakalpakstan must be in accordance with the Constitution of the Republic of Uzbekistan.

Article 72. The laws of the Republic of Uzbekistan shall be binding on the territory of the Republic of Karakalpakstan.

Article 73. The territory and boundaries of the Republic of Karakalpakstan may not be altered without the consent of Karakalpakstan. The republic of Karakalpakstan shall be independent in determining its administrative and territorial structure.

Article 74. The Republic of Karakalpakstan shall have the right to secede from the Republic of Uzbekistan on the basis of a nation-wide referendum held by the people of Karakalpakstan.

Article 75. Relationship between the Republic of Uzbekistan and the Republic of Karakalpakstan, within the framework of the Constitution of the Republic of Uzbekistan, shall be regulated by treaties and agreements concluded by the Republic of Uzbekistan and the Republic of Karakalpakstan.

Any disputes between the Republic of Uzbekistan and the Republic of Karakalpakstan shall be settled by the way of reconciliation.

Part five: Organisation of State Authority

Chapter 18: Oliy Majlis of the Republic of Uzbekistan

Article 76. The supreme state representative body shall be the Oliy Majlis of the Republic of Uzbekistan that exercises legislative power.

The Oliy Majlis of the Republic of Uzbekistan shall consist of two chambers - the Legislative Chamber (the lower chamber) and the Senate (the upper chamber).

The term of powers of the Legislative chamber and the Senate of the Oliy Majlis of the Republic of Uzbekistan— five years.

Article 77. The Legislative Chamber of the Oliy Majlis of the Republic of Uzbekistan shall consist of one hundred twenty deputies elected by territorial constituencies on a multiparty basis.

The Senate of the Oliy Majlis of the Republic of Uzbekistan shall be the chamber of territorial representation and consist of members of the Senate (senators).

Members of the Senate of the Oliy Majlis of the Republic of Uzbekistan shall be elected in equal quantity — in six persons — from the Republic of Karakalpakstan, regions and the city of Tashkent by secret ballot at relevant joint sessions of deputies of Zhokarghy Kenes of the Republic of Karakalpakstan, representative bodies of state authority of regions, districts, cities and towns from among these deputies. Sixteen members of the Senate of the Oliy Majlis of the Republic of Uzbekistan shall be appointed by the President of the Republic of Uzbekistan from among the most authoritative citizens with large practical experience and special merits in the sphere of science, art, literature, manufacture and other spheres of state and public activity.

A deputy of the Legislative Chamber of the Oliy Majlis of the Republic of Uzbekistan, as well as a member of the Senate of the Oliy Majlis of the Republic of Uzbekistan, may be a citizen of the Republic of Uzbekistan who has reached on the date of the elections twenty-five years of age and permanently residing on the territory of the Republic of Uzbekistan not less than five years. Requirements for candidates to be a deputy shall be determined by law.

One and the same person may not be simultaneously a deputy of the Legislative Chamber and a member of the Senate of the Oliy Majlis of the Republic of Uzbekistan.

Article 78. The joint conducting of the Legislative Chamber and the Senate of the Oliy Majlis of the Republic of Uzbekistan shall include:

1. adoption of the Constitution of the Republic of Uzbekistan, introducing amendments;
2. adoption of the Constitutional laws and laws of the Republic of Uzbekistan, introducing amendments;
3. adoption of decision on holding a referendum of the Republic of Uzbekistan and designation the date of its holding;
4. determination of the guidelines of home and foreign policies of the Republic of Uzbekistan, and adoption of strategic state programmes;
5. determination of the structure and powers of the bodies of the legislative, executive and judicial authorities of the Republic of Uzbekistan;
6. admission of new state formations into the Republic of Uzbekistan and approval of decisions to secede from the Republic of Uzbekistan;
7. legislative regulation of customs, currency and credit systems;
8. approval of the state budget of the Republic of Uzbekistan submitted by the Cabinet of Ministers of the Republic of Uzbekistan and control over its execution;
9. determination of taxes and other compulsory payments;
10. legislative regulation of the administrative and territorial structure, and alteration of the boundaries of the Republic of Uzbekistan;
11. formation, annulment and renaming of districts, towns, cities and regions, and alteration of their boundaries;

12. institution of state awards and titles;
13. ratification of decrees of the President of the Republic of Uzbekistan on the formation and abolition of ministries, state committees and other bodies of state administration;
14. formation of the Central Election Committee of the Republic of Uzbekistan;
15. consideration and approval, upon the nomination of the President of the Republic of Uzbekistan, of a nominee of the Prime Minister of the Republic of Uzbekistan;
16. election of an authorised person of the Oliy Majlis of the Republic of Uzbekistan for human rights and his deputy;
17. consideration of report of the Accounting Chamber of the Republic of Uzbekistan;
18. ratification of decree of the President of the Republic of Uzbekistan on announcement of condition of war in case of attack on the Republic of Uzbekistan or necessity of implementation of contractual obligations on mutual defence from aggression;
19. ratification of decrees of the President of the Republic of Uzbekistan on announcement of general and partial mobilisation, introducing, prolongation and discontinuance of the state of emergency;
20. ratification and denouncement of international treaties;
21. exercising of other powers specifed by the present Constitution.

The matters on joint conducting by the chambers shall be considered, as a rule, first by the Legislative Chamber and then by the Senate of the Oliy Majlis of the Republic of Uzbekistan.

Article 79. The exclusive powers of the Legislative Chamber of the Oliy Majlis of the Republic of Uzbekistan shall include:

1. election of the Speaker of the Legislative Chamber of the Oliy Majlis of the Republic of Uzbekistan and his deputies, chairmen of committees and their deputies;
2. ruling of matters on deprivation of immunity a deputy of the Legislative Chamber of the Oliy Majlis of the Republic of Uzbekistan submitted by the Procurator-General of the Republic of Uzbekistan;
3. adoption of decisions on matters relating to the organisation of its activity and the internal schedule of the chamber;
4. adoption of resolutions on those or other matters in the sphere of political, social and economic life, as well as matters of home and foreign policies of the state.

Article 80. The exclusive powers of the Senate of the Oliy Majlis of the Republic of Uzbekistan shall include:

1. election of the Chairman of the Senate of the Oliy Majlis of the Republic of Uzbekistan and his deputies, chairmen of committees and their deputies;
2. election, upon the nomination of the President of the Republic of Uzbekistan, of the Constitutional Court of the Republic of Uzbekistan;

3. election, upon the nomination of the President of the Republic of Uzbekistan, of the Supreme Court of the Republic of Uzbekistan;
4. election, upon the nomination of the President of the Republic of Uzbekistan, of the Higher Economic Court of the Republic of Uzbekistan;
5. appointment and relief of the Chairman of the State Committee of the Republic of Uzbekistan for Protection of Nature of his post upon the nomination of the President of the Republic of Uzbekistan;
6. ratification of decrees of the President of the Republic of Uzbekistan on appointment and relief of the Procurator-General of the Republic of Uzbekistan and his deputies of their posts;
7. ratification of decrees of the President of the Republic of Uzbekistan on appointment and relief of the Chairman of the National Security Service of the Republic of Uzbekistan of his post;
8. appointment and relief of diplomatic and other representatives of the Republic of Uzbekistan to foreign states of their posts upon the nomination of the President of the Republic of Uzbekistan;
9. appointment and relief of the Chairman of the Board of the Central Bank of the Republic of Uzbekistan of his post upon the nomination of the President of the Republic of Uzbekistan;
10. upon the nomination of the President of the Republic of Uzbekistan adoption of acts of amnesty;
11. upon the nomination of the Procurator-General of the Republic of Uzbekistan ruling of matters on deprivation of immunity a member of the Senate of the Oliy Majlis of the Republic of Uzbekistan;
12. hearing reports of the Procurator-General of the Republic of Uzbekistan, the Chairman of the State Committee of the Republic of Uzbekistan for Protection of Nature, the Chairman of the Board of the Central Bank of the Republic of Uzbekistan;
13. adoption of decisions on matters relating to the organisation of its activity and the internal schedule of the chamber;
14. adoption of resolutions on those or other matters in the sphere of political, social and economic life, as well as matters of home and foreign policies of the state.

Article 81. The Legislative Chamber and the Senate of the Oliy Majlis of the Republic of Uzbekistan, after expiry of their terms of powers, shall continue their activity until the beginning of the work accordingly of the Legislative Chamber and the Senate of new convocation.

The first sittings of the Legislative Chamber and the Senate of the Oliy Majlis of the Republic of Uzbekistan shall be convoked by the Central Election Committee accordingly not later than in two months after the elections to the Legislative Chamber and not later than in one month after the formation of the Senate.

Sittings of the Legislative Chamber of the Oliy Majlis of the Republic of Uzbekistan shall be convoked during sessions. Sessions shall be convoked, as a rule, since the first working day of September till the last working day of June of the next year.

Sittings of the Senate of the Oliy Majlis of the Republic of Uzbekistan shall be convoked as required, but not less often than three times a year.

Sittings of the chambers of the Oliy Majlis of the Republic of Uzbekistan shall be empowered if not less than half of the total number of all deputies, senators paticipiate in their work.

At adoption of the constitutional laws, presence of not less than two- thirds of the total number of all deputies, senators shall be obligatory.

The President of the Republic of Uzbekistan, the Prime Minister, members of the Cabinet of Ministers, the Chairmen of the Constitutional Court, the Supreme Court and the Higher Economic Court, the Procurator-General of the Republic, the Chairman of the Board of the Central Bank shall have the right to attend sittings of the Legislative Chamber and the Senate of the Oliy Majlis of the Republic of Uzbekistan, as well as sittings of their bodies. The Chairman of the Senate shall have the right to attend sittings of the Legislative Chamber of the Oliy Majlis of the Republic of Uzbekistan and its bodies, the Speaker of the Legislative Chamber—sittings of the Senate of the Oliy Majlis of the Republic of Uzbekistan and its bodies.

The Legislative Chamber and the Senate of the Oliy Majlis of the Republic of Uzbekistan shall convoke separately.

The joint sittings of the Legislative Chamber and the Senate of the Oliy Majlis of the Republic of Uzbekistan shall be convoked upon taking the oath by the President of the Republic of Uzbekistan, making speeches by the President of the Republic of Uzbekistan on major matters of social and economic life, home and foreign policies of the country, making speeches by heads of foreign states. As agreed by the chambers the joint sittings of the chambers may be convoked on other matters.

Article 82. The Legislative Chamber and the Senate of the Oliy Majlis of the Republic of Uzbekistan, on matters relating to their conducting, shall adopt resolutions.

Resolutions of the Legislative Chamber and the Senate of the Oliy Majlis of the Republic of Uzbekistan shall be adopted by a majority of votes of the total number of deputies of the Legislative Chamber or members of the Senate except for cases stipulated by the present Constitution.

Article 83. The Oliy Majlis of the Republic of Uzbekistan shall pass laws, decisions and other acts. Any law shall be adopted when it is passed by a majority of the total voting power of the deputies of the Oliy Majlis.

Promulgation of the laws and other normative acts shall be a compulsory condition for their enforcement.

Article 84. The law shall come into effect when it is adopted by the Legislative Chamber, approved by the Senate, signed by the President of the Republic of Uzbekistan and issued in the official publications in specified by law procedure.

The law, adopted by the Legislative Chamber of the Oliy Majlis of the Republic of Uzbekistan, not later than ten days from the date of adoption, shall be addressed to the Senate of the Oliy Majlis of the Republic of Uzbekistan.

The law, approved by the Senate of the Oliy Majlis of the Republic of Uzbekistan, within ten days, shall be addressed to the President of the Republic of Uzbekistan for signing and promulgation.

The President of the Republic of Uzbekistan, within thirty days, shall sign the law and promulgate it.

The law, rejected by the Senate of the Oliy Majlis of the Republic of Uzbekistan, shall be returned to the Legislative Chamber of the Oliy Majlis of the Republic of Uzbekistan.

In case of the second consideration of the rejected by the Senate of the Oliy Majlis of the Republic of Uzbekistan law and approval the law anew by the Legislative Chamber, by a majority in two-thirds of votes of the total number of deputies, it shall be considered to be adopted by the Oliy Majlis of the Republic of Uzbekistan and addressed by the Legislative Chamber to the President of the Republic of Uzbekistan for signing and promulgation.

On the rejected by the Senate of the Oliy Majlis of the Republic of Uzbekistan law the Legislative Chamber and the Senate, on a par with, may form from among deputies of the Legislative Chamber and members of the Senate a conciliatory commission for overcoming the occured disagreements. At adoption by the chambers proposals of the conciliatory commission the law shall be subject to consideration in ordinary procedure.

The President of the Republic of Uzbekistan shall have the right to return the law with his objections to the Oliy Majlis of the Republic of Uzbekistan.

In case of approval of the law in the earlier adopted edition by a majority not less than two-thirds of votes of the total number accordingly of deputies of the Legislative Chamber and members of the Senate of the Oliy Majlis of the Republic of Uzbekistan, the law shall be subject to signing by the President of the Republic of Uzbekistan within fourteen days and promulgation.

Publication of laws and other normative-legal acts shall be an obligatory condition for their application.

Article 85. The Legislative Chamber of the Oliy Majlis of the Republic of Uzbekistan shall elect from its composition the Speaker of the Legislative Chamber and his deputies.

The Speaker of the Legislative Chamber of the Oliy Majlis of the Republic of Uzbekistan and his deputies shall be elected by a majority of votes of the total number of deputies by secret ballot for the term of powers of the Legislative Chamber.

The Speaker of the Legislative Chamber of the Oliy Majlis of the Republic of Uzbekistan may be recalled before the appointed time by decision of the Legislative Chamber adopted by more than two-thirds of votes of the total number of deputies of the Legislative Chamber by secret ballot.

The Speaker of the Legislative Chamber of the Oliy Majlis of the Republic of Uzbekistan shall:

1. convoke sittings of the Legislative Chamber, preside at them;
2. exercise the general direction over a preliminary review of matters to be submitted for consideration by the Legislative Chamber;
3. coordinate the work of the committees and commissions of the Legislative Chamber;
4. organize the control over the implementation of laws of the Republic of Uzbekistan and resolutions of the Legislative Chamber;
5. direct the work on interparliamentary relations and the activity of the groups of the Legislative Chamber connected with the work of international parliamentary organisations;

6. represent the Legislative Chamber in interrelation with the Senate of the Oliy Majlis of the Republic of Uzbekistan, other state bodies, foreign states, international and other organisations;
7. sign resolutions of the Legislative Chamber;
8. exercise other powers stipulated by the present Constitution and legislation.

The Speaker of the Legislative Chamber of the Oliy Majlis of the Republic of Uzbekistan shall issue ordinances.

Article 86. The Senate of the Oliy Majlis of the Republic of Uzbekistan shall elect from among its composition the Chairman of the Senate and his deputies. The Chairman of the Senate shall be elected upon the nomination of the President of the Republic of Uzbekistan.

One of the Deputies Chairman of the Senate of the Oliy Majlis of the Republic of Uzbekistan shall be a representative from the Republic of Karakalpakstan.

The Chairman of the Senate of the Oliy Majlis of the Republic of Uzbekistan and his Deputies shall be elected by a majority of votes of the total number of senators by secret ballot for the term of powers of the Senate.

The Chairman of the Senate of the Oliy Majlis of the Republic of Uzbekistan may be recalled before the appointed time by decision of the Senate adopted by more than two-thirds of votes of the total number of senators by secret ballot.

The Chairman of the Senate of the Oliy Majlis of the Republic of Uzbekistan shall:

1. convoke sittings of the Senate, preside at them;
2. exercise the general direction over a preliminary review of matters to be submitted for consideration by the Senate;
3. coordinate the work of the committees, commissions of the Senate;
4. organize the control over the implementation of laws of the Republic of Uzbekistan and resolutions of the Senate;
5. direct the work on interparliamentary relations and the activity of the groups of the Senate connected with the work of international parliamentary organisations;
6. represent the Senate in interrelation with the Legislative Chamber of the Oliy Majlis of the Republic of Uzbekistan, other state bodies, foreign states, international and other organisations;
7. sign resolutions of the Senate;
8. exercise other powers stipulated by the present Constitution and legislation.

The Chairman of the Senate of the Oliy Majlis of the Republic of Uzbekistan shall issue ordinances.

Article 87. The Legislative Chamber of the Oliy Majlis of the Republic of Uzbekistan for the term of its powers shall elect from among deputies of the Legislative Chamber the committees for draftig laws, preliminary consideration and preparation of matters to be submitted to the Legislative Chamber, control over the implementation of laws of the Republic of Uzbekistan and decisions to be adopted by the Legislative Chamber.

The Senate of the Oliy Majlis of the Republic of Uzbekistan for the term of its powers shall elect from among senators the committees for preliminary consideration and preparation of matters to be submitted to the Senate, control over the implementation of laws of the Republic of Uzbekistan and decisions to be adopted by the Senate.

The Legislative Chamber and the Senate of the Oliy Majlis of the Republic of Uzbekistan, in case of necessity for the implementation of concrete tasks, shall organize commissions from among deputies, senators.

Article 88. To deputies of the Legislative Chamber and members of the Senate of the Oliy Majlis of the Republic of Uzbekistan expences, connected with deputy or senator activities, shall be compensated in the established procedure.

Deputies of the Legislative Chamber and members of the Senate, working in the Senate on a permanent basis for the period of their powers, may not be engaged in other paid activity except for research and pedagogical.

A deputy of the Legislative Chamber and a member of the Senate of the Oliy Majlis of the Republic of Uzbekistan shall have the right of immunity. They may not be brought to criminal responsibility, arrested or subject to measures of administrative penalty imposed in the judicial order, without the consent accordingly of the Legislative Chamber and the Senate.

Chapter 19: The President of the Republic of Uzbekistan

Article 89. The President of the Republic of Uzbekistan is the Head of the State and executive authority in the Republic of Uzbekistan.

Article 90. A citizen of the Republic of Uzbekistan not younger thirty five, being in full command of the state language and permanently residing on the territory of Uzbekistan for at least 10 years, immediately preceding the elections, may be elected the President of the Republic of Uzbekistan. One and the same person may not be the President of the Republic of Uzbekistan for more than two consecutive terms.

A citizen of the Republic of Uzbekistan not younger thirty five, being in full command of the state language and permanently residing on the territory of Uzbekistan for at least 10 years, immediately preceding the elections, may be elected the President of the Republic of Uzbekistan. One and the same person may not be the President of the Republic of Uzbekistan for more than two consecutive terms.

The President of the Republic of Uzbekistan shall be elected by citizens of the Republic of Uzbekistan on the basis of the universal, equal and direct suffrage by secret ballot for the term of seven years. The procedure for electing the President shall be defined by law of the Republic of Uzbekistan.

Article 91. The President, during his term of office, may not hold any other paid post, serve as deputy of representative body, engage in commercial activity.

The President shall enjoy personal immunity and protection under law.

Article 92. The President shall be regarded as having assumed office upon taking an oath of the following content at sitting of the Oliy Majlis of the Republic of Uzbekistan:

"I do solemnly swear to faithfully serve the people of Uzbekistan, to strictly follow the Constitution and laws of the Republic, to guarantee the rights and freedoms of its citizens, and to conscientiously perform the duties vested on the President of the Republic of Uzbekistan."

Article 93. The President of the Republic of Uzbekistan shall:

(1) guarantee observance of rights and freedoms of citizens, the Constitution and laws of the Republic of Uzbekistan;

(2) take necessary measures on the protection of sovereignty, security and territorial integrity of the Republic of Uzbekistan, implementation of decisions regarding its national-state structure;

(3) represent the Republic of Uzbekistan within the country and in international relations;

(4) conduct negotiations and sign treaties and agreements of the Republic of Uzbekistan, ensure the observance of the negotiated by the Republic treaties, agreements and the assumed by it obligations;

(5) receive letters of credence and recall from diplomatic and other representatives accredited to him;

(6) present to the Senate of the Oliy Majlis of the Republic of Uzbekistan nominees for appointment of diplomatic and other representatives of the Republic of Uzbekistan to foreign states;

(7) present to the Oliy Majlis of the Republic of Uzbekistan annual reports on major matters of social and economic life, home and foreign policies of the country;

(8) form the office of executive authority and direct it; ensure interaction of the supreme bodies of authority and administration of the Republic; form and abolish ministries, state committees and other bodies of state administration with subsequent submission of decrees on these matters for approval by the chambers of the Oliy Majlis of the Republic of Uzbekistan;

(9) represent to the Senate of the Oliy Majlis of the Republic of Uzbekistan a nominee for the election on the post of the Chairman of the Senate;

(10) represent for consideration and approval by the chambers of the Oliy Majlis of the Republic of Uzbekistan a nominee of the Prime Minister of the Republic of Uzbekistan and relieve him of his post;

(11) approve, upon the nomination of the Prime Minister of the Republic of Uzbekistan, members of the Cabinet of Ministers of the Republic of Uzbekistan and relieve them of their posts;

(12) appoint and relieve the Procurator-General of the Republic of Uzbekistan and his deputies of their posts with their subsequent approval by the Senate of the Oliy Majlis of the Republic of Uzbekistan;

(13) represent to the Senate of the Oliy Majlis of the Republic of Uzbekistan nominees on the posts of the Chairman and judges of the Constitutional Court, the Chairman and judges of the Supreme Court, the Chairman and judges of the Higher Economic Court, the Chairman of the Board of the Central Bank of the Republic of Uzbekistan, the Chairman of the State Committee of the Republic of Uzbekistan for Protection of Nature;

(14) appoint and relieve judges of regional, interdistrict, district, city, martial and economic courts of their posts;

(15) appoint and relieve khokims of regions and the city of Tashkent of their posts with their subsequent approval by relevant Kenghashes of people's deputies. The President shall have the right to relieve, by his decision, khokims of districts and cities of their posts, should they violate the Constitution, laws or perform acts discrediting the honour and dignity of a khokim;

(16) suspend and repeal acts passed by bodies of state administration, as well as khokims;

(17) sign and promulgate laws of the Republic of Uzbekistan; shall have the right to return a law, with his objections, to the Oliy Majlis of the Republic of Uzbekistan for the second discussion and vote;

(18) announce condition of war in case of attack on the Republic of Uzbekistan or in case of necessity of the implementation of contractual obligations on mutual defence from aggression and within seventy-two hours submit the adopted decision for approval by the chambers of the Oliy Majlis of the Republic of Uzbekistan;

(19) in exceptional cases (real outside threat, mass disturbances, major catastrophes, natural calamities, epidemics) in the interests of ensuring citizens' security introduce the state of emergency on the entire territory or in the particular localities of the Republic of Uzbekistan and within seventy-two hours submit the adopted decision for approval by the chambers of the Oliy Majlis of the Republic of Uzbekistan. Conditions and the procedure for introducing the state of emergency shall be regulated by law;

(20) serve as the Supreme Commander-in-Chief of the Armed Forces of the Republic of Uzbekistan, appoint and relieve the supreme command of the Armed Forces of the post and confer the highest millitary ranks;

(21) award orders, medals and certificates of honour of the Republic of Uzbekistan, confer qualification and honorary titles of the Republic of Uzbekistan;

(22) rule on matters of citizenship of the Republic of Uzbekistan and granting political asylum;

(23) put to the Senate of the Oliy Majlis of the Republic of Uzbekistan submission on adoption of acts of amnesty and effectuate pardoning of persons condemned by courts of the Republic of Uzbekistan;

(24) form the National Security Service of the Republic of Uzbekistan, nominate and relieve the Chairman of the National Security Service of his post with the subsequent submission of decrees on these matters for approval by the Senate of the Oliy Majlis of the Republic of Uzbekistan;

(25) exercise other powers stipulated by the present Constitution and laws of the Republic of Uzbekistan.

The President shall not have the right to transfer exercising of his powers to state bodies or officials.

Article 94. The President of the Republic of Uzbekistan shall issue decrees, resolutions and ordinances binding on the entire territory of the Republic on the basis of and for enforcement of the Constitution and laws of the Republic of Uzbekistan.

Article 95. The Legislative Chamber, the Senate of the Oliy Majlis of the Republic of Uzbekistan may be dissolved, by the decision of the President of the Republic of Uzbekistan adopted as agreed with the Constitutional Court of the Republic of Uzbekistan, in case of insuperable disagreements within the Legislative Chamber or the Senate putting under threat their normal functioning or numerous adoption by them decisions contradicting the Constitution of the Republic of Uzbekistan, as well as insuperable disagreements between the Legislative Chamber and the Senate putting under threat the normal functioning of the Oliy Majlis of the Republic of Uzbekistan.

In case of dissolution of the Legislative Chamber and the Senate of the Oliy Majlis of the Republic of Uzbekistan, the new elections shall be held within three months.

The Legislative Chamber and the Senate of the Oliy Majlis of the Republic of Uzbekistan may not be dissolved during the state of emergency.

Article 96. Should the President of the Republic of Uzbekistan fail to perform his duties due to poor health confirmed by a certificate of a State Medical Commission formed by joint decision of the chambers, an extraordinary joint sitting of the chambers of the Oliy Majlis shall be held within ten days. This sitting shall elect an acting President of the Republic of Uzbekistan from among its deputies, senators for the term up to three months. In this case the general elections of the President of the Republic of Uzbekistan shall be held within three months.

Article 97. The President, upon completion of his term of office, shall be a lifetime member of the Senate.

Chapter 20: Cabinet of Ministers

Article 98. The executive authority shall be exercised by the Cabinet of Ministers of the Republic of Uzbekistan. The Cabinet of Ministers of the Republic of Uzbekistan shall be composed of the Prime Minister of the Republic of Uzbekistan, his deputies, ministers, chairmen of state committees.The Head of the government of the Republic of Karakalpakstan shall be a member of the Cabinet of Ministers.

The composition of the Cabinet of Ministers shall be formed by the President of the Republic of Uzbekistan. The nominee of the Prime Minister of the Republic of Uzbekistan shall be considered and approved by the chambers of the Oliy Majlis of the Republic of Uzbekistan upon the nomination of the President of the Republic of Uzbekistan.

Members of the Cabinet of Ministers shall be approved by the President of the Republic of Uzbekistan upon the nomination of the Prime Minister of the Republic of Uzbekistan.

The Cabinet of Ministers shall provide the direction of the effective functioning for the economic, social and spiritual spheres, the implementation of laws of the Republic of Uzbekistan, decisions of the Oliy Majlis, decrees, resolutions and ordinances of the President of the Republic of Uzbekistan.

The Cabinet of Ministers in accordance with the current legislation shall issue resolutions and ordinances binding on all bodies, enterprises, institutions, organisations, officials and citizens on the entire territory of the Republic of Uzbekistan.

The Prime Minister of the Republic of Uzbekistan shall organize and direct the activity of the Cabinet of Ministers being responsible for efficiency of his work, preside at sittings of the Cabinet of Ministers, sign its decisions, upon the nomination of the President of the Republic of Uzbekistan represent the Cabinet of Ministers of the Republic of Uzbekistan in international relations, exercise other functions stipulated by laws of the Republic of Uzbekistan, decrees, resolutions and ordinances of the President of the Republic of Uzbekistan.

The President of the Republic of Uzbekistan shall have the right to preside at sittings of the Cabinet of Ministers, adopt decisions on matters relating to the competence of the Cabinet of Ministers, as well as to abolish resolutions and ordinances of the Cabinet of

Ministers, ordinances of the Prime Minister of the Republic of Uzbekistan proceeding from Article 89 and Article 93 of the present Constitution. The Cabinet of Ministers, in its work, shall be responsible before the President of the Republic of Uzbekistan and the Oliy Majlis of the Republic of Uzbekistan.

The Cabinet of Ministers shall tender its resignation to the newly-elected Oliy Majlis.

The procedure for the organisation of the work and competence of the Cabinet of Ministers shall be defined by law.

Chapter 21: Fundamental Principles of Local Bodies of State Authority

Article 99. The Kenghashes of people's deputies, led by khokims, are the representative bodies of authority in regions, districts, cities and towns (except towns subordinate to district centres, as well as city districts). They shall act upon matters within their competence in accordance with the interests of the state and citizens.

Article 100. The joint conducting of the local bodies of authority shall include:

- ensurance of legality, legal order and security of citizens;
- matters of economic, social and cultural development within their territories;
- formation and implementation of the local budget, determination of the local taxes and fees, formation of non-budget funds;
- direction of the municipal economy;
- protection of the environment;
- ensurance of the registration of civil status acts;
- adoption of normative acts and exercising of other powers which are not contrary to the Constitution and legislation of the Republic of Uzbekistan.

Article 101. The local bodies of authority shall enforce laws of the Republic of Uzbekistan, decrees of the President, decisions of the higher bodies of state authority, participate in the discussion of matters of national and local significance.

The decisions of the higher bodies, adopted within their competence, shall be binding on the subordinate bodies.

The term of office of the Kenghashes of people's deputies and khokims is five years.

Article 102. The khokim of region, district, city and town shall serve as the head of the representative and executive authorities of his relevant territory.

The khokim of region and the city of Tashkent shall be appointed and relieved of his post by the President of the Republic of Uzbekistan and approved by the relevant Kenghash of people's deputies.

The khokims of districts, cities and towns shall be appointed and relieved of their posts by the khokim of the relevant region and approved by the relevant Kenghash of people's deputies.

The khokims of city districts shall be appointed and relieved of their posts by the khokim of the relevant city and approved by the city Kenghash of people's deputies.

The khokims of towns subordinate to district centres shall be appointed and relieved of their posts by the khokim of the district and appropved by the district Kenghash of people's deputies.

Article 103. The khokim of region, district, city and town shall exercise his powers in accordance with the principle of one-man management and shall bear personal responsibility for decisions and actions of bodies directed by him.

The organisation of the work and powers of khokims and local Kenghashes of people's deputies, as well as the procedure for the elections to the local Kenghashes of people's deputies, shall be regulated by law.

Article 104. The khokim within his vested powers shall adopt decisions which are binding on all enterprises, institutions, organisations, associations, as well as officials and citizens on the relevant territory.

Article 105. Self-governing bodies in settlements, kishlaks and auls, as well as in makhallas of cities, towns, settlements, kishlaks and auls, shall be assemblies of citizens electing Chairman (aksakal) and his advisers for the term of two and a half years.

The procedure for the elections, organisation of the work and powers of self-governing bodies shall be regulated by law.

Chapter 22: Judicial Authority in the Republic of Uzbekistan

Article 106. The judicial authority in the Republic of Uzbekistan shall function independently from the legislative and executive authorities, political parties, other public associations.

Article 107. The judicial system in the Republic of Uzbekistan shall consist of the Constitutional Court of the Republic of Uzbekistan, the Supreme Court of the Republic of Uzbekistan, the Higher Economic Court of the Republic of Uzbekistan, the Supreme Courts of the Republic of Karakalpakstan on civil and criminal cases, the Economic Court of the Republic of Karakalpakstan elected for the term of five years, regional and Tashkent city courts on civil and criminal cases, interdistrict, district and city courts on civil and criminal cases, martial and economic courts for the same term.

The organisation and procedure for the operation of courts shall be specified by law.

The formation of extraordinary courts shall be inadmissible.

Article 108. The Constitutional Court of the Republic of Uzbekistan shall hear cases relating to the constitutionality of acts of the legislative and executive authorities.

The Constitutional Court shall be elected from political and legal scholars and shall consist of the Chairman, Deputy Chairman and judges of the Constitutional Court including a representative from the Republic of Karakalpakstan.

No member of the Constitutional Court, including the Chairman, shall have the right to simultaneously serve as a deputy.

The Chairman and members of the Constitutional Court may not be members of political parties and movements nor hold any other paid posts.

The judges of the Constitutional Court shall have the right of immunity.

The judges of the Constitutional Court shall be independent in their work and subordinate solely to the Constitution of the Republic of Uzbekistan.

Article 109. The Constitutional Court of the Republic of Uzbekistan shall:

1. define the compliance of the Constitution of the Republic of Uzbekistan, laws of the Republic of Uzbekistan and resolutions of the chambers of the Oliy Majlis of the Republic of Uzbekistan, decrees of the President of the Republic of Uzbekistan, enactments of the government and local bodies of state authority, interstate treaties and other obligations of the Republic of Uzbekistan;

2. conform the compliance of the Constitution of the Republic of Karakalpakstan to the Constitution of the Republic of Uzbekistan, laws of the Republic of Karakalpakstan — to laws of the Republic of Uzbekistan;
3. interpret the norms of the Constitution and laws of the Republic of Uzbekistan;
4. hear other cases relating to its competence in accordance with the Constitution and laws of the Republic of Uzbekistan;

The judgements of the Constitutional Court shall take effect upon publication. They shall be final and not subject to appeal.

The organisation and procedure for the work of the Constitutional Court shall be specified by law.

Article 110. The Supreme Court of the Republic of Uzbekistan shall be the supreme judicial body of civil, criminal and administration proceedings.

The adopted by it acts shall be final and binding on the entire territory of the Republic of Uzbekistan. The Supreme Court of the Republic of Uzbekistan shall have the right to supervise the administration of justice of the Supreme Courts of the Republic of Karakalpakstan, regional, city, interdistrict, district and martial courts.

Article 111. Any economic and management disputes, that may arise between enterprises, institutions and organisations based on different forms of ownership, as well as between entrepreneurs, shall be settled by the Higher Economic Court and economic courts within their competence.

Article 112. Judges shall be independent and subject solely to law. Any interference in the work of judges in administering law shall be inadmissible and punishable by law.

The immunity of judges shall be guaranteed by law.

Judges may not be senators, deputies of the representative bodies of state authority.

Judges may not be members of political parties, participate in political movements, as well as be engaged in any other paid activity except for research and pedagogical.

Before the completion of his term of office, a judge may be relieved of his post only on grounds specified by law.

Article 113. Examination of cases in all courts shall be open to the public. Hearings in camera shall be allowed only in cases prescribed by law.

Article 114. Court verdicts shall be binding on all state bodies, public associations, enterprises, institutions, organisations, officials and citizens.

Article 115. Legal proceedings in the Republic of Uzbekistan shall be conducted in Uzbek, Karakalpak or in a language spoken by the majority of the population in the locality. Persons participating in court proceedings, who do not know the language in which it is being conducted, shall have the right to be fully acquainted with the materials of the case, participate through an interpreter in proceedings and address the court in their native language.

Article 116. An accused shall be ensured the right to defence.

The right to legal assistance shall be guaranteed at any stage of investigation and legal proceedings. Legal assistance to citizens, enterprises, institutions and organisations shall be given by the College of Barristers. The organisation and procedure for the work of the College of Barristers shall be specified by law.

Chapter 23: Electoral System

Article 117. Citizens of the Republic of Uzbekistan shall have the right to elect and be elected to the representative bodies of state authority. Every elector shall have one vote. The right to vote, equality and freedom of expression of will shall be guaranteed by law.

The elections of the President of the Republic of Uzbekistan, to the Legislative Chamber of the Oliy Majlis of the Republic of Uzbekistan and Jokarghy Kenes of the Republic of Karakalpakstan, to the representative bodies of state authority in regions, districts, cities and towns shall be held accordingly on the year of expiration of the constitutional term of their powers— on the first Sunday of the third decade of December. The elections shall be held on the basis of the general, equal and direct suffrage by secret ballot. The right to elect have the citizens of the Republic of Uzbekistan who have reached eighteen years of age.

Members of the Senate of the Oliy Majlis of the Republic of Uzbekistan shall be elected by secret ballot at relevant joint sittings of deputies of Jokarghy Kenes of the Republic of Karakalpakstan, the representative bodies of state authority in regions, districts, cities and towns from among these deputies not later a monthly term after their election.

Citizens, who have been legally certified as insane, as well as persons in prisons, may neither elect nor be elected.

Any other direct or indirect infringement on citizens' voting rights shall be inadmissible.

A citizen of the Republic of Uzbekistan may not simultaneously be a deputy in more than two representative bodies of state authority.

The procedure for the elections shall be specified by law.

Chapter 24: Procurator's Office

Article 118. The Procurator-General of the Republic of Uzbekistan and the procurators subordinate to him shall supervise the strict and uniform observance of laws on the territory of the Republic of Uzbekistan.

Article 119. The Procurator-General of the Republic of Uzbekistan shall direct the centralised system of bodies of the procurator's office.

The Procurator of the Republic of Karakalpakstan shall be appointed by the supreme representative body of the Republic of Karakalpakstan as agreed with the Procurator-General of the Republic of Uzbekistan.

The procurators of regions, districts, cities and towns shall be appointed by the Procurator-General of the Republic of Uzbekistan.

The term of office shall be five years for the Procurator-General of the Republic of Uzbekistan, the Procurator of the Republic of Karakalpakstan, the procurators of regions, districts, cities and towns.

Article 120. Bodies of the Procurator's Office of the Republic of Uzbekistan shall exercise their powers independently of any state bodies, public associations and officials, and shall be subject solely to law.

Procurators for the term of their powers shall suspend their membership in political parties and other public associations pursuing political goals.

The organisation, powers and procedure for the work of bodies of the Procurator's Office shall be specified by law.

Article 121. On the territory of the Republic of Uzbekistan shall be prohibited establishment and functioning of private, cooperative organisations, public associations and their branches independently conducting any operational work, investigations, inquiries and other functions connected with combatting crime.

Public associations and citizens may render assistance to the law-enforcement bodies to safeguard legality and order, rights and freedoms of citizens.

Chapter 25: Finance and Crediting

Article 122. The Republic of Uzbekistan shall have independent financial, monetary and credit systems.

The state budget of Uzbekistan shall consist of the national budget, the budget of the Republic of Karakalpakstan and local budgets.

Article 123. The Republic of Uzbekistan shall have a single taxation system. The right to determine taxes shall belong to the Oliy Majlis of the Republic of Uzbekistan.

Article 124. The banking system of the Republic of Uzbekistan shall be directed by the Central Bank of the Republic.

Chapter 26: Defence and Security

Article 125. The Armed Forces of the Republic of Uzbekistan shall be formed to defend the state sovereignty and territorial integrity of the Republic of Uzbekistan, peaceful life and security of its population.

The structure and organisation of the Armed Forces shall be specified by law.

Article 126. The Republic of Uzbekistan shall maintain the Armed Forces to ensure its security at a level of reasonable sufficiency.

Part six: Procedure for amending the Constitution

Article 127. The Constitution of the Republic of Uzbekistan shall be altered by law adopted by a majority, not less than two-thirds of the total number accordingly of deputies of the Legislature Chamber and members of the Senate of the Oliy Majlis of the Republic of Uzbekistan, or by referendum of the Republic of Uzbekistan.

Article 128. The Oliy Majlis of the Republic of Uzbekistan may adopt law on alterations and amendments to the Constitution within six months after submission of a relevant proposal, with regard for its broad discussion. Should the Oliy Majlis of the Republic of Uzbekistan reject a proposal on alteration of the Constitution, it may be renewed not earlier than in a year.

APPENDIX II.A

BTI COUNTRY REPORT 2014: RANK AND SCORE OF EACH COUNTRY UNDER STUDY:[1]

		India	*Kazakhstan*	*Kyrgyzstan*	*Tajikistan*	*Turkmenistan*	*Uzbekistan*	*Russia*
Ranking Status Index		26	83	66	113	115	118	77
Democracy Status SI		8.10	3.85	5.80	3.60	2.78	2.85	4.40
Stateness		7.8	8.5	7.5	7.3	7.8	7.3	7.8
Political Participation		9.3	2.8	6.3	2.8	1.3	1.8	3.5
Rule of Law		7.5	3.0	4.5	3.0	2.3	2.3	4.3
Stability of Democratic Institutions		8.5	2.0	5.5	2.0	1.0	1.0	2.5
Political and Social Integration		7.5	3.0	5.3	3.0	1.7	2.0	4.0
Level of Socioeconomic Development		4.0	5.0	4.0	3.0	4.0	3.0	6.0
Currency and Price Stability		7.5	7.5	7.5	4.0	5.0	3.5	9.0
Private Property		7.5	6.0	6.5	4.0	3.0	3.0	4.0
Welfare Regime		4.5	6.0	5.0	3.5	3.5	4.0	5.5
Economic Performance		8.0	7.0	5.0	4.0	7.0	4.0	7.0
Sustainability		5.5	5.5	3.5	3.0	4.0	3.5	4.5
Status Index	Score	7.19	5.05	5.61	3.59	3.45	3.09	5.24
	Rank	26	83	66	113	115	118	77
Political Transformation	Score	8.10	3.85	5.80	3.60	2.78	2.85	4.40
	Rank	20	102	64	108	123	122	86
Economic Transformation	Score	6.29	6.25	5.43	3.57	4.11	3.32	6.07
	Rank	45	47	70	113	104	116	48
Management Index	Score	6.32	4.67	4.69	3.58	2.19	1.79	3.90
	Rank	20	75	74	110	122	125	104

Source: Table prepared by Author with help of data from BTI country Reports, www.bti project.org and www.bti-project.de . Accessed 27 June 2014.

*scale: 1-10; Rank: out of 129 countries

1. The Bertelsmann Stiftung's Transformation Index (BTI) analyzes and evaluates the quality of democracy, a market economy and political management in 129 developing and transition countries. It measures successes and setbacks on the path toward a democracy based on the rule of law and a socially responsible market economy. In-depth country reports provide the basis for assessing the state of transformation and persistent challenges, and to evaluate the ability of policymakers to carry out consistent and targeted reforms. The BTI is the first cross-national comparative index that uses self-collected data to comprehensively measure the quality of governance during processes of transition. The Status Index ranks the countries according to their quality of democracy and market economy as of January 31, 2013. www.bti-project.org Also see, http://www.bertelsmann-stiftung.de. For details of methodology see appendix: II.A.i

APPENDIX II.A.1: METHODOLOGY

The Bertelsmann Stiftung's Transformation Index (BTI) analyzes and evaluates whether and how developing countries and countries in transition are steering social change toward democracy and a market economy. Guided by a standardised codebook, country experts assess the extent to which a total of 17 criteria have been met for each of the 129 countries. These experts ground the scores they provide in assessments that comprise the country reports, all of which are available online. A second country expert then reviews these assessments and scores. In a final step, consistency is assured by subjecting each of the 49 individual scores given per country to regional and interregional calibration processes. Standardising the analytical process in this way makes targeted comparisons of reform policies possible.

The BTI aggregates the results of this comprehensive study of transformation processes and political management into two indices: the Status Index and the Management Index. The Status Index, with its two analytic dimensions – one assessing the state of political transformation, the other the state of economic transformation – identifies where each of the 129 countries stand on their path toward democracy under the rule of law and a market economy anchored in principles of social justice. Focusing on the quality of governance, the Management Index assesses the acumen with which decision-makers steer political processes.

The BTI is published every two years. This biennial evaluation of transformation and development allows us to assess observed trends and identify the outcomes of transformation strategies. The BTI expands the available body of knowledge about how political processes are managed and decision-making is conducted, and makes this knowledge available to policymakers and other advocates of reform. Overall, the BTI officers a comprehensive body of data allowing a broad spectrum of actors to assess and compare the factors driving success in developing and transformation countries.

Within the BTI, transformation is understood as comprehensive and politically driven change in which an authoritarian system and a state-dominated or clientelist economic order evolve in the direction of democracy and a market-based economy. However, this implies neither linear, irreversible development nor a predetermined path of transformation, nor does it suggest that there is an ideal sequence of milestones to be passed. A return to authoritarianism and periods of stalling are possible, as are detours along the course of development and out-of-sync political and economic change processes. Indeed, democracy under the rule of law and a market economy anchored in principles of social justice represent goals, but not necessarily immediate priorities within complex development processes. Many states, in fact, pass through radical, sometimes even revolutionary developmental stages; others have yet to undergo comprehensive systemic change; and some states are, for the moment, not targeting transformation.

Analytical framework

The state of political transformation (democracy status) is measured in terms of five criteria, which in turn are derived from assessments made in response to 18 questions. The BTI's concept of democracy goes well beyond other definitions of democracy, which are limited primarily to basic civil rights and the conduct of free elections. Stateness, which is seen as a precondition to political transformation, is included in the BTI's definition of democracy and examined through questions specifically dealing with the state's monopoly on the use of force and basic administrative structures. It also includes an evaluation of the rule of law with an eye to the separation of powers and the prosecution of office abuse. In addition, it assesses the degree to which the democratic system is consolidated in terms of how deep its acceptance among the population runs, its capacity to represent a broad spectrum of interests, and the political culture upon which it is based.

The state of economic transformation (market economy status) is measured in terms of seven criteria, which are based on a total of 14 indicators. The BTI's concept of a market economy includes not only aspects such as economic performance, regulatory or competition policy and property rights; it also includes elements of social justice, such as social safety nets, equality of opportunity and sustainability. In BTI terms, comprehensive development not only aims at economic growth, but also requires successful poverty alleviation and the freedom of action and choice for as many citizens as possible.

The Management Index is comprised of five criteria, which are based on a total of 20 indicators. It focuses on how effectively policymakers facilitate and steer development and transformation processes. By examining and evaluating decision-makers' reform policies, the BTI sheds light on those factors determining success and failure on the way to democracy and a market economy. Successful transformation management implies that governments are consistent in pursuing their goals and use their resources wisely and effectively. It also implies that decision-makers cultivate the broadest possible consensus for their transformation goals and work reliably with external supporters and neighbouring states.

A government's management performance is weighted with the level of difficulty, which is derived from three qualitative and three quantitative indicators. It reflects the observation that each country's quality of transformation is influenced by structural conditions. In this way, difficult conditions and the scarcity of resources in a given country are factored into the equation for political management performance. With its focus on political actors' steering capacity, the BTI is the only index to analyze and compare governance performance with self-collected data.

Country selection

Because the BTI focuses on the normative goals of democracy under the rule of law and a market economy anchored in principles of social justice in its analysis, it excludes from its survey countries that might be considered long-consolidated democratic systems and in which economic development can be regarded as well-advanced. This is not to suggest that, with the achievement of these two goals, a static end-state is achieved. Rather, it reflects the observation that reform needs and priorities following the consolidation of democracy and a market economy will differ from those that emerge during transformation processes. In the absence of a clearly defined "threshold of consolidation," the Transformation Index therefore excludes all countries that were members of the Organisation for Economic Cooperation and Development (OECD) by the year 1989.

Small states with fewer than two million residents (until the BTI 2006: three million) are also not examined in the BTI. Exceptions to this rule have been made, however, to allow for the inclusion of particularly interesting examples of development and transformation. Bahrain, Bhutan, Estonia, Kosovo, Mauritius, Montenegro and Qatar.

Since 2003, the number of countries surveyed has increased from 116 to 129. They are divided into seven regional groups: South and East Africa (20 countries), West and

Central Africa (18), Asia and Oceania (21), Middle East and North Africa (19), Latin America and the Caribbean (21), Post-Soviet Eurasia (13) and East-Central and Southeast Europe (17).

The 129 countries surveyed by the BTI exhibit substantial differences with regard to size and economic power, level of socioeconomic development and political culture. In order to draw meaningful comparisons with respect to the state of transformation and the quality of governance, the BTI refers to variables that can be compiled in all countries. These variables – from the monopoly on the use of force and press freedom to bank regulation and education policy, and to the efficiency of resource use and conflict management – are relevant to national governments everywhere. This allows comparisons even between very different states to yield interesting insights into the operability of political institutions and the quality of management in transformation processes.

In the codebook upon which the survey is based, particular care has been taken to formulate questions without cultural or regional bias, thus ensuring their applicability to a broad diversity of states. However, because the BTI refers to nation-state frameworks, transnational developments and regional disparities at the subnational level are addressed only to a limited extent in the country reports and will largely escape quantitative assessment.

Criteria and indicators

1. **Stateness**

   There is clarity about the nation's existence as a state with adequately established and differentiated power structures.

   1.1 To what extent does the state's monopoly on the use of force cover the entire territory?

   1.2 To what extent do all relevant groups in society agree about citizenship and accept the nation-state as legitimate?

   1.3 To what extent are legal order and political institutions defined without interference by religious dogmas?

   1.4 To what extent do basic administrative structures exist?

2. **Political participation**

   The populace decides who rules, and it has other political freedoms.

   2.1 To what extent are political representatives determined by general, free and fair elections?

   2.2 To what extent do democratically elected rulers have the effective power to govern? To what extent are there veto powers and political enclaves?

   2.3 To what extent can individuals form and join independent political parties or civic groups? To what extent can these groups associate and assemble freely?

   2.4 To what extent can citizens, organisations and the mass media express opinions freely?

3. **Rule of law**

   State powers check and balance one another and ensure civil rights.

   3.1 To what extent is there a working separation of powers (checks and balances)?

   3.2 To what extent does an independent judiciary exist?

3.3 To what extent are public officeholders who abuse their positions prosecuted or penalised?

3.4 To what extent are civil rights guaranteed and protected, and to what extent can citizens seek redress for violations of these rights?

4. Stability of democratic institutions

Democratic institutions are capable of performing, and they are adequately accepted.

4.1 Are democratic institutions capable of performing?

4.2 To what extent are democratic institutions accepted as legitimate by the relevant actors?

5. Political and social integration

Stable patterns of representation exist for mediating between society and the state; there is also a consolidated civic culture.

5.1 To what extent is there a stable, moderate, socially rooted party system able to articulate and aggregate societal interests?

5.2 To what extent is there a network of cooperative associations or interest groups to mediate between society and the political system?

5.3 How strong is the citizens' approval of democratic norms and procedures?

5.4 To what extent have social self-organisation and the construction of social capital advanced?

6. Level of socioeconomic development

In principle, the country's level of development permits adequate freedom of choice for all citizens.

6.1 To what extent are significant parts of the population fundamentally excluded from society due to poverty and inequality?

7. Organisation of the market and competition

There are clear rules for stable, market-based competition.

7.1 To what level have the fundamentals of market-based competition developed?

7.2 To what extent do safeguards exist to prevent the development of economic monopolies and cartels, and to what extent are they enforced?

7.3 To what extent has foreign trade been liberalised?

7.4 To what extent have a solid banking system and a capital market been established?

8. Currency and price stability

There are institutional or political precautions to control inflation sustainably, together with an appropriate monetary policy and fiscal policy.

8.1 To what extent do government and central bank pursue a consistent inflation policy and an appropriate foreign exchange policy?

8.2 To what extent do the government's fiscal and debt policies support macroeconomic stability?

9. Private property

There are adequate conditions to support a functional private sector.

9.1 To what extent do government authorities ensure well-defined rights of private property and regulate the acquisition, benefits, use and sale of property?

9.2 To what extent are private companies permitted and protected? Are privatisation processes conducted in a manner consistent with market principles?

10. Welfare regime

There are viable arrangements to compensate for social risks.

10.1 To what extent do social safety nets provide compensation for social risks?

10.2 To what extent does equality of opportunity exist?

11. Economic performance

The economy's performance points to solid development.

11.1 How does the economy, as measured in quantitative indicators, perform?

12. Sustainability

Economic growth is balanced, environmentally sustainable and future-oriented.

12.1 To what extent are environmental concerns taken into account in both macro- and microeconomic terms?

12.2 To what extent are there solid institutions for basic, secondary and tertiary education, as well as for research and development?

13. Level of difficulty

13.1 To what extent do structural difficulties constrain the political leadership's governance capacity?

13.2 To what extent are there traditions of civil society?

13.3 How serious are social, ethnic and religious conflicts?

13.4 GNI p.c. PPP rescaled (2011)

13.5 UN Education Index, rescaled (2011)

13.6 Stateness + Rule of Law (average of 2 BTI criteria scores)

14. Steering capability

The government manages reforms effectively and can achieve its policy priorities.

14.1 To what extent does the government set and maintain strategic priorities?

14.2 How effective is the government in implementing its own policies?

14.3 How innovative and flexible is the government?

15. Resource efficiency

The government makes optimum use of available resources.

15.1 To what extent does the government make efficient use of available human, financial and organisational resources?

15.2 To what extent can the government coordinate conflicting objectives into a coherent policy?

15.3 To what extent can the government successfully contain corruption?

16. Consensus-building

The political leadership establishes a broad consensus on reform with other actors in society, without sacrificing its reform goals.

16.1 To what extent do the major political actors agree on democracy and a market economy as strategic, long-term goals?

16.2 To what extent can reformers exclude or co-opt anti-democratic actors?

16.3 To what extent is the political leadership able to moderate cleavage-based conflict?

16.4 To what extent does the political leadership enable the participation of civil society in the political process?

16.5 To what extent can the political leadership bring about reconciliation between the victims and perpetrators of past injustices?

17. International cooperation

The political leadership is willing and able to cooperate with external supporters and organisations.

17.1 To what extent does the political leadership use the support of international partners to implement a long-term strategy of development?

17.2 To what extent does the government act as a credible and reliable partner in its relations with the international community?

17.3 To what extent is the political leadership willing and able to cooperate with neighbouring countries?

Does the BTI assume a necessary linkage between democratic and market-economic development?

The BTI's normative reference points – democracy under the rule of law and a market economy anchored in principles of social justice – are closely related both functionally and empirically. The high correlation in scores between the BTI's two dimensions addressing these processes underscores their interrelated nature. Similarly, the fundamental market-economic and democratic institutions are to a large extent interdependent. However, the fact of such interdependencies does not mean there is a predetermined, automatic course of development. Indeed, there is no scholarly consensus on the best path to democracy and a market economy; the focus on the goals of democracy and a market economy therefore implies no sweeping definitions or limitations on the content of reform programmes. Nor do we claim to know the optimal sequence of democratic and economic reforms– whether the introduction of the market economy should precede democratisation, for example, or vice versa.

Aren't the guiding principles of democracy under the rule of law and a market economy anchored in principles of social justice simply Western objectives?

Unlike many other research projects, the Transformation Index makes its normative positioning wholly transparent. The BTI holds that certain desires – to have a say in the composition of the government, to be free from arbitrary imprisonment or torture, and to have recourse to independent courts and inalienable rights, for example – are not limited to a particular cultural sphere. Our analysis is also premised on the belief that the aspiration to be free from hunger, poverty and disease is universal, that there is more to economic development than simply solid growth rates and economic freedom, and that social welfare and the sustainability of economic development must be respected. At the same time, the BTI is committed to no particular existing institutional model, such as the German model of the social market economy or specifically European models of constitutional democracy. Rather, the previously mentioned fundamental standards and functions of democracy under the rule of law and a market economy anchored in principles of social justice can be effectively embodied in a variety of ways.

Measurement and review process

Who are the BTI country experts, and how are they chosen?

The country reports form the foundation for all the BTI's evaluations and analyses; their quality is thus crucial for the reliability and validity of its use as a measuring tool. Careful selection of the experts is therefore of particular importance.

The Transformation Index has over the years built up a network of nearly 250 experts from leading universities and research institutions around the world (see list on pp. 134–135). In addition to scholars known for their county-specific expertise, this network includes experts from civil society organisations with several years of experience in a given country. These experts are chosen largely at the recommendation of the regional coordinators. Along with professional expertise, considerations of independence and impartiality are given particular weight in the selection of country experts.

The Transformation Index is based on a qualitative expert survey in which written assessments are translated into numerical ratings and examined in a multi-stage review process so as to make them comparable both within and across regions. This method enables those factors of political and economic development that elude purely quantitative assessments to be captured in the experts' qualitative appraisals. This method presents significant advantages as it allows, for example, a distinction to be made between rights granted de jure and their de facto implementation.

In addition, statements can be made about the magnitude of social capital and the extent to which civil society is integrated into political decision-making processes. Furthermore, the quality of governance can be assessed and compared. Facts such as constitutional provisions or official economic data can be interpreted and weighed in context. The resulting country assessments render fully transparent and verifiable the reasons behind each of the BTI's 6,708 individual scores.

Nevertheless, this type of qualitative expert survey will always contain a degree of subjectivity. The BTI survey process takes this into account during the preparation of reports and evaluations, as well as during the review of the data. It is designed to minimize subjective factors as far as possible throughout the process. The process of country assessment has both a qualitative and quantitative component, in each case performed by two country experts.

As a rule, one foreign and one local expert are involved in the evaluation process; this ensures that both external and internal perspectives are taken into account in the course of assessment and helps counteract subjective influence. In total, 246 experts from leading research institutions around the world contributed to the production of the country reports.

A standardised codebook serves as the foundation of the survey process, providing a single reference framework for the experts when answering the questions. The first expert drafts a detailed report on the basis of the criteria outlined in the codebook, referencing the qualitative indicators associated with each criterion. The second expert reviews, comments on and adds to this country report. In addition, in the course of answering 11 of the 49 questions (indicators), the country experts are required to draw upon a set of quantitative indicators (ranging from inflation rates to education spending). Independently of one another, the two country experts translate the assessment into a numerical rating on a scale of one (the lowest value) to 10 (highest value), structured by four levels of score-based categories contained in the codebook. In this way, countries are evaluated on the basis of whether and to what extent they comply with the specified rating levels and fulfill the BTI criteria.

In order to ensure the validity, reliability and comparability of the assessment, each individual score undergoes a multistep process of review by the country experts, the regional coordinators, the project team and the BTI board. The scores and responses provided by the experts for each of the 49 indicators are initially reviewed by regional coordinators, who examine the content to ensure it is both complete and consistent. The regional coordinators, all political scientists with expertise in comparative studies, participate in each step of the report creation process and apply their regional expertise to ensure the high quality of the country reports. They subsequently perform an intraregional calibration of their countries' scores, and then they join with the project team to carry out an interregional score calibration for all 129 countries, this time checking for across-the-board comparability and viability. Finally, all scores are discussed once again by the BTI board before being adopted. The BTI board, a panel of scholars and practitioners with long-term experience in the field of development and transformation, provides the project with ongoing support and advice (see also p. 133).

Who uses the BTI data?

Because of its approach and particular focus on governance, the BTI is recognised as one of the world's premier instruments for the systematic comparison of transformation processes. It is used, for example, by the German, British and US governments as a yardstick in assessing their partner countries. In addition, several international organisations, including the World Bank, the European Commission and Transparency International, use it in the course of their own analyses. The BTI has gained wide acceptance in academia and the media, and is also used by reform-oriented civil society groups and politicians worldwide as a tool facilitating critical

Index aggregation

Why does the BTI use rankings?

The high level of aggregation of individual scores and the use of rankings are primarily means of providing orientation and communicating findings to a broader public. Rankings necessarily reduce complexity in order to highlight particular differences between individual countries, call attention to trends in development and make factors key to progress more readily identifiable.

However, the focus on rankings and the isolated consideration of one or only a few questions cannot replace a more thoroughly articulated analysis of a country's strengths and weaknesses. The BTI's non-aggregated individual scores as well as the country reports and regional reports – all available free online – are therefore indispensable.

The Status Index is formed by calculating the average of the total scores given for the dimensions of political (democracy status) and economic (market economy status) transformation. The state of transformation in each analytic dimension is equivalent to the average of the scores of the associated criteria. Criterion scores are in turn based on the average scores of the equally weighted indicators that comprise the criterion. Combining the two analytical dimensions into a Status Index follows the normative premise of the BTI, under which transformation is always conceived as a comprehensive transition toward democracy and a market-economic system.

The Management Index is formed by calculating the average of scores given for the management criteria, which is then off-set against the assigned level of difficulty.

Democracies and autocracies

The indicators on the state of political transformation are also used in determining whether a country is classified as a democracy or autocracy. This analysis comprises more than just whether sufficiently free and fair elections are held. In accordance with the Transformation Index's comprehensive concept of democracy, six threshold values marking minimum requirements are considered. The country is classified as an autocracy if even one score falls short of the relevant threshold.

The group of autocracies also includes "failing states," defined as countries in which the state's monopoly on the use of force and basic administrative structures are lacking to such an extent that the government is severely limited in its capacity to act (the average of scores given for questions 1.1 and 1.4 is less than three).

If a country is classified as an autocracy in the BTI, there are consequences in the evaluation of other democracy-related questions. For instance, if decision-makers are not selected through sufficiently free and fair elections, the effective power to govern does not, by defi nition, lie in the hands of democratically elected leaders, even if the government is otherwise stable. The performance and acceptance of democratic institutions will be similarly poorly assessed even if recognised and effective institutional structures are in place, as they would lack democratic legitimacy.

In the Management Index, one of the four criteria takes the BTI's normative goals into account: The "steering capability" criterion consists of questions dealing with the capability of a specific government to set and maintain strategic priorities, implement related reform policies and be flexible and innovative in terms of policy formulation and implementation. In the course of this evaluation, it is considered whether a government pursued both democracy and a market economy as overriding goals; this is done to ensure that effective prioritisation, implementation and learning capacity in the service of authoritarian regime consolidation is not rewarded with a positive rating.

APPENDIX II.B
GDP-PER-CAPITA

Country	*GDP per-capita (PPP $) 2005-2011*									
	1980	*1990*	*2000*	*2005*	*2006*	*2007*	*2008*	*2009*	*2010*	*2011*
India	879	1,210	1,722	2,209	2,378	2,573	2,635	2,813	3,039	3,203
Kazakhstan	—	7,089	5,406	8,699	9,529	10,259	10,469	10,318	10,916	1,568
Kyrgyzstan	—	2,523	1,507	1,721	1,756	1,888	2,027	2,060	2,008	2,126
Tajikistan	—	2,961	969	1,500	1,251	1,505	1,801	1,846	1,938	2,052
Turkmenisatn	—	3,749	2,322	4,762	5,245	5,795	6,567	6,881	7,422	8,055
Uzbekisatn	—	2,002	1,632	2,001	2,121	2,290	2,456	2,611	2,754	2,903
Russian Federation	—	2,626	8,613	11,853	12,878	14,016	14,767	13,615	14,199	14,808

Source: Prepared by the Author with help of data from **https://data.undp.org/dataset/GDP-per-capita-2005-PPP-/navj-mda7**, accessed on 27 June 2014.

APPENDIX II.C
WORLD DEVELOPMENT INDICATORS: LABOUR FORCE STRUCTURE

	Labour force participation rate % (ages 15 and older)				*Labour force (ages 15 and older) % of labour force*			*Labour force Growth (%)*
	Male		*Female*		*Total*	*Female*	*millions*	
	2000	*2012*	*2000*	*2012*	*2000*	*2012*	*2012*	*2002-12*
India	83	81	34	29	405.2	484.3	25.3	1.2
Kazakhstan	76	78	65	68	7.5	9.04	9.5	1.6
Kyrgyzstan	74	79	56	56	2.1	2.6	42.7	2.1
Tajikistan	75	77	58	59	2.3	3.5	43.6	3.3
Turkmenistan	74	77	48	47	1.7	2.3	39.2	2.2
Uzbekistan	72	75	47	48	9.2	13.0	39.6	2.9
World	79	77	52	51	2,766.4	3,280.4	39.8	1.4

Source: Table prepared by Author with help of data from World Bank Report http://wdi.worldbank.org/table/2.2. May 2, 2014.

APPENDIX II.D

Table 2.8a

Country	*Life Expectancy at Birth*[1]		*Infant Mortality Rate*[2]		*Youth Literacy Rate*[3]		*Adult Literacy Rate*[4]	
	2012		*2012*		*2005-12*		*2005-12*	
	Male	*Female*	*Male*	*Female*	*Male*	*Female*	*Male*	*Female*
India	65	68	43.5	44.3	88	74	31	75
Kazakhstan	65	74	19.3	14	100	100	96	100
Kyrgyzstan	66	74	26.3	20.6	100	100	..	100
Tajikistan	64	71	54.3	43.5	100	100	97	100
Turkmenistan	61	70	51.7	37.6	100	100	..	100
Uzbekisatn	65	72	39.2	29.3	100	100	..	100
Russia	65	76	9.8	7.8	100	100	97	100
Norway	00	84	2.5	2	..	..	..	..

Source: Table(2.8a) prepared by Author with help of data from sources mentioned below:

1. http://data.worldbank.org/indicator/SP.DYN.LE00.FE.IN/countries; 2. (Relevance to gender indicator: Infant mortality rates are higher for boys than for girls in countries in which parental gender preferences are insignificant) http://databank.worldbank.org/data/views/reports/tableview.aspx; www.childmortality.org.; 3. http://wdi.worldbank.org/table/2.13; 4. http://wdi.worldbank.org/table/1.5

Table 2.8b

The labour force structure of women as according to WDI

Country	*Labour force participation*[1]			
	2000		*2012*	
	Male	*Female*	*Male*	*Female*
India	83	34	81	29
Kazakhstan	76	**65**	78	**68**
Kyrgyzstan	74	56	79	56
Tajikistan	75	58	77	59
Turkmenistan	74	48	77	47
Uzbekisatn	72	47	75	48
Russia	68	54	71	57
Norway	72	**60**	70	**62**

Table 2.8c

Country	*Population (millions)*			*HDI Rank*	*Female population as % of total*[#]
	2000	*2012*	*2025*		*2012*
India	1,042.3	1,236.7	1,418.7	136	48.3
Kazakhstan	14.9	16.8	18.6	69	51.8
Kyrgyzstan	4.9	5.6	6.7	125	50.7
Tajikistan	6.2	8.0	10.5	125	49.8
Turkmenistan	4.5	5.2	6	102	50.8
Uzbekisatn	24.7	29.8	33.9	114	50.3
Russia	146.3	143.5	135.7	55	53.8
Norway	4.5	5.0	5.6	1	50

Source: Table(2.8b,c) prepared by Author with help of data from sources mentioned below:
1. (2009)http://databank.worldbank.org/data/views/reports/tableview.aspx; (2000& 2012) http://wdi.worldbank.org/table/2.2
http://wdi.worldbank.org/table/1.5

APPENDIX II.E

SOCIAL INSTITUTIONS AND GENDER INDEX REPORT*

According to Social Institutions and Gender Index report **India** is ranked 56th out of 86 in the 2012 and was ranked 96th out of 102 in 2009. The 2011 Human Development Index (HDI) score for the country is 0.547, placing it in 134th place out of 187 countries. The Gender Inequality Index score is 0.617. India's Global Gender Gap Index rating for 2011 was 0.6190, placing it in 113rd place out of a total of 135 countries. **Kazakhstan** is ranked 14 out of 86 in the 2012 and was ranked 3rd out of 102 in the 2009. The country is ranked 68th in the 2011 Human Development Index (HDI), with a score of 0.745, and has a Gender Inequality Index value of 0.334. Kazakhstan was ranked 49th in the 2011 Global Gender Gap Index, with a score of 0.7010.

The Kyrgyz Republic is ranked 33 out of 86 in the 2012 Social Institutions and Gender Index. The country was ranked 30 out of 102 in the 2009 Social Institutions and Gender Index. In 2011, the Kyrgyz Republic had a Human Development Index (HDI) score of 0.615, placing it in 126th place (out of a total of 187 countries). The Gender Inequality Index for the same year was 0.370 (66th place out of 146 countries). Kyrgyzstan

* http://genderindex.org

is ranked in 44th place in the 2011 Global Gender Gap Index, with a score of 0.7036. **Tajikistan** is ranked 40 out of 86 in the 2012 Social Institutions and Gender Index. The country was ranked 35 out of 102 in the 2009 Social Institutions and Gender Index. Tajikistan is ranked 127th in the 2011 Human Development Index (out of 187 countries) with a score of 0.607, and has a Gender Inequality Index score of 0.347. Under the 2010 Global Gender Gap Index, Tajikistan has a score of 0.6526, placing it in 96th place (out of 135 countries). **Turkmenistan** is not ranked in the 2012 Social Institutions and Gender Index due to missing data for one or more SIGI variables. However, the country note below sets out information and data relating to variables where this is available information. i.e., Discrim. Fam. Code Rank 2012: 7; Discrim. Fam. Code Value 2012: 0.0338; Early Marriage: 0.059 and for others variables no Data available like Legal Age of Marriage: 0; Parental Authority: 0; Inheritance: 0. Turkmenistan was ranked in 102nd place in the 2011 Human Development Index (HDI), with a score of 0.686, but has no gender inequality rating. Turkmenistan is not ranked in the 2011 Global Gender Gap Index.

Uzbekistan is ranked 57 out of 82 countries in the 2012 Social Institutions and Gender Index. In 2011, Uzbekistan had a Human Development Index score of 0.641, placing it in 115th place out of a total of 187 countries. UNDP does not provide a gender inequality score for Uzbekistan for 2011.Uzbekistan is not ranked in the 2011 Global Gender Gap Index.

APPENDIX III.A
WOMEN IN PUBLIC SPHERE

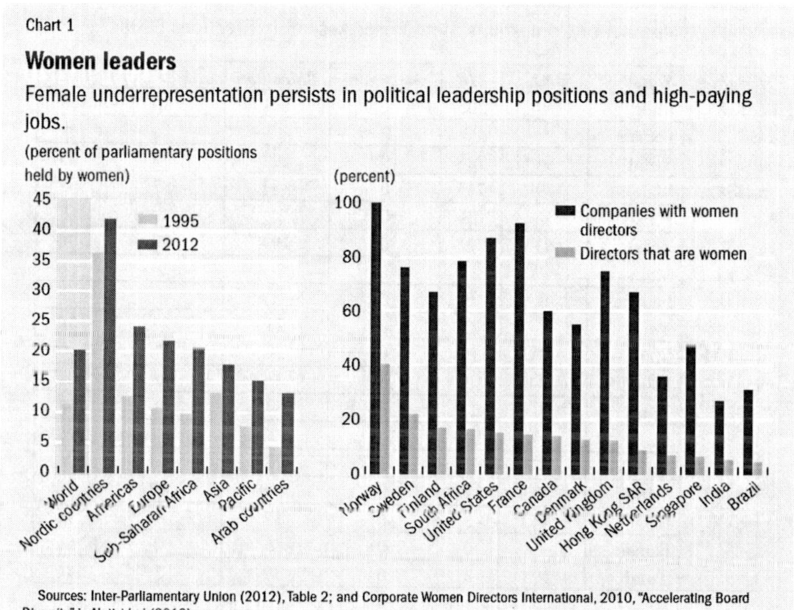

Source: https://www.imf.org/external/pubs/ft/fandd/2013/06/pdf/pande.pdf. Accessed on 6 May, 2014.

APPENDIX III.B
WOMEN'S REPRESENTATION IN PARLIAMENT

Year	*Total Seats*	*Lok Sabha*	*Percentage*	*Total Seats*	*Rajya Sabha*	*Percentage*
1952	499	22	4.4	219	16	7.3
1957	500	27	5.4	237	18	7.5
1962	503	34	6.8	238	18	7.6
1967	523	31	5.9	240	20	8.3
1971	521	22	4.2	243	17	7.0
1977	544	19	3.4	244	25	10.2
1980	544	28	7.9	244	24	9.8
1984	544	44	8.1	244	28	11.4
1989	517	27	5.3	245	24	9.7
1991	544	39	7.2	245	38	15.5
1996	543	39	7.2	223	20	9.0
1998	543	43	7.9	245	15	6.1
1999	543	49	9.0	245	19	7.8
2004	539	44	8.2	245	28	11.4

Source: http://www.indiastat.com/, See Kamala K. "Political participation of women in India", in Alok Kumar Gupta and Asha Bhandari, Ed. "Women and Political Participation in Indian Democratic System", Author's Press, 2010. pp. 72-85.

APPENDIX III.C
POLITICAL PARTIES AND WOMEN

Table:

Number of Contestants State Wise: Assembly Elections 2008

Parties	*States*	*J&K*	*MP*	*Mizoram*	*Rajasthan*	*Chhattisgarh*	*Delhi*
BJP	Male	59	205	7	161	80	65
	Female	5	23	2	32	10	4
	Total	**64**	**228**	**9**	**193**	**90**	**69**
BSP	Male	79	215	0	187	82	68
	Female	4	13	0	12	8	2
	Total	**83**	**228**	**0**	**199**	**90**	**70**
CPI	Male	7	21	0	20	20	68
	Female	0	0	0	1	1	2
	Total	**7**	**21**	**0**	**21**	**21**	**70**
CPM	Male	8	12	0	34	8	4
	Female	0	0	0	0	0	0
	Total	**8**	**12**	**0**	**34**	**8**	**4**
INC	Male	74	199	39	177	77	62
	Female	4	29	1	23	10	8
	Total	**78**	**228**	**40**	**200**	**87**	**70**
NCP	Male	18	3	6	37	3	16
	Female	1	0	0	2	0	0
	Total	**19**	**3**	**6**	**39**	**3**	**16**

Source: Election Commission of India, 2009; See Kamala K. "Political participation of women in India", in Alok Kumar Gupta and Asha Bhandari, Ed. "Women and Political Participation in Indian Democratic System", Author's Press, 2010, pp. 72-85.

APPENDIX III.D
WOMEN IN NATIONAL PARLIAMENTS 2010

Country	*Rank*	*Elections held*	*Lower or Single House*			*Upper House or senate*			*% of women*
			Seats	*women*	*% of women*	*Elections held on*	*Seats*	*women*	
India	100	April 09	545	59	10.8%	July 07	233	21	9.0%
Kyrgyzstan	35	Dec 07	90	23	25.60%	-	-	-	-
Tajikistan	65	Feb 05	63	11	17.50%	March 05	34	8	23.5%
Uzbekistan	65	Dec 04	120	21	17.50%	Jan 2005	100	15	15%
Turkmenistan	68	Dec 08	125	21	16.8%	-	-	-	-
Kazakhstan	73	Aug 07	107	17	15.90%	Oct 2010	47	2	4.3%

Source: Table prepared by the Author with help of data from http://www.ipu.org/pdf/publications/wmnmap14_en.pdf; http://www.indiastat.com. Also See Kamala Kumari, "Globalisation and Women in India", Tuesday, 27 July 2010, paxindica.in/.

APPENDIX III.E
SIGNIFICANT WOMEN POLITICIAN IN ASIA

(A)

List of the first female holders of political offices in India Central Government

India

British India

Leader of a Major Party - Annie Besant - 1917

Member of Provincial Legislative Assembly – Dr. Muthulaksmi Reddy – 1921

Provincial Minister – Vijaya Lakshmi Pandit – 1938

Member of Central Legislature – Radhabai Subbaroyan – 1937

Member of National Defence Council – Begum Jahanara Shahnawaz – 1942

Minister of Health – Rajkumari Amrit Kaur – 1946

Independent India

Deputy Chairperson of the Rajya Sabha (Upper House)– Violet Alva – 1964

Prime Minister – Indira Gandhi – 1966

Foreign Minister – Indira Gandhi – 1967

Chief Election Commissioner of India – V. S. Ramadevi – 1990 (In office 26 November-12 December 1990); Also, former Karnataka and Himachal Pradesh Governor

Leader of Opposition – Sonia Gandhi - 1998

President – Pratibha Patil – 2007

Governor – Sharada Mukherjee (earlier Sharda Pandit) – Governor of Andhra Pradesh from 05-05-1977 to 14-08-1978 and then Gujarat

Governor – Sharada Mukherjee-1978-1983

Home Minister of Andhra Pradesh- Sabita Indra Reddy (2009) and latour minister in newly created Telangana State

Chief Minister – Syeda Anwara Taimur Chief Minister of the Indian state of Assam from 6 December 1980 to 30 June 1981. She was a leader of the Indian National Congress party in Assam.

Chief Minister – Rabri Devi – 1997, Bihar

Delhi

Chief Minister – Sushma Swaraj – 1998 Delhi

Justice of the High Court - Justice Leila Seth- 1978

Himachal Pradesh

Governors – Sheila Kaul – 1995

Chief Justice of the High Court - Leila Seth – 1991

Karnataka

Governor – V.S. Ramadevi – 1999

Kerala

Governor – Jothi Venkatachalam – 1977

Justice of the High Court - Anna Chandy 9 February 1959- 5 April 1967

Justice Anna Chandy, was the first female judge (1937). She was, in fact, one of the first female judges in the British Empire next to Emily Murphy.

Madhya Pradesh

Chief Minister – Uma Bharati – 2003

Maharashtra

Governor – Vijayalakshmi Pandit – 1963

Orissa

Chief Minister – Nandini Satpathy – 1972

Punjab

Chief Minister – Rajinder Kaur Bhattal 1996

Rajasthan

Chief Minister – Vasundhara Raje – 2003

Governor – Pratibha Patil – 2004

Tamil Nadu

Chief Minister - Janaki Ramachandran- 1989(24 days in January 1989)

Jayaram Jayalalithaa- six time from 1991 to 2015

Governor – M. Fatima Beevi- 1997-2001

Uttarakhand

Governor - Margaret Alva- 2009

Uttar Pradesh
Governor – Sarojini Naidu – 1947
Chief Minister – Sucheta Kriplani – 1963

West Bengal
Governor – Padmaja Naidu – 1956
Chief Minister – Mamata Banerjee – 2011

Russia/USSR/Central Asia

1917 Aleksandra Michailovna Kollonta, Peoples' Commissar of Social Affairs, Russia. Countess Sofia Vladimirovna Panina was Vice Minister of State Welfare and Vice Minister of Education earlier in 1917.

1930-40 Polina Semenovna Zemcuzina, People's Commissar of Fishery Economy USSR.

Before her Vavara Nikoleavna Iakovleva was Deputy People's Commissar of Education, 1920-29 and Minister of Finance in Russia. 1929-36, Polina was Soviet Deputy People's Commissar of Food Industry.

1932-37 Mar'yam Tugambayeva, Vice-Chairperson of the Central Executive Committee Kyrgyzstan. 1937 Joint Acting Chairperson, Central Executive Committee with Mikhail Ivanovich, She was also known as Mariya Tuganbayeva, (1907- 86).

1947-57 Rajkumari Amrit Kaur, (1889-1964, Minister of Health), India
1951 Minister of Communication
1952 Minister of Communication (from ca. 1955 Forth in cabinet)
1957-64 Member of Rayja Sabha (Upper House).

1959-62 Khally Nazarova, Minister of Social Affairs, Turkmenistan
1963-65 Deputy Premier Minister
Deputy Minister of Public Service in 1958

1959-63 Zaure S. Omarova, Deputy Premier Minister Kazakstan
1966-80 Minister of Social Affairs
Deputy Chairperson of the Government of Alma-Ata 1963-66.

1960-65 A.N. Atanepesova, Deputy Premier Minister, Tajikistan

Turkmenistan

Republic of Turkmenistan/ Türkmenostan Jumhuriyäti (Female suffrage 1922/27) The Turkmen Nation settled in the area in the 15th century, 1886 it became part of the Russian Empire, 1918 an Autonomous Socialist Republic and Independent 27.1.91

The Supreme Soviet became the Peoples Council- Khalk Maslakhaty and Assembly- Majlis in 1992

CA. 1963-? Vice-Chairperson A.K. Babayeva
CA. 1963-? Member of the Presidium A.M. Rebrikova

1975-CA. 78 Vice-President Shemshat Annaeva

1975-89 Secretary K.O. Nazarova

1975 Vice-President N.N.

In 1975 Deputy Premier Minister, 1975-89 Member of the Presidium of Supreme Soviet. (b. 1933-)

1975-89 Member of the Presidium Roza A. Bazarova

1988-90 President of the Republic Roza Atamuradovna Bazarova (13.8-19.1)

In 1989 President of the Republic

1976-89 Vice-President Rosa M. Karyeva

1990-ca. 92 Member of the Presidium Maya Gosel Aymedova

1990-ca. 92 Member of the Presidium Geukher B. Geldyyeva

1990-ca. 92 Member of the Presidium Svetlana F. Lagshikina

Ca. 1992-95 Deputy Chairperson Abad Sakhatovna Rezaeva (Rizacva)

Afterwards vice-premier and Minister of Education.

1999-2003 Deputy Chairperson Gozel Nuralyyeva

Vice-Premier 2003-04.

2001- Secretary General of the Majlis Enegul B. Dollayeva

2003- Deputy Chairperson Akja Tajiyevna Nurberdiyeva

2006-07 Acting Chairperson (22.12-23.02.)

2007- Chairperson

Other versions of her name is Akdja or Akça and Nurberdyyeva.

Turkmenistan Ministers

1958 Deputy Minister of Public Service Khally Nazarova

1959-62 Minister of Social Affairs

1963-65 Deputy Premier Minister

1960-77-? Minister of Social Welfare Anzurat Mullabavna Rakhimova

1963-67 Deputy Minister of Education Bibi Palvanova

1967-77-? Minister of Education

1965-71 Minister of Social Affairs D. Moumedova

1969-76 Head of the Central Committee Department of Culture S. Annanurova

1971-76 Deputy Premier Minister and Secretary of the Communist Party Central Committee Department of Propaganda and Agitation Maria Molaeva

1975 Vice-President N.N.

1975 Deputy Premier Minister Roza Atamuradovna Bazarova

1988-90 President of the Republic (13.8-19.1)

Between 1975-89 Member of the Presidium of Supreme Soviet. (1933-)

1976-80? Head of the Communist Party Central Committee Department of Culture A.A. Karlieva

1977-79 Minister of Local Industry Annabibi Baimakhanova

1979-88 Minister of Light Industry

1979-89 Minister of Education Meredgul Aliyevna Aliyeva

1990-92 Minister of Education

1985-88 Deputy Minister of Health Aksotlan Toreyevna Ataeva

1990-94 Minister of Health

1994-96 Minister of Social Affairs

Ambassador to the United Nations from 1996.

1988-93 Deputy Premier Minister Tuvakbibi Amagl'dyeva

1988-90 Minister of Foreign Affairs

1995-98 Deputy Premier Minister Abad Sakhatovna Irzayeva Rizaeva

1999-2004 Minister of Education

Former Vice-President of the Parliament

Other versions of her surnames are Sehedovna, Sehedana and Risaveva.

1997-2006 Member of the Cabinet and Prosecutor General Gurbanbibi Sinirenovna Atajanova

One of President Saparmurat Niyazov (Saparmurat Turkmenbasy the Great)'s strongest supporters she relently procecuted all opponents in "show-trials" throughout her years in office. Officially she resigned for health reasons but later "confessed" on national TV that she had been taking bribes and stealing national property. (b. 1948-).

Ca. 1998-99 Minister of Consumer Goods Djamal Aymurandovna Geklenova

1999-2002 Deputy Premier Minister in charge of the Chamber of Industry and Commerce and Turkmen Statistics and Forecasts Committee

1999-2002 Minister of Textile Industry and Foreign Trade

2007 State Minister and Chairperson of the state joint-stock corporation "Turkmenhaly"

2007- Minister of Textile Industry

Her name is also transcribed Jemal Goklenova

Ca. 2000-04 Deputy Minister of Social Maintenance Ejegyz Rozyeva

Ca. 2000-04 Deputy Minister of Health Ema Rejepovna Dovletsakhatova

2001 Minister of Social Affairs and Labour Enebay Geldiyevna Atayeva

2001-04 Minister of Economy and Finance

2002-04 Deputy Premier Minister responsible for the Banking Sector, Costums and Imports and Governor of Ahal Region (Ca. 2003-04)

2006-07 Minister of Culture and TV and Radio Broadcast

Before 2001 and from 2004 Head of the Central Council of Trade Unions and Head of the Women's Association. Her name is also transcribed as Ataeva Enebay Gelgievna

2002-03 Deputy Prime Minister responsible for Culture, Tourism, and Sports Gurbansoltan Handurdyeva Head of the state-television system in 2003.

2002-04 Member of the Cabinet and Chairperson of the National Bank

2005 Acting Chairperson of the National Bank and Acting of the State Development Fond Sekersoltan Kakalyyevna Muhammedova

Another version of her name is Shakersoltan Mukhammedova. Like so many other government officials she was fired by the country's excentric dictator, Saparmyrat Nyyazov Turkmenbasy (Father of Turkmen) during a direct news broadcast. She was later appointed Acting Governor until she was fired again

2003-04 Deputy Premier and Minister of Culture and Information Gozul Nuralieyeva

She was Vice-Chairperson of the Majlis.

2003-04 Deputy minister of Economy and Finance Bibitac Vekilova

2004-05 Minister of Economy and Finance

2005-07 Minister of Social Security

After firing her predesessor during a TV-transmission, he appointed her acting minister for a six month test period after which she was confirmed in the office. She was fired by President Niyazov during a Cabinet Session, who instucted her to join the agricultural joint-stock association as a deputy to control revenues and expenditures there. At the same session he fired a number of other ministers. She was later re-appointed to the Cabinet.

2004-06 Minister of Culture, Information, TV and Radio Broadcasting Maral Basimovna Basimova Until her appointment she was Mayor of Abadan City (Former Bezmein)

2004- Deputy Minister of Culture Jamal Saparova

2005 1. Deputy Minister of Foreign Affairs Annagul Sapargylyjovna Rejepova Appointed Director of the National Institute of Democracy and Human Rights for a six months trial period in March 2005, but was fired in June.

2005-06 Deputy Minister of Education Semsat Allaberdiyevna Tatova

2006-07 Minister of Education Semsat Amangylyjovna Annagylyjova

2007- Deputy Prime Minister in Charge of Culture, Media and Health Care Issues Maysa Yazmuhammedova

Former Deputy Governor of the Ahaol Region and Trade Union leader.

Tajikistan

Heads of State of Tajikistan/ Jumhurrii Tojikiston/Tocikiston (Female suffrage 1922) Became part of the Russian Empire 1868, part of the Central Asian Emirate as Bukhara Emirate 1917, a Soviet Republic 1818, Part of Uzbekistan 1924-29 before becoming an Autonomous Republic, independent 9.9.91

Ca. 1960-65 Vice-President K. Alueva

1984 Acting President N. Zaripova (January-17/2)

Tajikistan Ministers

Ca. 1960-65 Vice-President K. Alueva

Ca. 1960-65 Deputy Premier Minister A.N. Atanepesova

1965-(70) Deputy Premier Minister M.K. Karimova

1966-78 Secretary of the Communist Party Central Committee Department of Propaganda and Agitation Ibodat Rakhimova Vice-President 1955-66 and Secretary 1978-89 of the Supreme Soviet

1969 Head of the Central Committee General Affairs Department L.I. Volkova

1974-81 Minister of Trade Raisa M. Grishiha

1981-(89) Deputy Premier Minister

1975-78 Deputy Head of the Central Committee Department G. Bobosadykova. She was also First Secretary of the Gorkom of Dshaibe (The Capital).

1974-90 Minister of Public Service Adolat T. Kasymova

1990-92 Minister of Social Affairs

1977-80? Head of the Communist Party Central Committee Light and Food Industry Department V.I. Kozlova

1978-89/90 Minister of Social Affairs Karomat Mirzoalieva

1984 Acting President Nizoramo Zaripova as Vice-President of the Supreme Soviet, she acted as Republic Head during a vacancy. (b. 1923).

1990-92 Minister of Culture Tamara M. Abdushurova

1992-93 Minister of Social Affairs M. Abdemakhmanova

1992-93 Minister of Health Inumzada Jura

1992-94 Minister, Chairperson of the State-Committee of Youth, Sports and Tourism Zebiniso S. Rustamova

1993-94 Minister of Education Bozgul Dodkhudoeva

1994 and 1996-99 Deputy Premier Minister

1993-? Deputy Minister of Industry Bikhodzhal Rakimova

1993-? 1. Deputy Minister of Information Anora Astaova

1993-94 Deputy Minister of Labour Munira Abdulloyevna Inoyatova

1994-96 Deputy Premier Minister

1994-99 Minister of Education

1999- Presidential Advisor of Social Affairs

1993- Deputy Minister of Social Affairs Durslton Shonazirova

1995-2000 1. Deputy Minister of Economy and Foreign Economic Relations Larisa Smeyanova

2000- Deputy Minister of Justice

1995- Deputy Minister of Health Zukira Mirzoyeva

1996-97 Chairperson of the State Committee for Youth, Sport and Tourism Zebiniso Rostannova

1997-2000 Chairperson of the State Committee for Construction Rafiqa Ganievna Musaeva

2000-01 Minister of Labour and Employment

2001- Minister of Labour and Social Welfare

Also known as Rafika Musovea or Museyeva

1997-2004 Chairperson of the State Committee for Women and Family Affairs Latofat Nasriddnova. The Deputy Chairperson was Mukarramhon Bursurukova

1999-2004 Deputy Premier Minister in charge of Women's Issues Nigina Sharapova

2004- Deputy Minister of Health

1999-2000 Minister of Social Security Qimmat Rustamovna Rustamova

Ca. 1999 Chief of the Legal Department of the President's Office Tochinisso Azizova

2000- Deputy Minister of Culture and Information Guljon Mirsoeva Around 2001 Deputy Minister of Labour and Social Protection Adolat Uzakova

2002- Deputy Minister of Education Sabokhat Radzhabova

2004- Deputy Prime Minister Khayrinisso Mavlonova Former Deputy Chairperson of the Soghd Region and Deputy Chairperson of the Leninobod Regional administration.

Ca. 2004- Chairperson of the State Committee for Women and Family Affairs Rukiya Kurbonova

2006- Deputy Minister of Finance Gulmira Khamrokulova

2006- Deputy Minister of Energy Mavjuda Keldiyerova

2006- Deputy Minister for Water Resources Aikhon Sharipova

2006- Minister of Health Rano Abdurakhmanova

2009- Deputy Minister of Foreign Affairs Ozoda Rahmonova

The only one of President Rahmon Nabiyev's 9 children to hold public office. Married to Deputy Finance Minister Jamollidin Nuraliev

Kyrgyzstan

Heads of State of Kyrgyzstan/Kirgistan/Kyrgyz Respublikasy (Female Suffrage 1918/22) The Mongol-Turkish Tribe of Kirghiz became part of the Russian Empire in the 1860s and 1870s. Part of the Soviet Union 1920 and Declared independent 31.8.91, member of the United Nations 1992. The Qara Khitai Empire covered parts of present day's Kyrgyzstan, Kazakhstan, China and Mongolia.

Supreme Soviet and afterwards Majlis

1938-? Secretary (Faith) Evmenevna Kutareva

1947-49 Vice-Chairperson Kulpina Konduchalova

Among other posts 1953-59 Deputy Premier, 1953-63 Minister of Foreign Affairs, 1969-82 of Culture.

1949-ca.70 Vice-Chairperson R. Ryskolova

1950-67 Secretary Zurakan Imankalykova

1959-ca. 70 Member of the Presidium Rakemova

1965-? Member of the Presidium B. Baislova

1968-1975 Member of the Presidium D. Abdraeva

1959-ca. 70 Member of the Presidium T. Edilbayeva

1975-81 Member of the Presidium Zhanilya Tumenbaeva

1981-87 Secretary of the Presidium S. Omarkulova

1984-91 Vice-Chairperson K. Saginbaeva

1987-90 Member of the Presidium A. Myrzalieva

2007- Deputy Speaker of the Majlis Cholpon Baekova

Former President of the Constitutional Court.

Kyrgyzstan Ministers

1932-1937 Vice-Chairperson of the Central Executive Committee Mar'yam Tugambayeva

1937 Joint Acting Chairperson of the Central Executive Committee (16.09-0 4.10)

Марьям ТУГАМБАЕВА acted jointly with Mikhail Ivanovich Us. Also known as Mariya Tuganbayeva, she lived (1907- 86).

1938 Acting Chairperson of the Central Executive Committee Kalima Amankulova (15.05-18.07)

The second female acting Head of State of the Autonomous Republic (b. 1915-)

1952-61 Deputy Minister of Finance Sakin Bergmantrovna

1961-80 Deputy Premier Minister

1966-80 Minister of Foreign Affairs

In 1962-66 Vice-Chairperson of Council of Nationalities in USSR-Supreme Soviet.

1953-59 Deputy Premier Minister Kuluipa Konduchalovna Konduchalova

1953-63 Minister of Foreign Affairs

1969-82 Minister of Culture

Кондучалова Кулуйпа was vice-Chairperson of the Executive Committee of Tien-Shan Regional Council 1940-43, Secretary of the Presidium of the Supreme Soviet 1948-49, Deputy Chair of Supreme Soviet 1949-52, Secretary of the Central Committee of Communist Party 1952-53, Member of the Politburo the Communist Party of Kyrgyzstan 1952-62 and Vice-Chairperson of the Federal Council of the Supreme Soviet of the USSR 1958-66. She lived (1920-2013).

1953-56 Minister of Social Affairs Batysu Salieva

1973-89 Minister of Social Affairs

Between 1966-74 Chairperson of the Committee for Social Affairs and Health in House of Nations in the Supreme Soviet of the USSR.

1959-(70) Vice-President B. Musuralieva

1980 84 2. Deputy Premier Minister Deizamal Cheybekova

1980-82 Minister of Foreign Affairs

1982-92 Minister of Consumers' Protection Shakira B. Al'dasheva

1989-91 Deputy Premier Minister

1982-89 Minister of Culture Dzhumagul Nusupovna Nusupova

1986-89 Deputy Premier Minister and Minister of Foreign Affairs Roza Isakovna Otunbaeva

1992 Deputy Premier Minister and Minister of Foreign Affairs

1994-96 Minister of Foreign Affairs

2005 Acting Minister of Foreign Affairs

2005 Designate Minister of Foreign Affairs

2010 Chairwoman of the Provisional Government

2010-11 President

Other versions of her surname are Otunbaeva, Otunbayeva or Otunbajewa. In 1983-86 Secretary of the Municipal Communist Central Committee of Frunze, 1991 Ambassador of the USSR to Malaysia, 1992-93 Ambassador to USA and Canada, 1994 to Turkey and 1996-2004 Ambassador to the United Kingdom of Great Britain and Deputy Head of the United Nations special mission to Georgia 2002-04. She and some other oppsition-members were barred from standing in the February-elections, and this trickered a peoples revolution that brought the downfall of President Aliev and the opposition to power. After the elections he nominated her as Foreign Minister, but she was rejected by the parliamentary majority. MP from 2007 Parliamentary Leader of the Social Democrats 20009-10 and following re-newed riots in 2010 she took control and assumed the role of Head of State and Government after the former President was ousted. Her title is Chairwoman of the Provisional Government of the Kyrgyz Republic (Kyrgyz Respublikasynyn Ubaktyluu ôkmôtùnùn tôrajymy). (b. 1950-).

1989-92 Deputy Premier Minister Shanyl Tumenbayevna Tumenbayeva

1992-93 Minister of Education Chynora S. Dzhakipova (Chinara Kakypova) From 1999 Leader of the Democratic Bloc, which consists of a number of opposition-parties.

1994-96 Deputy Minister of Finance Uktomkhan Abdullaeva

1996-99 First Deputy Finance Minister

1999-2001 First Deputy Labour and Social Protection Minister

2001-07 Deputy Labour and Social Protection Minister

2007-09 Minister of Labour and Social Development

2009 Deputy Prime Minister

2010-11 Deputy Prime Minister for Social Affairs

Her name is also transcribed as Ouktomkhane Avavovna Abdoullaeva. (b. 1949-).

1995-96 Minister of Justice Larisa Gutnichenko

1996-98 Deputy Premier Minister for Social and Cultural Policy

From 1999 Resident Representative of the Government in the Jogorku Kenesh (Parliament)

1996-98 Deputy Premier Minister Mira Jangaracheva

1998-2000 Minister of Labour and Social Welfare

In 1992-95 Deputy Mayor of Bishkeh, 1995-96 Presidential Advisor of Social Affairs. (b. 1952-)

1997-98 Minister of Labour and Social Security Asygul Abdurkhmenova

1997-2000 and 2005 Minister of Justice Nellia Nikolayevna Beyshenalieva

1998-2000 Chairperson-Minister of the Social Fond Roza Mavletovna Uchkempirova

From 2000 Chairman of the Supreme Court

1999-2002 Chairperson of the State Committee of Women's Affairs Sagyn Ismailova

1999-2002 Deputy Minister of External Trade and Industry Nina M. Kirichenko

2000-02 Minister of Education and Culture Kamila Sharshekeyeva

She was dean at the American University in Kyrgyzstan until her appointment.

2000-05 Minister of Labour and Social Welfare Roza Aknazarova

2000-02 Chairperson of the State Commission of Business Development Kamilya Kenenbaeva

2000-05 1. Deputy Minister of Labour and Social Affairs Uktomkhan Avazovna Abdoulaeva. Her name is also transcribed as Uktamjhan Abdullayeva

2001-07 First Deputy Minister of Foreign Affairs Lidia Adamkalyjevna Imanaliyeva Ambassador to Poland from 2007.

2001-05 Deputy Minister of Communication and Transportation Valentina Davidova

2002-04 Minister of Education and Culture and Science Ishengul Sadykovna Boljurova

2005 Minister of Education

2005 1. Deputy Prime Minister for Social Issues

2006-07 Acting Deputy Prime Minister

2007-09 Minister of Education and Science

Also known as Ishenkul Boldzhurova or Boldjurovashe, she has been Co-Chairperson of the Popular Movement in 2004. Rejected by the Parliament as minister after the "tulip revolution" in the autum of 2005. Rector of the National University. (1951-)

2002-05 Deputy Minister of Health Lyudmila Vasilyevna Shteinke

2002-05 Deputy Minister of Industry and Foreign Trade Janyl Tumenbaeva.

Until 2002 Deputy of the Jalal-Abad Province

2004-05 Deputy Prime Minister Toktobubu Djekshenovna Aytikeeva

Deputy Head of the Social Department in the Presidential Administration and Secretary of the State Educational Programme and 2002-04 president of the National TV and Radio Corporation.

Around 2004 Deputy Minister of Economic Development, Foreign Trade and Industry Nina Mikhailovna Kirichenko

2004-05 Deputy Minister of Finance Olga Lavrova

2012- Minister of Finance

Chair of the Social Fund and later exceutive of Gazprom (b. 1956-)

2004-05 Deputy Minister of Education Gaisha Ibragimova

Previously worked in the Presidential Administration. She required the required amount of signatures but did not register as presidential candidate in 2005.

2005 Minister of Health Fnu Aytimbekova

2005 Designate Minister of Culture Toktokan Borombaeva

Leader of the Elmuras (People's Legacy) since 2002, she was nominated for the cabinet by the President but rejected by the Parliament

2005 Designate Minister of Social Affairs and Labour Alevtina Pronenko

Also rejected by the Parliament.

2005-10 Chairperson of the State Commission on Migration and Employment Aigul Maratbekovna Ryskulova

2006-07 Deputy Minister of Finance Tazhikan Kalimbetova

2007-09 Minister of Finance

2009-10 Deputy Prime Minister

2007-08 Deputy Minister of Foreign Affairs Elmira Sultanovna Ibraimova

2008-09 Deputy Prime Minister

2010 Coordinator of the Social Sector, Public Relations and Media of the Provisorial Government

Worked at Moscow State University in the Economy Department until 1999, Ambassador and Permanent Representative to the United Nations 1999-2992 and Leader of the parliamentary faction of Ak Zhol in 2007. (b. 1962-).

2009 Minister of Labour and Social Development Nazgul Askerovna Tashpaeva

2009-10 Minister of Labour, Employment and Migration Aigul Ryskulova

2011 Minister of Social Welfare

Former Chief of the State Migration and Employment Committee.

Ca. 2009-11 and 2011-12 Deputy Minister of Finance Dinara Shaydieva

2011 Acting Minister of Finance

2012- Minister of Health

2010 Provisoric Minister of Health Damira Abaskanovna Niyazalieva

2010 Provisoric Minister of Education and Science Irina Jur'evna Karamuškina

2011-12 Deputy Prime Minister for Social Issues Gulnara Asymbekova

2012-14 Deputy Prime Minister for Social Affairs Kamila Abdyrazakovna Talieva

2014- Minister of Culture, Information and Tourism

2014- Deputy Prime Minister Elvira Kubanychbekovna Sarieva

Journalist and MP

Heads of state of Kyrgyzstan

1144-51 Khanum Regnant Tabuyan T'a-Pu-Yen Gantian Huanghou of Qara Khitai (Turkistan)

Possibly successor of her husband, Yelü Dashi, who reigned as Emperor Dezong 1124-1144 as leader of the Central Asian Khanate – in what today is partly Kyrgyzstan and partly Chinese Turkistan the region Sinkiang Uighur Autonomous Region/Xinjiang Uygur Zizhiqu. She was mother of Yelü Yilie, who ruled as emperor Liao Renzong in 1151-1164 and possibly also mother of Khanum Regnant Yelü Pusuwan Chengtian Taihou who ruled in 1164-1178.

1164-78 Dowager Khanum Regnant Yelü Pusuwan Chengtian Taihou of Qara Khitai (Turkestan)

Also known as Empress Chengtian, Cheng Tian Hou) of Qara Khitai she was sister of Yelü Yilie, who ruled as emperor Liao Renzong in 1151-64. In the 1120s China's Liao Dynasty was ousted by the Liaos, or Khitans, and were driven west into Central Asia, where, after defeating the Seljuq Turks of Persia under the Sultan Sanjar in 1141, they founded the Qara-Khitai Empire with Samarkand as its capital covering present day's Mongolia, Northern-China, Kyrgyzstan and other Central Asian territories. The khanate was weakened in about 1200 by attacks from the Khwarizm Shahdom and in 1218 it collapsed precipitately when the Mongols invaded. The governmental institutions of Qara Khitai were taken over by the Mongols to form the foundations of their own imperial administration.

1242-46 Regent Dowager Khanum Ebüskün of Qara Khitai (Turkestan)

For Qara Hülägü

1252-61 Regent Dowager Khanum Organa Hatum of Qara Khitai (Turkestan)

Her name also spelled as Orqina Khatum. Qara Khitai also covered parts of present day's Turkmenistan, and she was also ruler of the Chagataiid Horde in Mongolia and the Khanate of the Eastern Turkiut (Xinjiang)

Around 1850 Tsarina Kurmandjan Datka of Alay

Also known as Kurmanjan Mamatbai Kyzy, or Alai Queen, she was an outstanding leader of Kyrgyz nation. She had refused to live with the husband she was forced to marry and ruled the country alone when her second husband died, during the gloomy time of feudal despotism she could maintain a free spirit of independent nomad's life, traditional way of living and Kyrgyz culture in Alay region. She was respected by all the foreign rulers she met during her reign, even by Kokand Khan – guardian of Muslim norms. At that time, it was considered astounding that a woman could govern such a huge territory as the Fergana valley. After the Kirgis territory was annexed by Russia in 1876, she continued the resistance movement. She lived (1811-1907)

1959-(70) Vice-President B. Musuralieva

2010 Chairwoman of the Provisional Government Roza Isakovna Otunbaeva

2010-11 President

Former Foreign Minister and long time political opposition leader

Uzbekistan

Republic of Uzbekistan/Özbekiston Jumhuriyäti (Female suffrage 1922/38).

Formed the most important part of the Turkestan-Khuhstan Empire, split up into three Khanates of Khiva, Kokand and Bukhara remained independent until 1921 other parts of the territory was incorporated in the Turkestan Soviet Republic 1918, 1922 the Uzbek Autonomous Soviet Republic was formed. Parliament of Uzbekistan/ Ozbekiston Independent 31.8.91

Supreme Soviet was renamed Olys Majlis after the independence.

1959-63 Member of the Presidium S. Pulatova

1959-63 Member of the Presidium T.M. Poznyankova

1959-63 Member of the Presidium O. Rafikova

1963-67 Member of the Presidium R. Abdullayeva

1971-ca. 84 Vice-Chairperson

1963-67 Member of the Presidium Zufira Israilova

1971-ca. 84 Vice-Chairperson

1963-? Member of the Presidium S.A. Kharova

1963-? Member of the Presidium K. Khasanova

1963-? Member of the Presidium M.Y. Yuldashova

1963-89 Vice-Chairperson A. Kh. Babeva

1971-ca.84 Secretary Khakima M. Putatsava

Ca. 1984-89 Secretary G.K. Khaidorova

1995-? Deputy Chairperson of the Olys Majlis Boritosh Shodiyeva

2005-08 Deputy Speaker of the Legislative Chamber of Oliy Majlis Diloram Gafurjanovna Tashmukhamedova 2008- Speaker

Her name is also transcribed as Dilorom Tashmukhamedova. She was First Secretary of the Political Council of Social and Democratic Party of Uzbekistan "Adolat" ("Justice"). Presidential Candidate in 2007 and received 2,9% of the vote.

2010- Vice-President of the Senate of the Oliy Majlis Mavjuda Rajabova

Uzbekistan Ministers

1952-59 Deputy Premier, Minister of Construction Industry Yadar Sadykovna Nasriddinova

1959-70 President

Between 1959-70 Vice-Chairperson of the Supreme Soviet and 1970-74 President of the Federation Council of the Supreme Soviet of the USSR. She lived (1920-2006).

1955-56 1. Deputy Minister of Culture Zakha Rakhimbabaeva

1963-67 Minister of Culture

1981-89 Minister of Culture

1956-78? Minister of Social Affairs Vasiha Sadykovna Sadykova

1959-63 Vice-President U. Ibadulayeva

1963-(70) Vice-President P. Yezhanova

1967-89 Minister of Public Service Anna Brodova

Between 1963-67 Deputy Chief of Government of Tashkent.

1970-(89) Minister of Justice Mamlikat S. Vasikova

1971-(89) Deputy Premier Minister Rano Kh. Abdullaeva

1971-75 Head of the Central Committee Department of Culture

Between 1961-62 First Secretary of Samarkand. (b. 1935-)

1971-74 Head of the Central Committee Department of Propaganda and Agitation Kh. Iu. Asletdinova

1974-89 Deputy Premier Minister Kudratilla A. Akhmedova

In 1963-64 In Charge of Agriculture of Tashkent, 1969-71 Vice-President of the Soviet of Tashkent, 1971-74 Ditto of Syr Paria and First Secretary of the District Communist Party.

1974-? Deputy Minister of Building Material Mme. Nasriddinova

1981-89 Minister of Social Affairs Mme. Saerumarovna Sultanova

Between 1971-81 First Secretary of the Communist Party of Frunze.

1989-93 Minister of Social Affairs Sanobar A. Khodzhayeva

1991-92 Minister of Foreign Affairs Shakhlo N. Makhmudova

The first post-independence foreign minister. She later worked in the Ministry of Foreign Affairs.

1991-94 Vice-Chairperson of the State Committee for Women's Affairs

1994-2004 Chairperson of the State Committee for Women's Affairs

1995-2003 Deputy Premier Minister Dilbar Mukhammadkhonovna Gulomova (Gulyamova or Ghulomova)

1998-2000 Deputy Premier Minister of Analysis and Information Galina Karimovna Saidova

2000-05 and 2010 1. Deputy Minister of Economy

2005-06 Chairperson of the Anti Monopoly State Commission

2010-11 Minister of Foreign Economic Relations, Investments and Trade

2011- Minister of Economy

Ca. 1998-2001 Deputy Minister of Health Bakhtiyar Nuyazmatova

2001- Deputy Minister of Economic Relations S.N. Burkhanova

Before 2000- Deputy Minister of Foreign Economic Relations Shakhlo Abdullaeva

2004-08 Deputy Premier Minister, Head of the Social Protection of Family, Maternity and Childhood Complex and Chairperson of the Women's Committee Svetlana Tursunovna Inamova

2004-05 Minister of Education and Culture Ishengul Sadykovna Boldjurova

2004-05 Minister of Labour and Social Roza Korchubekovna Aknazarova

2004-05 Chairperson of the State Commission on Enterprise Development Kamilya Najitmudinovna Kenenbaeva

2008-11 Deputy Prime Minister and Chairperson of the Women's Committee Farida Akbarova

Former Deputy Governor of Tashkent Region and Vice-Chairperson of the National Women's Committee 2007-08 until her appointment as Deputy Prime Minister and Chairperson of the Committee.

2008 Deputy Minister of Foreign Affairs Gulnara Islomovna Karimova

Minister-Counsellor to Russia 2003-05, Ambassador and Permanent Representative of Uzbekistan to the United Nations Office and other International Organisations in Geneva since 2008 and Ambassador to Spain from 2010, leader of a number of NGO's and owner of a number of large companies. Daughter of President Islom Karimov and believed to be his designated heir. (b. 1972-)

2011- Deputy Prime Minister and Chairperson of the Women's Committee Elmira Irkinovna Basitkhanova

Uzbekistan Heads of State

674-710 Princess Qabaq Hatun of Bahura

976-77 Regent Dowager Princess of Samarqand and of Buhara

For al-Malik II

1170/72 Regent Turhan of Uiguristan

Till 1218 Ruler Salbak Tarhan of Uiguristan

1257 Regent Boraqcin of Hwarizim Sali (A Mongol Tribe)

Regent for Ulagci. She died 1257.

1865/75-85 Khanum Qurban Gan Danca Alimgul of Alay Qaancasy (The Khanate of the Alayan Ruleress)

She was given the area as a dowry and established a firm rule making it an independent principality

1959-70 President Yadar Sadykovna Nasriddinova (24.3-25.9)

In 1952-59 she was Deputy Premier, Minister of Construction Industry Between 1959-70 Vice-Chairperson of the Supreme Soviet, 1970-74 President of the Federation Council of the Supreme Soviet of the USSR and 1974-? Deputy Minister of Building Material. She lived (1920-2006).

1959-63 Vice-President U. Ibadulayeva

1963-(70) Vice-President P. Yezhanova

B
Women Who Made a Change in Politics

India

Indian women had always been active even during the British rule. For example, Annie Besant, Dr. Muthulaksmi Reddy, Vijaya Lakshmi Pandit, Begum Jahanara Shahnawaz,

Rajkumari Amrit Kaur etc. after independence also the same continued. Violet Alva, Indira Gandhi, V. S. Ramadevi, Sonia Gandhi, Pratibha Patil etc

Indira Gandhi, Prime Minister for fifteen years. Indira Gandhi, India. Prior to this she was the President 1959-60 and 1966-77 Leader of the Congress Party. She was Minister of Information 1964-66 and member of Rajya Sabha 1964-67 and of Lok Sabha 1967-77, 1978 and 1980-84. In 1975 she declared a state of emergency and ruled as a dictator. She lost the 1977-elections and imprisoned. After her release she was leader of Congress (I) 1978-84 and as Premier she also held posts of Minister of Foreign Affairs, Defence, Finance, Home Affairs etc.

First woman mayor of Kochi, India: Mercy Williams,2005, "The Hindu". The Hindu. 2005-10-07. Retrieved 2013-04-29.

Sonia Gandhi is an Italy-born Indian politician, who has served as President of the Indian National Congress party since 1998. She is the widow of former Prime Minister of India, Rajiv Gandhi who belonged to the Nehru-Gandhi family. Within 62 days of joining as a primary member, she was offered the party President post which she accepted. She contested Lok Sabha elections from Bellary, Karnataka andAmethi, Uttar Pradesh in 1999. In Bellary she defeated veteran BJP leader, Sushma Swaraj. In 2004 and 2009, she was re-elected to the Lok Sabha from Rae Bareli in Uttar Pradesh.

Mayawati, served four terms as Chief Minister of Uttar Pradesh as head of the Bahujan Samaj Party, which focuses on a platform of social change.

Mamata Banerjee, Chief Minister of West Bengal since 2011. She is the first woman to hold the office. Nickname: Didi. She is the President of All India Trinamool Congress party. Banerjee pulled off a landslide victory for the All India Trinamool Congress (AITMC) or (TMC) in West Bengal by defeating the world's longest-serving democratically-elected communist government, the Communist Party of India (Marxist)-led Left Front government, bringing to an end 34 years of Left Front rule in the state. Banerjee previously served as a Minister of Railways twice, Minister of Coal, and Minister of State for Human Resource Development, Department of Youth Affairs and Sports and Women and Child Development in the cabinet of the Indian government. She opposed forceful land acquisition for industrialisation by the then communist government in West Bengal for Special Economic Zones at the cost of agriculturalists and farmers. In 2012, the Time magazine named her one of the "100 Most influential People in the World".

Jayalalithaa Jayaram, commonly referred to as Jayalalithaa, chief minister of Tamil Nadu, a state in southern India, since 2011. President, All India Anna Dravida Munnetra Kazhagam (AIADMK) party. Prior to this she had a marvellous career in films/Awards: Filmfare Award for Best Actress – Tamil, Filmfare Award for Best Actress – Telugu.

Sushma Swaraj, Leader of Opposition in the 15th Lok Sabha. She has been elected six times as a Member of Parliament and three times as a Member of the Legislative Assembly. She is of Bharatiya Janata Party.

Pratibha Patil, Former President of India, who served as the 12th President of India from 2007 to 2012; she was the first woman to hold the office.

Russia/USSR/Central Asia

First woman mayor in former Russian Empire and first female mayor of Anapa: Maria Skobtsova

During the soviet time in Kazakhstan, Foreign minister – Akmaral Arystanbekova – 1989. in Kyrgyz republic, Chairman of the Supreme Soviet- Maryam Tugambayeva – 1937 and Foreign Minister – Roza Otunbayeva – 1992 and

President – Roza Otunbayeva – 2010

Roza Otunbayeva, Kyrgyzstan President 7 April 2010-1 December 2011 1 year, 238 days 07.04.2010-19.05.2010 Head of the Interim Government

1983-86 Secretary of the Municipal Communist Central Committee of Frunze, 1986-89 Deputy Prime Minister and Foreign Minister in the Kyrgyz SSR, 1991 Ambassador of the USSR to Malaysia, 1992 Kyrgyz Deputy Premier Minister and Minister of Foreign Affairs, 1992-93 Ambassador to USA and Canada and 1994 to Turkey, Foreign Minister 1994-96, Ambassador to the United Kingdom of Great Britain 1996-2003, Deputy Head of the United Nations special mission to Georgia 2002-04, Acting Foreign Minister 2007, Parliamentary Leader of the Social Democrats 2009-10.

Grand Duchess Olga Konstantinovna Romanova of Russia, she was acting head of state during a vacancy at the throne. She lived (1851-1926)

In Turkmenistan, General Secretary of the Communist Party of the Turkmen SSR – Anna Mukhamedova – 1937

In Uzbekistan, Chairman of the Presidium of the Supreme Soviet – Yagdar Nasriddinova – 1959

Republic of Uzbekistan after independence, Foreign Minister – Shakhlo Makhmudova – 1991

APPENDIX IV
WOMEN WHO MADE A MARK IN WOMEN'S CAMPAIGN FOR CHANGE IN THEIR RESPECTIVE COUNTRIES

Note: These are not the only ones; there are many other women as well, who made a difference in Women's campaign for change both in India as well as in Central Asia.

Sampat Pal Devi: The founder of The Gulabi Gang is a symbol of an extraordinary women's power. As mentioned above the movement formed in 2006 by Sampat Pal Devi in the Banda District of Uttar Pradesh in Northern India. Today she with the help of her Gulabi Gang helps destitute women in this region.

D. Sharifa Khanam, Founder STEPS, Women's Development Organisation, India. D. Sharifa Khanam founded STEPS Women's Development Organisation in 1987. Ms. Khanam's work for the past two decades has been devoted to the protection of women. The organisation provides short-term residence for battered women and works with both the local community and police to protect abused women. Ms. Khanam's dedication to women, particularly Muslim women, began in 1999 when she created the first network of Muslim women in southern India, the Tamil Nadu Muslim Women's Jamaat Committee. The group, comprised of poor and working class women, functions as a community tribunal to aid local women. Ms. Khanam is currently working to build the first mosque exclusively for Muslim women in India. She hopes the mosque will become the center of a vibrant Islamic feminist and democratic culture.

Naish Hasan, Women's rights activist, writer, India, Naish Hasan is the founder and president of Muslim Mahila Aandolan (Indian Muslim Women's movement) which has been working in India since 2007. She is chief editor of "Musalman Auratein (Muslim women)" and writes on issues of Muslim women in a number of journals and magazines. She is committed to raising the voices of Muslim women in India through written and visual media. For over a decade Naish Hasan has been working in the women's rights field in India, and specifically with Muslim women. She is a passionate advocate for Muslim women's identity in India. Her aim is to protect Indian Muslim women who experience simultaneous exploitation by their male counterparts in the name of religion and by the government due to their minority status. Naish has conducted trainings on the subjects of gender violence, women's law, women's rights, and women's rights in the Qur'an. Her goal is to create society free of discrimination and gender based exploitation where human rights, dignity, and secularism are the foundation of one's existence.

Marfua Tokhtakhodjaeva is an author and a journalist who writes about women's rights in Uzbekistan. From 1995 to 2005, Dr. Tokhtakhodjaeva was Chairperson of the Women's Resource Center in Tashkent (TWRC), one of the first civil society organisations to talk about the rights of women and the social problems of urban and rural women. TWRC collected and distributed information about cases of discrimination against women, domestic violence, trafficking and income generating opportunities. TWRC also held seminars and events for the enlightment of women. In 2005, after the Andijan revolt, TWRC was closed as were most independent NGOs. A long time leader of the women's movement in Uzbekistan, Marfua Tokhtakhodjaeva is a founding member and co-director of the Women's Resource Center (WRC) in Tashkent, an NGO founded in 1991 to work towards economic and social stability, democratisation, and increased awareness of women's human rights in the region. Dr. Tokhtakhodjaeva has written extensively on the status of women in Central Asia in post-communist societies and was formerly a Regional fellow at the Kennan Institute of the Woodrow Wilson Center in Washington, DC. She received her PhD in Architecture, specialising in city planning and the restoration of architectural monuments. In 2003, she was voted "Woman of the Year" by the United Nations agencies in Uzbekistan.

Galiya Khassanova is a director of the UNDP Gender in Development Bureau in Kazakhstan. She is currently a fellow of the Contemporary Issues Fellowship Programme and is researching the role of women in the creation of democratic institutions in Kazakhstan.

Svetlana Shakirova, Director of the Research Department, Almaty Management University,1.09.2011-2015; 1998-2011, Director, Center for Gender Studies (NGO) (Almaty). President, 1995-2001 Feminist League (NGO) (Almaty). 1989-1991 Ministry of People's Education of Kazakh SSR. Teaching methods department(Alma-Ata). Applied sociologist

Roza Sarabayeva, Professor, KAZGU, Almaty, Kazakhstan. She has worked on women issues and other related issues and has many publications to her name.

Sofia R. Kasymova is the director at Gender Education Center Dushanbe, Tajikistan. She has worked on numerous projects related women's issues in Tajikistan right from education, polygamy, migration, violence etc.

Dr. Nurgul Djanaeva is a founder of the Forum of Women's NGOs of Kyrgyzstan (a women's network), author of the book "Kyrgyzstan women in transition," and a member of several women's networks, including AWPP, APWLD and the Central Asian Forum of women's NGOs. Nurgul has her PhD in social philosophy from Leningrad State University.

Dinara Alimdjanova, Director, Gender Study Center, Uzbekistan: Dinara Alimdjanova is a trainer of Socio-Economic and Gender Analysis methodologies. For the last 14 years, Ms. Alimdjanova has worked on promoting gender with regard to the programming framework and strategies developed by the United Nations. More specifically, she has organised gender awareness trainings and developed specific methodological and analytical tools to promote gender equality at the government level in Muslim societies. She worked on the development and implementation of the National Action Plans on Improving Women's Status in Tajikistan, Turkmenistan. She also provided advisory services to the National Council of Women's Organisations, governments, and women's movements. Ms. Alimdjanova is the author of several publications and analytical papers, presented worldwide. Her areas of interest include: human development, women's and gender issues, engendering macroeconomics, gender and trade, methodologies of socio-economic and gender analysis, gender and religion, etc.

APPENDIX V

Анкета

Уважаемый респондент,

Данная анкета является частью моей пост-докторской работы под названием "Политическое участие женщин в Индии и в Центральной Азии». Я из Индии, и я буду использовать ваши ответы как источник первичной информации для анализа социально-политических, экономических и культурных изменений в обществе, которые произошли с 1991 года в Центральной Азии. Этот опрос не имеет юридической силы. Это информация будет использована только для моих научных исследований. Если вы не хотите писать свое имя, то вы можете оставить столбец пустым. Я прошу, чтобы вы были откровенны и честны в ответах, и я уверяю вас, что любая информация, предоставленная Вами, будет рассматриваться как строго конфиденциальная.

Искренне благодарю вас за сотрудничество.

1. Имя респондента (по желанию):

2. Возраст:
   (а) 20-25 лет (б) 25-30 лет
   (в) 30-35 лет (г) свыше 35 лет ☐

3. Пол: (а) мужской (б) женский

4. Профессия (выберите из списка):
   (а) из академической среды
   (б) СМИ (в) Государственный сектор
   (г) Частный сектор (д) Самозанятый
   (е) Студент (ж) Домохозяйка (з) Безработный
   (и) Пенсионер (к)Другое ☐

5. Образование
   (а) Среднее (б) Выпускник
   (в) Высшее (г) Профессиональная квалификация
   (д) другие ☐

6. Месячный доход (приблизительно
   (а) Менее 3 000 Сом (б) 3 000 - 6 000 сом
   (в) 6 000 -9 000 Сом (г) более чем 9 000 Сом ☐

7. Сколько времени вы проводите на рабочем месте и дома каждый день
   (А) дома____ часов (б) на работе ____ часов ☐

8. Какие из проблем, интересуютвас? Ранжируйте их соответствующим образом.
   (а) Здоровье ☐ (б) Социальные ☐
   (с) экономические ☐ (Г) Культурное ☐
   (е) политические ☐ (F) Семейные ☐
   (Г) Спорт ☐ (Я) Иностранный язык ☐

9. (I) Считаете ли вы,что распад СССР повлиял на ежедневную деятельность женщин?
   (а) Да (б) нет ☐ (в) Не могу сказать, ☐

   (II) Если да, то пожалуйста, оцените их соответственно:
   (а) на заработную плату ☐ (б) медицинские услуги ☐
   (в) на детях ☐ (г) на ☐
   (д) на безопасность/рост преступности ☐
   (е) другие ... ☐

10. Как бы вы описали вашу политическую деятельность?
    (а) Активный ☐ (б) неактивный ☐
    (с) отношусь благожелательно ☐

11. Как вы думаете, женщины могут играть роль в политике?
    (а) Да (б) нет (с) не могу сказать, ☐

12. Просьба указать некоторые изменения, которые произошли в политической деятельности женщин:
   1. Улучшение политического сознания
      (а) Да (б) нет (в) остались такими же (г) Не могу сказать, ☐

   2. Повышение политического участия:
   (I) на местном уровне:
      (а) Да (б) нет (в) остались такими же (г) Не могу сказать, ☐
   (II) на региональном уровне:
      (а) Да (б) нет (с) остались такими же (г) Не могу сказать, ☐
   (III) На национальном уровне:
      (а) Да (б) нет (в) остались такими же (г) Не могу сказать, ☐

13. Каково ваше мнение о женщинах и политике?
   (I) Имеют ли женщины более сбалансированную перспективу, чем мужчины?
      (а) Да (б) нет (в) Не могу сказать, ☐
   (II) Являются ли они более искренни и честны?
      (а) Да (б) нет (с) Не могу сказать, ☐
   (III) Они лучше, принимают решения?
      (а) Да (б) нет (с) Не могу сказать, ☐

14. Какие из перечисленных ниже организаций, являются более эффективными для укрепления политической осведомленности и участия женщин? (Ранжировать их в соответствии с их компетенцией)
   (а) правительства ☐
   (б) политические партии ☐
   (в) Женские организации ☐
   (Г) Неправительственные организации ☐
   (д) транс-национальные организации ☐

15. Как распада СССР отразился на экономическом состоянииженщин?
   (а) Улучшилось (б) не улучшилось
   (с) ухудшилось (г) Не могу сказать ☐

16. Повлиял ли распад СССР на женское движение?
   (а) Да (б) нет (в) Не могу сказать ☐

17. По вашему мнению, играютли женщины эффективную роль в политике в вашей стране?
   (а) Да (б) нет (в) Не могу сказать ☐

18. Делаетли правительство достаточно, чтобы содействовать участию женщин во всех сферах жизни?
    (а) Да (б) нет (в) Не могу сказать ☐

19. Пожалуйста, кратко изложите идею укрепления политического участия женщин.

20. Какие меры могут быть приняты для вовлечения женщин в более значимую и конструктивную роль в социально-экономическом развитии страны?

21. Пожалуйста, укажите некоторые изменения в экономической активности женщин из-за распада Советского Союза.

22. Каковы последствия распада СССР на социально-культурный статус женщин в обществе, дайте сравнение советской и пост советской эпохе

Исследователь
КамалаКумари,
Центр русской и центральноазиатских исследований
Школы международных исследований,
Университет Джавахарлала Неру, Нью-Дели, Индия.

Index

F

G

K

L

M

T

Y

Z